D0576529

Kitchen Planning

Guidelines • Codes • Standards

Julia Beamish Ph.D., CKE, Kathleen Parrott Ph.D., CKE, JoAnn Emmel Ph.D. and Mary Jo Peterson, CKD, CBD, CAPS

NKBA
The Finest Professionals in the Kitchen & Bath Industry
National Kitchen & Bath Association℠

Professional Resource Library

About The National Kitchen & Bath Association

As the only non-profit trade association dedicated exclusively to the kitchen and bath industry, the National Kitchen & Bath Association (NKBA) is the leading source of information and education for all professionals in the field.

NKBA's mission is to enhance member success and excellence by promoting professionalism and ethical business practices, and by providing leadership and direction for the kitchen and bath industry.

A non-profit trade association with more than 36,000 members in North America and overseas, it has provided valuable resources for industry professionals for more than 40 years. Its members are the finest professionals in the kitchen and bath industry.

NKBA has pioneered innovative industry research, developed effective business management tools, and set groundbreaking standards for safe, functional and comfortable design of kitchens and baths.

NKBA provides a unique, one-stop resource for professional reference materials, seminars and workshops, distance learning opportunities, marketing assistance, design competitions, consumer referrals, job and internship opportunities and opportunities for volunteer leadership activities.

Recognized as the kitchen and bath industry's education and information leader, NKBA provides development opportunities and continuing education for all levels of professionals. More than 100 courses, as well as a certification program with three internationally recognized levels, help kitchen and bath professionals raise the bar for excellence.

For students entering the industry, NKBA offers Supported and Endorsed Programs, which provide NKBA-approved curriculum at more than 47 learning institutions throughout North America.

NKBA helps members and other industry professionals stay on the cutting-edge of an ever-changing field through the Association's Kitchen/Bath Industry Show, one of the largest trade shows in the country.

NKBA offers membership in four different categories: Industry, Associate, Student and Honorary. Industry memberships are broken into 11 different industry segments. For more information, visit NKBA at www.nkba.org.

THANK YOU TO OUR SPONSORS

The National Kitchen & Bath Association recognizes with gratitude the following companies who generously helped to fund the creation of this industry resource.

PATRONS

www.americanwoodmark.com

www.kohler.com

BENEFACTORS

www.monogram.com

www.subzero.com   www.wolfappliance.com

CONTRIBUTOR

www.groheamerica.com

SUPPORTERS

www.nyloft.net

www.showhouse.moen.com

www.totousa.com

DONORS

Rev-A-Shelf   **Viking Range Corp.**   **Whirlpool Corp.**

This book is intended for professional use by residential kitchen and bath designers. The procedures and advice herein have been shown to be appropriate for the applications described; however, no warranty (expressed or implied) is intended or given. Moreover, the user of this book is cautioned to be familiar with and to adhere to all manufacturers' planning, installation and use/care instructions. In addition, the user is urged to become familiar with and adhere to all applicable local, state and federal building codes, licensing and legislation requirements governing the user's ability to perform all tasks associated with design and installation standards, and to collaborate with licensed practitioners who offer professional services in the technical areas of mechanical, electrical and load bearing design as required for regulatory approval, as well as health and safety regulations.

Information about this book and other association programs
and publications may be obtained from the
National Kitchen & Bath Association
687 Willow Grove Street, Hackettstown, New Jersey 07840
Phone (800) 843-6522
www.nkba.org

Copyright © 2006 by the National Kitchen & Bath Association.

ISBN 1-887127-56-9

First Edition 2006

Illustrations and Drawings: Jean Anguiano, Jessica Best,
Nicole Daniels, Karen Dorian, Jerry Germer and Bridget Miller

Top cover photo courtesy of Peter Ross Salerno, CMKBD – Wyckoff, New Jersey
Bottom cover photo courtesy of Gerard Cirrarello, CMKBD – Westbrook, Connecticut

Published on behalf of NKBA by Fry Communications, Irvine, CA

Peer Reviewers

Timothy Aden, CMKBD	Jim Krengel, CMKBD
Julia Beamish, Ph.D, CKE	Chris LaSpada, CPA
Leonard V. Casey	Elaine Lockard
Ellen Cheever, CMKBD, ASID	Phyllis Markussen, Ed.D, CKE, CBE
Hank Darlington	Chris J Murphy, CKD, CBD, CKBI
Dee David, CKD, CBD	David Newton, CMKBD
Peggy Deras, CKD, CID	Roberta Null, Ph.D
Kimball Derrick, CKD	Michael J Palkowitsch, CMKBD
Tim DiGuardi	Paul Pankow, CKBI
Kathleen Donohue, CMKBD	Jack Parks
Gretchen L. Edwards, CMKBD	Kathleen R. Parrott, Ph.D, CKE
JoAnn Emmel, Ph.D	Al Pattison,CMKBD
Jerry Germer	Les Petrie, CMKBD
Pietro A. Giorgi, Sr., CMKBD	Becky Sue Rajala, CKD
Tom Giorgi	Betty L. Ravnik, CKD, CBD
Jerome Hankins, CKD	Robert Schaefer
Spencer Hinkle, CKD	Klaudia Spivey, CMKBD
Max Isley, CMKBD	Kelly Stewart, CMKBD
Mark Karas, CMKBD	Tom Trzcinski, CMKBD
Martha Kerr, CMKBD	Stephanie Witt, CMKBD

INTRODUCTION . . . . **XIX**

CHAPTER 1: KITCHEN HISTORY AND TRENDS. 1

   A Brief History of the Kitchen 1

   The Colonial Kitchen   2

       Hearth and Beehive Ovens   2

   The Modern Kitchen   3

       The Victorian Kitchen   3

   The Beecher Kitchen   4

       The Plumbed Sink   4

   Standardization: The 1900s   5

       The Laboratory Look   5

   Major Kitchen Trends Through the 1900s. 6

       Early 1900s   6

       The 1920s   7

       The 1930s   9

       The 1940s   10

       The 1950s   11

       The 1960s   12

       The 1970s   12

       The 1980s   13

       The 1990s   15

   Current and Continuing Design Trends – The 2000s 18

   Demographic and Population Trends 18

       Population Diversity   18

       An Aging Population   19

       Household Composition   19

   Consumer References. 20

   Space Usage Trends 21

   Environmental Awareness Trends 24

   Activity Trends 24

   Location Trends 27

Product Trends 28

Summary 28

CHAPTER 2: KITCHEN DESIGN RESEARCH **29**

Early Studies 29

Studies at Mid-Century 30

    Guides For Arrangement Of Urban Family Kitchens   31

    Energy Saving Kitchen   31

    Kitchen Guidelines   32

Kitchen Research in the 1990s 32

Virginia Tech Kitchen Research 33

    Someone's In The Kitchen   33

        Content Analysis   34

        Personal Interview and Cooking Activity   34

        National Telephone Survey   34

        Results and Implications   35

    Kitchen Storage Research Project   40

        Kitchen Inventory Survey   40

Kitchen Design Research 41

    Measuring for Storage Needs   41

        Implications   42

Summary 42

CHAPTER 3: INFRASTRUCTURE CONSIDERATIONS **43**

Codes 43

Structural Issues 44

Floors 44

    Oversized Appliances   45

    Stability and Evenness   46

    Moisture Control   48

Walls 48

    Load-Bearing Walls   48

    Uneven Walls   49

    Insulation   50

Doors and Windows 50

    Door Choices   51

    Window Options   53

Plumbing 55

    Plumbing Fixtures   55

    Water Delivery   56

    Drain/Waste/Vent Pipes   57

        Septic Systems   59

    Hot Water   59

Summary 60

CHAPTER 4: ENVIRONMENTAL CONSIDERATIONS **61**

Green Building 61

Energy Management in the Kitchen 63

Energy Star 63

Water Quality 64

Water Quality Standards 64

Primary Drinking Water Standards 64

Secondary Drinking Water Standards 65

Canadian Water Quality Guidelines 65

Other Water Contaminants 66

Water Quality Testing 67

Solving Water Quality Problems 68

Water Treatment Equipment 69

    Filters   69

    Water Softeners   69

    Iron Removal Equipment   70

    Neutralizers   70

    Distillation Units   71

    Reverse Osmosis Unit   71

    Disinfection Methods   71

Summary 72

Water Conservation 72

Air Quality 73

Source Control 73

    Indoor Air Quality and Construction   74

    Renovation Hazards   74

Air Cleaning 75

Ventilation Systems and Filters 75

Moisture Problems 76

Moisture from Kitchens 77

    Moisture Basics   77

Molds and Moisture 78

    Molds and Health   79

Preventing Moisture Problems 79

Waste Management in the Home 82

Planning for Waste in the Kitchen 82

    Community Practices and Regulations   83

    Waste Management Appliances   83

A Recycling Center 84

Noise 86

Sound Insulating Construction Techniques 89

CHAPTER 5: HUMAN FACTORS AND UNIVERSAL DESIGN IMPLICATIONS 91

Anthropometry 91

    Structural Anthropometry   92

Functional Anthropometry 95

    Reach Ranges   99

    Range-of-Joint Motion   100

Mobility Aids 101

Comfort Zone 104

Anthropometry of Children 104

Ergonomic & Universal Design 105

    History and State of the Art   106

    Equitable Use   107

    Flexibility in Use   108

    Simple and Intuitive Use   109

    Perceptible Information   110

    Tolerance for Error   111

    Low Physical Effort   112

    Size and Space for Approach and Use   113

Dispelling Myths 115

U.S. Access Codes, Laws and Standards 116

    American National Standard For Accessible and
    Useable Buildings and Facilities (ANSI A117.1)   116

    Uniform Federal Accessibility Standards (UFAS)   117

    Fair Housing Act Accessibility Guidelines   117

"Safe Harbors"   117

Americans with Disabilities Act Accessibility Guidelines   118

Canadian Policies and Practices 118

Ontarians with Disabilities Act   119

ODA   119

Residential Rehabilitation Assistance Program   119

Incorporating Human-Based Kitchen Design 120

CHAPTER 6: ASSESSING NEEDS **121**

Elements of a Design Program 122

Interviewing the Client. 122

Prepare for the Interview   122

Needs Assessment Forms   123

Client Information Forms   123

Job Site and House Information Forms   124

Personal Information   124

Getting To Know Your Client (Form 1) 124

Getting to Know Your Client's Home (Form 2) 125

Type of Home   126

The Home of the Future   127

Activities in the Kitchen (Form 3) 127

Storage in the Kitchen (Form 4) 128

Your Client's Kitchen (Forms 5 and 6) 129

Appliances   130

Client Preferences and Specifications   130

Budget   131

The Job Site   131

New Construction   131

Job Site Inspection (Form 7) 132

Dimensions (Forms 8 Through 13) 132

Preparing the Client 134

Establish A Plan   134

Ready For the Design Program? 135

Form 1: Getting to Know Your Client   136

Form 2: Getting to Know Your Client's Home   143

Form 3: Checklist for Kitchen Activities [Client Checklist]   145

Form 4: Kitchen Storage Inventory [Client Checklist]   150

Form 5: Cabinetry, Surfaces, and
Kitchen Features Checklist [Client Checklist]   166

Form 6: Appliance Preference Checklist [Client Checklist]   179

Form 7: Job Site Inspection   189

Form 8: Dimensions of the Kitchen – Floor Plan   196

Form 9: Dimensions of the Kitchen – Elevations   197

Form 10: Dimensions of Mechanical Devices   198

Form 11: Window Measurements   199

Form 12: Door Measurements   200

Form 13: Fixture and Appliance Measurements   201

CHAPTER 7: KITCHEN PLANNING **203**

Location and Types of Kitchens 203

Location of Kitchen   203

Work Zone   203

Social Area   204

Types of Kitchens   204

Closed Arrangements   205

Open Arrangements   208

Size of Kitchens   213

The Center Concept 214

Designing Kitchen Centers   221

Background on the Guidelines   221

Access Standards   222

Food Preparation Centers and Guidelines 222

Traffic and Work Aisles   223

Entry   223

Work Aisles   225

Circulation   227

Sink Center 228

Food Preparation Activities   228

Cleanup Activities   229

Other Activities   230

Recommendations   230

Refrigeration Center 241

Recommendations   241

Cooking Centers 244

Recommendations   245

Combining Centers 257

   Arranging the Centers   257

   Counter Areas   261

   Storage   266

   Cabinet Calculations   282

Serving and Dining Guidelines 292

   Recommendations   293

   Dining   296

   Recommendations   296

That's Entertaining 301

   Kitchens for Caterers   301

   Outdoor Kitchens   302

      Location   302

      Equipment   303

      Space Planning   305

A Kitchen Where You Need It 306

   Morning Kitchen   306

   Mini Kitchen   306

   Considerations   306

Summary 308

CHAPTER 8: MECHANICAL PLANNING **309**

Wiring/Electrical 309

   Wiring   309

   Receptacles   312

   Ground Fault Circuit Interrupters   313

   Special Wiring Needs   343

   Communications   315

Gas 316

Heating 316

   Types of Heaters   316

Considerations for the Kitchen 320

Cooling 321

   Natural Cooling   322

   Mechanical Cooling   322

Ventilation 323

   Updraft Ventilation Systems   326

Microwave Ovens and Ventilation System Combinations   328

Downdraft Ventilation Systems   328

Ventilation Efficiency   329

Ducts   330

Fan Size   330

Replacement Air   332

Noise   332

Controls and Features   333

Lighting 333

Natural or Daylighting   334

Types of Artificial Lighting   335

General or Ambient Lighting   335

Task Lighting   338

Accent Lighting   338

Lighting Fixtures   338

Location   340

Controls   342

Low Voltage Lighting   343

Safety   344

CHAPTER 9: MORE THAN A KITCHEN **345**

The Family Foyer or Mudroom 345

Designing the Family Foyer/Mudroom   349

Coats, Jackets, Hats, and Other Outerwear   349

Seating Area   352

Design Details   353

Materials   353

Mechanical Systems   353

Home Planning Center 354

Locating the Home Planning Center   355

The Desk Area   356

Desk Area Storage   358

Clearance Around the Desk Area   359

Lighting   360

A Standing Desk   360

Household Communications   361

Computer Workstation   362

A Laundry Area. 364

    What Type of Laundry?   364

    Laundry Equipment   366

        Utility Service   368

    Space Planning in the Laundry Area   369

        Laundry in Transition   371

        Storage   373

        Ironing   374

A Craft/Hobby Area 376

A Gardening Area. 379

    Planning the Indoor Garden Area   379

        Work Counter Area   379

        A Garden Sink   381

        Storage   382

    A Growing Area   383

Social Spaces 383

    The Kitchen Sitting Area   383

Summary 392

CHAPTER 10: A CLOSER LOOK AT YOUR CLIENT **393**

    Addressing Differences 393

    Design Considerations for Users 394

        Across The Lifespan   394

    Children 395

    Middle Years. 399

    Aging 400

        Physical Changes   400

    Mobility 404

        Kitchen Design Implications   405

        Refrigeration Center   411

        Flooring   412

    Dexterity/Strength/Balance/Stamina. 413

        Kitchen Design Implications   413

            General   413

            Sink Center   414

            Cooking Center   415

            Refrigeration Center   416

            Storage   416

Vision 417

    Kitchen Design Implications   418

        Lighting   418

        Color and Cueing   419

        Storage   421

        Controls   421

        Sink Center   422

        Cooking Center   422

Hearing and Speech 422

    Kitchen Design Implications   424

        General   424

        Noise Control   425

        Visual Cueing   425

Cognition 425

    Kitchen Design Implications   426

        General   426

        Refrigeration Center   428

        Storage   428

Summary 428

CHAPTER 11: PUTTING IT ALL TOGETHER **429**

The Design Process 430

The Design Program 432

    Goals and Purpose   433

    Objectives   433

    Activities and Relationships   433

        Relationship Matrix   436

        Bubble Diagram   437

The Design Drawing 438

    Templates   438

    Room Outline   441

    Visual Diagrams   445

    Three Dimensions and Vertical Relationships   445

    Priority Areas   446

        A Sample Design Drawing   447

    Finishing The Floor Plan   456

        Adjusting the Dimensions   456

Vertical Relationships   458

Evaluating and Checking   461

Putting It All Together – A Sample Project 466

A Sample Design Program   467

Goals and Purpose   467

Scope of the Project   468

Objectives and Priorities   468

Activities and Relationships   469

The Design Solution   469

Leah and Matthew's Kitchen   472

CHAPTER 12: KITCHEN PLANNING GUIDELINES WITH ACCESS STANDARDS. . . . 475

Kitchen Planning Guideline 1: Door/Entry 476

Kitchen Planning Guideline 2: Door Interference 477

Kitchen Planning Guideline 3: Distance Between Work Centers 478

Kitchen Planning Guideline 4: Separating Work Centers. 479

Kitchen Planning Guideline 5: Work Triangle Traffic 480

Kitchen Planning Guideline 6: Work Aisle 481

Kitchen Planning Guideline 7: Walkway 484

Kitchen Planning Guideline 8: Traffic Clearance at Seating 485

Kitchen Planning Guideline 9: Seating Clearance 487

Kitchen Planning Guideline 10: Cleanup/Prep Sink Placement 489

Kitchen Planning Guideline 11: Cleanup/Prep Sink Landing Area 490

Kitchen Planning Guideline 12: Preparation/Work Area 491

Kitchen Planning Guideline 13: Dishwasher Placement. 492

Kitchen Planning Guideline 14: Waste Receptacles 493

Kitchen Planning Guideline 15: Auxiliary Sink. 494

Kitchen Planning Guideline 16: Refrigerator Landing Area 495

Kitchen Planning Guideline 17: Cooking Surface Landing Area 496

Kitchen Planning Guideline 18: Cooking Surface Clearance 498

Kitchen Planning Guideline 19: Cooking Surface Ventilation 499

Kitchen Planning Guideline 20: Cooking Surface Safety 500

Kitchen Planning Guideline 21: Microwave Oven Placement 501

Kitchen Planning Guideline 22: Microwave Landing Area. 502

Kitchen Planning Guideline 23: Oven Landing Area 503

Kitchen Planning Guideline 24: Combining Landing Areas. 504

Kitchen Planning Guideline 25: Countertop Space 505

Kitchen Planning Guideline 26: Countertop Edges 506

Kitchen Planning Guideline 27: Storage 507

Kitchen Planning Guideline 28: Storage at Cleanup/Prep Sink 509

Kitchen Planning Guideline 29: Corner Cabinet Storage. 510

Kitchen Planning Guideline 30: Electrical Receptacles. 511

Kitchen Planning Guideline 31: Lighting. 512

GLOSSARY **513**

APPENDIX **520**

LIST OF PHOTOS **540**

LIST OF ILLUSTRATIONS **542**

REFERENCES **545**

RESOURCES **547**

INDEX **551**

INTRODUCTION

Our goal, our hope, is that this book will help you to be a better designer—more creative, more knowledgeable and more successful.

This is not the type of book that you sit down to read cover-to-cover. Rather, it is a book to be used again and again.

This is a book for your studio, office, or showroom —wherever you are at your creative best. We hope it finds a place on a shelf near your drawing board, computer or table, and eventually gets worn, with your comments written in the margins and "sticky notes" coming out in all directions.

This book was developed around the National Kitchen & Bath Association's Kitchen Planning Guidelines and the related Access Standards. With these guidelines as a core, we incorporated the infrastructure, environmental, electrical and mechanical considerations needed to apply the Planning Guidelines. We included discussions on historical and consumer trends in kitchens, plus research on kitchen design and planning. We added sections on assessing clients and gathering the information necessary to design a kitchen. In addition, we provided ideas for designing spaces related to kitchens, such as planning centers, laundries, craft, hobby and social areas. Finally, throughout the book, we emphasized understanding client needs and we integrated knowledge of universal design.

We organized and presented this book as if we were talking to a new designer, just starting a career. At the same time, we offered information, ideas, suggestions and tips for the more experienced kitchen designer. We firmly believe we can all learn something new—as we certainly did in writing this book!

We provided lots of references as to where to go for more industry information. In addition, we cross-referenced other books in the National Kitchen & Bath Association's Professional Resource Library series that contain additional information on such topics as construction, mechanical systems, cabinetry and graphics standards.

Design is visual, and therefore, a book on design must be visual. We included many drawings, diagrams and dimensioned plans to aid you in understanding the concepts presented. We added many photographs to show how the content is integrated into "real life" settings and to spark ideas of your own.

There are many worksheets and checklists to use in your work and with your clients. Feel free to use them as is or to adapt them to be useful to you. We are excited that we have been able to provide these worksheets and checklists in an electronic form on the CD that comes with this book. The electronic format will enable you to use them on a computer or edit them for your business before printing.

CHAPTER 1: Kitchen History and Trends

A BRIEF HISTORY OF THE KITCHEN

The kitchen and its place in family life have changed throughout history, in conjunction with the evolving lifestyles, economic conditions, values and attitudes of its users. The overall look, feel, location and relative importance of the kitchen in the home have been emblematic not only of the era, but also of the particular circumstances of the families they served.

So a brief walk through the history of kitchens will help the designer understand the ever-changing and complex interconnection between this room and the various roles it plays in domestic life. As the demographics and attitudes of our society change, so will the kitchen, to keep up with the needs of the users.

The history of the modern home kitchen begins with the need for a place of family food preparation, usually centered on the source of heat and light. This source has changed over time, but for ages the open fire in a hearth reigned supreme. It served as the sole heat source for the home until late in the 17th Century. This meant that most family living and activities took place in the one room that contained the fireplace.

The first known kitchen separated from the living area was in 13th Century Flanders, along the coast of what is now Belgium. Flemish kitchens contained tables on trestles for food preparation. Horizontal boards placed above the table provided a place to store kitchen utensils. These storage elements developed into display dressers used in 15th Century Flanders, where the number of shelves on the dresser was an indicator of social rank.

THE COLONIAL KITCHEN

The colonists in North America brought many ideas for kitchen design from Europe. Although established as a separate room in many homes, the standard kitchen of the 17th Century continued to serve as the dining room for the middle class, and occasionally as a bedroom and social area. Equipped with perhaps the only heat source in the home, a hearth, the kitchen was the focus of the family, providing for material and social needs.

In the warm Southern Colonies, the heat from cooking was not desired, so the kitchen served as a work area only and was often a separate structure located near the house. These simple 17th Century kitchens often contained a trestle table or bench, storage chest, corner cupboard and occasionally a separate worktable. Wooden floors were sprinkled with sand, which helped to keep them from absorbing odors.

Hearth and Beehive Ovens

The typical 18th Century kitchen was large, and included a six-foot wide and four-foot deep fireplace. The fireplace contained massive wrought andirons with racks, spits, and lug-poles to transfer pots into and out of the fire. Beehive ovens were built into the sidewall of the hearth. A table and chairs, as well as a worktable, were included. Because it was the most comfortable room in the home, the kitchen was often used for family bathing as well. In wealthier households, the kitchen was used by servants and was often located on the lower level or in a separate building. A summer kitchen consisting of a lean-to or annex to the main house kept extra heat out of the house.

Later in the Century, wood and coal cast iron stoves which enclosed the fire and transferred heat through the metal became available. These stoves were less of a fire hazard, but provided less heat for cooking. Benjamin Franklin designed one such stove, built to fit into the fireplace.

Most kitchens of the period were all unadorned wood, but by the second quarter of the 18th Century, paint was used—more as a preservative than for decorative purposes. As paint became more popular, stenciling, marbling and graining techniques were used on walls, woodwork and cabinetry.

THE MODERN KITCHEN

The modern kitchen has been influenced by two major trends that roughly coincide with the 19th and 20th centuries. The 19th Century brought industrialization, with social and technological changes. In the 20th Century, standardization surfaced, with a focus on work simplification and efficiency.

Houses and the kitchens associated with them changed as the country evolved into an industrialized nation that developed numerous new products and redefined the role of women and family life. In addition, democracy, joined with the industrial age and the rising middle class, discouraged the formation of a permanent servant class, so live-in household help was less available or often not reliable. This meant that the woman of the home had to take on many activities to manage and run the house.

The Victorian Kitchen

The Victorian kitchens were large and often located in the rear of the house or the basement. Many included a summer kitchen behind the main kitchen to prevent overheating in the warmer months. If the family was wealthy, servants would perform most of the cooking and household chores. The kitchens were usually not attractive, covered with institutional green or cream-colored enamel paint. Some had wainscoting, plate racks and glass door cabinets. They were not very comfortable or convenient.

The range, sink and table in the Victorian kitchen were all freestanding pieces. The pantry, located between the kitchen and dining room, contained large, wall-to-wall and floor-to-ceiling stationary cabinets that served as both a storage and a preparation area. These oak "pantry dressers" housed china behind glass doors on the top, with counters and usually a sink below.

THE BEECHER KITCHEN

Recognition that kitchens were not very functional and an interest in the development of the servant-less household led to the work of pioneers in the field of kitchen design. By 1870, Catherine Beecher and her sister, Harriet Beecher Stowe, a noted author and abolitionist, had written a book, *American Woman's Home Companion*, which made recommendations for all concerns of women at the time.

The kitchen they advocated used a ship's galley as the model. It featured work centers and used the latest technology. Storage was close by and compartmentalized. Open shelving was shallow to allow only one row of food items, and bins for flour and other products were planned into the design. Two work centers were present in the room for storage/preservation and cooking/serving. The cooking stove stood away from the work areas, while the other units incorporated work surfaces and shelves. Windows provided natural light. Painted walls and floors were easier to clean. They recommended placing the pantry between the kitchen and dining room to keep out noise and heat.

The Plumbed Sink

The development of water and sewer systems in the larger cities began to change the way households functioned. Early in the century, the kitchens contained a dry sink, but eventually households were able to hand-pump water and then the plumbed sink appeared late in the century. The Beechers' model kitchen used a plumbed faucet to distribute water. By the late 19th Century, campaigns to improve health conditions promoted the idea of cleanliness and sanitation in the home. The ability to obtain water and remove wastewater was critical to this development. Much of the emphasis on kitchen design and materials, too, was focused on sanitation and cleanliness.

The food preparation equipment of the 1800s began to reflect the emerging industrial revolution, and goods were designed with more utility and variety. These products were mass produced and available to the emerging middle class through mail order catalogs. Although the 19th Century began with open hearths and beehive ovens, large cast iron stoves fueled by coal or wood soon became the norm. These ranges often included tall, cylindrical hot water heaters that left scars in the kitchen floor. The Beechers encouraged the use of technology to simplify tasks and actually designed a stove that would achieve multiple tasks efficiently. By the late 1800s, electrification was possible in many locations, but electric rates were not affordable and most homes were not wired until the next Century.

STANDARDIZATION: THE 1900s

Several societal, economic and technological factors influenced the path of American women and the design of the home at the beginning of the 20th Century. The expansion of industrial jobs resulted in the reduced availability of household labor. Less help in the home was compounded in the 1930s by the economic constraints of the Great Depression. These factors, along with the introduction of improved appliances, led to the designing of more efficient kitchens that were reduced in both size and cost to accommodate the household's head cook, the housewife.

Home economists and others were involved in helping to research and study the equipment and work center concepts and in sharing this information with consumers. Sanitation was of prime importance in the kitchen. Around 1912, home economist Christine Frederick was concerned with the efficiency of the home and published articles about home tasks in the *Ladies Home Journal*. She borrowed the work principles of the factory and applied them to tasks in the home. In the 1930s, motion expert Lillian Gilbreth studied the number of steps necessary to prepare meals within certain kitchen arrangements. She felt that appliance manufacturers knew little about the needs of housewives in the kitchen.

The Laboratory Look

The new kitchens of the era, with their continuous work space and closed storage, looked very much like a laboratory designed for one person. The concept relied on standardized components that could be bought and added end-to-end to produce a kitchen of the desired length. With continuous base cabinets, a sink and built-in wall cabinets above, these new kitchens began to resemble the former serving pantries. The popularity and demand for the assembled kitchen concept led to growth in the mass production of building materials and kitchen cabinets. The full mechanization of appliances allowed them to be built in with the working surfaces as an integral part of this assembled kitchen.

Many guidelines were developed, based on the analysis of kitchen work tasks that recommended counter space and storage requirements. Research bulletins were published for farm families. The work triangle concept was developed. It utilized sink, range and refrigeration centers to act as a guide to create an efficient kitchen space. The U-shape, L-shape, corridor and one-wall kitchen were all layouts that could utilize the work triangle concept. More about the research into kitchen design can be found in Chapter 2 – Kitchen Design Research.

MAJOR KITCHEN TRENDS THROUGH THE 1900s

Throughout the 20th Century, kitchen design evolved rapidly as lifestyles changed, and new products and technologies were developed. Elements of some of these designs are now being revived and adapted for today's kitchens. Following are some of the highlights of kitchen design from the early 1900s to the 21st Century.

Early 1900s

Kitchens were decorated and furnished in a simple manner. Domestic scientists of the time described the kitchen as a gleaming, light-colored laboratory.

Around the turn of the Century a desire and need for more efficient storage appeared and cabinets that did exist were hung high on the wall.

Two new types of wooden cabinets appeared: the broom cabinet and the "linen" cabinet. The latter was used to store foodstuffs like cereals and canned goods.

The baking table evolved into a self-contained, upright cabinet work center with all the needed tools for baking. The "Hoosier" (or "Dutch") cabinets which typically came in oak or painted white enamel were marketed by manufacturers located mostly in Northern Indiana. The list of manufacturers included such names as G.P. McDougall & Sons, Kompass & Stoll Co., the Hoosier Manufacturing Co., Coppes Brothers and Zook.

Sheet metal cabinets promoted by the metal industry replaced wooden cabinets. These cabinets came to be known as the "Youngstown" cabinets.

Armstrong Cork Company began production of cork floor tile in 1904 in a limited number of colors. Cork usage declined in the 1930s.

For many homes, the fireplace was still the heat source for cooking and heating in the early 1900s. It was soon replaced, however, by coal- and wood-burning stoves and almost immediately followed by gas and kerosene stoves, as well as combination gas and coal ranges.

Although a prototype of the electric kitchen was exhibited in 1893, the electric stove did not move into the kitchen until 1909. This cooking surface without a flame was quite the novelty to many. By 1915, thermostats made electric and gas stoves "automatic."

Families with electric lighting were the envy of the neighborhood. If power was available, the lighting typically consisted of a bare, shade-less bulb hanging from the middle of the room on a cloth-covered cord.

The 1920s

The kitchens of the 1920s were a series of awkwardly connected, dark spaces removed from the family activities with little consideration given to the cook's view. It included as many as three small rooms used for various purposes. Most cabinets and appliances were white, often giving the appearance of a sanitized laboratory.

Pine, oak, maple and fir were favorite countertop materials. Wood was also used as a drain board for the sink. Once tile, steel and laminate became fashionable, consumers quickly switched from wood.

The farmhouse kitchen typically included a Hoosier cabinet, lots of open shelves, a pantry, a dish cupboard, a freestanding range, console sink and large kitchen table. Countertops and work surfaces were usually covered with enameled sheet metal or linoleum. In some homes, Hoosier or other built-in baking cabinets covered an entire wall. The Hoosier was gone by the 1940s.

Figure 1.1 Kitchens in the 1920s typically included an electric range with storage and cooking surface, open shelves, a dish cupboard and console sink. (Courtesy of *Reeves Journal*)

In the homes of the wealthy, the kitchen was the domain of servants. A trash disposal chute, foldout ironing board, bell indicator and intercom system became part of the more sophisticated kitchens.

Cast iron sinks were the most popular, along with earthenware sinks, which were enameled white on the inside and glazed brown on the exterior. Some sinks of the 1920s were made of a copper/nickel mix called Monel, a lightweight, white metal.

Appliances of the era included an icebox, gas stove and the new motor-driven wringer washer. Between 1925 and 1927 ranges came in colors, including black, white, red, green, buff, blue and gray.

In the late 1920s, the kitchen was first included into the decorative scheme of the home, creating colorful rooms for living and not just working.

Color in the kitchen was attributed to two legendary merchandisers: Abraham & Straus and Macy's. From the 1920s and into the 1930s, cobalt blue and silver color schemes were very popular. Black and white with pale tones of yellow and blue were also used. A yellow wall with a double band of blue just under the ceiling moulding was one combination.

Floors were most often covered with sheet linoleum or linoleum tiles, usually in a black-and-white checkered pattern. Colors also ranged from beige and brown to brilliant scarlet and navy blue. Patterns included Art Deco, Modern, and Colonial Revival. Embossed inlaid linoleum became available in 1925. In 1927, the Formica Company developed its first light-colored faux wood grain laminate.

The Tudor style was popular and included stonework, wood paneling, carvings, decorative mouldings and wooden beams.

The first all-steel refrigerator had furniture-like legs for aesthetic purposes, as well as being easier to clean under. The GE Monitor top was built in 1926 and cost $525. The round top design was named after the Monitor submarine. In 1929, Kelvinator turned the design into a box with no legs and a concealed compressor.

Common kitchen accessories included the electric toaster, coffeepot, Bakelite-handled cutlery and Clarice Cliff's "Bizarre" line of ceramics.

The 1930s

A "typical" 1930s kitchen featured porcelain-topped kitchen worktables and a Hoosier cabinet. An "atypical" kitchen of the time featured the boxy, built-in cabinetry. The built-in, "continuous kitchen" design, with its sequence of work stations and unbroken activity flow, resembled the production line of the modern factory. This highly organized kitchen, beginning in 1935, was known as the streamlined kitchen. The kitchen began to resemble a scientist's lab more than the heart of the home. Westinghouse ads showed kitchens with three designated work centers: refrigeration and preparation center; range and serving center; and sink and dishwasher center.

Later in the decade, wall-to-wall white steel cabinets, as well as standardized prefab wooden cabinets, were backed by rectangular white tile on the walls. New Porta-Bilt built-in cabinets promoted the idea of being able to build in cabinets and then take them with you when you moved. The breakfast nook was in vogue.

The introduction of non-porous materials for improved sanitation followed the cleanliness movement taking place in the bathroom. Countertops used oversized hexagonal tiles in olive green, black and beige. Another look was the white and/or pale yellow four-inch square tiles on diagonal with accent trim in black, dark blue, green or maroon.

Black and white tile remained a standard on floors. Linoleum continued to be installed in sheet and tile forms, and tile designs combining different colors began to increase in popularity.

Figure 1.2 This 1930s kitchen with free-standing appliances features a monitor-top refrigerator and electric range. (Courtesy of The Henry Ford Museum)

Vinyl made its debut as vinyl/asbestos called Vinylite, but was not widely marketed until the late 1940s.

Lighting consisted of a single, flush-mount ceiling fixture in the center of the room. Sinks were large and freestanding. They included a double bowl and drain board.

Popular colors of the day included Art Deco bright pastels, white, cream, coral red, sky blue, pearl gray, peach and mint green. Entering a '30s kitchen, you might see light gray cabinets with light green panels and peach walls.

Chromium was widely used on appliances and fixtures. Although the cooling coil-crowned electric refrigerator was available, many households still used the icebox. Chlorofluorocarbon was produced under the name of Freon by DuPont. Electric refrigerators were also shown with legs to allow easy cleaning beneath. Dishwashers were portable and mostly top-loading models. The Tappan "table top" range, a combination of white-enameled range, cupboard and worktable, was produced. Electric toasters toasted one side of bread at a time. The first electric powered ironer and food waste disposer were introduced.

Fiestaware and Harlequin dinnerware were popular kitchen accessories.

The 1940s

Popular colors were white, pale green, light gold, forest green and gray with maroon accents.

Kitchens of the era included cabinets that created a seamless, uniform wall of doors and drawers above and below a continuous counter. A range and sink were incorporated into the continuous counter. These modular cabinets were available in painted wood or metal. Custom kitchen cabinets were also marketed.

Stainless steel became popular for sinks. Linoleum or laminate materials covered the countertops and linoleum continued to be used on floors. Black and white linoleum tile remained popular, but a range of patterns and colors, as well as cork and asbestos tiles, became available after World War II. Vinyl was heavily marketed in the later part of the decade.

Appliances in the kitchen included a rounded electric refrigerator, a dishwasher and an electric range. Auto defrost in refrigerators was developed. In 1947, the "Radarange" was the first microwave on the market, used mostly by restaurants and hotels. Disposers, mostly in the batch model, became available. The popularity of small appliances began with the introduction of the electric skillet, blender and portable mixer.

Colonial maple furniture and Priscilla curtains were typical accessories, often in black and white with red accents. Franciscan Dinnerware had its beginning.

The 1950s

New housing of the time formalized the trend for built-in kitchens and often included an informal eating area.

Colorful linoleum reigned supreme until the 1950s, when asbestos and ceramic tiles became the standard. Asphalt-asbestos tile was the most widely used resilient floor covering on the market. Semi-flexible vinyl asbestos tile was also popular. Emerging materials were fiberglass, cast aluminum, acrylics and resins. Glass became a popular material used in glass-chip terrazzo floors and countertops. Colorful laminates were used on countertops and cabinets.

Steel cabinets remained popular, but the idea of the factory-built cabinet was born. Merillat Industries and Wood-Metal (now Wood-Mode) cabinet companies were founded, as was the National Institute of Wood Kitchen Cabinets in 1955. (It is now KCMA – The Kitchen Cabinet Manufacturers Association.) Dramatic colors were introduced; among them pink, gray, pastel greens, turquoise and sky blue.

Refrigerators were large spaceship-like units in bright colors with a top-mount freezer. Bottom freezers were also available, and Amana patented the first self-defrost model in 1954. The first icemaker was introduced in 1953 by Servel and consumed one-third of the freezer space. Gas-powered refrigerators were marketed and GE introduced the "wall refrigerator" to integrate refrigeration with the continuous cabinet look of the kitchen. All cold food storage was now at eye level.

The wall oven was developed, and Tappan produced the first domestic microwave wall oven in 1952. It sold for $1,295.

Front-loading, portable dishwashers were developed, followed by built-in models of either the top- or front-loading type. Continuous feed disposers came on the market. In 1953, automatic clothes washer sales topped those of the wringer washer for the first time and Bendix introduced its Duomatic combination washer/dryer.

Accessories included colorful molded plastic furniture with chrome trim, Russel Wright American Modern dinnerware and Tupperware.

The 1960s

Great rooms with an adjacent open kitchen reflected the more casual lifestyle of the time. Although "space age kitchens of the future" were publicized, they were not really taken to heart by consumers.

Pop Art colors, like acid green, orange, pink, red, yellow, bright blue, black and white were the look of the 1960s.

New no-wax, sheet vinyl and ceramic tile in bright colors and strong patterns covered floors. Brick and wood floors were also used. Furniture designer Paul McCobb designed "Eurostyle" cabinetry with aluminum extruded legs and cabinet dividers from the Mutschler Brothers in the Midwest. Cheerful painted metal cabinets were teamed with laminate surfaces in brightly mixed colors and highly patterned wallpaper.

In 1963 the self-cleaning oven was developed, and in 1967 Raytheon, after acquiring Amana in 1965, introduced the first countertop microwave oven. By 1969, all built-in dishwashers were of the front-loading type. Chilled water and crushed ice dispensers were now available in refrigerators.

Accessories found in the 1960s kitchen were the "Smile" cookie jar, Pop Art posters, and super graphic Venetian blinds.

The 1970s

Colors such as brown, orange, avocado green and harvest gold were all the rage while dark wood cabinets, as well as cream laminate "Euro" cabinets with oak trim, were beginning to become popular.

Cabinet companies experimented with wood-like alternatives, and some adopted particleboard for cabinet components. In-cabinet storage accessories, like the vertical knife drawer, were becoming increasingly available.

Energy consciousness was imposed due to the oil embargo and the resulting energy crisis. The U.S. government began to look at the energy efficiency of appliances and developed the Energy Guide labels to help consumers find energy-efficient appliances and equipment. Meanwhile, built-in and black glass-front appliances, the trash compactor, the over-the-range microwave oven and the food processor were introduced. Jenn-Air launched the indoor grill. And microwave oven sales were accelerating.

Patterned laminates and butcher block were common on counters. The solid surface counter with integral sink was now available in four colors, which were thought to be all the choices consumers and designers could possibly need. Mylar wallpaper was in style.

Fluorescent lighting was used to save energy and track lighting was added for flexibility and to increase the amount of light. Floors were covered with no-wax vinyl, ceramic tiles, and indoor/outdoor kitchen carpeting in various patterns.

Accessories found in the homes of the 1970s included Styrofoam "wood" beams for the ceiling, Tiffany lamps and antiques.

The 1980s

The 1980s was somewhat of a transition period and an era of difficult economic times, high interest rates and higher energy prices. Because of this, many households were remodeling rather than building and saving costs in their kitchen projects by making cosmetic changes, like resurfacing cabinets or changing hardware.

Figure 1.3 Islands became popular during the 1980s, along with neutral colors. (Courtesy of Wood-Mode, Inc.)

Kitchens continued to open up into other rooms so that families could spend more time together. The great room was more common. Eating bars on peninsulas became popular as an informal eating space. Some kitchens included islands.

Cabinets continued to be influenced by sleek European designs. The Euro-style, frameless cabinet was gaining popularity in the American market. Laminate cabinets with oak trim continued to be in vogue. Appliance garages began to appear. At the opposite end of the spectrum, the 1980s also saw the country look and old world styling used.

Neutral and earth tone solid colors with little texture covered surfaces, while almond joined white and black for appliance colors. Glass block returned and granite began to appear on countertops. Overall, solid surface counters gained in popularity. Color-through laminates became available for counter surfaces and many households chose stainless steel sinks.

Side-by-side refrigerators, along with icemakers, became the popular style. Trash compactors began to appear in more kitchens, but they never developed into a major trend. The microwave oven became a standard kitchen appliance. Sealed gas burners and halogen heating elements appeared on the market. Induction cooking technology was also available and promoted as the cooking method that would reign supreme, but it never thrived in the North American market.

The 1990s

Kitchens continued to open up and expand. These larger kitchens accommodated more people and more family activities.

Kitchen designs on the upswing included the unfitted kitchen, a look comprised of individual pieces of furniture to replace cabinetry, each serving a specific purpose in the kitchen. Kitchens were also designed with many new shapes and configurations. Islands became highly desirable. The integrated kitchen with hidden major appliances was beginning to emerge.

White cabinets were widely used, along with the many natural woods, including cherry, oak, maple and hickory. A combination of painted and natural wood was also popular.

Figure 1.4 A mix of painted and wood finishes, and cabinetry configured to look like unfitted furniture, were two style trends that emerged in the 1990s and are still popular today. (Courtesy of Julie A. Stoner, CKD, ASID – Wayne, Pennsylvania)

Numerous storage and task areas were built into the kitchen cabinetry. Consumers desired a built-in desk or paperwork area in the kitchen. Drawer configurations were adapted to refrigerators and dishwashers. Work spaces were improved with the inclusion of under-cabinet lighting to illuminate work surfaces. Low voltage lighting and compact fluorescent lights provided for more flexibility because of their smaller size.

Solid surface materials were considered the ultimate in countertops and they were also incorporated into floors and cabinet panels. Granite counters became more common in high-end kitchens.

Almond was a popular appliance color, but was replaced by a new color called bisque or biscuit. White and black were still strong, with stainless steel emerging.

More households installed an additional refrigerator in the kitchen, wet bar, family room or elsewhere.

Warming drawers for residential use came on the market, along with electronic controls.

As Baby Boomers looked towards retirement, the idea of incorporating universal design features in their homes gained interest.

After a move by consumers to install restaurant-grade appliances into their home, the appliance industry developed professional-style appliances to provide consumers with a safer alternative. For high-end kitchens, the professional look was extremely popular.

A return to the look of the 1930s, 1940s, 1950s emerged with retro-styled appliances that contained all of the technologies of modern appliances.

Energy standards demanded that appliance manufacturers design and build models that were increasingly more energy and water efficient. The International Energy Star program began.

Figure 1.5 Professional-style appliances were developed in the 1990s and remain popular today. (Courtesy of GE)

CURRENT AND CONTINUING DESIGN TRENDS – THE 2000s

Clearly, styles, designs, colors and materials go in and out of fashion, often rapidly. New technology is constantly providing new products. So the professional designer should make a regular practice of attending trade shows and reading trade and consumer publications and on-line materials to stay up to date. For more information on today's most popular kitchen (and bath) styles and how to create and adapt them, consult *Design Principles* in NKBA's Professional Resource Library.

Aside from design and material trends, however, there are over-arching demographic and lifestyle factors worth noting that are influencing kitchen planning in this new millennium. Today's casual lifestyle finds more household members working together in the kitchen and carrying on a wider variety of activities. There is often a more relaxed style of entertaining and guests help with the food preparation. Both trends call for a kitchen where people can interact and where two or more cooks can work.

DEMOGRAPHIC AND POPULATION TRENDS

A study of the demographic and population trends for North America, as well as specific population groups, provides valuable insight into market potential as well as influences on kitchen space use and design. Two major trends emerging are an increasingly more culturally diverse population and a larger number of older people. Other trends of interest may be changes in household composition. All of these affect consumer buying trends.

Population Diversity

According to the State of the Nation's Housing 2002, a publication of the Joint Center for Housing Studies of Harvard University, almost two-thirds of the household gain in the U.S. has involved minorities, and one in five U.S. households is headed by either a foreign-born individual or a first-generation American. The disproportionately large increase in minority households is due to immigration. A diverse population is also present in Canada.

This increasing diversity means a wider range of lifestyles, and design criteria, to be considered for clients of varying backgrounds.

An Aging Population

It is projected that by 2030, 22 percent of the American population will be 65 years of age and older and 25 percent of that population will be minorities. Thirteen percent of the Canadian population is 65 years of age and older, an increase of 10.2 percent since 1996. This is twice the growth of other age groups.

Increased life expectancy is credited with some of the increase. In the 18th Century, the average North American was expected to live to the age of 35, but by 2000 that increased to 77.1 years of age for residents of the United States and 79.4 for residents of Canada.

These demographic trends open up a large market of individuals who will have an increased interest in kitchens that are safe, comfortable and ergonomically designed, and accessible design will be critical for those with disabilities. See Chapter 10 for additional characteristics of this population and design applications appropriate for them.

Household Composition

Other demographic trends noted by the National Association of Home Builders and the Joint Center for Housing Studies of Harvard University that could impact the design market include the changes in household composition.

From 1974 to 2000, the number of dual-employed couples increased from 43 percent of the household population to 57 percent. Busier households, where two adults as well as children are trying to prepare breakfast in the morning, need a well-designed and functional kitchen in which to work and to interact.

The number of non-family households, with either two unrelated individuals or a single-person, rose 11 percent between 1996 and 2001. Family households headed by an unmarried person, typically a single parent, increased 8 percent. These population groups may not need as large a space, but they may desire more personal touches that fulfill their needs.

The one household category that experienced the smallest increase was married-couple families, which grew by only 3 percent between 1996 and 2001. Similar trends are occurring in Canada.

CONSUMER REFERENCES

In terms of what consumers today want in their kitchens, a recent National Association of Home Builders study indicated their top preference for kitchen arrangement (40%) was having the kitchen and family room visually open but separated by a half wall. Other choices included:

- The kitchen and family room completely open (23%)

- The kitchen and family room in separate areas of the home (18%)

- The kitchen and family room side by side but separated by a full wall (9%)

The top features considered to be "must haves" by consumers in a NAHB survey were a walk-in pantry (85%) and an island work area (77%).

In a National Family Opinion survey, almost 70 percent of respondents with a pre-1946 home gave extra cabinet space top priority. A high proportion of these households also desired to upgrade their wiring, change or add plumbing fixtures, change the floor plan and remove walls.

The primary goal of households who are remodeling a kitchen, according to a *Kitchen & Bath Design News* survey of kitchen dealers, designers and remodelers, is to update the appearance and add new features (78%). Also important are a more efficient or accessible layout (65%) and additional storage space (42%).

Overall it is evident that convenience and organization are an important part of what consumers want in a design. A well-planned kitchen with good storage that allows for easy food preparation is more important than the newest kitchen trends.

Here are additional ways demographic and lifestyle trends are affecting kitchen planning today.

SPACE USAGE TRENDS

• **Command central.** As the kitchen continues to be the hub of activities in the home, the space it occupies continues to expand and open into other rooms. Combining the kitchen with a dining area, family room and/or den creates one large living space or great room. Often this gathering space includes a fireplace. Sometimes a portion of the great room replaces the formal dining room.

Figure 1.6 This kitchen is completely open to a family room area. (Courtesy of Gerard Cirrarello, CMKBD – Westbrook, Connecticut)

- **Islands.** Consumers' desire for an island in the kitchen remains high and today's larger kitchens can easily accommodate one. These islands vary greatly in size, shape and usage and may include multiple levels. The island may be used solely as a prep area, or contain a variety of appliances and fixtures, including a cooktop, sink, or microwave oven. One portion may also serve as an eating bar for snacks and informal meals.

- **Multiple height counters.** Following the principles of universal design, multiple counter heights provide work space for a variety of activities and users. Counters that are higher than the standard 36 inches make for comfortable work spaces for taller individuals while lower-than-standard levels provide good surfaces for shorter or seated individuals.

- **Multiple cooks.** The multiple-cook kitchen is designed with enough space to accommodate a couple, or adults and children who enjoy cooking together.

Figure 1.7 Multiple height counters include an area higher than 36 inches for eating or for work spaces for taller users. (Courtesy of American Woodmark)

- **Center or zone design.** An increase in cooks, activities and entertaining in the kitchen has led to a focus on activity-based centers or zones. Expanding on the three primary centers of the work triangle, this design can include multiples of the basic and ancillary zones in the space.

- **Windows.** A larger number of windows, as well as larger windows, increases natural light and adds to the feeling of openness. However, this decreases the area available for tall appliances and wall storage.

Opening up wall space for windows, art work, or an open space design has developed into a kitchen with minimal inclusion or complete absence of wall cabinets. All of the storage is placed in base cabinets or pantry type storage areas. A lack, or reduction in the number of, wall cabinets presents a new way to look at kitchen design.

Consumers want pantries more than ever. Pantries can be of different sizes, tall or walk-in and located in different parts of the kitchen. Many storage devices to make better use of pantry space are available.

Figure 1.8 This kitchen places most of the storage space in the pantry and base cabinets, providing only minimal wall cabinets. (Courtesy of Joel Leizan – Laguas, Puerto Rico)

ENVIRONMENTAL AWARENESS TRENDS

- **Recycling.** Whether by choice or necessity, many households include recycling in their daily routine. Because the kitchen is the source of many recyclable materials, creating space for temporarily storing bottles and cans, etc., is a growing trend.

- **Preserving natural resources.** Higher costs and environmental awareness have prompted many consumers to be conscious of natural resource usage in their homes. These consumers are looking for more water- and energy-efficient appliances.

- **Green building.** An increasing number of consumers consider themselves pro-environment and look for environmentally sound or "green" building products, including those made of recycled material. Consumers are avoiding endangered tropical hardwoods like mahogany, rosewood and teak.

ACTIVITY TRENDS

- **Hub of the home.** The kitchen has evolved into the hub of home where the family meets for meals, carries on conversations, entertains, completes homework assignments and conducts other activities too numerous to mention. All this activity calls for a space that is multi-functional and flexible.

- **Hobby cooking.** The popularity of cooking shows on television has sparked an interest in hobby cooking. As a departure from the day-to-day meal preparation, hobby cooking makes use of new techniques and appliances to prepare foods for meals at home or while entertaining guests. Hobby cooking often involves cooking as a form of entertaining, so a large kitchen that accommodates a crowd is necessary.

- **Health and wellness.** Many consumers are health conscious today and this is reflected in how they shop, prepare and store food. A concern over water safety and improved flavor has prompted many consumers to seek separate water filtration systems for drinking and cooking water in the kitchen. The filtering devices can be located at the sink, within the faucet housing or in the refrigerator.

- **Electronics.** As households congregate and spend more time in the kitchen, they begin to incorporate a television to keep up with the world's events, a computer for work, e-mail and networking, and home audio systems. Many parents also prefer to have their children use the computer in the kitchen so they can easily monitor their activities.

- **Technology.** Our fascination with technology extends to today's kitchens. From improved energy efficiency and water usage to high-tech controls, today's appliances are state-of-the art devices. Small computer-like components allow the consumer to choose from a wide variety of settings and preset start times. Appliances monitor multiple temperatures at one time, keep refrigerated food at the perfect temperature, sense when food is cooked or when dishes are clean, and even change from a cooling device to a cooking device. Refrigerators are available with a complete computer and/or television in the door, and Internet capabilities allow users to control appliances from remote locations.

Figure 1.9 Television and Internet access are now available in some refrigerator models. (Courtesy of LG Electronics)

25

Figure 1.10 Drawer configurations for dishwashers were first developed in the 1990s. (Courtesy of Burke Cheney – Wilton, Connecticut)

LOCATION TRENDS

- **Outdoor kitchens.** The popularity of grilling and the desire to expand the home to the outdoors has led to the development of the outdoor kitchen. New appliances and materials allow the designer to develop a complete kitchen outdoors including grills, burners, refrigerators, beer taps, woks, ice makers, warming drawers and even heaters and fireplaces.

- **Outpost kitchens.** The need and desire to prepare and serve food in areas of the home other than the kitchen has prompted the design of outpost kitchen spaces that can function as mini kitchens. Among the common locations are bedrooms, family rooms, basement recreation rooms or in an office area.

As part of the master or guest bedroom suite, many households are incorporating space for a small refrigerator and/or microwave oven to handle food, drink and health needs. Households are finding the outpost kitchen a convenient solution to the morning rush, as support stations when a family member is injured or ill, or a means for providing refreshments close at hand for the expanding number of activities that may take place in the bedroom and bathroom suite area.

Figure 1.11 Fully equipped outdoor kitchens now expand the living area. (Courtesy of Viking Range Corp.)

PRODUCT TRENDS

- **The second appliance.** Partly in response to the need for multiple work stations, multiple appliances are becoming a more common feature of today's larger, high-end kitchen designs. Consumers sometimes seek two dishwashers to accommodate their needs while entertaining or to help manage their busy lifestyles, using clean dishes from one dishwasher and placing them in the other to be washed. An extra small refrigerator or refrigeration drawers provide special use or additional cold storage. These refrigeration units can also be used in recreation rooms, family rooms, bedrooms, bathrooms, outdoor kitchens and wet bars. Double ovens provide more space for baking. Microwave ovens and other smaller appliances are also now found in many other rooms of the home.

- **Variety.** With such a large variety of sizes and styles, little is standard today when it comes to appliances. Although many appliances still come in standard sizes, more of the newer models are appearing in both larger and smaller sizes than before. These 48-inch refrigerators, 30-inch dishwashers and extra-wide ovens all require special planning considerations.

- **Controls.** Increasing numbers of appliances are incorporating electronic controls that only require a touch of the finger to use. Included on dishwashers, refrigerators, ranges and wall ovens initially, the controls are now moving to the glass ceramic and gas cooktops, where they allow expanded control of the cooking surface, along with built-in safety features like lock-out functions and surface sensors.

- **Multiple sinks.** Larger kitchens are now incorporating a smaller, second sink to serve as an additional work station for multiple cooks. These smaller sinks often function as a salad sink or a prep area for the second cook.

SUMMARY

With each previous era, new design trends emerged that incorporated the lifestyles and technologies of the time. Although certain styles and designs may go in and out of fashion during various periods of time, the current selection of colors, materials, styles, sizes and textures offers the consumer and designer an unlimited array of choices for a kitchen design plan. An important part of the kitchen designers' job is to stay abreast of the ever-changing array of products and the evolving lifestyle and design trends that affect their practice.

CHAPTER 2: Kitchen Design Research

Creating functional kitchen storage and counter workspaces has been the focus of educators and designers for decades. As early as 1870, Catherine Beecher and her sister Harriett Beecher Stowe were making recommendations for homemaking, including how to plan an efficient kitchen (Beecher & Stowe, 1869). Their plans included work centers and efficient storage ideas. By the early 1900s, the analysis of housework moved Christine Frederick to propose kitchen plans that would improve work efficiency (Frederick, 1913). Since her early works, numerous studies related to work efficiency, storage and energy use have resulted in recommendations for well-planned kitchens.

EARLY STUDIES

Some of the earliest known research was conducted by home economists at state universities who were funded by the U.S. Department of Agriculture's Agricultural Experiment Station (AES) to investigate ways to improve rural housing conditions. Findings from their studies were often published in AES Bulletins and then summarized in consumer pamphlets developed by the Cooperative Extension Service. These two agencies together had a large role in developing the first guidelines for the modern kitchen.

A 1932 bulletin by Deane Carter reports on several studies of housing that had been conducted by this time. Her work was funded by the AES and the President's Conference on Home Building and Home Ownership. She conducted personal interviews with farm families in Arkansas, reviewed more than 1000 kitchen plans and the catalogs of twenty cabinet manufactures in order to make recommendations for standard cabinet sizes. Some of her recommendations are tied to construction elements. For example, a wall cabinet should be as tall as a standard door height; a kitchen can have a 3-foot wide work aisle because that allows a door to be placed at the end; counter height should be at the most "commonly preferred height."

In New York, Ella Cushman published several Cooperative Extension bulletins to encourage work efficiency and good household management techniques. Her 1936 bulletin, "The Development of a Successful Kitchen," illustrated numerous ideas that would reduce the time and energy the homemaker spent in the kitchen. In this bulletin, work centers are introduced, work surfaces are at different heights, and cabinets are divided for convenience. The bulletin even illustrated a sink in an island.

By the late 1930s and early 1940s, the work of Maud Wilson began to illustrate a scientific awareness of the study of user needs in kitchen planning. Her analysis of The Willamette Valley Farm Kitchen (1938) involved surveys of farm families to determine the size and arrangement of kitchens in the homes of this region of Oregon.

First, the functions of the kitchen and other work areas in the homes were determined. Then the equipment and other items used to accomplish the tasks and functions were determined. An analysis was made of the items to group them according to use. Work distances were developed for completing the tasks. Finally, recommendations for the various centers were made according to this analysis. Wilson and Helen McCullough also published a bulletin that specified A Set of Utensils for the Farm Kitchen (1940), which encouraged "fewer and better utensils, wisely selected, well cared for, conveniently stored."

By the late 1940s, Maud Wilson developed two reports focused on the design and placement of kitchen cabinets (Patterns for Kitchen Cabinets [1947] and Considerations in Planning Kitchen Cabinets [1947]) based on her research during the past decade. She recommended work spaces beside the sink and range, various work heights depending on the task being completed, pull-outs to provide various work heights, and various cabinet arrangements to handle the many different items stored in the kitchen.

STUDIES AT MID-CENTURY

Standards from the 1948 study *Functional Kitchen Storage* (Heiner & McCullough, 1948) and the 1949 Small Homes Council (SHC) report, Cabinet Space for the Kitchen (McCullough, 1949) established the early guidelines for kitchen storage promoted by the Small Homes Council. McCullough (1949) compared the Small Homes Council standards with the Federal Housing Administration (FHA) Minimum Property Standards (MPS). The MPS were based on the number of bedrooms, while the Small Homes Council recommendations were based on family size. Generally, the SHC wall cabinet recommendations were less generous than the MPS and the base cabinet recommendations were more generous. McCullough cautioned to be sure the MPS were met.

Figure 2.1 Research in the 1950s showed that the sink was the most frequently used area of the kitchen. (Courtesy of Blanco)

Guides For Arrangement Of Urban Family Kitchens

Heiner and Steidel examined another aspect of kitchen design in their 1951 study of kitchen arrangements. They studied cooks preparing and serving meals and cleaning up in several kitchen arrangements. Some of their findings were: the sink is the most frequently used area; the range was second in use, but most often inspected; the mix center was third; and the refrigerator, dining, and serving areas tied for fourth. They recommended keeping work areas together, but cautioned that storage and work areas must be planned into the space.

Energy Saving Kitchen

A study by the Agricultural Research Service of Beltsville, MD, developed and evaluated energy saving kitchen designs. Based on a review of numerous studies of human energy expenditures during cooking activities, three kitchens with three variations each, were developed and built so that cooks could work in them and the arrangements and storage could be studied. The kitchens included seated work areas, carts, and pull-outs, and specially designed storage features, such as revolving base cabinet shelves, slant-front wall cabinets and floor-to-ceiling open dish storage. The kitchens were demonstrated in magazines and through Cooperative Extension bulletins.

Kitchen Guidelines

During the 1960s, the Small Homes Council continued to issue updated guidelines (Kapple, 1964; Wanslow, 1965) largely based on the earlier research. They concluded that the optimum kitchen space in a home would depend on a family's belongings and living habits, and be limited by the amount of space available. Thus, multiple standards based upon home size (minimum, medium, and liberal) were established due to a wide variety of requirements.

In 1975, NKBA joined the Small Homes Council in issuing the *Kitchen Industry Technical Manual*, Volume 5 (Jones & Kapple, 1975), which made recommendations for minimum- and liberal-sized kitchens. The 21 guidelines listed in this publication became the basis for the Certified Kitchen Designer exam. The Technical Manuals were issued in a second edition in 1984 (Jones & Kapple).

KITCHEN RESEARCH IN THE 1990s

In the late 1980s and early 1990s, NKBA sponsored two research projects that impacted their kitchen planning guidelines (Cheever, 1992). In 1991, Yust and Olsen (1992) completed a study entitled "Residential Kitchens: Planning Principles for the 90s." They surveyed clients of Certified Kitchen Designers about their kitchens and scored their kitchens based on the 1984 guidelines. A large portion of the kitchens scored poorly, indicating that the guidelines were not reflecting the current trends and needs of kitchen design.

The results of the Yust and Olsen study led NKBA to conduct a Utensil Survey Project (Cheever, 1992), the results of which were incorporated into the guidelines used by the kitchen design industry. NKBA's project consisted of:

1) developing a new core list of items typically found in a North American kitchen;

2) identifying the base/wall cabinet and countertop frontage required to accommodate these items;

3) comparing these new dimensional requirements with the existing information listed in the Small Homes Council *Kitchen Industry Technical Manual*, Volume 5 (Jones & Kapple, 1975); and

4) developing new industry standards for acceptable kitchens in two categories: kitchens under 150 square feet and kitchens over 150 square feet.

The Cheever study used only 25 households, but found that the number of items stored in the kitchen had increased 110% from the number reported in the research of Heiner and McCullough (1948). The findings from both of these NKBA-sponsored studies resulted in significant changes in the Kitchen Planning Guidelines in 1992. The guidelines were updated again in 1996 to incorporate universal design recommendations. Although many space requirements changed, the basic recommendations for the amount and type of storage did not change from the 1992 NKBA recommendations (Cheever, 1996).

VIRGINIA TECH KITCHEN RESEARCH

As NKBA began to review guidelines in 2000, they recognized a need to reexamine kitchen use and storage requirements. The first study, "Someone's in the Kitchen" (Emmel, Beamish, & Parrott, 2001), was actually a combination of several studies: content analysis, interviews and observations of cooking activities, and a national telephone survey. The second study, "Kitchen Storage Research Study" (Parrott, Beamish, & Emmel, 2003) was an inventory of items kept in recently designed kitchens.

Someone's In The Kitchen

The project had the following objectives:

1) to identify the types of foods, utensils, appliances and products that are stored and used in today's kitchens.

2) to identify activities which occur in today's kitchens.

3) to determine how kitchen storage and counter space are utilized and organized.

4) to classify different styles of food preparation and patterns of kitchen activities.

5) to analyze work center and work flow guidelines in relation to the styles of food preparation and patterns of kitchen activities.

6) to evaluate current criteria governing the use of cabinets and other storage devices in the kitchen to determine if they meet the needs of today's households.

The research project designed to address these objectives had three segments: a content analysis of shelter magazines, a personal interview and cooking activity and a national random telephone survey.

CONTENT ANALYSIS

One method for evaluating the design and components of contemporary kitchens is to analyze the kitchens featured in popular magazines. From a six-month period in 2000, nineteen different shelter, design and kitchen-related magazines were reviewed. A total of 104 articles were analyzed. The findings revealed information about kitchen design features, appliances and activities, as well as the lifestyle of the households using the kitchens. Islands and wall ovens were two of the most common features. The content analysis provided insight into contemporary kitchen design and usage, important to formulating the interview and telephone survey questions.

PERSONAL INTERVIEW AND COOKING ACTIVITY

A two-phase laboratory activity was developed to assess how families use kitchen space. A personal interview gathered information about the participants' household, food shopping and food preparation patterns and their present kitchen and its use related to storage, counter space and appliances. A cooking activity was designed to assess how individuals used kitchen space while preparing a set menu of foods that represented different types of cooking activities. Demographic and anthropometrical data were also collected.

The sample for the laboratory activity was drawn from the local area of Virginia Tech University. A purposive sample of males and females of varying heights, ages, and abilities, as well as different household types and cooking partners, was selected. The target sample size was calculated based on 75 menu preparations, but the total number of participants was greater due to multiple cooks sharing some preparation activities.

There were five different menus prepared in the cooking activity. Three different kitchens in the Center for Real Life Kitchen Design at Virginia Tech were used to provide variety. All cooking activities were videotaped for later analysis.

NATIONAL TELEPHONE SURVEY

A national telephone survey was conducted to further investigate patterns of kitchen use. The 52-question instrument gathered information about food buying, appliance usage and cooking patterns, as well as activities that take place in the kitchen. Demographic information about participants was also collected. The survey employed a random sampling design, using a national sampling firm. Telephone interviews of approximately sixteen minutes in length were completed with 630 adults over age eighteen. The interviews provided a representative sample of adults residing in households in the contiguous United States with a margin of error of ± 3.9% at the 95% level of confidence.

RESULTS AND IMPLICATIONS

The local and national samples in these studies were similar in their demographic make-up. A majority of the respondents in both samples (over 90%) were from households of fewer than four people. The most common types of households were a family or adult couple. Both samples included more females than males, within a wide variety of age and income brackets. Approximately 75% of each sample lived in single-family residences they owned. There was not a dominance of any particular age or size of residence. The national sample was equally divided among small town, rural, city and suburban residences.

Figure 2.2 Despite take-out and restaurant meals, researchers have found that people still cook on a regular and frequent basis. (Courtesy of KitchenAid)

The researchers found that kitchens are busy places, with frequent cooking and many other household activities. Key conclusions from the study can be grouped according to the following questions: What do people do in their kitchens? Who is cooking? How do people cook? What do people have in their kitchen? and What do people want in their kitchens?

What Do People Do in Their Kitchens?

- People cook on a regular and frequent basis, especially in family or couple households. For example, over 70% of the national sample prepared a meal five or more times a week.

- People cook, eat, socialize, manage their household, and engage in recreational activities in their kitchens. Around 80% talked on the telephone and took medicines and vitamins. Over 70% planned meals in the kitchen and had conversations with friends and families.

- Many activities in the kitchen require counter or table space and seating. Multiple people may be in the kitchen, involved in various activities, even if they are not all participating in cooking activities.

- Eating in the kitchen is a common activity (almost 2/3 of participants), and most people consider it important to have an eating area in the kitchen. Even people who do not regularly eat in the kitchen consider an eating area important.

Who is Cooking?

- The most common cooking pattern, in 67% of households in the national phone survey, was for one person to do most of the cooking. However, other people may be in the kitchen during food preparation.

- When there are two cooks in the household, they are more likely to take turns cooking or follow the teacher-student model of cooking. Only a small minority of households (13% in the national sample) has members that actually cook together. This trend was reported in both the national phone survey and personal interview with the local sample, as well as being observed during the laboratory cooking activity.

- Two cook patterns of preparation observed in the cooking activity were the teacher-student model and the independent cook model. In the teacher-student model, two cooks stood side-by-side to work on one task together. The independent cooks worked on separate tasks in separate areas.

- Singles cook less frequently and use their kitchens less than other types of households.

How Do People Cook?

- The microwave oven is a major cooking appliance and is used frequently. For example, 63% of the local sample reported using their microwave oven as much or more than the range/cook top. The microwave oven becomes a central point in the flow of work in the kitchen and adjacent counter space is frequently used for food preparation.

- The sink is also a major focal point for food preparation. People in the laboratory cooking activity used the counter space adjacent to the sink for a variety of food preparation activities as well as for clean up.

- Most people use and need a generous amount of counter space. Cooks observed in the laboratory typically had a primary and a secondary preparation area. Extra counter space was needed to assemble ingredients.

- The trash is frequently accessed during food preparation. People in the laboratory cooking activity wanted the trash to be centrally located, and easily accessible, preferably under or immediately adjacent to the sink. In addition, many people (approximately one third of the national sample) are storing recyclables in the kitchen.

Figure 2.3 Hand washing some dishes at the sink is still a frequent activity, research has shown. (Courtesy of Moen)

- Hand dishwashing of at least some items is frequent, especially in smaller households. As an example, over half of the local sample did some hand dishwashing daily. Pre-rinsing dishes in the sink, before loading the dishwasher, was common to almost all study participants.

- The types of food preparation activities were diverse. Preparing food from scratch, baking, and grilling outdoors were the most frequently cited types of cooking. Food preparation activities that were more complex or required special ingredients, techniques or equipment were less frequent.

- Most people are frequent users of fresh produce. In the national sample, the frequent users of fresh produce were more than twice the number who were frequent users of canned or frozen produce.

- Use of convenience foods was less than might be expected. Close to one half of both samples indicated that they rarely, if ever, use boxed or frozen convenience foods.

- Also surprising was the fact that most people are only occasional users of carryout food, with over 40% of the national sample reporting that they "rarely" or "never" use carryout food.

What Do People Have in Their Kitchens?

- Almost every household has a refrigerator, range and microwave oven in their kitchen.

- Dishwashers and garbage disposers are common in kitchens. Built-in ovens and cooktops are found in only a minority of kitchens.

- People have many small appliances (an average of twelve per household), and use some of them frequently. Some small appliances are stored on countertops (four is typical), but many people have to store them outside of the kitchen as well.

- Pantry or tall storage closets are found in over half the kitchens and are considered desirable.

- People store many items on their kitchen counters, only some of which are food preparation tools. Participants in the local sample had an average of seven items stored on their countertops, in addition to the small appliances reported above.

What Do People Want in Their Kitchens?

- People generally express satisfaction with their kitchens, even if they want improvements. People who had input into their kitchen designs, or have had an opportunity to remodel their kitchens, are more satisfied.

- Many people do not "fit" their kitchens. Some people have trouble reaching wall cabinets; others find shelves in base cabinets difficult to access. Standard counter heights may be too high or too low. Better, more accessible, and more efficient storage in the kitchen is a frequently expressed need.

- If people had a chance to improve their kitchens, they simply want MORE—more space, more storage, more cabinets, and more counter space. Efficiency and organization are also considered desirable.

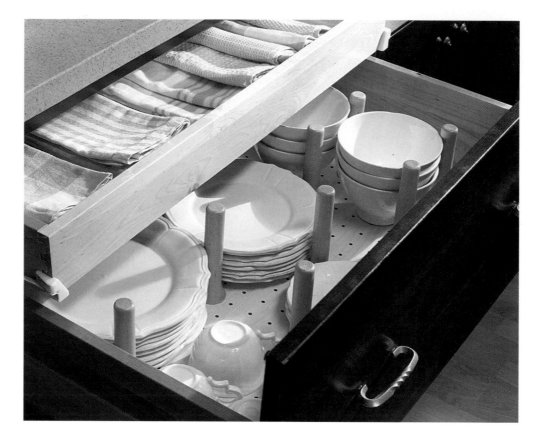

Figure 2.4 Research has shown that consumers want more storage, efficiency and organization in their kitchens. (Courtesy of Diamond Cabinets)

Kitchen Storage Research Project

A second Virginia Tech study was conducted to help develop further background for revised kitchen storage guidelines. The purpose of this study was to investigate the number and type of items kept in recently designed kitchens and to determine the amount of shelf and drawer storage needed to store these items effectively.

KITCHEN INVENTORY SURVEY

An inventory survey instrument was developed to record information about items stored and used in residential kitchens. The instrument included questions about demographic and housing information, kitchen activities, and cooking patterns. A lengthy checklist of items stored in the kitchen was developed to identify the number, location and frequency of use of the stored items. The inventory checklist listed 550 different items in 16 different categories, plus major appliances.

KITCHEN DESIGN RESEARCH

NKBA cooperated in the study by asking all Certified Kitchen Designers to volunteer to interview recent clients and conduct an inventory of their kitchens. Designers were asked to conduct an interview with a client that had a small kitchen and one that had a large kitchen. They received continuing education credits for each completed questionnaire. The interviews often required several hours to complete. The surveys were conducted in the winter and spring of 2003.

A total of 87 useable inventory surveys were returned. Of these, 81% of the respondents prepared five or more meals per week and most often, one person did the cooking (76%). The respondents often took medicine in the kitchen (64%), did major shopping once a week (63%), prepared food from scratch (56%) and planned meals in the kitchen (56%).

Three kitchen sizes were used in analyzing the data: small kitchen (150 square feet or less) – n = 31; medium kitchen (151-350 square feet) – n = 31; and large kitchen (over 350 square feet) – n = 24. The number of items stored in the kitchen increased with the size of the kitchen. There were an average of 655 items in the small kitchen, 820 items in the medium kitchen, and 1019 items in the large kitchen. As the kitchen size increased, people tended to have both a greater variety of items and multiples of the same items.

Measuring for Storage Needs

After tabulating the surveys, and identifying items stored in 25% or more of the kitchens, examples of these items were gathered and arranged in a 12-inch deep x 12-inch high linear mock-up space. This mock-up was used to calculate the amount of storage required for the sixteen categories of items and for the total amount of storage needed in the kitchen. The mock-ups with items were photographed. Calculations were made to determine the amount of wall, base, drawer, pantry, counter, and miscellaneous storage needed in the various sized kitchens.

The total number of linear storage inches required was: 1141 inches in the small kitchen, 1376 inches in the medium kitchen, and 1552 inches in the large kitchens. Storing food required the most space. Other items requiring significant amounts of storage were small appliances, preparation items, small utensils, pots and pans, and baking ware.

Small kitchens had noticeably fewer dishes, baking ware and bulk storage items, while small and medium kitchens had fewer pots and pans and storage containers. Medium and large kitchens required similar amounts of storage for the following: small appliances, preparation items, baking ware, dishes, flatware, management /home office supplies and miscellaneous items. Large kitchens needed more storage for food, pots and pans and serving pieces than the other sized kitchens. All sized kitchens had similar requirements for linens.

Most storage was located in base cabinets, followed by drawer storage, wall cabinets, pantry storage and counter space. Food, glasses and drinking items, dishes and serving pieces were most likely stored in wall cabinets. Small utensils, flatware, linens and management/home office supplies are more likely kept in drawers. Pots and pans are also kept in drawers, especially in large kitchens. Pantries stored food and bulk items. About one-fourth of the small appliances were kept on the counter, as well as small utensils, serving pieces, cleaning supplies, management/home office supplies and miscellaneous items. The amount of counter space used for storage was greatest in the small kitchen where there were fewer storage options. Miscellaneous storage included open shelves, carts, tables, furniture and wall cabinets above the standard cabinet height.

IMPLICATIONS

Information from this study was used to calculate recommendations for storage. The Kitchen Planning Guidelines discussed in Chapter 7 reflect the findings from the study. The major change calls for the designer to prescribe storage based on a linear shelf/drawer frontage, rather than wall and base cabinet requirements. The new guidelines provide designers with flexibility to plan storage that is both accessible and located where needed. The recommendations are based on kitchen size.

SUMMARY

Research has helped to shape the design of kitchens for many years. Approaching food preparation and cleanup as work and studying how to perform the work more efficiently has guided the study of kitchen design. The planning guidelines for kitchens have consistently reflected the findings from research and continue to keep kitchen design appropriate for the lifestyles of the times. Studies will need to be done more frequently to reflect continually changing food preparation patterns and lifestyles.

CHAPTER 3: Infrastructure Considerations

Early in the design process, you will need to consider the infrastructure of the kitchen space and related areas in the home. In Chapter 6, **Form 7: Job Site Inspection** guides you through a needs assessment of many of the infrastructure considerations. No matter what types of structural changes are made, you must take time to carefully plan infrastructure needs and double check your list so that nothing is forgotten. Mistakes or oversights may not only be difficult to change later, but most likely expensive, as well.

This chapter provides an overview of the structural and plumbing elements you should consider while designing. Two other volumes of the NKBA Professional Resource Library go into more detail on these subjects. *Residential Construction* covers codes and overall exterior and interior home construction. *Kitchen & Bath Systems* also covers building codes, as well as mechanical, electrical and plumbing systems. Please refer to these two companion volumes for the specifics that this chapter cannot address.

CODES

The fundamental guidelines, which govern the types of materials that can be used in home construction, as well as how they may be used, are called building codes. Although you will be working with a plumber, contractor or other construction professional who is familiar with these codes, your own understanding of the codes helps you to be aware of restrictions or requirements as you develop a kitchen plan. Building codes are legally binding, and inspectors are required to assure compliance. Becoming familiar with the codes used in your client's area is essential.

In addition to residential construction codes, your kitchen project may be covered by one or more codes targeted to making buildings accessible to people with disabilities. Accessibility codes and laws for the United States and Canada are discussed in Chapter 5, Human Factors and Universal Design Implications.

Plumbing codes are a specialized part of the building codes and regulate the type, size and length of pipe, as well as the methods and location for installing them.

43

In new construction, complying with the codes is a matter of the plumbing contractor selecting the materials and methods allowed for the area. For remodeling projects, however, it may take a little more planning to evaluate the situation, decide what changes are feasible and make certain the changes reflect the current plumbing codes.

Electrical code considerations are discussed in Chapter 8 – Mechanical Planning.

STRUCTURAL ISSUES

Whether you are working with new construction or on a remodeling project, special structural considerations are relevant to each phase and element of the project. Again, a building contractor or other building professional should be well aware of these issues, but careful planning and examination of the current structural components in the kitchen will be critical when making decisions about design options.

If you have the original construction plans, you can begin with them as a guide, but eventually you will need to verify that the structure is actually built as indicated on the plans. Following are some of the structural considerations to keep in mind.

FLOORS

If the floor will be changed, it is important to know more about the structure and what is hidden within or below that floor. Begin by examining the floor joists to determine how the floor was constructed, if any damage exists and the size of the framing members. This helps to determine the strength of the floor or its ability to hold weight. If the flooring material is over a slab foundation, check for moisture and cracks that require sealing.

While examining the floor structure, make note of the components contained within the floor structure so that you do not damage them during the remodeling process. Concealed air ducts, wiring, or plumbing pipes may already be present. Because some of these items may be difficult and expensive to relocate, knowledge of exactly what is there will help you decide which items you may want to leave as is. Verify the direction and size of the floor joists or trusses to provide a better idea of how to proceed with plans for new plumbing, wiring or heating components that need to be located in the floor.

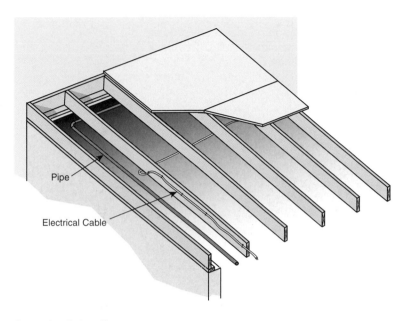

Pipe

Electrical Cable

Figure 3.1 Piping or wiring contained within the floor structure must be identified before remodeling so that they are not damaged during the process.

Oversized Appliances

If you are considering the addition of a commercial sized range, large cast iron range, or oversized refrigerator, these items can exert a great deal of pressure on a floor because of their weight. In new construction, the contractor will need to determine if extra supports must be added in order to handle this extra weight.

In older homes, however, a careful evaluation of the present floor structure is essential for determining current strength and condition of the floor for such loads. One way to accurately evaluate the floor structure is to strip the floor down to the joists to see if they are large enough or spaced appropriately to hold these heavy, oversized appliances. While the floor is open, this would be an excellent time to investigate the plumbing, ductwork and other components that may be concealed in the floor joists.

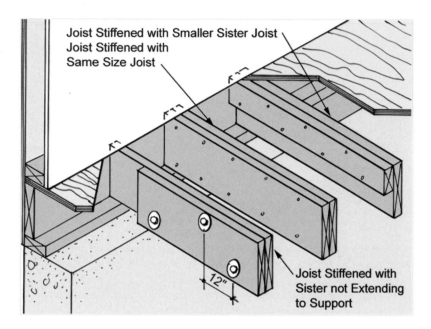

Figure 3.2 Extra floor supports may be needed when installing heavy or oversized appliances.

Floors in older homes were typically not built to hold these extremely heavy, oversized appliances, and therefore reinforcing the floor will most likely be necessary.

Stability and Evenness

Whether poorly constructed, weakened from age, or sagging because of a settling foundation, floors can become uneven. Stable and even floors are essential for many kitchen applications.

Cabinets require a sound and flat foundation on which to rest so that all the edges fit perfectly together in a continuous line. Uneven floors may cause gaps to form between cabinets or cabinetry may not line up from front to back. Although shims and fillers can take care of some of these openings or misalignments, a flat and level floor will make the cabinet installation go more quickly and smoothly.

Appliances, like cabinetry, will not fit together properly on an uneven floor. Many appliances are intended to snug up against the cabinetry or another appliance when installed, but an uneven floor causes appliances and cabinetry to tilt to one side, forming gaps between them. Most appliances have legs for adjusting the level, but an even floor foundation will save time and tedious adjustments.

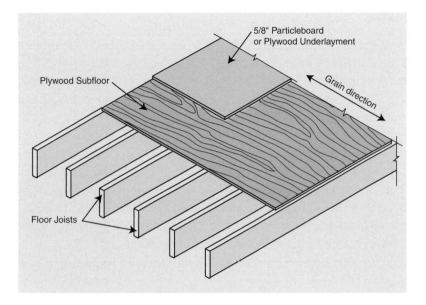

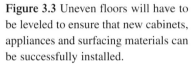

Figure 3.3 Uneven floors will have to be leveled to ensure that new cabinets, appliances and surfacing materials can be successfully installed.

Levelness is also important for appliances to function properly and for client satisfaction with the use of the appliance. For example, clothes washers that are not level may begin to vibrate excessively when the washer begins its spin cycle. Your client may also find it frustrating to see the oil run to one side of a pan while cooking, or to discover a lopsided dessert in the refrigerator.

Level, even floors are important for the successful installation of many surfacing materials. For example, ceramic tile must have a flat surface to avoid tile breakage and cracked grout with use.

Uneven floors can also squeak, which is annoying as well as noisy.

More information on leveling floors and on preparations for installing new floors is contained in *Residential Construction*.

Moisture Control

If the kitchen is located on the main floor over a crawl space or on a slab, moisture may migrate through the floor structure and damage the flooring. Vapor barriers should be in place to prevent this migration, but if you are not sure whether a vapor barrier is present, you can conduct a simple test. After the floor is stripped down to the floor boards, tape pieces of plastic sheeting (minimum 12 inches x 12 inches) to the floor in various parts of the room. After about a week, check to see if moisture has become trapped beneath the plastic. If there is no moisture build up, the floor has probably been sealed against vapor transmission. Signs of moisture mean you need to take measures to seal the slab or the floor and crawl space. Details about adding vapor barriers can be found in *Residential Construction.*

WALLS

Many times, remodeling projects call for altering the wall or wall surface. Whenever walls are to be removed or exposed, do not break into them until you know what is behind them. Walls may hide wiring, plumbing, drain and vent pipes, and even heating, air conditioning and air return ducts in some older homes. Any damage to these could not only be expensive, but disastrous.

Load-Bearing Walls

Load-bearing walls are the walls that support the roof and upper levels of the structure. These, along with the non-bearing partition walls, make up the frame or skeleton of the house that keeps the structure standing even through wind storms and snow loads. The ends of the ceiling joists must connect to the load bearing walls for support. If this skeleton is not strong and stable, it will shift and cause the walls to crack, floors to sag, and windows and doors to stick and not move smoothly. Over time it can cause the house to be out of square.

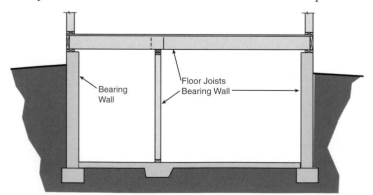

Figure 3.4 A load-bearing wall runs perpendicular to the joists.

Before you remove any walls, determine which type you have—load bearing or non-bearing. One way to tell whether a wall is load bearing is to check the ceiling joists above the space, either in the attic or by an access panel to the joists. If the joists run in the same direction as the wall you want to remove, it is probably not a load-bearing wall. Load-bearing walls tend to run perpendicular to the joists. If you do not have ready access to the joists, you may either need to remove some moulding or drill holes in the ceiling to determine where the joists are located.

Load-bearing walls can be removed or modified. If your design calls for alterations to this type of wall, work with your contractor to make sure it can be accomplished successfully. Refer to *Residential Construction* for more details on load-bearing walls.

Uneven Walls

Uneven walls and out of square corners can be a problem in both new and older construction. Such walls may make it difficult to properly install wall finishes and cabinetry. Walls can become uneven for a number of reasons. Over time, old plaster walls crack, and in an effort to restore them, the surface may become distorted. Wallboard may be damaged and not properly repaired. Or, perhaps walls were not installed square when initially built or they have shifted over time.

When these original walls or wall surfaces are to be retained in new projects, problems can arise whenever uneven surfaces interfere with the installation of a product. For example, if you are adding tile or stone to the walls, the pieces may not lay flat to provide an even surface. Stone or tile designed to have an irregular surface may be a good choice here. Cabinets will also not fit flat against the walls and therefore will not line up properly. This will either cause gaps to form between the cabinet pieces, or the face of the cabinets will not be flat. Once again, fillers and shims may help even out the installation, but it could be a more complex process.

If you do not plan to replace the walls, find surface treatments that will help smooth them out enough to meet your purposes. Refer to NKBA's book *Residential Construction* for more details, but be aware that some methods of doing this shrink the size of your room.

Walls that are not square are especially problematic when installing cabinetry and appliances in corners. Placing a square unit in a less than square corner will surely cause gaps to form somewhere. This problem may be difficult to correct, so you will probably need to rely on cabinet fillers to take care of any gaps that appear.

Insulation

Wall insulation is beneficial in both interior and exterior walls of a kitchen. For interior walls, insulation produces a sound barrier. The kitchen creates many noises that can echo into the adjoining rooms. In addition, kitchens are typically furnished with many hard surfaces, like cabinets and appliances, that do not absorb sounds. By insulating the interior walls of a kitchen, you can better isolate the noises that may move into unwanted areas. See Chapter 4 – Environmental Considerations for more information on noise issues, as well as *Residential Construction*.

Most homes, with the exception of those built before energy was an issue, contain insulation in the exterior walls. The purpose of this insulation is to prevent heat from transferring into and out of the home. An additional benefit of insulated exterior walls is to help control moisture. Moisture control is covered in more detail in Chapter 4 – Environmental Considerations. Details on insulating walls are covered in *Residential Construction*.

Insulation can be added in interior walls or increased in exterior walls during remodeling. If the wallboard is being replaced or you are working with new construction, it will be easy to add insulation to the wall cavity. Consider adding insulation in all kitchen walls that adjoin another room and extra insulation on exterior walls. For inside walls that have a closet or other built-in storage that can serve as a buffer for noise, wall insulation may not be necessary.

DOORS AND WINDOWS

Door and window areas are very important components of the room structure. For new construction, discuss with the client the type and amount of window space they desire and the type of door(s) that best fits their design and room configuration.

For remodeling projects, examine the windows and doors carefully to decide whether they need to be replaced or just refurbished. Use Forms 11 and 12 in Chapter 6 to gather information and measurements on existing doors and windows. Information on window and door styles and choices can be found in *Residential Construction*.

Door Choices

A kitchen can easily have multiple entry or exterior doors opening to the garage, patio or deck.

Interior doors may lead to the dining room, family room, stairwell or other area of the home. It is not uncommon to have as many as six doors opening into the kitchen. Not all of those doorways may have an actual door attached, but may instead be an opening or archway into another room.

When you decide to replace a door or modify a room entry, be sure the new plan fits with the other components of the room or other changes. For example, a new door size may mean a new door swing that could interfere with the placement of such items as cabinets, appliances, or dining furniture.

Consider which direction the doors should swing. Bi-fold doors are smaller and thus may be a good alternative where the door swing space for a standard sized door is an issue. Pocket doors slide into the wall cavity and are useful for opening up rooms without the worry of a door swing. They do, however, need adequate wall cavity space that is free from plumbing, electrical, or HVAC (heating, ventilation and air conditioning) components to enclose the pocket. When a pocket door is not possible, or perhaps too costly, consider a "barn" door—hardware that allows the door to slide along a wall.

Adequate door clearances should be maintained. See Chapter 7 for more information on door openings. Other kitchen modifications can also affect the door fit. For example, some floor covering applications like tile or stone, or floor heating systems, may raise the floor level enough that the doors will need to be trimmed in order to clear the floor.

Doors are discussed in detail in *Residential Construction*.

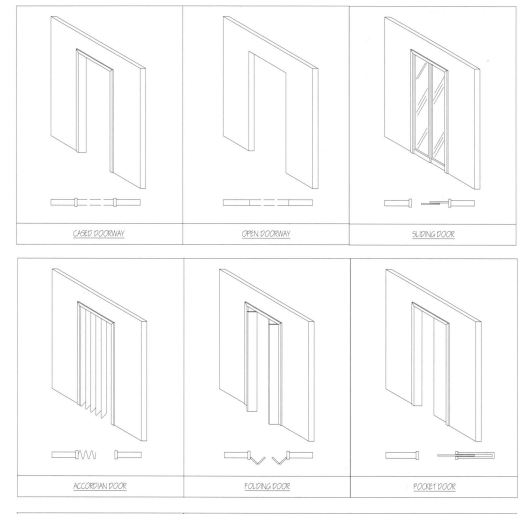

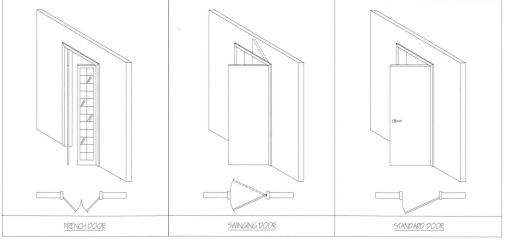

Figure 3.5 Select a door style and swing that fit the purpose and design.

Window Options

Windows serve many important functions in the kitchen, including providing quality daylight for the space, supplying fresh air when needed and allowing a view of the outdoors to watch children play in the backyard or to enjoy the scenery.

For new construction, plan the placement of windows early so that other components of the kitchen can be arranged around them. Once framed in, windows may be difficult to relocate. For remodeling projects, this may be the opportunity to help your client find a better arrangement or sizing for the windows. Carefully examine the current windows and discuss their placement and condition with your client.

Simply replacing a window with one of the same dimensions will not usually require changes in the wall structure. However, if you decide a window needs to be moved or increased in size, carefully examine the wall space where the changes will be made. Be aware of any structural issues that need consideration, such as studs that must be removed or moved, vent stacks that might be present, or headers that need to be modified. The removal of any studs to add a larger window will mean the addition of a larger header over the window to help support the weight of the structure.

With any type of replacement window, consider the fenestration pattern of the windows; that is, the placement of the window openings on the exterior of the home. You want the new window to blend with the other windows of the home, especially if this replacement window faces the street.

Considerations for selecting new windows, including energy efficiency, and information on improving existing windows is covered in NKBA's *Residential Construction*.

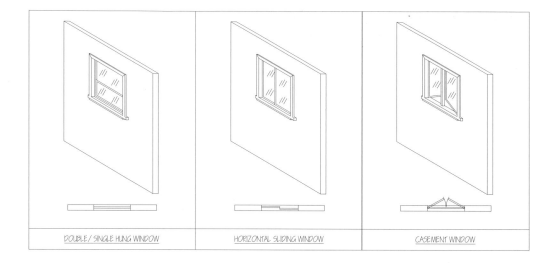

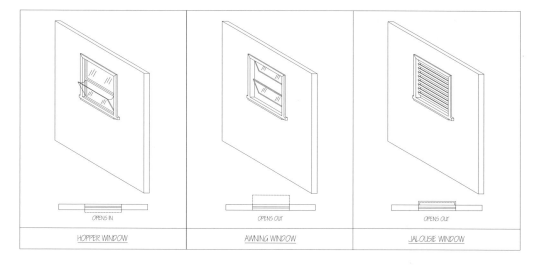

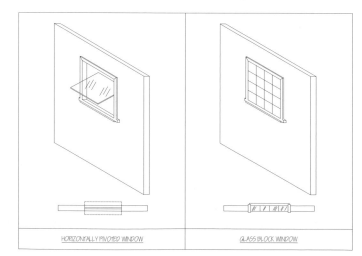

Figure 3.6 A variety of window design options are available.

PLUMBING

In addition to the standard kitchen sink and dishwasher, a kitchen may need water for a second sink or dishwasher, a steam oven, coffee system, water filtration system in a refrigerator, ice maker, or pot filler faucet. To assure they all function properly, water delivery should be evaluated. If your client is currently having a problem with inadequate water volume, water pressure or the amount of available hot water, help them investigate ways to remedy these issues and, as a result, improve the functioning of kitchen equipment, as well as the water system of the entire home.

Water quality related to water hardness can also impact water delivery when it leads to problems with appliance operation. Chapter 4 – Environmental Considerations provides information on hard water and other water concerns and offers suggestions on how to remedy water problems.

In new construction, the plumbing system can be planned with the new kitchen in mind. If you are working on a remodeling project, however, many decisions will need to be made related to relocating the current fixtures or deciding where new water and drain lines must be added, and the difficulty of that process. Because pipe is bigger and less flexible to work with than wire, it is a good idea to schedule the plumber before you schedule the electrician.

Plumbing Fixtures

A new kitchen means selecting all new fixtures, but when a client is remodeling, you could, on occasion, have a client who wishes to reuse some of the present fixtures. These fixtures may have been recently replaced, or perhaps they are special vintage fixtures that your client wishes to keep in the kitchen design. Reusing current fixtures involves investigating whether or not they can be successfully removed and reinstalled, or relocated if the new plan calls for a new location. Refer to Form 13 in Chapter 6 to collect information and measurements on existing fixtures and water-using appliances.

When new fixtures are desired in the current location, decide if they can be installed using the old plumbing lines or if new lines and fittings need to be added. Talk with the client about the fixtures they have in mind and the options that might be available for that fixture. For example, sinks come in many sizes and configurations, and faucets and accessories can vary widely in style, as well as the many mounting locations on and near the sink. Discuss the pros and cons of each type with your client to ensure they end up with the look and function they desire.

55

For more details see *Kitchen & Bath Systems* and *Kitchen & Bath Products*. Both books are part of the NKBA's Professional Resource Library.

Water Delivery

Consider the following when planning water delivery in the kitchen:

- To help cut costs in new construction or remodeling projects, locate the kitchen near another room with plumbing, like a bathroom or the laundry room, to take advantage of clustered plumbing lines.

- New flexible water supply piping makes it possible to easily reposition fixtures, such as a sink. Before you count on using this type of piping, check local codes to make sure it is allowed.

- Sinks come equipped with water shut-off valves, but when multiple water use appliances are incorporated into the kitchen, also consider locating a central shut-off somewhere in or near the kitchen to control water to that entire area.

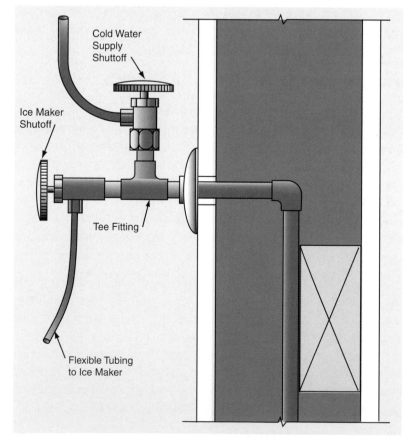

Figure 3.7 Water shut-off valves at the sink stop water delivery when necessary. If an appliance water supply line is connected, like an icemaker, it may also have a shut-off valve.

- Water delivery lines to some appliances, called a supply line, can be merely a small plastic tube. Care needs to be taken so that the line does not kink or is not punctured by other kitchen components. Hard water minerals can also easily clog these lines because they are very small.

- Outdoor kitchens also include sinks, and so provisions need to be made to ensure that the plumbing lines are protected against freezing in the winter.

Drain/Waste/Vent Pipes

As you examine the plumbing in the kitchen you are remodeling, you may notice that current code requirements for the size, type and/or height of plumbing drain/waste/vent components may require structural changes.

Codes set a minimum diameter for stack and vent pipes in relation to the number of fixtures installed. If the home is quite old, a careful examination may find that the current configuration of pipes does not meet these codes, so you must decide what it will take to make the necessary changes. Basically each sink will need to have a provision for a vent pipe. It may be more difficult to accommodate vents for sinks located on interior walls or in islands.

When relocating a sink, there is a five-foot limit for the changeover of a vent. If the distance from the sink to the vent location is greater, you will need to open more wall space to install a new vent or to re-vent.

If the house is built on a slab, reconfiguring plumbing will involve additional challenges. In order to move or add new pipes, you may need to chip into the concrete to get at the current pipes and/or make channels where new pipe must be laid. In this case, consider changes carefully, as they may make the project more difficult and add to its cost for your client.

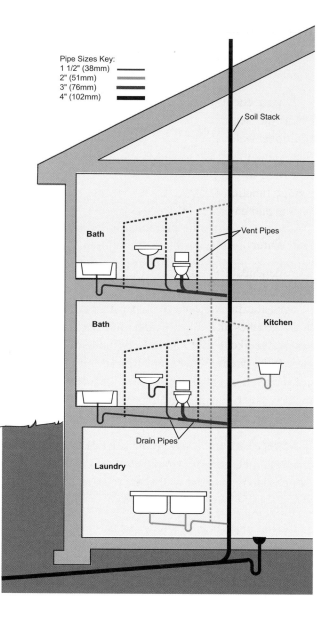

Pipe Sizes Key:
1 1/2" (38mm)
2" (51mm)
3" (76mm)
4" (102mm)

Soil Stack

Bath

Vent Pipes

Bath

Kitchen

Drain Pipes

Laundry

Figure 3.8 The location and size of drain, waste and vent pipes all have to be considered when remodeling a kitchen or bath.

Septic Systems

One other consideration for clients who are not connected to a municipal waste system is the septic tank.

If your client plans to install a garbage disposer, you will need to check the septic system capacity to make sure it can handle the additional water and waste. It may be that you will need to add a larger septic tank to accommodate the extra waste. If the tank is too small, it will need to be emptied regularly. With too much waste, the system cannot function adequately, leading to a break down of the septic system and environmental consequences.

Hot Water

A dependable and readily available supply of hot water is essential for the kitchen. A large amount of water is wasted when the user needs to open the faucet valve for an extended period of time before hot water reaches the faucet. A nearby hot water supply ensures that appliances like the dishwasher fill first with hot water rather than cold. How quickly that hot water arrives to the kitchen fixtures can vary depending on the location of the water heater in relation to the kitchen. If this appears to be an issue, a second water heater located near the kitchen would be a good idea.

Other types of systems, like recirculating hot water and on-demand water heaters, may also be good solutions for ensuring instant hot water. These units vary in capacity, so make sure they meet the water demands of the fixtures they serve.

On-demand, also called instantaneous, hot water systems may be desirable at or near the sink. These systems are designed for preparing instant coffee, tea, or instant soups. If your client would like to locate the hot water system on the sink, an extra hole will need to be ordered or drilled in the surface of the sink. Counter-mounted units will also need to have an opening ready for installation. No matter the type of installation, a water supply line will need to be installed under the sink for the heating unit.

If water filtration is included along with the hot water faucet in a dual device, space will be needed for the filtration unit as well. Also keep in mind that the filter will need to be replaced periodically, so locate it where the client can access it without too much inconvenience.

In-depth information on all these aspects of plumbing systems is included in *Kitchen & Bath Systems*.

Figure 3.9 On-demand water heaters provide instant hot water in rooms located a long distance from the central water heater source.

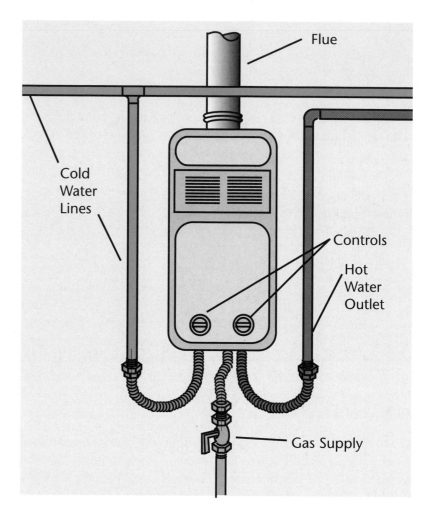

Flue

Cold Water Lines

Controls

Hot Water Outlet

Gas Supply

SUMMARY

Whether you are helping clients plan a new kitchen or remodel their current one, carefully investigate the basic structural components that are so essential to a successful project.

Floors, walls, windows and plumbing may pose problems or require special structural considerations that must be identified and dealt with before all the new products are specified and installed. In Chapter 8 – Mechanical Planning, additional considerations for mechanical systems are examined. The more you know about these issues, the fewer changes your client will need to make later on and the more functional your plan will become. Your client will also be more satisfied with the results.

CHAPTER 4: Environmental Considerations

Good design includes planning spaces that are environmentally friendly and healthy for the user. Often these considerations require that designers have in-depth knowledge concerning water and air quality, waste management, energy-efficient products and more, which are discussed in *Residential Construction*, *Kitchen & Bath Systems* and *Kitchen & Bath Products* all part of NKBA's Professional Resource Library.

This chapter provides an overview of these issues from the standpoint of the choices and considerations you, the designer, must make, as well as the impact they have on your client.

GREEN BUILDING

Green building encompasses energy efficiency, water quality and conservation, air quality, and waste management and recycling. Green building includes specific practices, products, and techniques. It is also a philosophical approach that guides design and business decisions.

In recent years, the term "green building" has come to represent policies and practices that are environmentally responsible. There is not a precise definition of green building, although the U.S. Green Building Council (www.usgbc.org) is taking leadership in describing and promoting green building practices. Green building practices are recognized to:

- promote healthy places to live and work

- enhance and protect natural ecosystems and biodiversity

- improve air and water quality

- reduce solid waste

- conserve natural resources

The Canada Mortgage and Housing Corporation's (CMHC) Healthy Housing program (www.cmhc-schl.gc.ca) subscribes to many of the same green building practices.

61

For the kitchen designer, there are many opportunities to implement green building or healthy housing policies and practices. Some general suggestions include:

- Specify environmentally healthy building and interior finish materials, including non-toxic, sustainably harvested, recycled, or renewable resource products.

- Specify materials and products from local sources that do not have an energy or pollution "cost" for transportation.

- Specify products that are energy efficient, such as Energy Star qualified appliances or windows.

- Specify plumbing fixtures and appliances that conserve water.

- Maximize the use of daylight and specify energy-efficient light sources.

- Plan window placement to maximize passive solar gain through south facing windows, minimize heat loss through north windows and limit heat gain though west windows.

- Plan the layout of the kitchen to maximize the use of standard size materials and products, and minimize the amount of construction waste.

- Investigate and implement opportunities to recycle construction and demolition waste. Encourage clients to donate serviceable cabinetry, appliances and fixtures removed in renovations to charitable organizations.

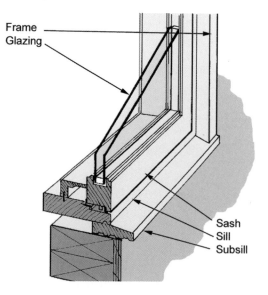

Figure 4.1 Double-glazed windows cut heat loss in half, compared to a single-glazed window.

ENERGY MANAGEMENT IN THE KITCHEN

Energy efficiency involves selecting the right materials, installing them properly, and understanding how the natural elements impact home energy use and comfort.

Selecting energy efficient appliances is a major part of a kitchen energy plan. Appliance manufacturers have made vast improvements in the energy efficiency of their products, but there is still a range of efficiencies from which to choose. The most energy efficient appliances may be more expensive initially. However, buying efficiency up front will save many times the extra money invested through lower energy costs over the life of the appliance.

Lighting is another area where consumers can impact their energy usage. Selecting energy efficient lighting types and using the lighting efficiently will help reduce energy costs while still providing adequate light.

There are guides to help consumers select energy efficient products. Both the United States and Canadian governments have established energy ratings for appliances, water heaters, furnaces and air conditioners to help consumers compare similar products on the market. These ratings are discussed in the book *Kitchen & Bath Products*, part of the NKBA's Professional Resource Library.

ENERGY STAR

Another energy-usage guide that covers a wider range of consumer products is the international symbol for energy efficiency, the Energy Star. Products covered by this program include insulation, windows, lighting, appliances, and heating and cooling equipment, to name a few. The program certifies that these products exceed the minimum standards for energy efficiency. When consumers see the Energy Star label, they can be assured that this product is among the most energy efficient of its type. Use of the label requires no calculations or product comparisons, so it is an easy guide for consumers to use. A complete list of Energy Star rated products and a list of qualifying models can be found on both the United States (www.energystar.gov) and Canadian (www.oee.nrcan.gc.ca/energystar) Energy Star web sites.

Figure 4.2 The Energy Star logo is found on qualified products.

WATER QUALITY

It is important for you, the designer, to discuss water quality with your client. The kitchen faucet is typically the main source of water for cooking, drinking and washing the dishes. The water must be safe and healthy, as well as smell, taste and look good. Water should work well for all kitchen uses and not contribute to maintenance problems.

This section discusses issues of water quality–water that is safe, healthy and functional for drinking, cooking and washing.

WATER QUALITY STANDARDS

The U.S. Environmental Protection Agency (EPA) establishes drinking water standards.

There are two types of water quality standards in the United States. The first assures that water is safe to drink or ingest. These standards are called "Primary Drinking Water Standards" and are enforced by law. The second type of standard is to assure that water is functional and aesthetic for various uses, such as bathing and washing. These standards are referred to as "Secondary Drinking Water Standards" and they are voluntary.

All municipal or public water systems are required to meet the primary standards. These systems must regularly test and, if necessary, treat their water to assure that it meets the primary standards. Individual or small private water systems (defined by the number of households connected to the water system) are not required to meet any water quality standards. However, owners of private systems are encouraged to use the EPA standards as benchmarks for testing and treatment of their water systems.

PRIMARY DRINKING WATER STANDARDS

The Primary Drinking Water Standards are based on the maximum contaminant levels (MCLs), or highest concentration of pollutants, allowed in public drinking water. The pollutants that are regulated by the primary standards are those that are known to cause adverse health effects and for which there is information available about chronic or acute health risks. There are three classes of pollutants for which there are MCLs.

- **Disease-causing organisms.** Most disease-causing organisms in water come from animal and human waste contamination, including bacteria and viruses. These organisms are very common in water supplies before treatment, especially if the water source is from surface water, such as lakes or rivers.

- **Toxic chemicals.** There are many toxic chemicals covered by the primary standards, including naturally occurring contaminants such as arsenic and copper; heavy metals such as cadmium, lead and mercury; agricultural by-products such as nitrates; industrial and manufacturing by-products and wastes such as asbestos, benzene and xylene; and pesticides and herbicides such as atrazine and lindane.

- **Radioactive contaminants.** Radium is an example of a radioactive contaminant. In addition, radon can be a radioactive water problem. Radon is a gas that is easily released when contaminated water is aerated, such as in a faucet sprayer. Radon then is breathed into the lungs, which can be a health threat. Breathing radon gas is usually considered a greater problem than ingesting radon contaminated water.

Under the provisions of the Safe Drinking Water Act, the Primary Drinking Water Standards are regularly reviewed. As new knowledge about health concerns emerges, or new technology to detect water pollutants is developed, the standards may be modified.

SECONDARY DRINKING WATER STANDARDS

Secondary Drinking Water Standards are based on the Secondary Maximum Contaminant Levels (SMCLs) of pollutants that affect the aesthetics and function of water. These are contaminants that impact water qualities such as appearance, taste, odor, residues or staining. Examples of secondary standard contaminants are chloride, iron, manganese, sulfur and pH. While these contaminants might not present a health threat, they can affect functional water use and can lead to maintenance problems. Secondary standards are voluntary and are not required. A public water system may choose to test and treat for some of the SMCLs.

CANADIAN WATER QUALITY GUIDELINES

Health Canada is the ministry responsible for drinking water standards in Canada and for educating Canadians about the importance of safe drinking water. The Healthy Environments and Consumer Safety division of the ministry (www.hc-sc.gc.ca/hecs-sesc/hecs/index.html) provides guidelines to assure that Canadian water is safe to drink as well as functional and aesthetic for household uses.

OTHER WATER CONTAMINANTS

Two water contaminants are not covered by the U.S. EPA standards, but can be a concern in kitchen.

- **Water hardness.** Water hardness is the most common water quality problem in North America. "Hard" water is water with a high mineral content, usually calcium and magnesium. Hard water is usually found in groundwater sources, such as water from wells. Both private and municipal systems can use groundwater.

Hard water creates problems with mineral deposits on fixtures, water-using appliances and plumbing. As these mineral deposits (sometimes called "lime scale") build up, pipes can become clogged and water flow is reduced. Heating elements and other parts of appliances and fixtures also can become coated with mineral deposits, reducing effectiveness and leading to mechanical failures. Hard water also reduces the effectiveness of cleaning products, including shampoos and soaps, and increases soap scum deposits.

However, hard water is safe for drinking and cooking. Some people believe that the minerals in hard water contribute to better tasting, healthier water.

Hard Water Classifications

Rating	Grains Per Gallon	Milligrams Per Litre (mg/L) Parts Per Million (ppm)
Soft	Less than 1.0	Less than 17.1
Slightly hard	1.0 – 3.5	17.1 – 60
Moderately hard	3.5 – 7.0	60 – 120
Hard	7.0 – 10.5	120 – 180
Very Hard	Over 10.5	Over 180

Figure 4.3 Water can be classified from soft to very hard, depending on the amount of calcium and/or magnesium present.

- **Iron bacteria.** Iron bacteria are a reddish brown slime that can clog pipes and fixtures. It is most likely to result when water is left standing. Typically, it is first noticed in the toilet tank, but can occur in water left standing in pipes, faucets and appliances. Iron bacteria are naturally occurring, and more common with well water. They are an unpleasant nuisance that can cause staining.

WATER QUALITY TESTING

The water in a new kitchen should not be a health threat. New fixtures and fittings need to be protected from staining, deposits, and other maintenance problems caused by water problems. Early in the design process, determine if water quality is a concern. Help your client get expert advice about water testing, and if needed, the selection of appropriate water treatment equipment.

If the project is a renovation, look for evidence of water concerns in the existing kitchen or a bathroom, such as fixture staining or hard water deposits. Check to see if the household uses filters in the kitchen for drinking water. Draw a glass of water and evaluate how it looks and smells.

If the home is, or will be, on a municipal water system, you can assume that the water is safe for drinking. If the home is on a private water system, ask your client about any testing or treatment they have done. Regular testing is the best method to help maintain a safe water system.

Most experts recommend that private water systems be tested annually for:

- Total coliform bacteria

- Nitrate

- pH

- Total dissolved solids

These contaminants are considered "marker" pollutants, meaning that a problem with one of these contaminants is usually evidence of more extensive problems. Other tests may be recommended, depending on the water source and recent water pollution problems in the area. A financial institution may require water testing before money is lent for any home improvements. The local, state or provincial health department is an excellent place to contact for further information about water testing.

Additional testing of the water supply may be recommended if there are nuisance problems in the water such as off-color, cloudy appearance, discoloration, unusual taste, odor or staining of fixtures. These problems can occur with both municipal and private water systems. If water problems are evident, and the home is on a public water system, start by contacting the local water authority. Some nuisance problems are temporary.

The local health department may test for nuisance pollutants or may recommend a private company. An independent company that follows a government-approved testing procedure should always do water testing. Never have a water test done by the same company that wants to sell water treatment equipment. Contact the water testing company and describe the water problem. It can recommend the necessary tests as well as the procedure for gathering the water sample.

SOLVING WATER QUALITY PROBLEMS

There are many options for solving water quality problems. Some may be as complex as having to locate a new water source, such as drilling a new well. Others may be as simple as attaching a filter to a faucet. It is important to match any water treatment equipment to the water problem and the pollutant to be removed.

Also, the amount of the contaminant in the water may determine the type of equipment as well as the size or capacity. Finally, if more than one water treatment device is needed, the order of installation may be important for the most effective operation.

Common Types of Water Treatment Methods

Water Treatment Method	Typical Contaminants Removed
Activated carbon filtration	Odors, chlorine, radon, organic chemicals
Anion exchange	Nitrate, sulfate, arsenic
Chlorination	Coliform bacteria, iron, iron bacteria, manganese
Distillation	Metals, inorganic chemicals, most contaminants
Neutralizing filtration	Low pH
Oxidizing filtration	Iron, manganese
Particle or fiber filtration	Disolved solids, iron particles
Reverse osmosis	Metals, inorganic chemicals, most contaminants
Water softening (cation exchange)	Calcium, magnesium, iron

Figure 4.4 This table is a brief summary of water treatment methods for common contaminants in household water.

WATER TREATMENT EQUIPMENT

As a kitchen designer, you may need to specify water treatment equipment, or at least incorporate it into your kitchen design. Following is a brief summary of the more common types of water treatment equipment used in homes.

Filters

Sometimes called carbon or charcoal filters, activated carbon filters are used to treat taste and odor problems, chlorine residue, organic chemicals and radon. When water flows through the carbon, contaminants adsorb or stick to the surfaces of the carbon particles.

Fiber filters or mechanical filters trap particles in the water, such as sand and soil, reducing turbidity and improving appearance.

Activated carbon filters and mechanical filters may be purchased separately or in a dual unit. Small filters that fit directly onto the kitchen faucet are available. Larger filter units fit under the sink. If desired, a filter can also be installed in a utility area that will treat the whole household water supply.

When a filter is installed in the kitchen, usually only the cold water line is filtered. A bypass feature on the faucet can allow the user to choose filtered or unfiltered water, and extend cartridge life. Sometimes, filters are installed with a dedicated faucet and may be combined with an instant hot water dispenser.

Water Softeners

Water softeners remove the calcium and magnesium that cause water hardness problems.

Water softeners are usually installed in a utility area, near the water heater. Because of the extensive problems that occur with hard water, typically all household water is softened. In some cases, people are concerned about the health effects of softened water, as the softening process increases the sodium content of the water.

In addition, the taste of softened water may not be desirable. A solution to these concerns is to soften only the hot water supply, so that the cold water lines provide untreated water. Another option is to provide a cold water line to the kitchen faucet that bypasses the water softener. These options should be discussed with a plumber.

Figure 4.5 Water filtration devices should be selected so that they eliminate the specific water problems and pollutants encountered by the client. (Courtesy of Everpure)

Iron Removal Equipment

Iron and manganese (which often occur together in water) do not cause health problems but can cause taste, odor, staining and appearance problems, even if they are present in very small amounts (0.3 mg/L for iron and 0.05 mg/L for manganese). Removal of iron can be complex because it depends on the form found in the water (dissolved or oxidized), the concentration of iron, and other pollutants in the water. Iron bacteria are actually microorganisms and often occur with iron-containing water. Iron removal equipment is generally installed in a utility area and is used to treat all the water coming into the household.

The options to remove iron include:

- **Iron filter.** Sometimes called a manganese green sand filter, this equipment operates in a similar way to a water softener.

- **Water softener.** Depending on the type of resin, a standard water softener will remove some iron.

- **Polyphosphate feeder.** This is effective only on cold water.

- **Chlorinator and filter.** A two-stage process, it also deals with iron bacteria.

- **Aerator and filter.** This is also a two-stage process.

Neutralizers

A neutralizer is used to treat low pH, or acidic, water. As water becomes more acidic, it is more reactive, and picks up more pollutants. Acidic water is also more corrosive to plumbing fixtures and water–using appliances. Neutralizers are usually used to treat all household water and are installed in a utility area.

Distillation Units

A distiller provides nearly pure water by boiling water until it evaporates, then condensing it. The resulting distilled water has almost no pollutants, but can taste very flat. A distillation unit might be installed in a kitchen, usually under the sink, and the potable water plumbed with its own faucet. Countertop units are also available. Distillers require an electrical connection to provide a heat source. Another consideration is how to vent the heat from the boiling process. Also, the distillation process takes time, so there needs to be a collection and storage container for the water. The size of the distillation unit, and in particular, the storage container, needs to relate to the demand for treated water.

Reverse Osmosis Unit

A reverse osmosis unit will remove many suspended or dissolved pollutants from the water. Usually, a reverse osmosis unit is installed under the kitchen sink, with a dedicated faucet. It can be used to treat drinking and cooking water only. A mechanical filter and an activated carbon filter are needed to pre-treat the water and to extend the life of the filtering membrane. As with distillation, reverse osmosis is a slow process, so a storage container is a necessary part of the equipment. A connection to a drain is required. Some reverse osmosis units require an electrical connection (to provide a pressure assist and speed the treatment process).

Disinfection Methods

A home on a private water system may need to disinfect water to make it safe to drink. The most common method is an injection pump using liquid chlorine (chlorine bleach). Ozone and ultraviolet light systems are also available. Disinfection methods are usually used to treat all household water and may be installed in a utility area, or even in the well house. Chlorinated water is often treated with an activated carbon filter to remove excess chlorine.

SUMMARY

When single water quality problems are identified, one water treatment device may be adequate. In many cases, however, more than one problem is present, requiring a combination of water treatment equipment. A household water treatment system should take into account the most practical and effective device to treat each problem, the order these devices should be placed in the system, and the intended use of the water—for drinking, cooking, laundry or other household uses.

Most types of water treatment equipment require regular maintenance to be safe and effective. If you specify or recommend this type of equipment, be sure to prepare your client, and assist them in making an appropriate choice in equipment.

For more details on water contaminants and how to remove them, consult NKBA's book *Kitchen & Bath Systems*.

WATER CONSERVATION

The kitchen designer also has a responsibility to plan for water conservation.

A good place to start is with aerators on faucets. The air added to the water increases the pressure and makes the flow seem greater so water use is reduced.

Several new options are now available in the residential market. For example, a faucet with an electronic, motion activator control will turn on only when you put a pot or your hands under the faucet. Foot controls make it easier to control the faucet, turning it on and off easily, to minimize water use. A leaning bar faucet controller installs beneath the edge of the sink counter, and water flow is controlled by the pressure of someone leaning against it. Many of these control systems also add convenience to the cook with messy hands or foster independence for the cook with limited muscle control.

Putting a secondary water heater in or near the kitchen or installing an in-line or on-demand water heater not only saves the water that would run down the drain waiting for hot water, but also the energy to heat the water.

The dishwasher is usually the major water-using appliance in the kitchen. However, depending on your client's habits, a dishwasher can actually be a more water-efficient method than hand dishwashing. A dishwasher with a choice of cycles allows water use to be matched to the load. Some dishwashers are available with sensors that adjust cycle length and water use to the soil level in the load.

Figure 4.6 A touchless faucet can save water because it is only activated when hands or an object are under it. (Courtesy of Gerber)

If a clothes washer is installed in or near the kitchen, look for a water-efficient model. Adjustable water levels allow less water to be used with smaller loads.

Another important factor in water conservation is eliminating leaks. Dripping faucets waste tremendous amounts of water. For example, the EPA estimates a faucet that loses one drop of water per second can waste 2,400 gallons of water in a year.

Talk to your client about selecting quality fittings and water-using appliances that are easy to maintain and less likely to develop leaks. These are not only a conservation measure, but will save money and reduce maintenance.

AIR QUALITY

Another part of the kitchen design process is to provide good indoor air quality, making a space pleasant to be in, healthy for the user and free of air pollution.

Providing good indoor air quality is a three-step process:

- **Source control** – minimizing or preventing the sources of indoor air pollution in a room or building.

- **Ventilation** – providing adequate air exchange, through natural or mechanical ventilation, to dilute the concentration of indoor air pollutants and assure that the space has a supply of fresh air.

- **Air cleaning** – when necessary, using filters or other devices to remove potentially harmful indoor air pollutants.

SOURCE CONTROL

In the kitchen, there are a number of sources of potential air pollution. Excess moisture is at the top of the list. Too much moisture not only creates a sticky, uncomfortably humid space, but can also lead to structural damage. A high level of moisture creates an environment that fosters the growth of biological pollutants such as molds, viruses and bacteria. Moisture control is discussed in more detail later in this chapter.

Cooking odors, grease, smoke, and by-products from gas combustion in cooking appliances are also common kitchen air pollutants. These pollutants not only affect air quality but can create maintenance problems as well. Effective and easy-to-use ventilation to remove pollutants is a must in a well-designed kitchen. Kitchen Planning Guideline 19 recommends a ducted ventilation system of at least 150 CFM (cubic feet per minute) with each cooking surface appliance.

Refer to Chapter 8 for more detailed information about kitchen ventilation systems.

Indoor Air Quality and Construction

Some of the air pollution in a kitchen can also come from building materials and interior finish materials. New building materials, such as paint, manufactured woods, varnishes, and plastics, can off-gas or emit chemicals into the air, as the materials age or cure. This is especially true of products made from, or with, volatile organic compounds (VOCs), such as some paints, particleboards or wood finishes. The heat and moisture in a kitchen can increase off-gassing.

Choose building materials that have low amounts of VOCs. Many alternatives are available, such as latex paints, water-based varnishes, or low-VOC wood products. Some building materials can be ventilated for 24 to 48 hours before installation, so that most off-gassing occurs outside your client's home. Increasing ventilation during and immediately after installation of new building materials is important to good indoor air quality.

Many building products, such as grout, joint compounds, plaster and latex paints, contain water. As these products dry and cure, water vapor is released. It is important that the kitchen is well ventilated while these products are drying, to prevent moisture problems.

Renovation Hazards

Make sure your client is aware of possible air quality problems that can result from demolition. Some things to consider and discuss with both the contractor and your client are:

- Will the demolition area be isolated from the rest of the home?

- Will the heating or air conditioning system be blocked in the demolition area, so that dust and debris are not circulated throughout the home?

- If the home was constructed before 1978, determine if there is any lead paint in the demolition area. Although lead paint was available until 1978, it was especially common in homes built before 1950. Disturbing lead paint can cause serious air pollution and health effects, especially to young children.

- Asbestos is another hazard in building materials in houses built before the late 1970s. Disturbing asbestos-containing materials can create airborne health hazards.

- Sometimes demolition uncovers things like dead animals and insects in walls, attics, and other spaces. This is part of the reason it is important to isolate the demolition area from the rest of the home.

- How will demolition waste be removed and disposed? Can any of the materials be recycled? Is any of the waste considered hazardous, such as asbestos-containing materials or preservative-treated wood? Are local regulations for disposal of construction waste being followed?

AIR CLEANING

Air cleaners are often incorporated into the heating, ventilating and/or air conditioning system of the home, where they are used to filter air, before it is returned, via ducts, throughout the house.

If an air cleaner is desired, choose a filtering medium that is effective for the type of pollutant the client wants removed. Look for information that the air cleaner has been tested and rated against an efficiency standard, such as ASHRAE's (American Society of Heating, Refrigeration and Air-conditioning Engineers) standard for in-duct cleaners. Finally, make sure the capacity of the air cleaner is matched to the size of the room.

VENTILATION SYSTEMS AND FILTERS

Most ventilation systems in kitchens are located above the cooktop (called a hood, canopy or updraft ventilation system) or near the cooking surface (called a proximity or downdraft ventilation system). A fan pulls air through a filter. As you can imagine, the filter catches a lot of grease. Maintenance of the filter is important—many are designed for easy removal and can be run through the dishwasher.

Most kitchen ventilation systems exhaust the air to the outside. However, sometimes a recirculating (ductless) system is used, which puts the air back into the room. An activated carbon type filter may be added, which helps to remove odors and smoke. Recirculating ventilation systems help to control grease and cooking odors, but do not remove moisture, heat, and combustion by-products. Recirculating ventilation systems are less expensive to purchase and install, but are less effective in controlling indoor air pollution in a kitchen. Therefore, exhaust ventilation systems are the better choice for good indoor air quality.

Refer to Chapter 8 for more detailed information about kitchen ventilation systems.

MOISTURE PROBLEMS

An interaction of many factors such as climate, lifestyle, construction, mechanical systems and ventilation, can create moisture problems. There are many potential sources of excess moisture in a home, including cooking, drying clothes, plants, and showering and bathing. The Canada Mortgage and Housing Corporation estimates that the various activities of occupants of a home will generate 2 to 10 gallons of moisture every day. The occupants themselves are a moisture source, with an estimated 3 pounds (pints) of water vapor produced daily by a typical household of four people.

Excess moisture is a potential problem for both the building and the people who live in it. Excess moisture in building materials leads to structural problems, such as peeling paint, rusting metal and deterioration of joists and framing. Damp building materials tend to attract dirt and therefore require more cleaning and maintenance. Even in a dry climate, excess moisture inside a building can lead to serious problems.

Damp spaces make good environments for the growth of many biological pollutants. Bacteria and viruses can thrive in moist spaces. Pests, from dust mites to cockroaches, need moisture to thrive. Wet building materials can also harbor mold growth, which leads to further structural damage. Mold can be a health threat for some people living in the home. Of course, mold growing on interior finish materials smells and is unattractive.

Cooking is a major source of moisture in the kitchen. Boiling or simmering food on a cooktop is particularly a problem. In addition, both microwave and conventional ovens remove moisture from food and vent it into the kitchen. The amount of moisture released in cooking depends on the type of food, whether or not the food is covered while cooking, and the length and temperature of cooking. Gas cooking appliances increase the moisture generated, because water vapor is a by-product of gas combustion.

Research conducted in the 1980s at the Cold Climate Housing Information Center at the University of Minnesota estimates that cooking a dinner for a family of four releases 1.22 pints of water into the air. The amount of moisture released more than doubles if a gas range is used, to 2.80 pints of water. Other moisture sources in a kitchen, identified by the Minnesota research, can include dishwashing (1.05 pints a day) and refrigerator defrosting (1.03 pints per day). To put this amount of moisture into context, consider that it takes only 4 to 6 pints of water vapor to raise the humidity level of a 1000 square foot house by 5 percent.

Many kitchens are open to other living spaces. While this allows some of the water vapor to disperse and reduce humidity in the kitchen, it also allows the water vapor to circulate throughout the home.

Moisture Basics

Water vapor is present in air in varying amounts. The amount of water vapor depends on the temperature. The warmer the air, the more water vapor it will hold. Humidity describes how much water vapor there is in air. Relative humidity, expressed as a percent, can be explained by the following formula:

$$\frac{\textit{Amount of water vapor in the air}}{\substack{\textit{Maximum amount of water vapor} \\ \textit{air can hold at that temperature}}} \; x \; 100 = \textit{Relative Humidity}$$

Note that the temperature of the air is an important factor in relative humidity. On a winter's day, when the outside temperature is 20 degrees Fahrenheit and the humidity is 70%, the air will actually be much drier than on a summer's day, when the outside temperature is 85 degrees Fahrenheit and the humidity is also 70%.

Condensation is the opposite of evaporation and occurs when water vapor returns to a liquid state. As the air cools, it can no longer hold as much water vapor, so the water condenses into a liquid. The temperature at which condensation occurs is referred to as the dew point. Everyone is familiar with the experience of fixing a cold glass of iced tea on a warm summer day and then finding that water condenses onto the cold exterior surface of the glass.

The cycle of water evaporating and condensing in a home can lead to moisture problems. For example, after preparing a meal, a kitchen is a warm, moist place. As the room cools and air from the kitchen moves throughout the home, the water vapor meets cooler surfaces, such as walls, and condensation can occur.

The air temperature inside the kitchen tends to be higher than the air temperature on the other side of the walls, floor and ceiling. This is especially true, in winter, of exterior walls and a ceiling with an attic above it. There is a natural tendency for warm air to move to cool air. This is nature's way of trying to maintain equilibrium. In a kitchen, warm, moist air will tend to move through walls and ceilings, moving from warm to cool. As the air moves through the wall or ceiling, it is cooled. At some point, condensation occurs. This hidden condensation, inside walls and attics, can be a particular nightmare for homeowners. As building materials get wetter, deterioration and mold growth can become extensive before the problem is noticed.

MOLDS AND MOISTURE

Molds are fungi. There are thousands of varieties of molds. Molds reproduce by spores, which blow out into the air. The spores can be dormant for years. Then, given the right conditions of food and moisture, the spores can begin to grow.

At any given time, there are typically mold spores in the air around us. Molds are a natural part of the ecosystem, and they play an important role in digesting organic debris such as dead leaves and insects. The problem occurs when there is an excess of mold growth and the organic matter they are digesting is part of the building structure.

Molds require moisture, oxygen and food to grow. How much of each of these elements is required will depend on the mold species. However, most molds start growing at a relative humidity of 70% or more. Molds can make food out of almost any organic matter, including skin cells, residues from food or textile fibers.

Cellulosic building materials such as paper, wood, textiles, many types of insulation, carpet, wallpaper and drywall, make an excellent environment for mold growth. The cellulosic materials absorb moisture, providing the right growth conditions, while the materials themselves provide the food for mold growth.

Molds grow fast. If cellulosic building materials get wet, mold growth will begin in 24 to 48 hours. Mold growth on the surface of non-cellulosic materials can start in the same time, as long as food and moisture are present.

Molds and Health

Molds can affect people in different ways. Some people are allergic to specific species of mold. Molds produce chemicals that are irritants to most people, and can cause problems such as headaches, breathing difficulties, and skin irritation as well as aggravating other health conditions such as asthma. Molds can sensitize the body so that the person is more susceptible to health effects from future exposures. Finally, some molds produce toxins. The likelihood of health effects increases with the amount of exposure to mold as well as the sensitivity of the individual.

PREVENTING MOISTURE PROBLEMS

Good ventilation in the kitchen not only avoids air quality problems, it also prevents moisture problems and mold growth by removing excess moisture and preventing condensation.

Energy efficient windows are important in preventing moisture problems. The interior surface of the energy efficient window is warmer, reducing the likelihood of condensation. Tight-fitting, insulated frames offer the same advantage.

Finish materials can contribute to, or help to prevent, moisture problems. After exposure to water and humidity, the more absorbent the material, the longer it stays damp. Specifying hard surface or non-absorbent materials, such as glazed tiles, solid surfacing, plastic laminate or engineered stone, reduces the likelihood of moisture problems. Materials that stay damp are much more likely to support mold growth. Specifying sealers for absorbent or porous materials, such as clay tiles, marble, or grout, can also reduce moisture absorption.

It is especially important that wall and ceiling finishes or materials block the flow of moisture into wall cavities or attics. This can be accomplished by selecting materials that are not moisture permeable, such as glazed tiles or vinyl wall coverings. Alternatively, a vapor retarder material, such as plastic sheeting, can be used in the wall construction. There are special considerations about the placement of a vapor retarder, depending on whether the climate is dominated by heating or cooling.

Low maintenance materials are also important to preventing mold growth. Materials that are kept clean are less likely to accumulate surface debris that can support mold growth. Avoid appliances, fixtures and fittings with cracks, seams, crevices and indentations that can accumulate residue from air borne grease, skin, body oils, spilled foods and cleaning products. All are organic materials that provide food for molds.

New products are becoming available with various types of anti-microbial finishes or additives. Generally, an anti-microbial finish means that the material is treated with a pesticide of some sort to protect the material or product itself. For example, paints with fungicides prevent mold growth in the paint itself. This does not mean that mold will not grow on the paint, in a moist environment, if a food source were to accumulate on the painted surface. Anti-microbial products may be desirable to minimize mold problems, but will not be an adequate substitute for good maintenance and moisture control practices.

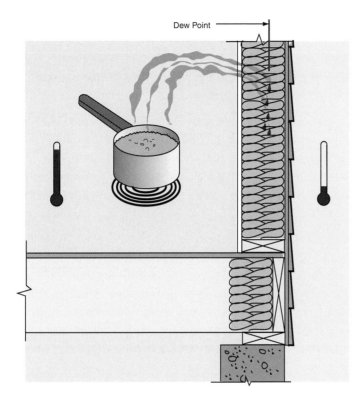

Figure 4.7 As warm, moist air moves through a wall, condensation will occur when the air is cooled to the dew point temperature.

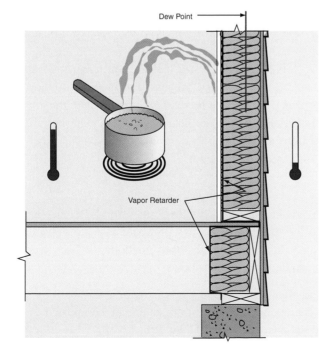

Figure 4.8 A vapor retarder prevents the flow of moisture from the kitchen into walls, where it can cause mold and other problems.

WASTE MANAGEMENT IN THE HOME

As a kitchen designer, you have a unique opportunity to encourage and facilitate your client's responsible waste management. Research continues to show that convenience motivates waste reduction behavior, in particular recycling. Through supportive design, you can make it easy to recycle.

Figure 4.9 Recycling systems should be planned for flexibility since community requirements will change over time. (Courtesy of KraftMaid Cabinetry)

A great deal of household waste is produced in the kitchen. As part of the preparation process, inedible or unappetizing parts of food—peels, seeds, bones, shells, rinds, fat, gristle and stems—are removed for disposal. All sorts of metal, glass, paper, cardboard or plastic packaging is accumulated. After a typical meal, food scraps remain.

Dealing with waste is part of the smooth flow of the food preparation process. For example, in the Virginia Tech research reported in Chapter 2, location of the trash receptacle was crucial to cooking participants. In Chapter 7, waste or trash collection is addressed from a space-planning perspective. Understanding that different types of waste can—and should—be managed differently creates opportunities for reducing the environmental impact of the waste generated in North American kitchens.

To practice recycling, items to be "recycled" are separated from items that are "thrown away." Recycled items may need to be disassembled or otherwise prepared so that different materials are separated. And recycled items often require temporary storage that is separate from the rest of the waste or trash. These are important distinctions to consider when designing a kitchen space.

Recycling is more than just separating out cans and bottles from regular trash. It is a complex process that includes finding uses for recycled materials and products. This means that the markets for recycled materials are volatile. Therefore which materials are recycled will vary from community to community, and over time. Plan for flexibility in a recycling system.

PLANNING FOR WASTE IN THE KITCHEN

Waste management planning in the kitchen begins by understanding the different types of waste that are generated in the kitchen and the different disposal methods. Waste from kitchen activities can be grouped as follows:

- **Food waste.** Most food waste is organic and so is biodegradable. Much food waste can be composted and not need be put into a landfill.

- **Packaging waste**. Packaging may need to be separated by material to facilitate recycling as much waste as possible.

- **Paper products**. In a typical home, a lot of paper becomes waste in the kitchen, much of which can be recycled, and some can be composted.

- **Miscellaneous waste**. Because of its central location, the kitchen trash can become the repository for waste from other rooms and activities. Even some of this miscellaneous waste can be recycled or composted.

Community Practices and Regulations

Waste management in the kitchen is influenced by community practices and regulations. Some communities require that certain materials be recycled and not be put into trash destined for the landfill. For example, aluminum cans, glass bottles or newspapers may be prohibited in trash pickups. In other communities, recycling may be voluntary. Some communities provide special containers for recycled items, and pick up recyclables on a regular schedule. Other communities provide collection points throughout the community for residents to drop off recycled items. Community recycling programs may allow recycled items to be co-mingled such as putting cans, bottles, and newspapers in the same containers for pickup. Other community programs require that recycled items be separated. Plastic soft drink bottles must be in separate containers from glass bottles, for example.

Some communities encourage recycling by limiting the amount of waste a household can have collected. Households may be limited on the size or weight of their refuse container, but may have unlimited amount of recyclables.

Become familiar with your client's community waste-management practices. These practices will determine how much space is needed to collect trash and recyclable items and how many separate containers are needed.

Waste Management Appliances

Two kitchen appliances can be part of the waste management process. Garbage disposers install under the sink drain, and grind up food waste so that it can be flushed into the sewage system. Trash compactors hold trash and compact it to reduce the volume.

83

For many people, garbage disposers are a convenient and sanitary way to handle food waste, minimizing odor and pest problems. However some communities do not allow garbage disposers. Environmentalists, who favor composting of food wastes, are critical of the amount of water used with garbage disposers.

Trash compactors reduce the volume of trash, but not the actual amount. This can be an advantage in a community where trash collection charges are by volume. However, there is no real environmental advantage to the compacted trash and its energy useage. Smaller households, especially those committed to recycling, are not likely to produce enough waste to find a trash compactor advantageous.

A RECYCLING CENTER

A recycling center can be a small area of the kitchen set aside for collecting, preparing and temporarily storing items for recycling. This may or may not be in the same location as the kitchen trash receptacle. Here are some suggestions for planning a recycling center.

- The best location for a recycling center is between the primary food preparation area (work triangle) and the exit to the garage, outdoors, or wherever the trash bins are kept.

  A typical scenario is that recyclables are collected inside the house for a limited period of time, and then taken to the larger storage bin, located in a garage or outside, adjacent to the regular trash bins.

  A recycling center could be located in a laundry area, mudroom, or utility room adjacent to the kitchen.

  Make sure that the recycling center is located in a well-ventilated area.

  Keeping the recycling center inside the house, in a heated or cooled space, makes it seem easier to use.

Figure 4.10 Recyclable items should be stored in containers that are easily accessible, such as roll-outs. The containers should also be easily removable. (Courtesy of Rev-A-Shelf)

- Storage for recyclable items should be accessible, such as in containers that roll-out, pull-out or swing-out. Containers need to be easily removed to transport the recyclable materials outside of the house.

  An alternative storage arrangement would be to include space for a community provided recycling container that could simply be lifted or wheeled outside for collection.

  Containers for recyclables need to be durable and easy to clean.

- Include a small sink in the recycling center or close by. Many items destined for recycling must be rinsed. A gooseneck or pullout style faucet adapts to different size containers.

- Provide storage for items used in preparing recyclables, such as twine for binding newspapers, scissors for cutting packaging, extra paper or plastic bags for sorting items, twist ties for closing bags, a magnet for testing metals, or can opener for removing lids.

- Provide space for a small trash can for non-recyclable items removed or discovered in the preparation of recyclable items.

- A small counter area will provide workspace for preparing and sorting recyclables.

- If the household uses and collects returnable bottles, incorporate storage for these into the recycling center.

If your client is interested in composting, try to incorporate some convenience features that encourage the practice. Include a food-scrap collection container into the recycling center. This container needs to be accessible, easily removed, and have a tight-fitting lid when not in use. Choose a container made of an easily washed, non-absorbent material so that odors are not a problem.

Alternatively, the compost scrap collection container might be kept in the food preparation area—where scraps are generated. A pull-out bin under a counter or even a removable section of countertop with a container underneath would make a convenient collection space for peels, trimmings and scraps. A compost collection container needs to be emptied regularly, so a large container is impractical.

Figure 4.11 A convenient compost bin is recessed into the kitchen counter adjacent to the sink for collecting food scraps. (Courtesy of Rev-A-Shelf)

Another idea for collecting food scraps for composting is to keep a container in the refrigerator or freezer. This helps control potential problems with odor or pests, if it is not possible to make an immediate trip to the compost area.

NOISE

A kitchen can be a noisy place. Typically, there is a lot of activity, pots and pans banging, appliance motors whirring, water running, and people talking. Even when people are not in the kitchen, appliances can continue to operate and the sound might be heard in adjacent spaces.

Noise is often defined as unwanted sound. Therefore, controlling noise is a matter of limiting the transfer of sound from one part of the home to another.

Sound moves by vibrations, which are transmitted through both air and building materials. Soft materials, like carpet and draperies, tend to absorb sound. Hard materials, like ceramic tile and stone, typically found in the kitchen, tend to reflect and/or transmit sounds. Noise is controlled in several ways:

- Reduce the amount of sound or noise that is generated.

- Isolate and buffer the sources of noise by space planning.

- Use construction techniques to insulate and stop sound transmission.

A first step to reducing noise problems in a kitchen is to choose appliances that operate quietly. In particular, specify a dishwasher that is well insulated for sound control. Make sure all appliances are level to reduce noise-generating vibrations.

Kitchen ventilation fans are necessary to control moisture, yet motors and air movement can be noisy. The quietest fans are those with the lowest sone rating. Selecting and installing kitchen fans to minimize noise is discussed in the section on ventilation in Chapter 8. A fan that is too loud simply will not be used, which may control noise, but lead to air-quality problems.

Laundry areas (See Chapter 9) are sometimes included in or near the kitchen. Noise transmission, especially to the social areas, should be considered before installing washers and dryers near or in the kitchen.

Motors, such as those used in ventilation fans, small appliances and washing machines, may vary in pitch (hertz). Many people perceive lower pitch noises to be less annoying. However, it is important for your client to "test listen" to different motors to determine their reaction to the noise before purchasing.

Line shelves in cabinets with cork, rubber or other sound-absorbing materials to reduce the "clatter" of dishes and other items. Cabinet doors and drawers should have cork or rubber bumpers to absorb the banging noise that can occur with closing.

If you have the opportunity to influence the home design beyond the kitchen space, look for ways to put sound-absorbing spaces between it and the adjacent quiet areas of the home. For example, a closet situated between a kitchen and a bedroom is an excellent way to buffer noise and to keep sleeping areas undisturbed. Built-in cabinets, bookshelves, stairways, and utility closets all make good sound buffers.

Another sound-buffering space planning technique is to back noisy area to noisy area. For example, put the dishwasher on the wall that is shared with the bathroom toilet, rather than the same wall that is shared with the bedroom.

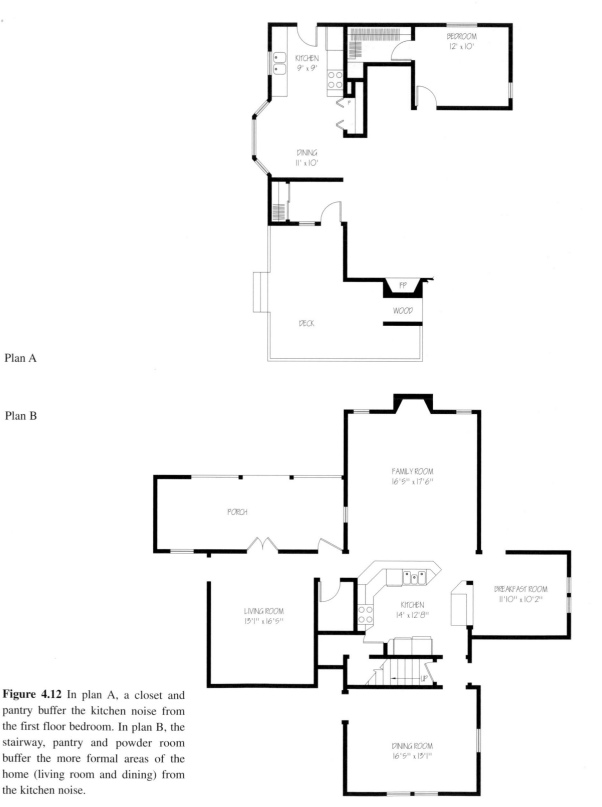

Plan A

Plan B

Figure 4.12 In plan A, a closet and pantry buffer the kitchen noise from the first floor bedroom. In plan B, the stairway, pantry and powder room buffer the more formal areas of the home (living room and dining) from the kitchen noise.

In new construction, or renovations that include building new walls, use sound insulating construction techniques to isolate kitchen noises. One simple approach is to use materials, such as acoustical tiles, cork, carpet, and other sound-muffling textiles. However, these softer and absorbent materials may not be the best choices in the kitchen, where water-, grease- and mold-resistance and easy cleaning are important. Therefore, look at wall construction techniques that reduce sound transmission.

To minimize the transmission of sound, avoid air paths between the kitchen and other spaces. For example, use resilient, non-hardening caulk to seal around receptacles, plumbing, light fixtures, and other openings in the walls and ceilings. Also, seal where the wall partition joins the floor and ceiling. If there are switches, receptacles and other openings on opposite sides of a wall, avoid locating them in the same stud space. If possible, separate these switches and receptacles, horizontally, by at least 24 inches.

There are several ways to construct the walls to minimize sound transmission. A standard stud wall could be insulated with fiberglass or a similar material to absorb sound. A sound-deadening gasket could be used between the studs and the drywall to minimize vibration and sound transmission. A double stud wall, with the studs on separate plates, reduces sound transmission by separating the two wall structures and limiting vibration. A staggered stud, double stud wall will be even more effective. Insulating material can be added to any of these special wall constructions. (See Figure 4.15)

Keep in mind that special, sound-insulating wall constructions do have several drawbacks, and the trade-offs need to be considered. Cost is increased for extra materials and time in construction. Floor space is lost, especially with the double walls. Also, the need to run plumbing, wiring, and ducts in the walls has to be considered, especially with a staggered stud, double wall.

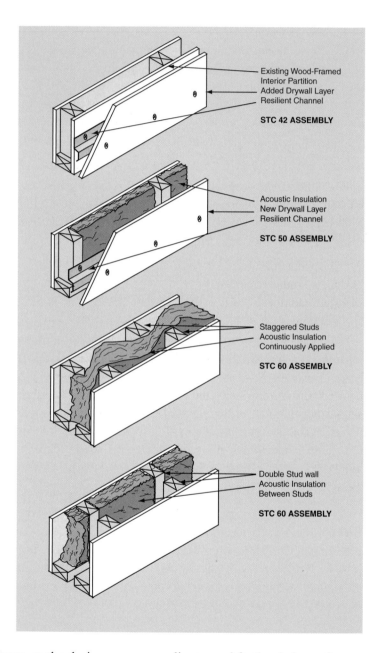

Existing Wood-Framed
Interior Partition
Added Drywall Layer
Resilient Channel

STC 42 ASSEMBLY

Acoustic Insulation
New Drywall Layer
Resilient Channel

STC 50 ASSEMBLY

Staggered Studs
Acoustic Insulation
Continuously Applied

STC 60 ASSEMBLY

Double Stud wall
Acoustic Insulation
Between Studs

STC 60 ASSEMBLY

Figure 4.13 Different building techniques can be used to reduce sound transmission through walls, which is measured in sound transmission units or STC.

If you, as the designer, or your client, need further information on environmental issues, contact the U.S. Environmental Protection Agency (EPA). A good place to start is the web site, www.epa.gov. Another excellent resource is the Canada Mortgage and Housing Corporation (CMHC), www.cmhc-schl.gc.ca, which provides information on many aspects of housing. Or contact the local office of your Cooperative Extension Service, health department, or water authority.

CHAPTER 5: Human Factors and Universal Design Implications

Like most principles and elements of design, universal design is an enduring approach that draws from both science and spirit. It is based solidly on human factors and, along with this quantitative information, places equal value on the aesthetics of a space or product. Universal design responds to our growing appreciation and respect for diversity in the spaces we design, and in the stature, age, abilities and culture of the people for whom we design.

The study of human dimensions and the design of spaces and products around human factors are solid steps toward good universal design. Traditionally, human factors-based design seemed to center on two extremes. It was either one-size-fits-all for the non-existent "average person" or totally custom design for each individual client's dimensions, abilities and needs. Universal design moves away from these extremes and builds on anthropometry and ergonomics in different ways. It embraces as broad a range of human factors as possible. One example is the placement of a wall switch that is dictated not by the reach range of the average height person, but by overlap of the reach ranges of the shorter and the taller among us. In addition, universal design places equal emphasis on aesthetics, acknowledging the importance of beauty and comfort in design solutions.

In this chapter, you will explore anthropometric and ergonomic information, as well as human factors studies, that help guide design of spaces and the basic concepts of universal design, which have become essential to good kitchen planning. Throughout this book, universal design concepts have been incorporated where applicable. Further information on access and specific user groups is covered in Chapter 10.

ANTHROPOMETRY

A basic understanding of the human body, including its limitations and capabilities, is helpful in any space planning, particularly in a room of such high function and activity as the kitchen. While you will often determine a client's particular dimensions and needs, there are general areas where standards, based on research, are useful.

Anthropometry, defined as the study of human measurements such as size and proportion, and parameters such as reach range and visual range, is a good starting point. While not an exact science, anthropometry uses populations grouped according to specific criteria, such as age, gender, or ability, to collect data on bodies at rest (structural or static) and bodies in motion (functional or dynamic). Much of the information offered here on anthropometric data is sourced from *Human Dimension & Interior Space* by Panero and Zelnick (1979), which is a generally accepted reference for interior space planning.

In this chapter, we will discuss various types of anthropometric information. In Chapter 6, which focuses on needs assessment, there is information about collecting anthropometric information on your specific clients. Included in Chapter 6 is **Form 1: Getting to Know Your Client**, which provides graphics to guide you in collecting anthropometric dimensions (part 1.2), reach and grasp profiles (part 1.3), and anthropometric dimensions with mobility aids (part 1.5).

Structural Anthropometry

Also called static anthropometry, structural anthropometry includes many dimensions relating to the body at rest. Figure 5.1 illustrates those dimensions that clearly impact kitchen space planning and will be important to the design applications detailed in Chapter 7.

The dimensions presented in Figure 5.1 are defined by Panero and Zelnick as follows:

- Stature is the vertical distance from the floor to the top of the head. It influences such spatial considerations as minimum height of door openings or ceiling.

- Eye height is the vertical distance from the floor to the inner corner of the eye. It dictates and affects such things as sight lines or the height of wall sconces, mirrors, wall art or windows.

- Elbow height is the vertical distance from the floor to the depression formed at the elbow. This affects such things as comfortable counter heights and sink heights.

- Sitting height is the vertical distance from the sitting surface to the top of the head when a person is sitting erect. This influences the height of such things as cabinets over a dining counter.

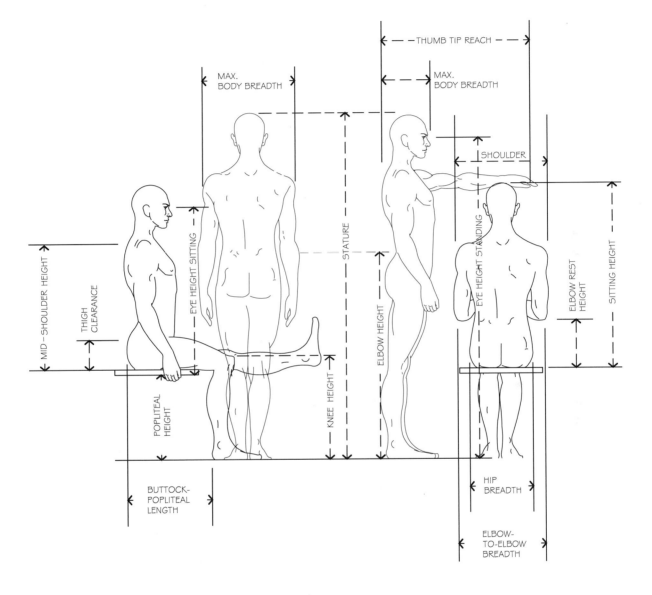

Figure 5.1 These are some of the body measurements that influence interior space planning. (Redrawn from *Human Dimension & Interior Space* by Julius Panero and Martin Zelnik [1979, Watson-Guptill Publications] pg. 30)

- Eye height while sitting is the vertical distance from the sitting surface to the inner corner of the eye with the subject sitting erect. This measurement dictates the sight lines that influence dining counter lighting or window mullion heights.

- Mid-shoulder height sitting is the vertical distance from the sitting surface to the point of the shoulder midway between the neck and acromion (end of shoulder blade). It influences the location of neck- or head-rests or backing for seating.

93

- Shoulder breadth (width) is the maximum horizontal distance across the deltoid muscles, and is important in determining necessary clearance between dining chairs.

- Elbow-to-elbow breadth is the horizontal distance with the elbows flexed and resting against the body, affecting clearances for dining space.

- Hip breadth is the width of the body measured across the widest portion of the hip, and it influences bench or seat width and passageways.

- Elbow rest height, measured from the top of the sitting surface to the bottom of the tip of the elbow, influences such things as armrests and counter heights.

- Thigh clearance is the vertical distance from a sitting surface to the top of the thigh at the point where the thigh and abdomen intersect. This is important when planning full-depth knee spaces, including the apron or drawer height.

- Knee height is the vertical distance from the floor to the midpoint of the kneecap and is useful when planning partial knee space.

- Popliteal height (behind knee) is the vertical distance from the floor to the underside portion of the thigh just behind the knee while a person is seated. This influences the height of benches and seats.

- Buttock to popliteal length is the horizontal distance from the rearmost surface of the buttock to the back of the lower leg. It indicates the necessary depth for benches and seats.

- Maximum body depth is the horizontal distance between the most anterior point, usually the chest or abdomen, to the most posterior, usually found in the buttocks or shoulder. It influences depth of floor space at work surfaces, clearance and passage. To accommodate groups of people who use mobility aids, this measurement must include the aid.

- Maximum body breadth is the distance, including arms, across the body. This measurement affects the widths of aisles, doors and doorways. To accommodate groups of people who use mobility aids, this measurement must include the aid.

Functional anthropometry is the measurement of the body in motion. It includes movement of body parts in relationship to one another, as well as measures of strength. Because it is more complex than structural anthropometry, it is more difficult to accurately measure. However, certain aspects are helpful to kitchen planning. This information focuses mainly on the reach range and the functional space of a person using a variety of mobility aids.

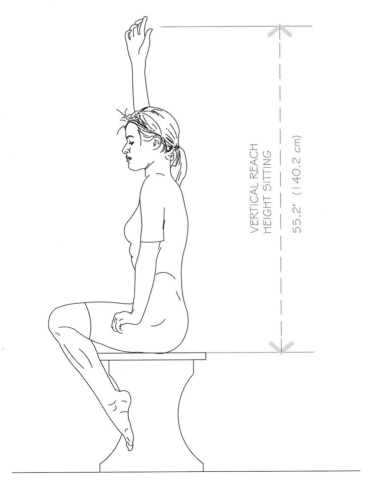

VERTICAL REACH HEIGHT SITTING

55.2" (140.2 cm)

Figure 5.2 As a population, women are shorter than men so adult female vertical reach height sitting is indicated. If a design accommodated this shorter reach, it would also include 95% of women and others, both men and women with a taller reach. (Redrawn from *Human Dimension & Interior Space* by Julius Panero and Martin Zelnik [1979, Watson-Guptill Publications] pg. 100)

- **Vertical reach height sitting** is the height above the sitting surface of the tip of the middle finger when the arm, hand and fingers are extended vertically. It impacts overhead storage.

95

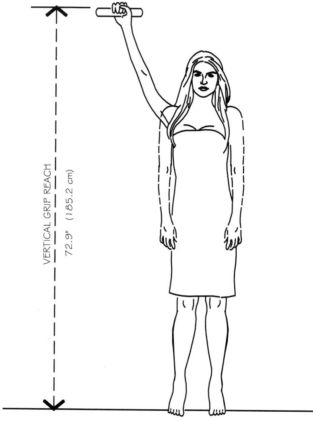

VERTICAL GRIP REACH

72.9" (185.2 cm)

Figure 5.3 The vertical grip reach is useful in determining maximum height for readily accessed storage. This drawing and related measurement are again based on the adult female in the fifth percentile, this time in a standing position. (Redrawn from *Human Dimension & Interior Space* by Julius Panero and Martin Zelnik [1979, Watson-Guptill Publications] pg. 100)

- **Vertical grip reach** is the distance from the floor to the top of a bar grasped in the hand, raised as high as it can be without discomfort, while the subject stands erect. It is important in planning the height of bookshelves, storage shelves or controls. Vertical grip reach from a seated position is also important in a design that accommodates operating from a seated position.

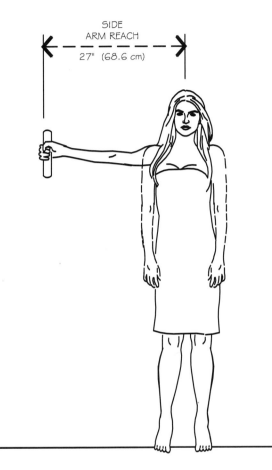

SIDE
ARM REACH
27" (68.6 cm)

Figure 5.4 Whether a person is seated or standing, the side arm grip reach will influence placement of stored items and controls. These measurements are based on a standing adult female in the fifth percentile. (Redrawn from *Human Dimension & Interior Space* by Julius Panero and Martin Zelnik [1979, Watson-Guptill Publications] pg. 100)

- **Side arm grip reach** is the distance from the centerline of the body to the outside surface of a bar grasped in the hand, stretched horizontally without experiencing discomfort or strain, while the subject stands erect. Like the vertical grip reach, this measurement helps determine a comfortable location for controls, general storage and the horizontal span of a work area. There seems to be more information available on this dimension for a standing person, but the data and its application involve the seated user as well.

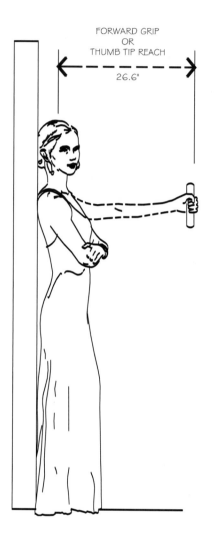

FORWARD GRIP
OR
THUMB TIP REACH

26.6"

Figure 5.5 Using the dimension for thumb tip reach based on adult females in the fifth percentile is a good basis for planning storage and work areas that are within the reach of most people. (Redrawn from *Human Dimension & Interior Space* by Julius Panero and Martin Zelnik [1979, Watson-Guptill Publications] pg. 100)

- **Thumb tip reach** is the distance from a wall directly behind the person to the tip of the thumb, measured with the subject's shoulders against the wall, and the arm extended forward with index finger touching the tip of the thumb. This dimension influences depth and height of work counters and shelves, as well as general storage above the counters.

Reach Ranges

Reach ranges vary according to stature, physical ability and obstructions. The height range within a person's reach is useful for planning functional storage, fixtures, appliances, and locating controls in the kitchen.

- The lower end of a forward reach range is 15 to 20 inches off the floor, depending on a person's ability to bend. The upper dimension can go as high as 72 inches for the average female (76 inches for the average male), but will depend on a person's stature and any obstruction, such as a counter or shelf.

- The average person who remains seated to maneuver in the kitchen has a forward reach range of 15 to 48 inches.

- A standing person who has difficulty bending may have a forward reach range of 24 to 72 inches.

- The person who uses crutches, a walker, or in some way needs their hands to maintain balance, has a slightly different reach range, depending on the mobility aid and physical ability.

A universal reach range of 15 inches to 48 inches has been suggested as a guide for both standing and seated users in a variety of situations. This range is generally accepted and used to guide placement of storage, controls and frequently used items.

	Seated User	Standing, Mobility Impaired Person	Standing Person 5' 3" – 5' 7"	Universal
Lower Limit–Bending	15"	15"	15"	15"
Lower Limit–No Bending	—	24"	24"	24"
Upper Limit	48"	72"	79 1/2"	48"

Figure 5.6 Working with the functional dimensions and reach ranges of a variety of people, universal design advocates use the reach range in the universal column to accommodate most people.

Range-of-Joint Motion

Range-of-joint motion is another aspect of human dimension that affects the design of the space and components within a kitchen. These include: movements of the hands, wrists and fingers; movement and flexibility of the shoulders and elbows; bending or twisting at the waist or spine; and movement of the knees. Because no joint operates in isolation, it is difficult to generate accurate and useful information regarding range of motion of joints. However, understanding the areas to consider will help in developing a space that works for a specific client. If you can observe and estimate a client's range-of-joint motion, your design and specifications can more accurately meet the client's needs.

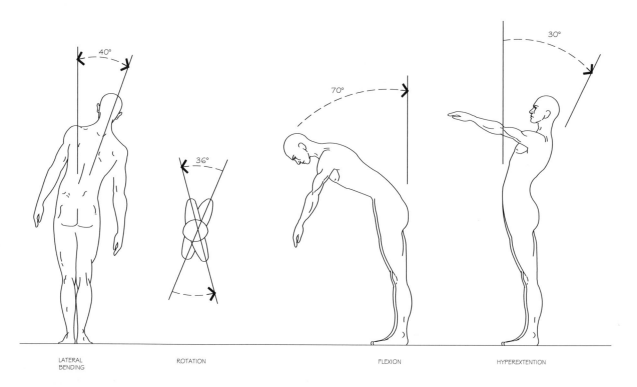

LATERAL
BENDING

ROTATION

FLEXION

HYPEREXTENTION

Figure 5.7 A person's range of motion in the spine and shoulders can affect the dimensions for a work center in the kitchen. (Redrawn from *Human Dimension & Interior Space* by Julius Panero and Martin Zelnik [1979, Watson-Guptill Publications] pg. 115)

MOBILITY AIDS

There is a growing amount of useful data related to movement and maneuvering, including information relating to walking or moving with an assistive device. Although these data seem less plentiful, Panero and Zelnick do offer minimal parameters. Access guidelines, such as those from the American National Standards Institute (ANSI) or Uniform Federal Accessibility Standard (UFAS), can be helpful. One critical rule: consider the person and the aid as one. And, just as for a person who does not use a mobility aid, these figures increase when the person using an aid goes from a static position to motion.

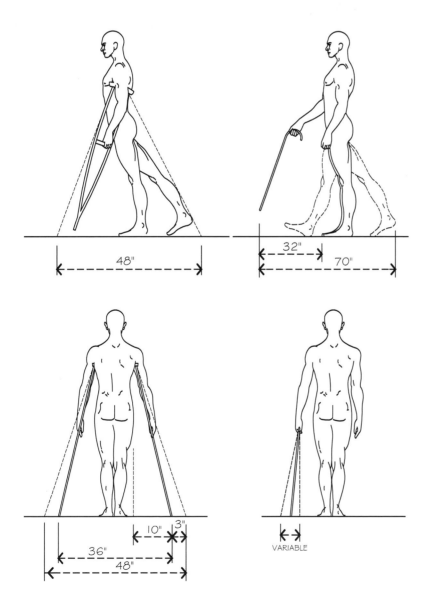

Figure 5.8 These minimum allowances will help in planning spatial clearances. Note that in this case, using the larger dimensions of percentile of adult males provides clearances for any human of smaller dimensions as well. (Redrawn from *Human Dimension & Interior Space* by Julius Panero and Martin Zelnik [1979, Watson-Guptill Publications] pg. 54)

101

Figure 5.9 The dimensions of a walker dictate the minimum clearances needed. (Redrawn from *Human Dimension & Interior Space* by Julius Panero and Martin Zelnik [1979, Watson-Guptill Publications] pg. 54)

28"
71.1 cm

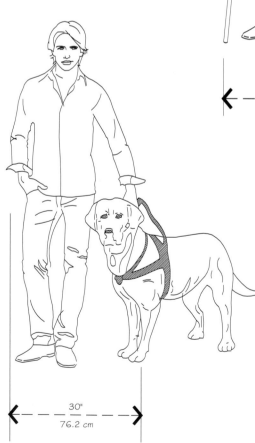

Figure 5.10 In this case, the clearance dimensions must be based on the actual user and dog, but the given dimension of 30 inches could be used as an absolute minimum. (Redrawn from *Human Dimension & Interior Space* by Julius Panero and Martin Zelnik [1979, Watson-Guptill Publications] pg. 54)

30"
76.2 cm

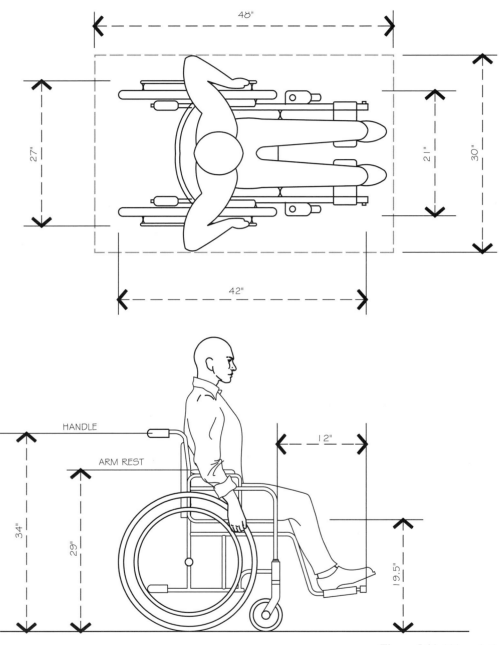

Figure 5.11 Although these measurements for a person using a chair are useful in general, it is much better to measure the person in the chair. The variables are greatly impacted by the person's size and ability, as well as the design and fit of the chair. The standard clear floor space used in planning spaces for a person in a wheelchair is 30 inches x 48 inches.

COMFORT ZONE

Based on psychological factors, we can also identify a body buffer zone or comfort zone. We maintain this personal space between others and ourselves who are walking, talking or just standing with us. While we maintain a greater distance with strangers, the personal or close zone will be most applicable to kitchen design.

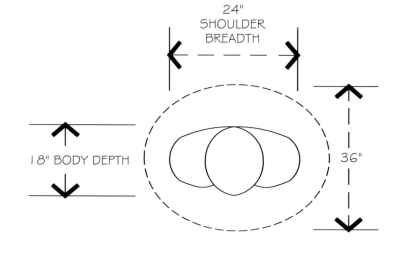

Figure 5.12 Based on a shoulder breadth of 24 inches and a body depth of 18 inches, a minimum area of approximately three square feet per person is a guide in a space to be shared. (Redrawn from *Human Dimension & Interior Space* by Julius Panero and Martin Zelnik [1979, Watson-Guptill Publications] pg. 41)

ANTHROPOMETRY OF CHILDREN

Historically there has been very little anthropometric data available regarding children. However, given the growing national focus on childhood health and safety, we can expect this to change. Although functional data would be most applicable, body dimensions of children are available and can be a starting point for the design of child-oriented spaces. The following chart is based on information from government data as well as Panero and Zelnick.

Stature (Height)		6 years	11 years	Hip Breadth		6 years	11 years
95 Percentile	Boys	50.4	61.8	95 Percentile	Boys	9.3	12
	Girls	49.9	62.9		Girls	9.3	13.3
5 Percentile	Boys	50.4	61.8	95 Percentile	Boys	9.3	12
	Girls	49.9	62.9		Girls	9.3	13.3
Sitting (Height)				Popliteal Height (to knee from floor when sitting)			
95 Percentile	Boys	27.4	31.7	95 Percentile	Boys	12.8	16.3
	Girls	27.1	32.8		Girls	12.6	16.4
5 Percentile	Boys	23.7	26.7	95 Percentile	Boys	10.4	13.3
	Girls	23.1	27.4		Girls	10.2	13.1
Elbow to Elbow Breadth				Buttock Popliteal Length (wall to back of knee when sitting)			
95 Percentile	Boys	11.3	14.7	95 Percentile	Boys	12.8	16.3
	Girls	11.1	14.7		Girls	12.6	16.4
5 Percentile	Boys	8.5	10.1	95 Percentile	Boys	11.3	14.5
	Girls	8.3	9.6		Girls	11.3	15

(Measurements in inches)

Figure 5.13 The height and breadth of children, both standing and seated, can be useful dimensions when planning a kitchen that must accommodate them as they grow. (Redrawn from *Human Dimension & Interior Space* by Julius Panero and Martin Zelnik [1979, Watson-Guptill Publications] pg. 106-107)

ERGONOMIC & UNIVERSAL DESIGN

Based on anthropometric data and other human factors, ergonomics is the study of the relationship of people to their environment. For us, ergonomic design is the application of human factors data to the design of products and spaces to improve function and efficiency. Universal design builds on ergonomics to improve the use of products, spaces and systems equally for people of a variety of size, ages and abilities. The relationship of people to their kitchens is the basis for the kitchen design guidelines and applications, detailed in Chapter 7 and throughout the book.

Universal design is inclusive and equitable, meeting the needs of a great number and variety of people. It is much more than the misconception that it is design limited to medical solutions for access challenges.

History and State of the Art

Since the end of World War II, awareness of the need for improved access and universal design has been growing. Currently, we are experiencing unprecedented interest, worldwide, in the design of environments and products that respect the diversity of human beings. Nowhere is this more true than in the kitchen, encompassing activities of daily life critical to every living person.

People are living longer, largely due to healthier lifestyles, better medicine, and vaccines and sanitation techniques that have virtually eliminated many killer infectious diseases. We are redefining retirement to encompass active adult living, and our designs must surely include the support that will enable active lifestyles. In addition, more people are living with disabilities and they want to live better. Wars have created a population of veterans with disabilities. And antibiotics and other medical advances have enabled people to survive accidents and illnesses that were previously fatal. According to the U.S. Census Bureau, Census 2000, 49.7 million people in the United States (19.3% of the population) had some level of disability and approximately 31.2 million (12%) had a severe disability. In addition, the National Center for Injury Prevention and Control estimates that for every 100,000 people age 55 to 85, over 3,500 had an unintentional fall in the year 2000. For people age 65 to 85, that number jumps to 4,652 unintentional falls per 100,000 people.

In short, universal design concepts must be applied to kitchen planning so that the kitchen will function for, and benefit, all the residents of, and visitors to, a home.

Ron Mace, FAIA, known as the father of universal design, defined it as "the design of products and environments to be useable by all people to the greatest extent possible". From 1994 to 1997, Mace led a research and demonstration project at the Center for Universal Design, funded by the U.S. Department of Education's National Institute on Disability and Rehabilitation Research (NIDRR), which included the development of universal design guidelines or principles.

Following is the Center for Universal Design's current list of the Seven Principles of Universal Design with applications added that apply to kitchens. You might find these principles a good checklist to use in the design process as additional criteria when choosing between options.

Equitable Use

Design is useful and marketable to people with diverse abilities.

- Provide the same means of use for all users: identical whenever possible; equivalent when not.

- Avoid segregating or stigmatizing any users.

- Provisions for privacy, security, and safety should be equally available to all users.

- Make the design appealing to all users.

Design Applications

- Rocker light switch

- Motion sensor lighting, ventilation or faucets

- Side-by-side refrigerator

Figure 5.14 Side-by-side refrigeration with bottom drawer freezer provides some storage within everyone's reach. (Courtesy of GE)

Flexibility in Use

Design accommodates a wide range of individual preferences and abilities.

- Provide choice in methods of use.

- Accommodate right- or left-handed access and use.

- Facilitate the user's accuracy and precision.

- Provide adaptability to the user's pace.

Design Applications

- Knee spaces with door and storage options, allowing for seated or standing use

- 48" work aisles, ensuring either a perpendicular or parallel approach to appliances

- Multiple counter heights

- Movable (portable) storage

- Storage for an optional stool

Figure 5.15 Providing a step stool is a design application that offers flexibility of use for individuals of varying heights. (Courtesy of Tom Trzcinski, CMKBD—Pittsburgh, Pennsylvania. Photography by Craig Thompson.)

Simple and Intuitive Use

Design is easy to understand, regardless of the user's experience, knowledge, language skills or current concentration level.

- Eliminate unnecessary complexity.

- Be consistent with user expectations and intuition.

- Accommodate a wide range of literacy and language skills.

- Arrange information consistent with its importance.

- Provide effective prompting and feedback during and after task completion.

Design Applications

- Operation of single-lever faucet that moves left for hot and right for cold

- Use of red to indicate hot and blue to indicate cold

- One-step controls on a microwave for preprogrammed recipes

Figure 5.16 This single-lever faucet is a great example of universal design, including the fact that right for cold, left for heat is intuitive. (Courtesy of Moen)

Perceptible Information

Design communicates necessary information effectively to the user, regardless of ambient conditions or the user's sensory abilities.

- Use different modes (pictorial, verbal, tactile) for redundant presentation of essential information.

- Provide adequate contrast between essential information and its surroundings.

- Maximize "legibility" of essential information.

- Differentiate elements in ways that can be described (i.e., make it easy to give instructions or directions).

- Provide compatibility with a variety of techniques or devices used by people with sensory limitations.

Design Applications

- Digital temperature control on faucets or ovens that sounds and blinks when temperature limits are reached (redundant cuing)

- Lighting controls that light up in the off position and go dark when the light is on

- Smoke detectors that sound and light the alarm

- Cooking controls that use numbers and pictures to indicate cooking mode/process

Figure 5.17 The controls on this range offer digital and pictorial communication. (Courtesy of GE)

Tolerance for Error

Design minimizes hazards and the adverse consequences of accidental or unintended actions.

- Arrange elements to minimize hazards and errors. Most used elements, most accessible; hazardous elements eliminated, isolated, or shielded.

- Provide warnings of hazards and errors.

- Provide fail-safe features.

- Discourage unconscious action in tasks that require vigilance.

Design Applications

- GFCI outlets that reduce risk of shock

- Temperature limiting faucets that prevent accidental scalding

- Timed automatic shut-off on faucets or ventilation

- Induction cooktops

Figure 5.18 An induction cooktop offers fail-safe features, such as its ability to shutoff if a pan is not on the element or if the pan boils dry. (Courtesy of Wolf Appliance Company)

111

Low Physical Effort

Design can be used efficiently and comfortably and with a minimum of fatigue.

- Allow user to maintain a neutral body position.

- Use reasonable operating forces.

- Minimize repetitive actions.

- Minimize sustained physical effort vigilance.

Design Applications

- Lever handles

- Remote controls for operating windows

- Remote controls for cooktop ventilation

- Motion activated appliances and controls

- D-pulls on cabinetry

- Conveniently located storage and appliances (raised dishwashers, counter height microwaves and ovens)

Figure 5.19 Dishwasher and laundry appliances are being designed higher off the floor to minimize bending. (Courtesy of GE)

Size and Space for Approach and Use

Appropriate size and space are provided for approach, reach, manipulation and use regardless of user's body size, posture or mobility.

- Provide a clear line of sight to important elements for any seated or standing user.

- Make the reach to all components comfortable for any seated or standing user.

- Accommodate variations in hand and grip size.

- Provide adequate space for the use of assistive devices or personal assistance.

Design Applications

- Split double ovens installed at comfort height

- Storage accessories installed within the universal reach range (15 to 48 inches above finished floor)

- Movable (portable) storage

- The 30" x 48" clear floor space in front of all appliances

- Knee space at a sink, cooktop, work counters or adjacent to tall appliances

Figure 5.20 Oven installed at comfort height is one design application that provides for easy approach, reach and use of the appliance regardless of user's body size, posture or mobility. Double ovens could be installed side-by-side the same way. (Courtesy of NY Loft)

The term universal design is sometimes inaccurately used as the politically correct description of compliance with the Americans with Disabilities Act (ADA) and other access codes or guidelines. While access codes and guidelines are important as a minimum, universal design is a broader approach that works to incorporate the needs of all users, not any one specific group. Universal design is an ideal, a way of thinking, whereas code compliance is often simply following a dictate.

A number of terms are used almost interchangeably with universal design.

- **Lifespan design** refers to the aspect of universal design that provides for the changes that may occur in the lifespan of the home, such as the birth and growth of children. It also refers to the changes that may occur in the lifespan of the owners, such as the return to home after a skiing accident that results in a broken bone.

- **Trans-generational design** refers to the design that acknowledges and supports the multiple generations living under one roof today.

- **Barrier-free design** is an older term, first used to refer to solutions that removed barriers in the environment. While removing barriers is still one important aspect, in North America universal design has been embraced as a broader, more positive approach and term.

- **Accessible design** or **accessibility** is a function of compliance with regulations or criteria that established a minimum level of design necessary to accommodate people with disabilities, i.e. "wheelchair accessible."

- **Adaptable design** refers to features that are either adjustable or capable of being easily added or removed to "adapt" to individual needs or preferences.

- **Visit-ability** refers to basic accommodations that will allow people of differing abilities to visit a home. In terms of kitchen design, visit-ability requires simply that doorways into the room be a minimum 32 inches clear.

• **FlexHousing** is a Canadian concept in housing that
incorporates, at the design and construction stage, the ability
to make future changes easily and with minimum expense,
to meet the evolving needs of its occupants. FlexHousing is
an approach to designing and building homes based on the
principles of adaptability, accessibility, affordability and
healthy housing. The FlexHousing concept of accessibility is
user-friendly and its features add convenience and practicality
to the functions of a home. Another consideration is the
reduction of potential hazards. Although the initial cost
of FlexHousing is slightly more than a conventional home,
FlexHousing features recover their investment over the long-
term because pre-engineered features allow for easy and
inexpensive change and renovation. The integration of healthy
building materials and innovative housing technology or
Healthy Housing protects both the health of the occupants
and the environment.

DISPELLING MYTHS

There are many misconceptions regarding universal design. Let us
put an end to the most common ones.

Myth 1: Universal design is nothing more than design for people
in wheelchairs.

Fact: The opposite is true. To be considered universal, a design
will be accessible not only to people in wheelchairs,
but also to people of most sizes, shapes and abilities.
Universal design applies to people tall or short, young or
old, left-handed or right-handed, visitors to an unfamiliar
city or home, parents with children, people carrying
packages, and more.

Myth 2: Universal design only helps people with disabilities and
older people.

Fact: Universal design extends the benefits of functional
design to many people including short or tall people,
large people, frail people, pregnant women, children or
even people traveling with much to carry or where there
is a language barrier—everyone eventually.

Myth 3: Universal design costs more than traditional design.

Fact: Many universal concepts are standard products and cost no more than traditional products. The degree of customization and quality of the products will have the greater impact on cost.

Myth 4: Universal design is stigmatizing because it looks medical.

Fact: The best universal design is invisible. When done well, universal design enhances both the appearance and personality of a space as well as the function of that space for a variety of users.

ACCESS CODES, LAWS AND STANDARDS

In the U.S., most existing access-related laws, codes and standards are intended as minimum criteria for access for people with disabilities. While this is not universal design, the related guidelines can serve as a starting point for universal thinking. The following might serve as a starting point for study of these references.

American National Standard For Accessible and Useable Buildings and Facilities (ANSI A117.1)

The first edition of the American National Standard for Accessible and Useable Buildings and Facilities (ANSI A117.1) standard was issued in 1961. Since then, the standard has been updated and revised several times. The last revision of the standard occurred in 2003.

Since the International Code Council (ICC) is the current secretariat for the standard, it is referred to as the ICC/ANSI standard and includes technical design guidelines for making buildings and sites accessible to, and usable by, people with disabilities. The ICC/ANSI standard is the referenced technical standard for compliance with the accessibility requirements of the International Building Code and many other state and local codes. Earlier editions of the ANSI standard are the referenced technical criteria for accessibility compliance required by the BOCA National Building Code, the Standard Building Code, the Uniform Building Code and other state and local codes.

The 1986, 1992 and 1998 editions of the ANSI A117.1 standard are also U.S. Department of Housing and Urban Development (HUD) approved "safe harbors" for compliance with the technical requirements of the Fair Housing Amendments Act of 1988 (accepted in place of these requirements), a federal mandate for accessibility in multifamily housing. "Safe harbors" and the Fair Housing Act are further discussed below.

Uniform Federal Accessibility Standards (UFAS)

First published in 1984, Uniform Federal Accessibility Standards (UFAS) includes criteria for the design and construction of federal buildings to provide access for people with disabilities. UFAS is the technical standard referenced by two federal mandates for accessibility: the Architectural Barriers Act (ABA) and Section 504 of the Rehabilitation Act of 1973. The ABA requires access to buildings constructed, altered, leased or financed in whole or in part by the United States; and Section 504 requires that federally financed programs and activities be accessible to people with disabilities. Section 504 also requires access to federally financed newly constructed and altered buildings. The technical provisions of UFAS are largely the same as the 1980 ANSI A117.1 standard. Updated guidelines are in review by the Department of Justice and HUD. When approved, they will be the ABA/ADA standards, available from the Access Board.

Fair Housing Act Accessibility Guidelines

First published in 1991, the Fair Housing Accessibility Guidelines (FHAG) provide architects, builders, developers and others, technical guidance for compliance with the accessibility requirements of the Fair Housing Amendments Act of 1988 (the Act). The Act covers newly constructed multifamily buildings containing at least four dwellings built for first occupancy on or after March 13, 1991.

"Safe Harbors"

In addition to the Guidelines, HUD has approved several "safe harbors" for compliance with the Act. A "safe harbor" is a standard that is legally recognized as compliant with the requirements of a code or guideline. The current "safe harbors" are:

- The 1986, 1992 and 1998 editions of the ANSI A117.1 standard, when used with the Fair Housing Act, HUD's Fair Housing Act regulations and the Guidelines.

- HUD's The Fair Housing Act Design Manual (1998).

- The Code Requirements for Housing Accessibility 2000 (CRHA), published by the International Code Council in October 2000.

- International Building Code 2000 (IBC), as amended by the IBC's 2001 Supplement to the International Codes.

"Safe harbor" standards constitute safe harbors only when adopted and implemented in accordance with the policy statement that HUD published in the Federal Register on March 23, 2000. That policy statement notes, for example, that if a jurisdiction adopts a model building code that HUD has determined conforms with the design and construction requirements of the Act (such as the IBC 2000, as amended by the IBC's 2001 Supplement to the International Codes), then covered residential buildings that are constructed in accordance with plans and specifications approved during the building permitting process will be in compliance with the requirements of the Act unless the building code official has waived one or more of those requirements or the building code official has incorrectly interpreted or applied the building code provisions. In addition, adoption of a HUD recognized "safe harbor" does not change HUD's responsibility to conduct an investigation if it receives a complaint.

Americans with Disabilities Act Accessibility Guidelines

First produced in 1991, the Americans with Disabilities Act Guidelines (ADAAG) are guidelines for compliance with the accessibility requirements of the ADA. The ADA addresses access to the workplace (Title I), state and local government services (Title II), and places of public accommodation and commercial facilities (Title III). It also requires phone companies to provide telecommunications relay services for people who have hearing or speech impairments (Title IV) and miscellaneous instructions for federal agencies that enforce the law (Title V). While not applicable to private residential spaces, the ADA and the ADAAG are noteworthy as the action that brought our society to attention regarding access.

CANADIAN POLICIES AND PRACTICES

The National Building Code (NBC) developed by the Canadian Codes Center of the Institute for Research in Construction (a branch of the National Research Center), is the standard on which many of the provincial regulations are based. The Canadian Standards Association (CSA) developed another standard, B651, the Barrier Free Design Standards, in 1975. This standard specifies minimum technical requirements, particularly relating to products, including a section that addresses kitchen and bathroom specifications. It has been revised several times. The standard's title has been changed to Accessible Design for the Built Environment (B651-04).

Ontarians with Disabilities Act

As is true in the U.S., this standard does not have the force of law unless mandated by a particular province, but it is effective in that many products targeted for universal design or access apply for CSA approval. In fact, most professionals look for this in products they specify. It is based on "average adult" dimension and to effectively use the concepts, a designer would need to consult with the end user.

Because of provincial jurisdiction, progress has been difficult in Canada in the development and enforcement of national civil rights or legislation related to housing, such as the ADA and the FHA in the United States. In 1982, the federal government enacted the Charter of Rights and Freedoms, including Section 15 prohibiting discrimination on the basis of mental or physical handicap. However, the Charter of Rights has not been as thoroughly implemented into specific enforceable legislation as the FHA and ADA in the U.S.

ODA

In Ontario, the building code includes specific requirements for accessible buildings, and in 2001, the Ontarians with Disabilities Act (ODA), was passed. The purpose of the ODA is to improve opportunities for people with disabilities and to enable them to become involved in the identification, removal and prevention of barriers faced by persons with disabilities.

Recognizing the difficulties in mandating change, the Canadian federal government, through Canada Mortgage and Housing Corp. (CMHC), has chosen to assist the development of housing through financial instruments such as grants, loans and insurance arrangements. CMHC assistance helps low-income and older Canadians, people with disabilities and Aboriginals with housing options and expenses.

Residential Rehabilitation Assistance Program

For example, in 1986 the Residential Rehabilitation Assistance Program (RRAP-D) for Persons with Disabilities was developed to offer financial assistance to homeowners and landlords to undertake accessibility work to modify dwellings occupied or intended for occupancy by low-income persons with disabilities. Another example is the Home Adaptations for Seniors' Independence (HASI) program, which helps homeowners and landlords pay for minor home adaptations to extend the time low-income seniors can live in their own homes independently.

In addition to these, most prominent access directives, there are many local access codes and guidelines. One that is gaining momentum relates to visibility, with a number of local rulings and proposed national legislation.

INCORPORATING HUMAN-BASED KITCHEN DESIGN

There is a wealth of information on which we can draw to plan kitchen spaces based on realistic human dimensions. Anthropometric studies give us basic dimensions for people of a variety of sizes and ages. An awareness of this information as we develop a plan for a client's kitchen helps to more accurately determine sizes and spatial relationships in each case.

In this chapter, you have also been presented with a short overview of federal access laws, codes, and standards. While this overview provides a level of familiarity, each kitchen that you design may fall under specific local regulations and you need to work with your local officials for guidance and technical assistance. For more information on housing accessibility, contact the U.S. Department of Housing and Urban Development (HUD). For ADA access issues, contact the U.S. Access Board. To increase your awareness of local access laws, contact the building inspector and consult local homebuilder associations. A list of resources begins on page 547.

As one universal design leader noted, "It is questionable whether accessibility standards will ever encourage designers to practice universal design." However, considering the long-term demographic trends pointing to an increase in older age groups, access needs will not disappear and universal design is a broad and beautiful way to achieve improved access without mandates.

CHAPTER 6: Assessing Needs

In today's homes, a kitchen is usually much more than a place to cook. It is likely a gathering and social space where many household activities take place. Household management, recreation, socializing and entertainment are examples of the many activities often accommodated in the kitchen space. However, even in this day of take-out food, restaurant meals and convenience foods, the kitchen is still very much a place to store, prepare, serve and eat food.

The multi-purpose nature of most kitchens presents a special challenge to the designer. It is a workspace, a personal space, a social space. To design a kitchen, begin by learning about your client(s) and how they use their kitchen.

This chapter focuses on assessing the needs of your client in preparation for developing a design. A needs assessment is the critical first step in the design process. Without knowing what your client wants and needs, you cannot know how to design the space. Listen to your client. Challenge your own assumptions about what is needed in a kitchen and tune into what your client tells you.

Design programming is the translation of the information about the client into a plan to guide the design process. Developing the design program allows you to make sure you have gathered—and understand—all the information you need to complete the design. In addition, the design program should be reviewed with your client to ascertain that both you and your client agree on the plan for the kitchen project. A design program can even be the basis of your contract.

Design programming is discussed further in Chapter 11, as part of the design process, and a sample program is shown there. However, a brief review of the parts of a typical design program is included here to help emphasize the need for careful and complete client information gathering.

ELEMENTS OF A DESIGN PROGRAM

Goal or Purpose. A statement that describes the project and the client, and defines the scope and the parameters of the project.

Objectives and Priorities. A list of the specific features, items, materials, layout or other details to include in the design project.

Activities and Relationships. A list of the different activities to be accommodated in the kitchen, and the appliances, fixtures, fittings, materials, cabinetry, lighting, furniture, storage and other details needed to support the activities. An explanation of how the different spaces of the activities relate, in terms of access, circulation, or flow of food preparation activities. Some designers may include charts, matrices or bubble diagrams in this section to illustrate the different spaces and the relationships among them.

INTERVIEWING THE CLIENT

From your first meeting with a potential client, you are gathering information. Informal conversations can help you learn more about their household, who will use the kitchen, and their goals and dreams for a new kitchen. However, you will soon want a more structured needs-assessment interview and information-gathering session with your client.

Prepare for the Interview

You may want to interview your client in your office or showroom. Alternatively, you may set an appointment and visit your client's home, which provides the opportunity to observe it firsthand. Even if your client is building a new home, a visit to their existing home can help you better understand what your client wants. Your client may feel more comfortable talking in their home, and their existing kitchen may give them clues about things to tell you. Finally, you may also be able to collect initial measurements during the same appointment.

Allow adequate time for the interview. Let the client know ahead of time that a typical interview might take two to three hours, including taking measurements. As you gain experience, you will be able to better estimate the needed time.

Alternatively, you may want to gather the client information in more than one session, so the process is less intense. For example, you may gather information about the client in one interview, and then focus on the home and job site in the second. Again, let your experience and sense of your client be your guide.

Recording the interview on audiotape gives you an accurate record of information and avoids the need to take notes while talking to the client. However, after the interview, it can be time consuming to transcribe information from the recording.

Needs Assessment Forms

Using a prepared interview format is helpful. This assures that you gather all the information you need and gives you a way to record, and later to organize, the responses. In some cases, you can give your client a checklist to complete in preparation for the interview.

The National Kitchen & Bath Association has a Kitchen Design Survey Form available to its members, and a completed example is included in the Appendix of this book. Familiarity with this Form is necessary for CKD certification.

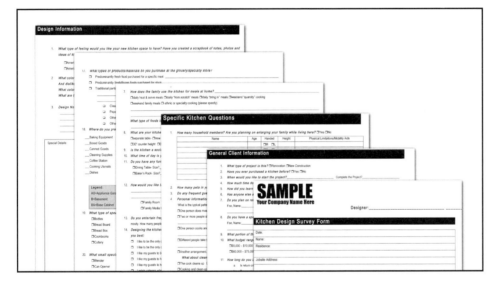

There are a number of forms created by the authors to use to gather information about your client, their home and the kitchen design project. These forms, found at the end of this chapter, provide an organized way to complete your interview and job site inspection.

Figure 6.1 Familiarity with the NKBA Kitchen Design Survey Form is necessary for certification. A completed example appears in the Appendix.

You might want to adapt the forms in this chapter to develop an interview format that works well on a computer and take a laptop with you to record information. All of these forms are found on the CD that comes with this book. The forms can be adapted as needed for your business or a particular client, and used in either an electronic or a printed format.

The following forms are included in this chapter:

Client Information Forms

Form 1: Getting to Know Your Client

Form 2: Getting to Know Your Client's Home

Checklists for Client Use

Form 3: Checklist for Kitchen Activities

Form 4: Kitchen Storage Inventory

Form 5: Cabinetry, Surfaces, and Kitchen Features Checklist

From 6: Appliance Preference Checklist

Job Site and House Information Forms

Form 7: Job Site Inspection

Form 8: Dimensions of the Kitchen – Floor Plan

Form 9: Dimensions of the Kitchen – Elevations

Form 10: Dimensions of Mechanical Devices

Form 11: Window Measurements

Form 12: Door Measurements

Form 13: Fixture and Appliance Measurements

Personal Information

In order to complete a client interview, you need to ask some questions about activities in the home, some of which may seem intrusive to your client. Adopt an open and frank approach to put your client at ease. Explain that some of the questions may seem personal, but the more information you have, the more successful your design.

During the interview, you will be asking about physical abilities. This can also be a sensitive subject. A client who is getting older may not recognize or accept the physical changes of aging. People with degenerative conditions may not be willing to yield to the impact of the disease on their bodies. Physical limitations can sometimes be hidden for short periods of time, especially with a relative stranger. Again, be open and stress the importance of fully knowing the client's physical situation, in order to develop the most supportive design. For more information on working with clients with special needs, refer to Chapter 10.

GETTING TO KNOW YOUR CLIENT (FORM 1)

The first thing you want to know is who uses the kitchen? Gather information about the users of the kitchen, their physical profiles and any specialized needs each may have. For instance, who are the primary cooks? How old are they? How tall are they?

You will want to collect anthropometrical (human measurement) information about your individual clients. This is especially important if your clients have any physical limitations or concerns about being able to function independently in the kitchen.

Review Chapter 5 to learn more about the importance of anthropometry and ergonomic design. **Form 1: Getting to Know Your Client** is a tool to collect anthropometric information about your client. Form 1 is also designed to help you collect information about any of your client's special needs with respect to activities in the kitchen. For example, do members of the household have any special physical needs? Do any of the cooks require a mobility aid, such as a wheelchair or cane?

Food-related activities are central to the design of a kitchen. Therefore, in addition to the anthropometric information and other special needs related to activities in the kitchen, you need to learn about how members of the household do, or do not, share cooking and cleanup activities. Form 1 can assist you in gathering information about cooking styles and patterns.

GETTING TO KNOW YOUR CLIENT'S HOME (FORM 2)

Start with the big picture. Where is the home located? How will the location influence the design of the kitchen? Location determines climate, telling you whether there are cold winters, hot summers or long seasons where the windows might be open to the outside air. Are there views of the ocean, a lake, mountains, trees or a city skyline, to be captured in the design? Or does the location determine that the kitchen design needs to be more inwardly focused, sheltered from things such as traffic noise or close-by buildings?

Location of the home can also give you a clue to your client's lifestyle. A kitchen in an urban apartment, a large ranch home in a rural area, or a condominium in a resort community represent different types of homes as well as lifestyles, and thus different types of kitchen design needs.

Finally, different countries, as well as different regions of the same country, can have variation in design trends. Vernacular housing describes housing styles that are typical or common to a region and that have been influenced by factors such as climate, available building materials and cultural heritage. Knowing something about the vernacular housing of the area where your client's home is located may give you some ideas about style, color or materials to use in the kitchen design.

Type of Home

Most kitchen designers work on projects in single-family homes—but not always. Especially in urban areas, a designer may work on a home that is an apartment, townhouse, or other type of multi-family structure. There may be some unique concerns in this type of home. For example, in many multi-family housing communities, plans for remodeling must be approved by a group such as the homeowners' association. You may be limited in making changes affecting the home's exterior. Likewise, plumbing changes may be limited. Carefully consider any possible factors that could occur in a multi-family project.

Often, even single-family housing may be in a community with a homeowners' association with rules that affect home renovations. In addition, sometimes there may be covenants in a property's deed that could influence a kitchen remodeling project, such as the size of an addition or the style and placement of windows.

While you consider these special and legal situations that can affect your design, also bear in mind the impact of the building permit process. Building codes and regulations may vary by location so make sure you reference the correct codes. *Residential Construction* and *Kitchen & Bath Systems* discuss building codes and permits in more detail.

If you are working on a remodeling project, ask to take a tour of the existing home. Take along a copy of **Form 2: Getting to Know Your Client's Home**. This form can be used to gather information about the "big picture" of your client's home and kitchen.

Observe the size, the number of bedrooms and bathrooms. Look at entrances and traffic flow, especially in and around the kitchen space.

A tour of your client's home will also be useful to get a sense of style and color. Ask your client to describe what they do and do not like about other rooms in the home. Use this information for clues about design preferences.

During the home tour, note what rooms are on the other side of the kitchen walls. This information might be useful as you think about potentially "borrowing" space from another room or relocating and reconfiguring plumbing. Look for details that might prevent surprises during the construction phase, such as the presence of heating or cooling ducts. You might want to make a sketch of the existing kitchen space, or do this as part of the job site inspection (See Form 7, page 189).

A camera can be a useful tool during a home tour. Use the camera (it helps to ask first) to make visual notes of features that will be useful to remember during the design process. A digital camera is particularly helpful for this type of documentation as pictures are easily transferred to a computer file. Also, take pictures of family members, favorite accessory items or views from windows. Later, you may be able to incorporate these items into presentation drawings for a personal touch.

The Home of the Future

Finish your understanding of the big picture by talking to your client about future plans for the home. Is this a home in which they plan to retire? Will they be likely to remodel or expand this home in the future?

While you are learning about future plans for their home, you can ask about the future of their family or household. "Expanding" households are typically, though not always, younger and are at the life stage where they can expect to add new household members, such as by marriage or birth. Sometimes a new household member is an older relative. "Launching" households are more likely to be older, with children who will soon be leaving. Future changes in household size or composition influence who uses the kitchen, as well as the activities that take place in that space.

ACTIVITIES IN THE KITCHEN (FORM 3)

Once you know something about who is using the kitchen, gather information about what they actually do there. As the research discussed in Chapter 2 indicates, most activities in the kitchen can generally be grouped as follows:

- Food preparation, cooking and serving
- Cleanup
- Other food-related activities
- Household management
- Relaxing and recreation
- Socializing

Since the potential kitchen activities are numerous, give your client an activity checklist to complete (Form 3). This can save time and may result in more complete information. Review the checklist with them, and then ask them to complete it at home. Alternatively, mail (or e-mail) the checklist to them in advance of the interview and then review it during the interview. Use the checklist included in this chapter, **Form 3: Checklist for Kitchen Activities**. The form also asks about location and frequency of activities—information that is extremely useful during the design process.

In addition to the information provided on the checklist, you may need clarification on certain activities. For instance, ask about activities that your client prefers to do while seated or standing. If your client has completed the checklist in advance, these issues can be discussed at the interview. Form 3 offers space to make notes after the client has completed the checklist.

STORAGE IN THE KITCHEN (FORM 4)

Talking about activities in the kitchen easily leads into a discussion of your client's storage needs. The number of items to be stored in the kitchen and the volume of space needed for storage can be a major issue in a kitchen design. What does your client want to store in the kitchen? Where will they use the different items? How frequently do they use each item? All that information is useful for planning kitchen storage.

A storage inventory checklist helps to determine your client's storage needs. **Form 4: Kitchen Storage Inventory** is a storage inventory your client can complete at home. It contains lists of 551 items in 16 different categories:

- Small electric appliances

- Food storage

- Preparation items

- Small utensils

- Pots and pans

- Baking ware

- Glasses and drinking items

- Dishes

- Serving pieces

- Flatware

- Linens

- Storage containers

- Cleaning supplies and tools

- Bulk storage

- Management/home office

- Miscellaneous

The items in this storage inventory are taken from the Virginia Tech Kitchen Storage Research Project (See Chapter 2), and represent those found in at least 25% of the 87 kitchens studied in this project. For each item on the storage inventory, there is space to indicate the number stored, the frequency of use and the type of storage location preferred. Additional space is provided in each category to list other items.

The Form 4 inventory is detailed, but is designed for ease of use. The fact that so many common kitchen items are already listed on the inventory saves your client time. This checklist will be helpful in the design process, so encourage your client to be thorough in completing it. As with the activity checklist, it is helpful if the client has completed this inventory in advance of the interview.

Compare **Form 3: Checklist for Kitchen Activities** with **Form 4: Kitchen Storage Inventory**. Are supplies needed for an activity that is not included on the storage inventory? Or do some of the storage items suggest activities that are not included on the checklist? If necessary, go back to the client for clarification.

YOUR CLIENT'S KITCHEN (FORMS 5 AND 6)

Once you have the big picture about your client's home, gather specific information about their kitchen project. At this point, ask your client about what they do and do not like in a kitchen—and what is feasible for their space and budget.

Begin with their current kitchen. Ask what they do not like about the space. Be very specific. Let your client volunteer information first, such as:

- There is not enough counter space.

- The space feels crowded.

- People bump into each other when sharing cooking activities.

Then ask about features that they do like, such as:

- The room is open to the family room

- The location of the refrigerator is convenient

Ideas suggested by your client, positive or negative, can indicate areas of strong feeling. Remember these ideas as you develop your design.

Next, ask your client to talk about what they want in their new kitchen. Let them suggest ideas, but be sure to cover the major features. **Form 5: Cabinetry, Surface and Kitchen Features Checklist** can help you and your client collect and organize information about their preferences. Form 5 can be completed during the interview or in advance of your meeting and then reviewed. Be aware—although Form 5 is designed as a client checklist, the number and detail of the choices and decisions on it can overwhelm an unprepared client. You may want to go over the form with your client first.

Appliances

Appliances are such an important part of a kitchen that the need or desire to replace them may be the motivation to remodel a kitchen. There are many choices on the market today. Use **Form 6: Appliance Preference Checklist** to help determine your clients' preference for appliances. As with some of the other forms, you may want to give this checklist to your client to complete in advance of the interview. Note that Form 6 is for new appliances. Form 13 is used to measure any existing appliances slated to remain in the kitchen.

Client Preferences and Specifications

Many clients think and dream about a kitchen project before it becomes a reality. They read shelter magazines, visit showrooms, or surf the Internet. Many collect ideas about design, products, fixtures, materials and other features. By asking questions about preferences—or definite specifications—you move from general ideas to the specific decisions to be made about the kitchen design.

In some cases, your client may have an item to include in the new kitchen from the current kitchen. Or they may have salvage pieces, such as cabinet or door hardware, to include in the new design. Ask if there are any pieces like this. Get detailed information, such as size, and any mechanical requirements such as plumbing connections.

Some clients may prefer to shop for and to select certain pieces, such as an appliance or a faucet, on their own. If the client is going to provide items for the new kitchen, this information will need to be specified in your contract. You and your client will need to agree on the specifications of the items they will provide. Timing will be important as well, so that the installation of the new kitchen is not delayed while waiting for a client-provided item.

Budget

At some point, you will need to discuss the project budget. Unless your client has carefully researched the issue before meeting with you, there is a good chance their budget is not in the same price range as their ideas. The farther their ideas are from their pocketbook, the more you will need to focus on priorities. Help your client think about what they really need, want and would like to have in their kitchen. The clearer these ideas, the easier it is to make budget decisions.

The Job Site

Before you can begin the actual design, make a thorough assessment of the job site. Structurally and mechanically, you need to know if your design ideas work.

You may want to review other volumes in the NKBA Professional Resource Library, including *Residential Construction* and *Kitchen & Bath Systems*. Also, review Chapter 3 – Infrastructure Considerations and Chapter 7 – Mechanical Considerations, in this book. Unless you are experienced in "reading" a house, and understanding its structural and mechanical systems, you may want to enlist the help of a contractor or other knowledgeable person to assist you.

New Construction

If your kitchen project is new construction or an addition, it is best to get involved in the planning before construction begins. Get a copy of all drawings that affect the kitchen design. Make sure that you have all dimensions and mechanical information that relate to the kitchen.

Study the plans for the new space. Find out what is fixed and what is flexible. For example, can an entry door be moved or a window relocated before construction begins? Or can an interior wall be increased in width to make it work as a plumbing or "wet" wall?

JOB SITE INSPECTION
(FORM 7)

If you are working on a remodeling project, you need to know all the structural and mechanical information as well, but it may be harder to find. A thorough and detailed inspection of the remodeled area and surrounding rooms will be necessary. If your client has plans or drawings of the space, this will be useful and can save time. However, you will need to verify that the rooms were actually built as drawn. You may want to make copies of client drawings, so that you can mark them up as needed.

Prepare for your site inspection by making an appointment with your client. Give them an idea of what you need to do, and make sure that you have access to all the areas of the home. You may do the site inspection at the same time you do the client interview, especially if you have to travel a distance to your client's home. Wear comfortable clothes that allow you to bend and stretch. Bring a sturdy measuring tape, graph paper, pencils and flashlight. A camera might also be useful to take pictures for future reference.

Your job site inspection needs to cover several areas: overall knowledge about the kitchen and its relationship to other spaces in the home—structure, mechanical systems, access, construction/ installation planning, and dimensions (discussed below). As with the client interview, if you use a prepared form or outline, you will be more likely to get all the information you need. Follow **Form 7: Job Site Inspection** to gain a thorough analysis of the information.

DIMENSIONS
(FORMS 8 THROUGH 13)

To collect dimensions of the job site, use:

- Form 8: Dimensions of the Kitchen – Floor Plan

- Form 9: Dimensions of the Kitchen – Elevations

- Form 10: Dimensions of Mechanical Devices

- Form 11: Window Measurements

- Form 12: Door Measurements

- Form 13: Fixture and Appliance Measurements

To collect accurate and complete measurements, follow these suggestions:

- Measure each wall. Take at least two measurements, one low, and one high on the wall, to help determine variations in corners. Use these measurements to make a to-scale ($1/2$" = $1'0$") drawing of the kitchen space. (See Form 8, page 196)

- Measure the ceiling height in several places. Layout a basic elevation of each wall. (See Form 9, page 197)

- If needed, prepare a reflected ceiling plan to note features on the ceiling, such as heat registers, beams or lighting.

- Measure any architectural features in the space, such as columns, arches, or beams. Locate these features on the floor plan (Form 8) or the elevations (Form 9), as appropriate.

- Measure the location and size of each heat register, radiator or other mechanical device. Include items on the walls, floor, and ceiling. Record these measurements on Form 10, page 198, and locate these features on the floor plan and/or elevations.

- Measure each window. Measure the size of the window, frame and overall size of the window with frame. Measure the location of the window from the floor, ceiling and corners of the room. Include the height of the stool (the sill and trim beneath it) (see Form 11, page 199). Note the location of each window on the floor plan and elevations.

- Measure each door, similar to a window. Locate the height of the door handle. Note the location of doors on the floor plan and elevations. Indicate the door swings (See Form 12, page 200).

- Measure the size of any appliances or fixtures to be removed. Include height, width and depth. Note any potential problems with removal (see Form 13, page 201).

- Measure the size and location of any appliances, fixtures, or furniture to remain. Include centerline dimensions to determine clearances (see Form 13, page 201). Note any details needed for re-installation.

If the new kitchen design will incorporate any additional existing space that is not now part of the kitchen, that space must be measured and inspected. For example, a porch, closet or breakfast area may be available to be incorporated into the new design. Follow the above guidelines for measuring and inspecting any space that will be part of the new kitchen design.

PREPARING THE CLIENT

The process for assessing the needs of your client and gathering information necessary to design their kitchen is extensive, but time spent on preparation will increase your success.

Now that you are prepared, spend a few minutes preparing your client. At the end of the interview and/or job site inspection, or when you present your design proposal, bid, or contract, discuss both the design process as well as the construction phase with your client.

Establish A Plan

First, discuss the time frame of the project. Present a realistic plan for each phase of the project. Indicate to your client what factors may delay the project and why. Discuss what you will do to keep the project on target. Suggest what your client can do to keep the project on time, such as minimizing change orders.

Talk to your client about what you will need from them. If they are going to do any of the work, such as tearing out or painting, be clear as to the time frame. At what point will they be needed to review plans and make color or design choices? When will they need to make decisions about appliances, fixtures and accessories? When will they need personal items removed from the workspace?

For detailed information on how to manage the construction phase of the project with your client, refer to *Kitchen & Bath Project Management.*

READY FOR THE DESIGN PROGRAM?

By now you have a detailed picture of your client and their ideas about the new kitchen. In addition, you know about the users of the kitchen, activities in the kitchen, and storage needs. It might be tempting to rush in and begin laying out your ideas. But first, think about the next step in the design process. You need to develop a design program.

Consider the design program a working document. After you review the program with your client, you may need to make changes as you fine-tune the project plan. Once you and your client agree on the design program, you may ask the client to sign off on the program. This will give you a firm basis for negotiating any change orders as the kitchen project progresses.

As you develop the design program, clarify your client's priorities. What do they need or require in the kitchen project? What do they want to have, and what would be desirable? Your goal is to provide all the "needs and requirements", most of the "wants," and some of the "desirables." You will find the time spent on a needs assessment, and gathering information about your client will benefit you in the completing the design program. If you and your client are clear on priorities, then it is easier to make compromises or trade-offs due to factors such as budget limitations, product availability or structural problems.

You and your client are now prepared for a successful kitchen project.

Forms 1 – 13 follow.

FORM 1: GETTING TO KNOW YOUR CLIENT

This form is an information fact sheet about your client. Use the parts that are appropriate to your design project. A custom design project, or a client with special needs, may require more detailed information.

1. Users of the kitchen:

   Name: _____ Age: _____

   Height: _____ Weight: _____ Handedness: ❏ Right ❏ Left

   Special needs or concerns: _____

   _____

   Name: _____ Age: _____

   Height: _____ Weight: _____ Handedness: ❏ Right ❏ Left

   Special needs or concerns: _____

   _____

   Name: _____ Age: _____

   Height: _____ Weight: _____ Handedness: ❏ Right ❏ Left

   Special needs or concerns: _____

   _____

   Name: _____ Age: _____

   Height: _____ Weight: _____ Handedness: ❏ Right ❏ Left

   Special needs or concerns: _____

   _____

   Name: _____ Age: _____

   Height: _____ Weight: _____ Handedness: ❏ Right ❏ Left

   Special needs or concerns: _____

   _____

2. Anthropometric Information

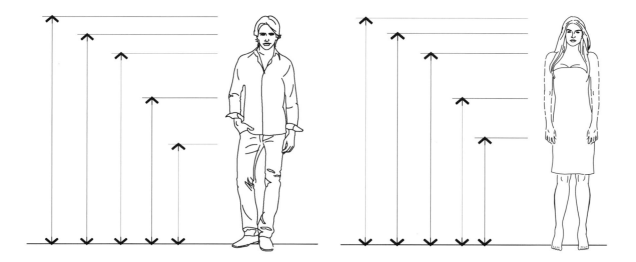

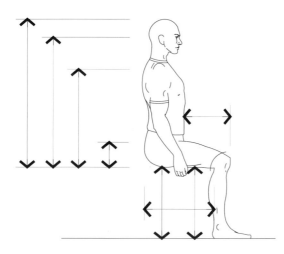

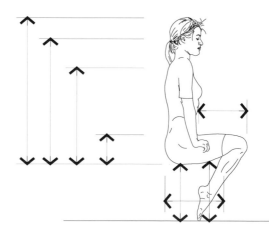

3. Reach and Grasp Profile

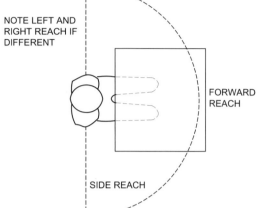

NOTE LEFT AND
RIGHT REACH IF
DIFFERENT

FORWARD
REACH

SIDE REACH

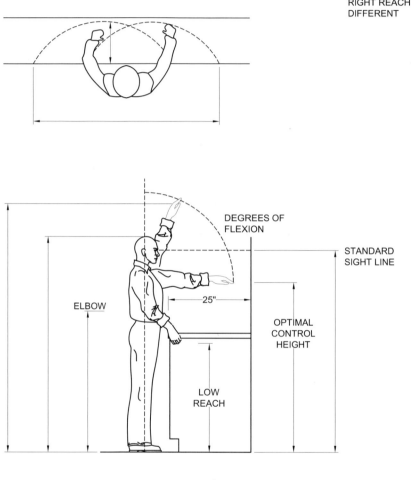

DEGREES OF
FLEXION

STANDARD
SIGHT LINE

ELBOW

25"

OPTIMAL
CONTROL
HEIGHT

LOW
REACH

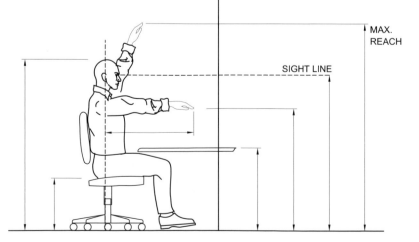

MAX.
REACH

SIGHT LINE

4. Physical Profile

Physical characteristic(s) affecting activities in the kitchen:

A. Sight: _____

Do you wear glasses for: ❑ Reading ❑ Distance

Are you taking medications that affect your sight? _____

Are you sensitive to light? _____

B. Hearing: _____

What issues regarding your hearing will affect your activities in the kitchen? _____

_____

C. Tactile/Touch: _____

Can you feel hot and cold? _____

D. Taste/Smell: _____

What issues regarding your sense of taste or smell will affect your activities in the kitchen?

_____

E. Strength and Function: _____

What can you lift? _____ Carry? _____

Do you have more strength on one side than the other? _____

Do you use both hands fully? _____ Palms only? _____

How is your grip? _____

Left side? _____ Right side? _____

F. Balance, Mobility and Assistance: _____

How is your balance: Standing? _____ Bending? _____

Does your mobility or balance vary by time of day?_____

Does an assistant help you: Sometimes? _____ All the time?_____

What adaptive equipment do you use? _____

_____

G. Prognosis: Is your condition stable? Is further deterioration anticipated? Is improvement anticipated?

_____

H. Other Physical Concerns: _____

_____

I. Special Safety Concerns: _____

_____

5. Mobility Aids

If a mobility aid, such as wheel chair, walker, or cane is used, it is important to collect information on the size of the mobility aid, as well anthropometric information about the client when using the mobility aid.

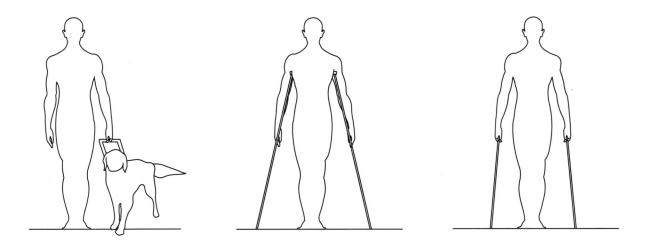

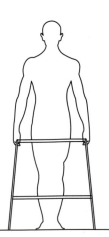

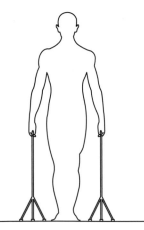

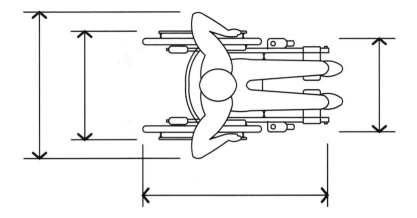

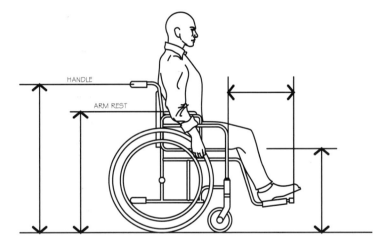

6. Personal Information about the Kitchen

    What is the typical pattern of cooking in your household?

    ❑ One person does most of the cooking. Who?_____

    ❑ Two or more people share most of the cooking. Describe. _____

    _____

    _____

    ❑ One person cooks and another person helps. Describe. _____

    _____

    _____

❏ Different people take turns doing the cooking. Describe. _____

_____

_____

❏ Another arrangement. Describe. _____

_____

_____

What about clean up?

❏ The cook cleans up.

❏ Cooking and clean up are shared.

❏ Clean up is done by someone who does not cook. Describe. _____

_____

❏ Another arrangement. Describe. _____

_____

_____

How often do you or someone in your household:

Do a major grocery shopping? _____

Do a convenience grocery shopping? _____

7. Future Plans

How long do you plan to live in this home? _____

_____

Do you anticipate changes in your household size or make-up? _____

_____

Will this affect activities in the kitchen? _____

_____

Is resale value of the home important? _____

_____

FORM 2: GETTING TO KNOW YOUR CLIENT'S HOME

This form can be used to collect general information about your client's home to help in developing your design. Specific structural and mechanical information is collected in other forms.

Location of home: _____

Type of neighborhood: _____

Type of home: ❏ single-family home ❏ duplex ❏ townhouse ❏ apartment/flat

❏ other _____

Structure of home: ❏ one-story ❏ two-story ❏ three-story ❏ ranch ❏ split-level

❏ split foyer/raised ranch ❏ other _____

Approximate size of home: _____

Number of bedrooms: _____ Number of bathrooms: _____

Style of home (exterior) _____

Is the home historic? What time period? _____

Are there historic covenants or restrictions affecting the home? _____

_____

_____

Is the home part of a homeowner's association? _____

Is there homeowner's association covenants or restrictions affecting the home? _____

_____

_____

Are there any other covenants or deed restrictions? _____

_____

_____

Style of home (interior): _____

_____

_____

Colors? _____

_____

Materials?_____

_____

Furniture?_____

_____

Accessories? _____

_____

Future plans for resale or remodeling? _____

_____

FORM 3: CHECKLIST FOR KITCHEN ACTIVITIES [CLIENT CHECKLIST]

Instructions: Review the list of activities in each section. If it is an activity that you do, or want to do in the kitchen, place a check in the first column. Then check the appropriate location and frequency columns. Extra lines are left in each section for you to add activities as needed.

✓	Activity	Location							Frequency	
		Sink	Cooktop	Oven	Microwave	Refrigerator	Prep Area	Other (Specify)	Often	Sometimes
	Bake: bread									
	Bake: foods made from mixes									
	Bake: foods made from scratch									
	Bake: frozen prepared foods									
	Broil foods									
	Can food: for preservation									
	Chop, carve, and slice foods									
	Cook: breakfast									
	Cook: dinner									
	Cook: lunch									
	Deep fry foods									
	Dehydrate foods: for preservation									
	Entertain: cook and serve meals for guests									
	Entertain: guests help cook									
	Entertain: pot luck/shared meals									
	Freeze food: for preservation									
	Freeze food: large quantity meals for later use									
	Freeze food: leftovers									
	Fry foods									
	Grill foods: indoors									
	Grill foods: outdoors									
	Hire a caterer: serve foods prepared elsewhere									
	Hire a caterer: prepare foods in your kitchen									

Food Preparation, Cooking, and Serving Activities

Food Preparation, Cooking, and Serving Activities, continued

✓	Activity	Location							Frequency	
		Sink	Cooktop	Oven	Microwave	Refrigerator	Prep Area	Other (Specify)	Often	Sometimes
	Make candy									
	Pack lunches or food to be eaten away from home									
	Prepare: drinks									
	Prepare: foods from complex recipes									
	Prepare: foods on a griddle									
	Prepare: foods with specialty ingredients									
	Prepare: fresh produce									
	Prepare: frozen convenience foods									
	Prepare: full meals									
	Prepare: items using a rolling pin									
	Prepare: kosher, halal or similar foods									
	Prepare: pre-packaged convenience foods									
	Prepare: snacks									
	Prepare: vegetarian meals									
	Reheat foods in microwave									
	Reheat foods in oven									
	Roast meats									
	Serve drinks									
	Serve food: buffet style									
	Serve food: family style									
	Serve food: individual plates									
	Serve food: carryout orders									
	Slow cook or simmer foods									
	Stir fry foods									
	Other activities:									

Cleanup and Waste Management Activities

✓	Activity	Location							Frequency	
		Sink	Cooktop	Oven	Microwave	Refrigerator	Prep Area	Other (Specify)	Often	Sometimes
	Air dry dishes or utensils									
	Compost food waste									
	Recycle: collect in kitchen									
	Recycle: not in kitchen									
	Recycle: sort in kitchen									
	Rinse dishes or utensils									
	Soak dishes, pans									
	Stack dishes or items for later washing									
	Trash: collect in kitchen									
	Wash dishes: dishwasher									
	Wash dishes: by hand									
	Wash pots and pans: dishwasher									
	Wash pots and pans: by hand									
	Other activities:									

Other Activities That Occur in The Kitchen

✓	Activity	Location							Frequency	
		Sink	Cooktop	Oven	Microwave	Refrigerator	Prep Area	Other (Specify)	Often	Sometimes
	Food Related Activities:									
	Eat meals									
	Eat snacks									
	Drink beverages									
	Plan meals									
	Take vitamins, medicines									
	Other:									
	Household Management Activities:									
	Homework/schoolwork									
	Laundry: air dry									
	Laundry: hand wash									
	Laundry: machine wash									
	Laundry: sort, fold									
	Paperwork, pay bills									
	Pet feeding, care									
	Polish shoes									
	Sort mail									
	Use a computer									
	Other:									

Other Activities That Occur in The Kitchen

✓	Activity	Location							Frequency	
		Sink	Cooktop	Oven	Microwave	Refrigerator	Prep Area	Other (Specify)	Often	Sometimes
	Relaxing and Recreation:									
	Computer games									
	Crafts									
	Display collections									
	Grow plants									
	Listen to music									
	Nails: clip, file, polish									
	Reading: newspaper, magazines									
	Reading: books									
	Sewing									
	Watch television									
	Other:									
	Social Activities:									
	Conversations with family, friends									
	Entertain									
	Play with children									
	Talk on telephone									
	Other:									
	Other Activities:									

FORM 4: KITCHEN STORAGE INVENTORY [CLIENT CHECKLIST]

Instructions: This inventory is divided into sections representing categories of items typically stored in kitchen cabinets and pantries. Many of the typical items found in kitchens are already listed. Check those items you want to store in the kitchen. Add any additional items needed. Complete the form, indicating how many of each item you have, how frequently you use it, and the type of storage you would like in your new kitchen. Blank lines are included for items you have that are not listed. A space for notes is at the end of each section. Include information about special size or space requirements, items that need to be stored away from children, or other important details.

Small Electric Appliances											
✓	Item to Store	How Many?	Frequency of Use		Type of Storage						
			Often	Sometimes	Wall Cabinet	Base Cabinet	Drawer	Pantry/Tall Cabinet	Counter Top	Other (describe)	
	Blender										
	Can opener										
	Chopper/blender (handheld)										
	Coffee grinder										
	Coffee maker, drip										
	Slow cooker										
	Food processor										
	Food processor blades										
	Fry pan or skillet										
	Juicer										
	Knife										
	Mixer, free standing										
	Mixer, hand										
	Pancake/griddle										
	Television										
	Toaster										
	Waffle iron										
	Additional items:										

Food Storage

✓	Item to Store	How Many?	Frequency of Use		Type of Storage					
			Often	Sometimes	Wall Cabinet	Base Cabinet	Drawer	Pantry/Tall Cabinet	Counter Top	Other (describe)
	Alcohol/liquors									
	Baking supplies, bottles									
	Baking supplies, boxes									
	Baking supplies, cans									
	Beers/soft drinks/water, bottles									
	Beers/soft drinks/water, cans									
	Beers/soft drinks/water, large bottles/cans									
	Beers/soft drinks/water, small bottles/pouches/boxes									
	Bread/bagels/rolls/muffins									
	Bread, packages									
	Bread, loaf									
	Canned foods, small									
	Canned foods, medium									
	Canned foods, large									
	Cereal boxes, small									
	Cereal boxes, medium									
	Cereal boxes, large									
	Flours/meals, bag									
	Flour/meals, box									
	Food in bags, small									
	Food in bags, medium									
	Food in bags, large									
	Food in canisters, small									
	Food in canisters, medium									
	Food in canisters, large									
	Food in jars, small									
	Food in jars, medium									
	Food in jars, large									
	Food in bottles, small									

Food Storage, continued

✓	Item to Store	How Many?	Frequency of Use		Type of Storage					
			Often	Sometimes	Wall Cabinet	Base Cabinet	Drawer	Pantry/Tall Cabinet	Counter Top	Other (describe)
	Food in bottles, large									
	Packaged drink mixes									
	Prepared/boxed mixes, small									
	Prepared/boxed mixes, large									
	Produce, fruit									
	Produce, vegetables									
	Ready-to-eat boxed foods, small									
	Ready-to-eat boxed foods, medium									
	Ready-to-eat boxed foods, large									
	Rice/grains, bag, small									
	Rice/grains, bag, large									
	Rice/grains, box									
	Spices/seasonings/herbs, bottles									
	Spices/seasonings/herbs, cans									
	Spices/seasonings/herbs, packages/boxes									
	Sugars, bag									
	Sugars, box									
	Wine									
	Additional items:									

Preparation Items

✓	Item to Store	How Many?	Frequency of Use		Type of Storage					
			Often	Sometimes	Wall Cabinet	Base Cabinet	Drawer	Pantry/Tall Cabinet	Counter Top	Other (describe)
	Baking/roasting bags									
	Bread board									
	Colander, small									
	Colander, medium									
	Colander, large									
	Cutting board, small									
	Cutting board, large									
	Measuring cup, 1 cup (wet)									
	Measuring cup, 2 cup (wet)									
	Measuring cup, 4 cup (wet)									
	Measuring cups, set (dry)									
	Measuring spoon set									
	Mixing bowl, small									
	Mixing bowl, medium									
	Mixing bowl, large									
	Mixing bowl, extra large									
	Molds									
	Muffin pan liners (pkgs.)									
	Salad spinner									
	Scale									
	Sifter									
	Storage canister, small									
	Storage canister, medium									
	Storage canister, large									
	Additional items:									

Small Utensils

✓	Item to Store	How Many?	Frequency of Use		Type of Storage					
			Often	Sometimes	Wall Cabinet	Base Cabinet	Drawer	Pantry/Tall Cabinet	Counter Top	Other (describe)
	Apple corer									
	Baster									
	Basting brush									
	Beater (flat rotary)									
	Bottle opener									
	Brush, soft (bottle)									
	Brush, stiff (vegetable)									
	Brushes									
	Can opener (handheld)									
	Cookie cutter									
	Fork (cooking)									
	Funnel									
	Garlic press									
	Grater/shredder									
	Ice cream scoop									
	Juicer (hand)									
	Knife block									
	Knife sharpener									
	Knife, bread									
	Knife, butcher									
	Knife, cake									
	Knife, carving									
	Knife, grapefruit									
	Knife, large									
	Knife, paring									
	Lemon zester									
	Mallet									
	Melon ball cutter									
	Mixing spoon (large)									

✓	Item to Store	How Many?	Frequency of Use		Type of Storage					
			Often	Sometimes	Wall Cabinet	Base Cabinet	Drawer	Pantry/Tall Cabinet	Counter Top	Other (describe)
	Pancake turner									
	Pasta server									
	Pizza wheel (cutter)									
	Potato masher									
	Rolling pin									
	Scissors (poultry)									
	Skewers									
	Slicer									
	Spatula/scraper									
	Spoon (wooden)									
	Strainer/sieve, small									
	Strainer/sieve, medium									
	Strainer/sieve, large									
	Thermometer, meat									
	Timer									
	Tongs									
	Wine bottle opener									
	Wire whip/whisk									
	Additional items:									

Small Utensils, continued

Pots and Pans

✓	Item to Store	How Many?	Frequency of Use		Type of Storage					
			Often	Sometimes	Wall Cabinet	Base Cabinet	Drawer	Pantry/Tall Cabinet	Counter Top	Other (describe)
	Double boiler insert									
	Dutch oven lid									
	Dutch oven/stew kettle									
	Griddle									
	Sauce pan, extra small									
	Sauce pan, small									
	Sauce pan, medium									
	Sauce pan, large									
	Sauce pan, extra large									
	Sauce pan lid, extra small									
	Sauce pan lid, small									
	Sauce pan lid, medium									
	Sauce pan lid, large									
	Sauce pan lid, extra large									
	Skillet/frying pan, small									
	Skillet/frying pan, medium									
	Skillet/frying pan, large									
	Spoon rest									
	Steamer, insert									
	Stock pot/pasta pot									
	Stock pot/pasta pot, lid									
	Tea ball									
	Tea kettle									
	Tea strainer									
	Additional items:									

✓	Item to Store	How Many?	Frequency of Use		Type of Storage					
			Often	Sometimes	Wall Cabinet	Base Cabinet	Drawer	Pantry/Tall Cabinet	Counter Top	Other (describe)
	Baking stone									
	Broiler pan									
	Cake pan, angel food									
	Cake pan, bundt									
	Cake pan, rectangle									
	Cake pan, round									
	Cake pan, square									
	Cake rack									
	Casserole dish w/ lid, small									
	Casserole dish w/ lid, medium									
	Casserole dish w/ lid, large									
	Casserole dish w/o lid, small									
	Casserole dish w/o lid, medium									
	Casserole dish w/o lid, large									
	Cookie sheet									
	Custard cups/ramekins									
	Loaf pan, small									
	Loaf pan, large									
	Muffin pan, mini									
	Muffin pan, six									
	Muffin pan, twelve									
	Pie plate									
	Pizza pan									
	Potholder, flat									
	Potholder, mitt									
	Quiche pan									
	Roasting pan w/ lid, medium									
	Roasting pan w/ lid, large									
	Roasting pan w/o lid, medium									
	Roasting pan w/o lid, large									
	Roasting rack									

Baking Ware

Baking Ware, continued

✓	Item to Store	How Many?	Frequency of Use		Type of Storage					
			Often	Sometimes	Wall Cabinet	Base Cabinet	Drawer	Pantry/Tall Cabinet	Counter Top	Other (describe)
	Spring form pan									
	Additional items:									

Glasses

✓	Item to Store	How Many?	Frequency of Use		Type of Storage					
			Often	Sometimes	Wall Cabinet	Base Cabinet	Drawer	Pantry/Tall Cabinet	Counter Top	Other (describe)
	Canned beverage insulator									
	Cups, stadium (plastic)									
	Glasses, juice									
	Glasses, highball									
	Glasses, iced beverage									
	Glasses, shot									
	Glasses, stemmed, Champagne									
	Glasses, stemmed, wine (small)									
	Glasses, stemmed, wine (large)									
	Glasses, water tumbler (plastic/glass)									
	Mugs, beer									
	Mugs, coffee/tea									
	Additional items:									

Dishes (may need to repeat if more than one set is stored separately in the kitchen)

✓	Item to Store	How Many?	Frequency of Use		Type of Storage					
			Often	Sometimes	Wall Cabinet	Base Cabinet	Drawer	Pantry/Tall Cabinet	Counter Top	Other (describe)
	Bowls, individual salad									
	Bowls, large cereal									
	Bowls, small cereal									
	Bowls, soup (w/o lid)									
	Plates, bread and butter									
	Plates, dessert/salad									
	Plates, dinner									
	Plates, luncheon									
	Plates, saucers									
	Coffee/tea cups									
	Additional items:									

Serving Pieces

✓	Item to Store	How Many?	Frequency of Use		Type of Storage					
			Often	Sometimes	Wall Cabinet	Base Cabinet	Drawer	Pantry/Tall Cabinet	Counter Top	Other (describe)
	Basket (wicker), small									
	Basket (wicker), medium									
	Basket (wicker), large									
	Bowl (serving), small									
	Bowl (serving), medium									
	Bowl (serving), large									
	Butter dish, w/ lid									
	Cake plate									
	Cheese board									
	Chip and dip plate									
	Coffee carafe/pot									
	Condiment dish									
	Creamer									
	Hot plate/trivet									
	Ice bucket									
	Pasta bowl									
	Pitcher, small									
	Pitcher, large									
	Platter, small									
	Platter, large									
	Salt and pepper shakers									
	Serving tray									
	Sugar bowl									
	Additional items:									

✓	Flatware									
	Item to Store	**How Many?**	**Frequency of Use**		**Type of Storage**					
			Often	Sometimes	Wall Cabinet	Base Cabinet	Drawer	Pantry/Tall Cabinet	Counter Top	Other (describe)
	Forks, dinner									
	Forks, salad									
	Forks, serving									
	Knives, butter									
	Knives, cheese									
	Knives, dinner									
	Knives, steak									
	Spoons, condiment									
	Spoons, iced tea									
	Spoons, serving/table									
	Spoons, soup									
	Spoons, sugar									
	Spoons, tablespoon									
	Spoons, teaspoon									
	Butter knife/spreader									
	Cake/pie server									
	Cheese spreader									
	Chop sticks									
	Corn holders									
	Gravy ladle									
	Ice tongs									
	Salad serving set									
	Additional items:									

Linens

✓	Item to Store	How Many?	Frequency of Use		Type of Storage					
			Often	Sometimes	Wall Cabinet	Base Cabinet	Drawer	Pantry/Tall Cabinet	Counter Top	Other (describe)
	Apron									
	Cloth napkins									
	Dish cloths									
	Dish towels									
	Hand towels									
	Placemats									
	Additional items:									

Storage Containers

✓	Item to Store	How Many?	Frequency of Use		Type of Storage					
			Often	Sometimes	Wall Cabinet	Base Cabinet	Drawer	Pantry/Tall Cabinet	Counter Top	Other (describe)
	Aluminum foil									
	Freezer paper									
	Plastic container lids, small									
	Plastic container lids, medium									
	Plastic container lids, large									
	Plastic containers, small									
	Plastic containers, medium									
	Plastic containers, large									
	Plastic storage bags (pkgs.), small									
	Plastic storage bags (pkgs.), large									
	Plastic wrap									
	Spice rack									
	Wax paper									
	Additional items:									

Cleaning Supplies and Tools

✓	Item to Store	How Many?	Frequency of Use		Type of Storage					
			Often	Sometimes	Wall Cabinet	Base Cabinet	Drawer	Pantry/Tall Cabinet	Counter Top	Other (describe)
	Brushes, small									
	Cleaning supplies, bottles									
	Cleaning supplies, boxes									
	Cleaning supplies, cans									
	Dish cloth, in use									
	Dish drainer									
	Dish towel, in use									
	Dust pan									
	Paper towel holder									
	Paper towel, in use									
	Pot scrubber holder									
	Pot scrubber									
	Rubber gloves									
	Sink strainer									
	Sponge									
	Trash can									
	Additional items:									

Bulk Storage

✓	Item to Store	How Many?	Frequency of Use		Type of Storage					
			Often	Sometimes	Wall Cabinet	Base Cabinet	Drawer	Pantry/Tall Cabinet	Counter Top	Other (describe)
	Coffee filters (pkg.)									
	Napkins, paper (pkgs.)									
	Paper lunch bags (pkgs.)									
	Paper towels, rolls not in use									
	Plastic/paper cups (pkgs.)									
	Plastic/paper, plates (pkgs.)									
	Plastic/paper, utensils (pkgs.)									
	Trash bags, plastic (pkgs.)									
	Additional items:									

Management/Home Office

✓	Item to Store	How Many?	Frequency of Use		Type of Storage					
			Often	Sometimes	Wall Cabinet	Base Cabinet	Drawer	Pantry/Tall Cabinet	Counter Top	Other (describe)
	Calculator									
	Cook book									
	Mail/bills									
	Miscellaneous "junk" drawer									
	Note pad									
	Pencil/pen									
	Recipe file box									
	Scissors									
	Stapler									
	Tape/tape dispenser									
	Telephone									
	Telephone directory									
	Additional items:									

✓	Item to Store	How Many?	Frequency of Use		Type of Storage					
			Often	Sometimes	Wall Cabinet	Base Cabinet	Drawer	Pantry/Tall Cabinet	Counter Top	Other (describe)
	Batteries									
	Candle holder									
	Candles, birthday									
	Decorative item									
	Fire extinguisher									
	Flashlight									
	Hand soap dispenser									
	Lotion									
	Matches (box)									
	Medications and/or vitamins, bottles									
	Medications and/or vitamins, boxes									
	Nut cracker									
	Plant									
	Straws (pkgs.)									
	Thermos bottle									
	Toothpicks (box)									
	Vase, small									
	Vase, large									
	Additional items:									

Miscellaneous

FORM 5: CABINETRY, SURFACES, AND KITCHEN FEATURES CHECKLIST [CLIENT CHECKLIST]

Kitchen design is made up of many details. This checklist helps you think about your preferences for many of the products and features for your new kitchen.

Instructions: We start with general questions about your kitchen and features that you might want. Then we move to the more specific checklists on kitchen products.

The checklists are divided into sections for different products and materials, such as cabinets, sinks and floors. Go through each section, indicating what you do and do not want. You will not have information for every column or row—only those that relate to you and your kitchen. If you are not sure about an item, make a note in the "Comments" column to discuss with your designer later.

In places, space is left for you to add information, describing your personal preference—for example, a color choice or an option that is not listed.

General Questions

What ideas do you have about arrangement of your kitchen? _____

_____

_____

Do you have ideas about areas that should be spacious or compact? _____

_____

_____

What areas should be open to another? _____

_____

_____

What will be the focal point? _____

_____

_____

Describe any preferences for style or color that you want to include in your kitchen. _____

_____

_____

Do you have any furniture that you want in your kitchen?

Dining table _____ Size? _____

Chairs _____ How many? _____

Hutch _____ Size? _____

Buffet _____ Size? _____

Baker's Rack _____ Size? _____

Easy chair _____ How many? _____

Sofa _____ Size? _____

Other items? _____

_____

Kitchen Features

Features	Preference			Comments
	Definitely want	Desirable	Definitely do NOT want	
Separate baking center				
Display area for collections				Describe:
Island				
Pantry				
Closed soffit				
Open soffit				
Raised eating bar (typical 42 inches)				
Counter eating bar (typical 36 inches)				
Table height eating area (typical 30 inches)				
Architectural details				Describe:
Special features:				

Cabinetry

Features	Preference			Comments
	Definitely want	Desirable	Definitely do NOT want	
Construction:				
Framed				
Frameless				
Door Type:				
Full Overlay				
Overlay				
Partial Overlay/Lip				
Inset				
Face Material:				
Wood – Species?				
Laminate				
Paint				
Acrylic/Thermofoil				
Metal				
Other				
Door Style:				
Describe:				
Color and Finish:				
Describe:				
Hardware:				
Knob				
Pull				
Finger pull				
Material				

Cabinetry, continued

Features	Preference			Comments
	Definitely want	Desirable	Definitely do NOT want	
Storage Accessories or Organizers:				Indicate preferred location of features by circling **B** for base cabinets, **W** for wall cabinets, and **P** for pantry cabinets. Not all types of accessories can be located in all types of cabinets.
Appliance garage				B　W　P
Bread box				B　W　P
Cutlery tray				B　W　P
Door shelf				B　W　P
Drawer divider/insert				B　W　P
Knife block				B　W　P
Lazy-susan/turntable				B　W　P
Plate rack				B　W　P
Pot rack				B　W　P
Pull-out bin				B　W　P
Pull-out cutting board				B　W　P
Roll-out cart				B　W　P
Roll-out shelf				B　W　P
Spice rack				B　W　P
Swing-out shelf				B　W　P
Tilt-down drawer				B　W　P
Trash can				B　W　P
Vegetable bin/basket				B　W　P
Other features:				
				B　W　P
				B　W　P
				B　W　P
				B　W　P
				B　W　P

Sinks and Other Fixtures and Fittings

SINK 1

Features	Preference			Comments
	Definitely want	Desirable	Definitely do NOT want	
Material:				
Enamel/cast iron				
Solid surface				
Stainless steel				
Other:				
Number of bowls:				
One				
Two				
Three				
Color:				
Describe:				
Mounting:				
Self-rimming				
Under-mount				
Integral				
Other:				
Special features:				

Sinks and Other Fixtures and Fittings
FAUCET

Features	Preference			Comments
	Definitely want	Desirable	Definitely do NOT want	
Material:				
Brass				
Brushed chrome				
Chrome				
Epoxy – Color?				
Gold				
Nickel				
Pewter				
Stainless steel				
Other:				
Style/Features:				
One handle				
Two handles				
Lever handle				
Knob handle				
"Goose" neck				
Pull-out spray				
Automatic operation				
Other features:				
DISPENSERS				
Dish detergent				
Hand lotion				
Hand soap				

Sinks and Other Fixtures and Fittings

SINK 2

Features	Preference			Comments
	Definitely want	Desirable	Definitely do NOT want	
Material:				
Enamel/cast iron				
Solid surface				
Stainless steel				
Other:				
Number of bowls:				
One				
Two				
Three				
Color:				
Describe:				
Mounting:				
Self-rimming				
Under-mount				
Integral				
Other:				
Special features:				

Sinks and Other Fixtures and Fittings
FAUCET

Features	Preference			Comments
	Definitely want	Desirable	Definitely do NOT want	
Material:				
Brass				
Brushed chrome				
Chrome				
Epoxy – Color?				
Gold				
Nickel				
Pewter				
Stainless steel				
Other:				
Style/Features:				
One handle				
Two handles				
Lever handle				
Knob handle				
"Goose" neck				
Pull-out spray				
Automatic operation				
Other features:				
DISPENSERS				
Dish detergent				
Hand lotion				
Hand soap				

Accessories				
Features	**Preference**			**Comments**
	Definitely want	Desirable	Definitely do NOT want	
Chilled water dispenser				
Compost bin				
Garbage disposer*				
Instant hot water				
Pot filler faucet				
Water filter				
Other accessories:				

*See Form 6 for further information on appliances.

Countertops				
Features	**Preference**			**Comments**
	Definitely want	Desirable	Definitely do NOT want	
Material:				
Butcher block/wood				
Ceramic tile				
Concrete				
Engineered stone				
Granite				
Marble				
Plastic laminate				
Soapstone				
Solid surface				
Other:				
Color or Pattern:				
Describe:				
Edge treatment:				
Bevel				
Bull nose				
Square				
Contrast color				
Other:				
Backsplash:				
Match to counter				
Full height				
Backsplash material:				
Describe:				

Floors				
Features	**Preference**			**Comments**
	Definitely want	Desirable	Definitely do NOT want	
Material:				
Bamboo				
Carpet				
Ceramic tile				
Cork				
Laminate				
Linoleum				
Vinyl – sheet				
Vinyl – tile				
Wood				
Wood – engineered				
Other:				
Color or Pattern:				
Describe:				

Walls

Features	Preference			Comments
	Definitely want	Desirable	Definitely do NOT want	
Material:				
Ceramic tile				
Paint				
Vinyl wall covering				
Wall paper				
Other:				
Color or Pattern:				
Describe:				

Ceiling

Features	Preference			Comments
	Definitely want	Desirable	Definitely do NOT want	
Material:				
Paint				
Vinyl wall covering				
Wall paper				
Other:				
Color or Pattern:				
Describe:				

Lighting				
Features	**Preference**			**Comments**
	Definitely want	Desirable	Definitely do NOT want	
Light sources:				
Fluorescent				
Halogen				
Incandescent				
Xenon				
Special features:				
Sink area				Describe:
Prep area				Describe:
Refrigerator area				Describe:
Cook area				Describe:
Serve and dining area				Describe:
Other				Describe:

FORM 6: APPLIANCE PREFERENCE CHECKLIST [CLIENT CHECKLIST]

Selecting and specifying appliances is an important part of a kitchen design. This checklist is designed to help you specify appliances and select the features that you want.

Instructions: In the preference column, simply check the column, or indicate the number of items or the size of the feature. Additional lines are provided to add features not listed. You will not have information in every column or row – only those that relate to your preferences. If you know the brand or model, add that information to the "Comments" column.

Range				
Range Features	Preference			**Comments**
	Definitely want	Desirable	Definitely do NOT want	
Fuel:				
Electricity				
Natural gas				
Propane				
Type:				
Free-standing				
Drop-in				
Slide-in				
Integrated				
Professional Style				

Range				
Range Features	**Preference**			**Comments**
	Definitely want	Desirable	Definitely do NOT want	
Electric surface units:				
Conventional coil				
Solid disk (electric hob)				
Sealed glass ceramic				
Magnetic induction				
Halogen unit				
Thermostatic controlled unit				
Dual size unit				
Gas surface units:				
Open-air (conventional)				
Sealed				
High Btu				
Surface controls:				
Electronic				
Conventional knob				
Other cooking surface features:				
Grill				
Griddle				
Oven features:				
Electric oven				
Gas oven				
Broiler				
Convection oven				
Pyrolytic (self-cleaning)				
Oven controls:				
Conventional knob				
Electronic				
Other range features:				

Cooktop (Separate)				
Cooktop Features	**Preference**			**Comments**
	Definitely want	Desirable	Definitely do NOT want	
Fuel:				
Electricity				
Natural gas				
Propane				
Professional style				
Electric units:				
Conventional coil				
Solid disk (electric hob)				
Sealed glass ceramic				
Magnetic induction				
Halogen unit				
Thermostatic controlled unit				
Dual size unit				
Gas units:				
Open-air (conventional)				
Sealed				
High Btu				
Controls:				
Electronic				
Conventional knob				
Other cooking surface features:				
Grill				
Griddle				

Ventilation System

	Preference			Comments
	Definitely want	Desirable	Definitely do NOT want	
Updraft/Canopy:				
Exhaust				
Recirculating				
Hood:				
Match to cooktop				
Match to cabinetry				
Custom design				Describe:
Slim line/telescoping				
Downdraft/Proximity:				
Surface mount				
Pop-up – behind cooktop				
Pop-up – beside cooktop				
Other ventilation features:				

Oven (Built-in)

Oven Features	Preference			Comments
	Definitely want	Desirable	Definitely do NOT want	
Single				
Double				
Wall installation				
Under-counter installation				
Professional style				
Broiler				
Convection cooking				
Steam cooking				
High-speed cooking				
Pyrolytic (self-cleaning)				
Controls:				
Conventional knob				
Electronic				
Other features:				
Height of installation?				

Microwave Oven				
Microwave Oven Features	**Preference**			**Comments**
	Definitely want	Desirable	Definitely do NOT want	
Installation:				
Free-standing				
Boxed/Built-in				
Integrated				
Drawer				
Microwave-ventilation combination				
Professional style				
Microwave-convection cooking				
Microwave-light cooking				
Features:				
Browning element				
Turntable				
Height of installation?				
Location?				

Food Storage Appliances

Refrigerator/ Freezer				
Refrigerator/ Freezer Features	**Preference**			**Comments**
	Definitely want	Desirable	Definitely do NOT want	
Type:				
Single door refrigerator				
Refrigerator-freezer:				
Side-by-side				
Top mount				
Bottom mount				
Modular units:				
Refrigerator				
Freezer				
Freezer:				
Upright				
Chest				
Installation:				
Freestanding				
Boxed/Built-in				
Integrated				
Under counter				
Decorative panels				
Professional style				

Refrigerator/ Freezer, continued

Refrigerator/ Freezer Features	Preference			Comments
	Definitely want	Desirable	Definitely do NOT want	
Features:				
Adjustable shelves				
Humidity controlled compartments				
Ice maker				
Ice dispenser (door)				
Mini-door				
Temperature controlled compartments				
Water dispenser (filter)				
Water dispenser (inside)				
Water dispenser (outside)				
Other features:				

Refrigerator/ Freezer

Other Food Storage Appliances	Preference			Comments
	Definitely want	Desirable	Definitely do NOT want	
Icemaker				
Wine cooler				

Dishwasher

Dishwasher Features	Preference			Comments
	Definitely want	Desirable	Definitely do NOT want	
Installation:				
Freestanding				
Built-in				
Integrated				
Decorative panels				
Professional style				
Drawers				
Size				
Interior finish:				
Plastic				
Stainless				
Dishwasher features:				
Adjustable shelves				
Electronic controls				
Flatware trays				
Hidden controls				
Multiple racks				
Special cycles				
Stem storage				
Other features:				
How many dishwashers?				

Other Cleanup Appliances

Other Waste Management and Cleanup Appliances	Preference			Comments
	Definitely want	Desirable	Definitely do NOT want	
Disposer:				
Batch feed				
Continuous feed				
Trash compactor				

Other Appliances

	Preference			Comments
	Definitely want	Desirable	Definitely do NOT want	
Built-in small appliances:				
Computer				
Intercom				
Radio				
Telephone				
Television				
VCR/DVD player				
Warming drawer				
Washer				
Dryer				
Other appliances:				

FORM 7: JOB SITE INSPECTION

The information on this form is collected by a thorough inspection of the existing structure and/or construction documents. Look for detailed information. Use this form to verify specifics at the actual site

Overall Kitchen

Begin with a floor plan sketch to understand the relationship of spaces and to make notes about structural and mechanical details. See the questions below for additional information to add to your sketch. Use standard graphic symbols on your sketch to minimize clutter.

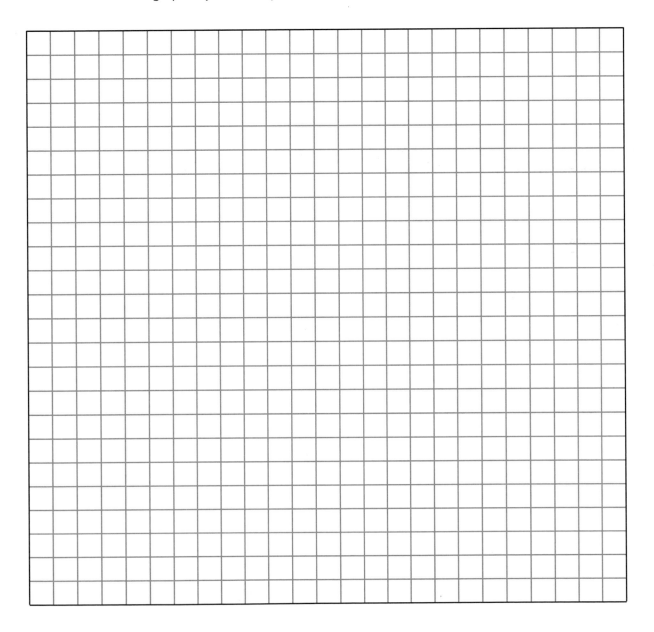

Note the following information on your kitchen sketch.

- How do people enter or exit the space?

- What rooms are above, below and around the existing kitchen space?

- Can any of the surrounding space be incorporated into the new plan? If so, how much – exactly?

- What walls can be changed – moved, removed or otherwise altered?

- Which windows and doors are to remain or be reused?

- What windows and doors can be changed – moved, removed or changed in size or type?

- What fixtures, appliance or furnishings are to remain? Are they to be left in the same location, or can they be moved?

- Is there cabinetry that is to be left in place or reused in the new design?

- Is the foundation concrete slab or wood construction?

- Which way do the floor joists run? Does the floor seem sturdy and stiff?

- Are there load-bearing walls to consider?

- Where does plumbing come into the space?

- Where are the existing gas lines, if any?

- Where are the drain/waste/vent pipes?

- Where are existing ducts and registers located? Can these be moved?

- What is the condition of finish materials – floors, walls, and ceilings?

- Are any of the finish materials to remain unchanged?

- Is there a view from the kitchen?

- Is view from the kitchen important?

Determine the following additional information about the kitchen.

Kitchen is on:　❑ north　❑ northeast　❑ east　❑ southeast　❑ south

　　　　　　　　❑ southwest　❑ west　❑ northwest

If new fixtures or appliances are to be installed, are they to be put in the same location as the old fixtures or appliances? _____

_____

If the remodeled kitchen project will affect the exterior
of the home, are there any restrictions to be considered? _____

_____

Will existing doors, windows, siding or roof materials be easy to match?

_____

Are there any home improvements or repairs to be incorporated
into the kitchen project, such as new siding or a roof replacement? _____

_____

If the home is older than 1978, could there be
lead-based paint or asbestos in the existing space? _____

_____

Structure

What is the construction of the house?

_____

What is the condition of the existing structure? Check for sound
and level floors, square corners, and materials in good condition. _____

_____

Is there evidence of water leaks or pest damage?

_____

If home is of wood construction, what size are the joists
and will they be adequate support for the new fixtures? _____

_____

Are windows and doors in good repair and do they operate smoothly? _____

_____

Are new or replacement windows and doors to match the
existing windows with respect to type, size, style, and material? _____

_____

Is the home well-insulated? _____

Are doors and windows energy-efficient? _____

191

Mechanical Systems

Can you relocate any plumbing pipes or gas lines?_____

_____

What is the capacity of the plumbing system?

_____

What size are the supply pipes? _____

_____

Is there adequate water pressure? _____

Is the water of good quality? _____

Will you be able to add additional fixtures or appliances, or
higher-capacity fixtures or appliances, to the existing plumbing? _____

_____

Where is the water heater? _____

What is the capacity?_____

Can the drain/waste/vent pipes be relocated if needed? _____

_____

Where are the traps, and what type are they? _____

_____

Is the home on a municipal or private sewage system? _____

Are there any concerns about system capacity, if the amount of wastewater is increased?_____

_____

How many electrical circuits come into the space, and what is the capacity? _____

_____

Do the circuits have GFCI (ground fault circuit interrupter) protection? _____

_____

Is the wiring in good condition? _____

_____

Can existing receptacles be moved? _____

_____

If needed, are 240-volt circuits available? _____

Where is the electrical service panel for the house? _____

_____

How many unused 110/120 volt and 220/240 volt circuits are available? _____

_____

If needed, can additional electrical circuits be added? _____

_____

How is the existing space heated and cooled? _____

_____

Is the current HVAC (heating, ventilating and air
conditioning) equipment in good condition and adequate in size? _____

_____

If there will be an increase in the size of the kitchen, will the HVAC system be adequate? _____

_____

Is there an exhaust ventilation system? _____

Is it adequate in size? _____

How is make-up air provided? _____

_____

Does all or part of the ventilation system need replacement? _____

_____

Access

What size are any doors between the kitchen and the exterior of the home? _____

_____

Are there narrow hallways or sharp turns? _____

_____

Will there be any problems in removing or bringing in large and/or heavy appliances? _____

_____

Is there finished living space above or below the kitchen?_____

_____

Will you be able to open up floors, ceilings, or walls to
get access to plumbing, electrical, and HVAC systems? _____

_____

Construction/Installation Planning

What part of the project, if any, do the clients want to do themselves?

_____

Is there any part of the project to be done by another professional?

_____

Contact information:

_____

_____

_____

What is the time frame of the project? _____

_____

Is there a deadline? _____

_____

Are there specific events that affect the project schedule?_____

_____

Are there specific times when the workers cannot have access to the kitchen space?

_____

Can appliances, cabinetry and materials be stored at the job site? _____

_____

How much space is there? _____

_____

Is the storage secure and protected from the weather? _____

_____

Where will trash be collected? _____

_____

How will workers get into and out of the jobsite? _____

_____

Is there carpeting or furniture that needs to be protected? _____

_____

Where can workers park? _____

_____

Where can they take breaks or eat lunch? _____

_____

Are smoking, playing music, eating and drinking allowed at the jobsite? _____

_____

Will there be bathroom facilities for workers to use? _____

_____

FORM 8: DIMENSIONS OF THE KITCHEN – FLOOR PLAN

Carefully measure the kitchen space and prepare a dimensioned drawing. Double check each dimension and record your numbers carefully. Note the location of all mechanical connections, including electrical and plumbing information. Double check each dimension and record your numbers carefully.

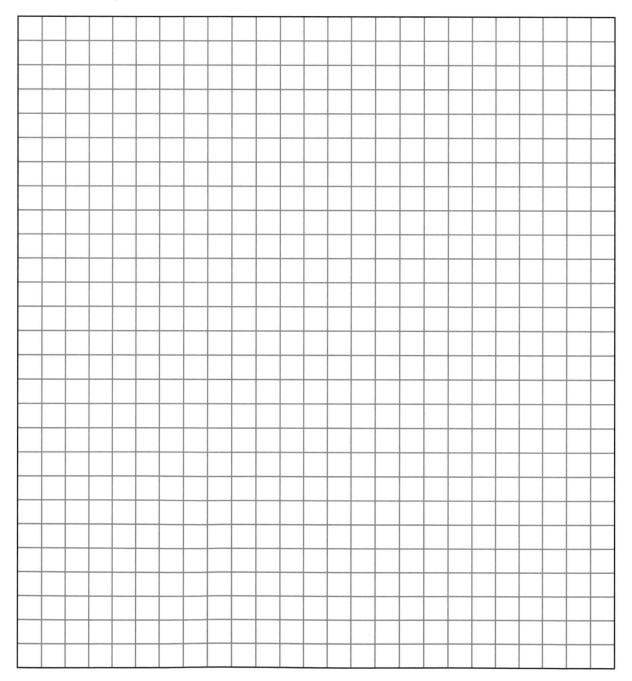

FORM 9: DIMENSIONS OF THE KITCHEN – ELEVATIONS

After taking an elevation of each kitchen wall, you will use these elevations to note the location of architectural features, mechanical devices (Form 10), windows (Form 11), doors (Form 12) and fixtures to remain (Form 13).

FORM 10: DIMENSIONS OF MECHANICAL DEVICES

Measure and locate each heat register, radiator or other mechanical devices. Note whether the location of these items is fixed.

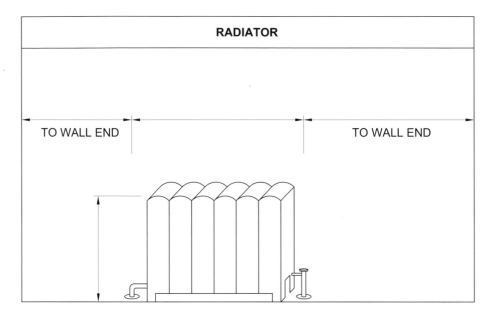

RADIATOR

TO WALL END   TO WALL END

REGISTER OR FAN - CEILING, WALL OR FLOOR							
NO.	A	B	C	D	E	F	G
1							
2							

E
TO WALL END   F   G   TO WALL END

D

A
TO CEILING

C

B

FORM 11: WINDOW MEASUREMENTS

Note the location of the window in relation to the floor, ceiling and both wall corners. Include the size of the window frame.

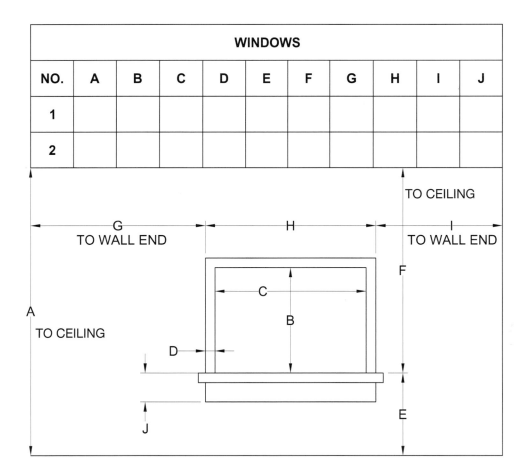

NO.	A	B	C	D	E	F	G	H	I	J
1										
2										

FORM 12: DOOR MEASUREMENTS

Note the location of the door in relation to both wall corners and the ceiling. Include the size of the door and the casing.

DOORS										
NO.	A	B	C	D	E	F	G	H	I	HANDLE L OR R?
1										
2										
3										

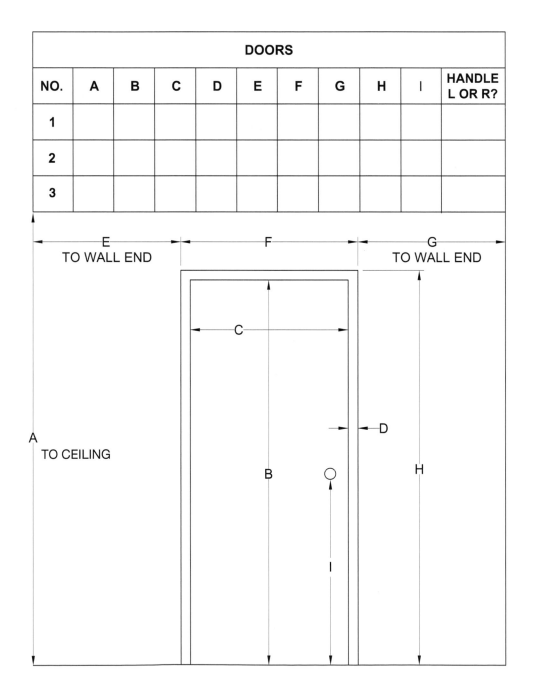

FORM 13: FIXTURE AND APPLIANCE MEASUREMENTS

Carefully measure existing fixtures and appliances that will remain. Also measure depth of handles.

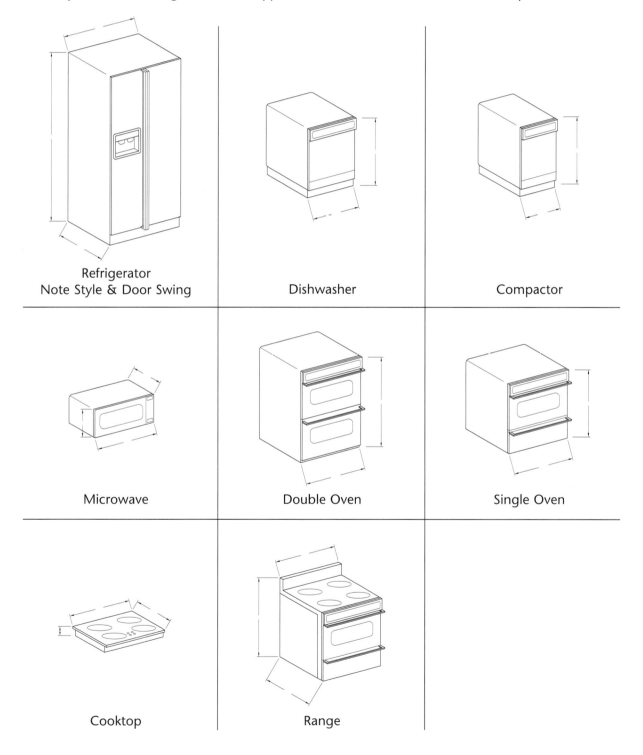

Refrigerator
Note Style & Door Swing

Dishwasher

Compactor

Microwave

Double Oven

Single Oven

Cooktop

Range

FORM 13: FIXTURE AND APPLIANCE MEASUREMENTS, CONTINUED

Carefully measure existing fixtures and appliances that will remain.

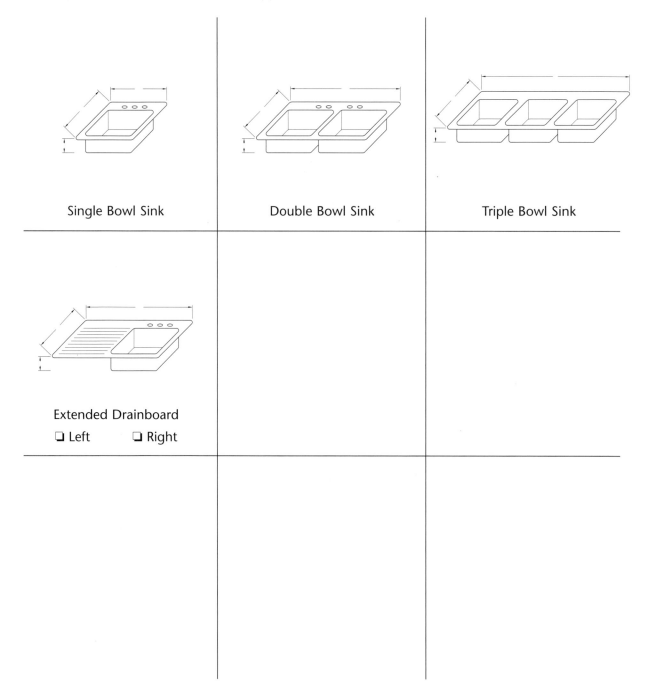

| Single Bowl Sink | Double Bowl Sink | Triple Bowl Sink |

Extended Drainboard

❏ Left   ❏ Right

CHAPTER 7: Kitchen Planning

Kitchens are essential spaces in most homes. In fact, building codes require that dwelling units must have a cooking area. How this essential room is designed can determine if the space meets the needs of the residents and is truly functional. This chapter presents information to help you consider how to plan the kitchen space to meet the needs of clients. Although each client's needs are unique, the basics of kitchen planning are based on research and the experiences of people preparing food. Anthropometric data and task analysis provide the designer with valuable information in planning kitchens.

LOCATION AND TYPES OF KITCHENS

Location of Kitchen

Some older homes were planned using the zoning paradigm, with the kitchen categorized in the work zone and the other areas characterized as private and social zones. From this perspective, food preparation is a task, along with other household jobs like laundry and mending. These task areas should be grouped together in one part of the house.

However, in many newer homes the kitchen is considered part of an informal social space. While food preparation is still important, other activities are also occurring in the kitchen (and surrounding areas) and should be accommodated by the space. Today's lifestyles seem to require an informal living space where family members and friends gather to share their lives on a regular basis. Time constraints mean that often several activities are occurring in the space at the same time. The kitchen is now often part of a social area.

WORK ZONE

Originally, the work zone allowed servants to perform household tasks without interruption and observation from the family living in other parts of the house. Even as servants became less common, the work areas remained consolidated into one part of the house. The homemaker was the typical worker and grouping these areas helped to make her job more convenient and remained a good planning concept.

The outcome of this concept was that the kitchen was often placed at the back of the house and close to a utility room or other work area. This location kept the kitchen separated from social and private spaces in the home. It was also close to outdoor play areas so that children could be observed. A formal dining area was adjacent to the kitchen and informal dining might be provided in the kitchen area or in a breakfast nook. The kitchen was located close to a service entry so that groceries and other products could be brought directly into the work area of the home.

SOCIAL AREA

When the kitchen is considered a part of an informal living space, a different arrangement becomes necessary. More activities occur in the space, not just food preparation. Meals may be served in the social kitchen area regularly. Children's play and homework can take place in this space. It may become the communications headquarters where messages are taken and schedules are kept. Watching television, using the computer, talking and visiting with friends and family will take place in the kitchen area. The kitchen may be an important space for entertaining as people help with the preparations or visit with the cook/host. The task of food preparation no longer occurs in isolation.

The kitchen can be located in a variety of places within the home, not just the back of the house. It will still need to be located close to a service entry, but access to a guest entry may be important as well. With the many and varied activities taking place, the kitchen requires more space that is adjacent and open to dining and living spaces. Environmental factors, like noise, moisture and lighting must be considered. The aesthetic appeal of materials and equipment may become important since the kitchen will be exposed to people in the social spaces. Often, more than one user will need to access some or all of the kitchen space, influencing the layout and arrangement of the kitchen. Kitchens that incorporate universal design principles can help to meet the needs of a variety of users.

Types of Kitchens

Whether or not the kitchen is considered a work area or a social space may also influence what type of arrangement is planned. Traditional planning has suggested that there were a few common arrangements of kitchen areas and that these could be planned into a variety of spaces. In fact, certain arrangements lend themselves to either a closed arrangement, typical of a work-type kitchen, or an open arrangement, typical of a social kitchen with centers or zones for multiple activities. The physical space and the ability to renovate may dictate which is used.

CLOSED ARRANGEMENTS

A closed arrangement indicates that the kitchen is probably best suited for one cook who works in isolation. These arrangements do not lend themselves to other family members or guests moving about, in or through the space. The following arrangements fall into this category:

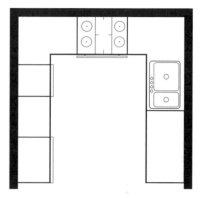

- **U-shaped kitchen** – This arrangement has two parallel cabinet/counter/work areas with a third area joining them, forming an arrangement similar to a U. Typically, a different type of work area is on each section: cooking, sink and refrigeration. This can be a very convenient arrangement for one person moving in between the various areas. Depending on the distance of the work aisle, it can be fairly difficult for more than one person at a time to use it. However, a wide U-shaped kitchen that includes an island can be a good layout for a multi-cook space.

Figure 7.1 A U-shaped kitchen has two parallel cabinet/counter/work areas. (Courtesy of American Classics by RSI)

- **Parallel or galley kitchen** – This arrangement offers two parallel cabinet/counter/work areas, typically with a wall at the end, so that traffic does not go through the kitchen. At least two work areas have to be on the same side. Again, depending on the size of the work aisle, the arrangement might be best suited for only one cook.

Figure 7.2 This parallel or galley kitchen locates the sink opposite the cooktop with refrigerator and ovens on opposite ends of the wall. (Courtesy of Robin Rigby-Fisher, CKD, CBD – Portland, Oregon)

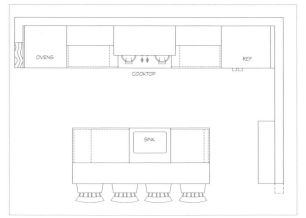

- **G-shaped kitchen** – This arrangement is a wide U-shaped kitchen, with a fourth arm turning back into the center of the space. This results in a fairly tight work area that lends itself to one cook, unless secondary work areas are planned along the outer arms.

All of these arrangements can be planned to feel more open by increasing the distance between the sides of the space and by creating a pass-through or peninsula counter. Dining areas or other social spaces might be planned at the open end of the arrangements to increase access.

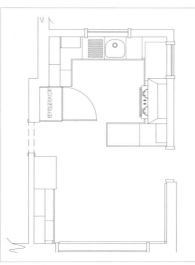

Figure 7.3 This G-shaped kitchen places the sink and range at a right angle to each other with a peninsula open onto the adjoining space. (Courtesy of Rebecca G. Lindquist, CMKBD – Duluth, Minnesota)

OPEN ARRANGEMENTS

Open arrangements are more likely to be used if there are two cooks, or if there will be several people in the kitchen area. Often these arrangements can combine with social spaces to create a multi-use space. These arrangements include:

- **L-shaped kitchen** – This arrangement has two arms of work areas joined together at one end to form an L-shape. Often one person could work on one side and another on the other side without too much interference. The open side of the arrangement might lend itself to a dining space, a seating arrangement or a work aisle.

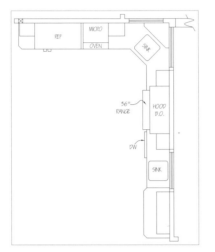

Figure 7.4 The L-shaped kitchen has one side open, allowing for another use in the open area, perhaps dining or seating. (Courtesy of Mark White, CKD – Annapolis, Maryland)

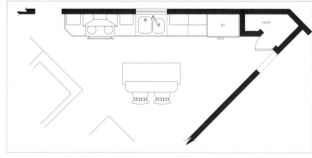

Figure 7.5 One-wall kitchen. This award-winning kitchen has the work areas on one-wall and uses an island for seating and storage (Courtesy of Beverly A. Alig, CKD – Annapolis, Maryland)

- **One-wall kitchen** – This arrangement puts all of the work areas on one wall. It can be an inconvenient kitchen because of the distance between the work centers on opposite ends of the wall, or if the distance is not too great, the amount of storage and counter space may be limited. It does allow for an open space opposite the kitchen wall that could be used for dining and social areas.

- **Corridor kitchen** – This arrangement is similar to the parallel kitchen, except that both ends are open. This allows for traffic through the work areas, which is not desirable. However, if alternate traffic can be arranged so that the traffic is only for the cook(s), then the arrangement may work for single or multiple cooks.

Figure 7.6 With both ends open, people can move through the living area, leaving the kitchen work areas uninterrupted by major traffic. (Courtesy of Toshie Lim, CKD, CBD – Alameda, California)

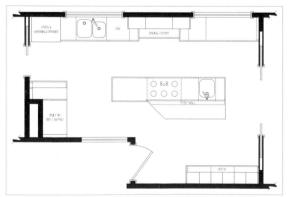

- **Island kitchen** – A separate work area or island can be incorporated into most of these kitchen configurations, provided there is room for the proper clearances in the work and traffic aisles. Island kitchens can be arranged in many different ways. The island is usually a workspace and may be combined with another activity area, such as dining. At least one side of the island faces a work area with a work aisle in between. The other side is more likely to be a traffic aisle or seating area, but it could be a work aisle as well.

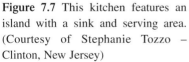

Figure 7.7 This kitchen features an island with a sink and serving area. (Courtesy of Stephanie Tozzo – Clinton, New Jersey)

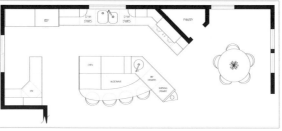

Figure 7.8 This kitchen features a triangular pantry and angled island. (Courtesy of Margie Little, CMKBD – Pleasant Hill, California)

Kitchens may come in even more shapes. Work areas can be placed at 45° angles. Curved arrangements may have no angles. Each work area may be unattached in an unfitted kitchen. No one shape is ideal and the designer will want to make sure that the needs of the user and the requirements of space are being met.

Size of Kitchens

Kitchens come in all sizes. Often this is dependent on the space allocated within a house, but it might also be a factor of the number of cooks or others using a kitchen at one time. Kitchens can be too small to be effective for adequate storage, workspace and workflow. They can also be too big, with work centers spread out so far that a cook has problems preparing a meal without expending a great deal of energy moving about the space. In some larger spaces, multiple prep centers or zones can be planned to create a smaller work area within the larger space.

Research indicates Certified Kitchen Designers (CKDs) are designing kitchens in ranges that could be categorized as follows:

- Small kitchen – less than 150 square feet

- Medium kitchen – 151 to 350 square feet

- Large kitchen – greater that 350 square feet

Determining the size of the kitchen you are working with will be an important first step in planning the design and layout of the space. In particular, storage requirements are specified according to kitchen size. All food preparation areas of a kitchen arrangement should be measured to determine the size of the kitchen. Figure 7.9 contains an example of how the size of the kitchen should be determined in order to calculate storage requirements.

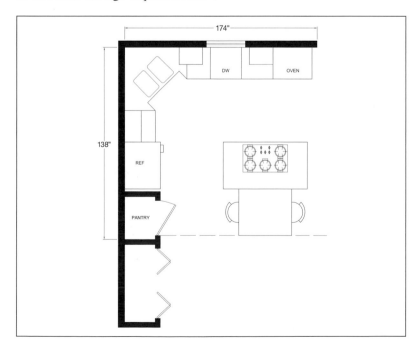

Figure 7.9 The main food preparation areas define the size of the kitchen. To calculate the size of this kitchen, include the pantry storage and the eating area that is used as a seated preparation area.

THE CENTER CONCEPT

A work center or zone is an area where a particular task occurs. Using the center concept is a comprehensive way to design an area that will be used for a certain task. There are three primary centers in the kitchen for food preparation and clean up: sink, refrigeration and cooking. Various secondary centers might be created for certain tasks like baking or salad preparation, if the client's activities and the space allow for it. Serving and dining areas should also be provided and are discussed separately. Other areas or centers may be needed for specific tasks that take place in the kitchen: communications, laundry or office. Ideas and requirements for these non-food activities are presented in Chapter 9.

In this book, the approach used to design kitchen work centers considers the following elements: the actual tasks and activities being conducted, the user(s) working in the center, the appliance or fixture that anchors and/or supports the center, required floor space, needed storage for items used and work surfaces necessary to complete the tasks.

- **Tasks and Activities** – Often multiple activities and tasks are occurring in one center. For example, food preparation and clean up are two primary tasks that occur at the sink. However, other activities, such as taking medications, also occur within the sink center and should be considered. The tasks and activities may drive decisions about the design requirements that must be met, such as counter height or amount of storage.

- **Users** – Consider the size and abilities of the cook when planning a center. Other user considerations include the number of cooks and the individual tasks they perform. In addition, individuals have different cooking styles that could affect the plan for the kitchen.

Several anthropometric measurements are explained in Chapter 5. The user's reach range over a cabinet is an important measurement needed for designing a kitchen. (Figure 7.10). While the average woman can reach a shelf over a base cabinet that is as high as 69 inches, the most comfortable reach range for most standing users will be between 25 and 59 inches. A more universal reach range of 15 to 48 inches accommodates standing and seated users.

Another important anthropometric consideration is the horizontal work area (Figure 7.11). The average person requires at least 30 inches to stand with elbows slightly extended and can use at least 48 inches of work surface with a depth of 16 inches.

More information about specific user requirements is presented in Chapter 5.

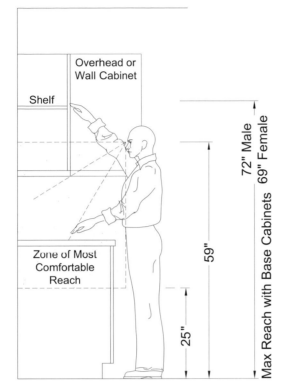
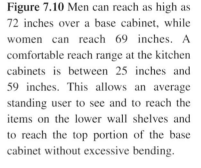

Figure 7.10 Men can reach as high as 72 inches over a base cabinet, while women can reach 69 inches. A comfortable reach range at the kitchen cabinets is between 25 inches and 59 inches. This allows an average standing user to see and to reach the items on the lower wall shelves and to reach the top portion of the base cabinet without excessive bending.

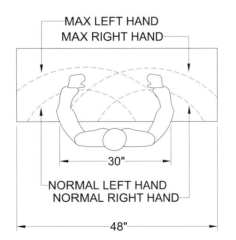

Figure 7.11 A work surface should be wide enough to fit the user and the task.

- **Appliance/Fixture** – Each center typically contains a basic appliance or fixture for which it is named. However, some tasks use multiple appliances or fixtures. For example, a range or cooktop may anchor the cooking center and other cooking appliances, i.e. wall oven and microwave may form secondary cooking centers. An auxiliary sink is another example of a secondary center, which can be combined with a work surface to create a second prep zone.

- **Floor Space** – Clearances are required at each center to assure that cooks can move around effectively in the space and operate the appliances and fixtures. These clearances will be discussed later in this chapter.

- **Storage** – All of the tasks that occur in the kitchen require space to store the things that are used in the center. There are several types of storage designed for placement in the kitchen and the designer can create special storage systems and products if needed. For more information on specifying cabinets see the NKBA book *Kitchen & Bath Products.*

Base cabinets – A base cabinet is the bottom cabinet and is usually 24 inches deep and 34 $1/2$ inches high with a $1^1/2$-inch high countertop bringing the total cabinet height to 36 inches. Standard base cabinets are typically sized in 3-inch linear measurements starting at 9 inches (tray storage) with the largest size of 48 inches, and custom cabinetry can be made in any size.

Typically a base cabinet has a 4- to-5-inch high x 3-inch deep toekick at the base, which allows a user to stand close to the cabinet. Some furniture type cabinets do not include a toekick and the user may need to lean into the cabinet to work at the counter surface. Toekicks may need to be raised to at least 9 inches and have the depth increased to 6 inches to accommodate the foot rests of a wheelchair or scooter.

Base cabinets can be customized to a lower height to accommodate shorter or seated people.

Drawers – A standard base cabinet comes with a drawer approximately 3 inches deep at the top of the cabinet, but a base cabinet can be designed with three to four drawers to accommodate all types of items in an accessible way. Base cabinets also may have pull-out shelves and trays that function like drawers.

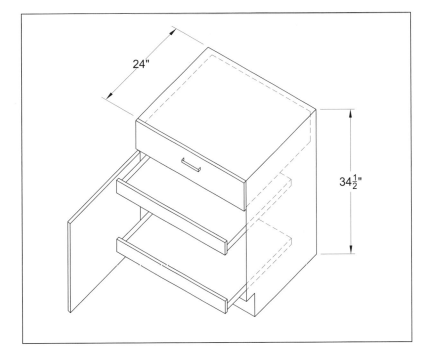

Figure 7.12 Base cabinet with pull-outs.

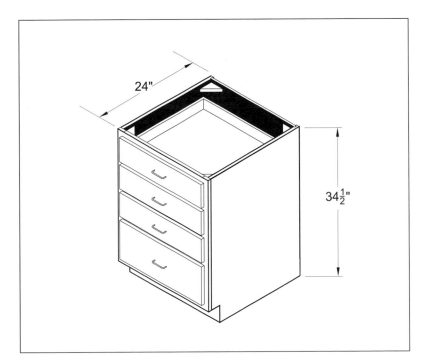

Figure 7.13 Drawer base with four drawers.

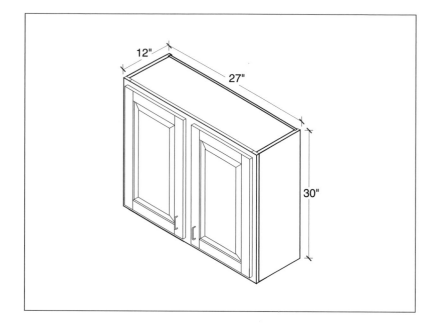

Figure 7.14 Typical wall cabinet

Wall cabinets – The standard wall cabinet depth is 12 inches, although 15 inches is also used to accommodate larger plates. The standard cabinet height ranges from 30 to 36 inches. Shorter cabinet sizes are used in certain applications, for example over an appliance or peninsula. Taller or stacked wall cabinets have become more common as ceiling heights have gone up. The linear width of standard or stock wall cabinets increases in 3 inch increments. The wall cabinet is placed 15 to 18 inches above a standard counter height of 36 inches. This puts two or three wall shelves within the reach of the average user and leaves a useable clear space above the work surface.

Tall cabinet/Pantry/Utility – There are several designs and arrangements for a tall cabinet or a pantry. This storage might be a closet or small room or it might be an elongated cabinet, 12, 18 or 24 inches deep with shelving and/or pull-outs. There are also fold-out shelving units that increase accessible storage capacity.

Other storage – Base and wall cabinets can include a variety of accessories that enhance the usability of the storage devices. Also, other storage pieces can add to the storage capacity of the kitchen. Pot racks, open shelving and furniture pieces can provide valuable storage areas in some kitchens.

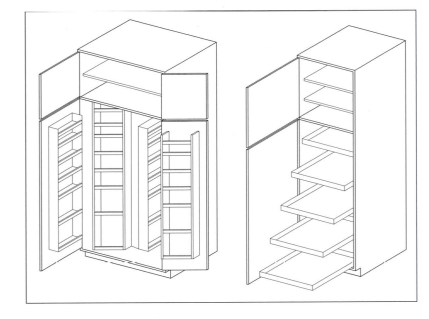

Figure 7.15 Tall cabinets can include fold-out storage or pull-out shelves.

Figure 7.16 Pot racks and open shelving can add to the storage capacity of a kitchen. (Courtesy of KraftMaid Cabinetry)

Work surface – Countertop space provides work surface needed to perform tasks in the center. Usually, the countertop surface corresponds to the base cabinet depth and will be +/- 25 inches, depending on the door thickness and countertop overhang needed to clear the cabinetry. Less deep areas are useable for some tasks, because the front 16 inches is the most comfortable work area. The rear 8 inches of the countertop is within reach of most users and is often used for permanent or temporary storage.

While the standard work area is 36 inches high, the ideal work surface height should be planned to be a few inches below the cook's elbow. A comfortable distance is usually considered to be 3 inches, but some tasks, like kneading bread, might require the arm to be extended in a way that suggests the need for a lower work surface. Use the client's measurements and cooking style to help you determine what height is best. While some specialized work heights are helpful to specific users or tasks, standard 36 inch high counters should also be provided, since they are considered a standard height that is useable by most people.

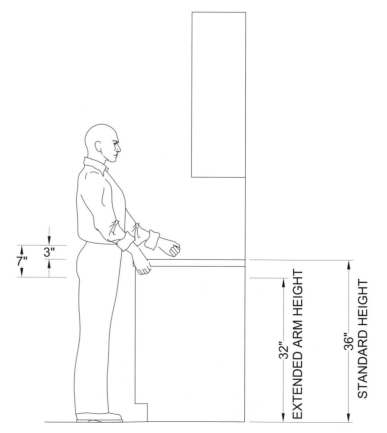

Figure 7.17 Standard work-surface height is 36 inches. Ideally, the height should be 3 to 7 inches below the user's elbow.

Designing Kitchen Centers

In the following sections, some general recommendations for circulation and work aisles are presented. Then each center is discussed separately, but comprehensively. The tasks and activities are identified and requirements associated with completing tasks safely and conveniently are detailed, followed by design recommendations. Combining centers, planning for adequate storage, and recommendations for dining and serving meals are also presented. The NKBA Kitchen Planning Guidelines and related Access Standards are important for the safe and comfortable use of the kitchen, and are discussed within these sections. For reference, all of the NKBA Kitchen Planning Guidelines and Access Standards are at the end of this book in Chapter 12.

Universal design concepts and ideas are presented and integrated throughout this chapter to encourage you to think about various user needs while planning the space. Thinking broadly about client's needs, now and in the future, can help you develop a thoughtful design that anticipates changes that will occur over the client's lifespan. In Chapter 10 you will find expanded ideas and recommendations for designing for specific user groups.

Background on the Guidelines

NKBA has been providing information on the design of kitchens since the Kitchen Industry Technical Manuals were first issued in 1975. The Kitchen Planning Guidelines have always had a very strong focus on safety and the building code requirements associated with kitchens. The guidelines have been reviewed and updated periodically to include new information, such as universal design. In 2003, an ad hoc committee of NKBA developed the current guidelines and these are incorporated into this book.

The examination of the guidelines incorporated a review of current housing trends and an analysis of the 2003 International Residential Code (IRC). Space recommendations are based on documented ergonomic considerations, and code requirements are highlighted. The IRC has been adopted by many states and localities, but designers should check the local building codes in their area to make sure they are in compliance with the jurisdiction they are working in. The Kitchen Planning Guidelines are intended to serve as a reference tool for practicing designers and an evaluation tool for kitchen designs. Designers taking the Certified Kitchen Designer Exam will be expected to know the guidelines and apply them to the designs they create for the exam. Students in NKBA Endorsed College Programs should learn the guidelines and be able to apply them in their design projects.

NKBA leads the building industry in promoting universal design and awareness. Their 1996 Kitchen Planning Guidelines included recommendations that would make the kitchen universal and accessible, many based on ANSI 117.1 guidelines and the Uniform Federal Accessibility Standards (UFAS). Many of the universal points included in the 1996 guidelines continue to be incorporated in the updated guidelines.

Access Standards

In this edition, the Access Standards include planning information that will improve a client's access to the kitchen. Because the International Building Code (IBC) references it, the 1998 edition of Accessible and Useable Buildings and Facilities (ICC/ANSI 117.1) has been used as the basis for the specific Access Standards. These ICC/ANSI standards serve as one of several safe harbors for designers and builders of multi-family housing who must be in compliance with the Fair Housing Amendments Act. If you are designing kitchens that are covered by the Fair Housing regulations, please check the sources mentioned in Chapter 5 to make sure you are in compliance with these federal standards.

Following many of the NKBA Kitchen Planning Guidelines there is a corresponding Access Standard. While these Access Standards and the ANSI standards on which they are based provide a great starting point, designers planning a kitchen for a particular client should closely examine the needs of that client to ensure that the kitchen is truly useable, not just meeting minimum requirements. The assessment forms presented in Chapter 6 should be used to gather information about the client's needs, and the suggestions according to user groups in Chapter 10 should help you.

FOOD PREPARATION CENTERS AND GUIDELINES

In this section, ideas for designing the kitchen work areas are discussed in detail, along with the Kitchen Planning Guidelines and Access Standards that relate to the work area. All the Guidelines and Access Standards are presented in Chapter 12.

Traffic and Work Aisles

Circulation and movement throughout the kitchen is one of the first areas that must be considered. Adequate traffic and work aisles are important for the safe and efficient use of the other centers. As you analyze the space that you will be designing, consider the traffic flow and the recommended circulation spaces. A specific kitchen layout, like a U-shape or an island design, may not be possible because there is not enough work or circulation space.

ENTRY

There will likely be several entries into the kitchen, depending on adjacent spaces that need to be accessed, i.e. dining area, social area, service entry, garage, mud room, outdoor social spaces. Considering the location of these entryways and how they affect the traffic pattern in the kitchen will be an important first step in planning the kitchen. Sometimes the entries have to stay where they are, but often you may be able to move, eliminate or create entries to enhance the layout of the kitchen.

Door openings should be at least 32 inches wide. This will provide an accessible entry to most people and equipment that will need to be placed in the kitchen. The 32-inch clearance is a clear opening and a 2-foot, 10-inch door is required to accomplish this opening. A 36-inch door with a 34-inch clear opening is preferred, especially for persons using a mobility aid.

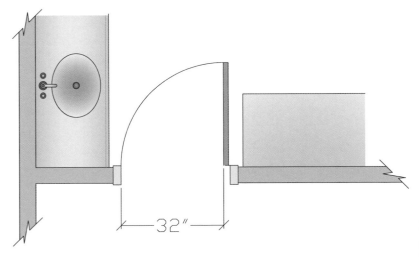

Figure 7.18 Allow 32 inches of clear space at each door opening in the kitchen. (Kitchen Planning Guideline 1)

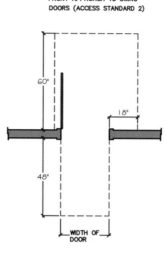

Figure 7.19 For a door to be useable by a person with a mobility aid there should be at least 18 inches of clear space beside the door opening. (Kitchen Planning Access Standard 2)

Space is needed beside the door to assure that it can be opened. This is especially true for a person using a mobility aid. Access Standards recommend a clearance on the pull side of a door that extends the width of the door plus 18 inches x 60 inches. A 48-inch deep clearance is needed on the push side of the door (See Figure 7.19.)

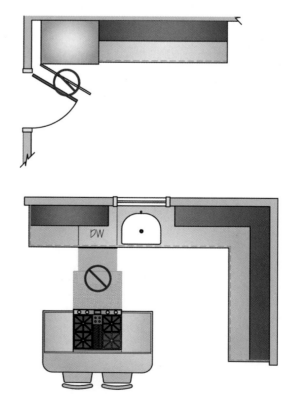

Figure 7.20 An entry door should not interfere with an appliance door opening and appliance doors should not open into each other. (Kitchen Planning Guideline 2)

Doors should not interfere with the operation of any appliance. For example, make sure an oven placed at the corner of the kitchen does not coincide with a door swing, as this is dangerous to the person using the oven when the door opens. Likewise, appliance doors should not interfere with each other. For example, as you lay out the placement of appliances, make sure oven and dishwasher doors do not open into one another, so that you cannot use one without closing the door of another.

WORK AISLES

Working in the kitchen requires space to move about between work areas. When work areas are across from each other they create a work aisle. When the kitchen is planned for one cook at least 42 inches is required for a work aisle. A 48-inch work aisle will provide room for the cook to stand in front of an open dishwasher and the oven door. If two cooks are going to be working in the kitchen then plan at least 48 inches for the work aisle. A work aisle of 60 inches to 66 inches will allow for a standard work aisle and room for someone to pass around the work area. It will also provide an adequate clearance for a cook with a mobility aid to maneuver a 360° turn (See Figure 7.23).

Either a 42- or a 48-inch work aisle would be acceptable for access standards that require a 30-inch x 48-inch clearance at each appliance or fixture for either a parallel or forward approach. Make sure the clear space is planned so that the appliance is useable. For instance, the clear space should be planned beside the dishwasher so that the door can be opened. Similarly, the clear space should be off-set at the refrigerator to allow for opening the door and accessing the interior space.

Figure 7.21 A kitchen planned for one cook should have 42-inch minimum work aisles, while a kitchen for two or more cooks should have work aisles of at least 48 inches. (Kitchen Planning Guideline 6)

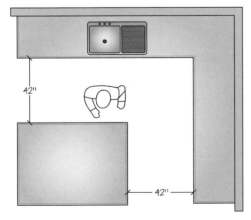

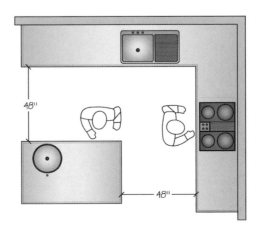

Figure 7.22 Access Standards require 30-inch x 48-inch clear space in front of each appliance for either a parallel or forward approach. (Kitchen Access Standard 6)

30" x 48"
CLEAR FLOOR SPACES AND
KNEE SPACES MAY OVERLAP

Another accessibility criterion is to allow room for turning around. A 60-inch turning radius is especially important in a U-shaped kitchen, where a person in a wheelchair might need to turn to reach all work areas. A space for a T-turn, including a knee clearance, can also provide access. See Chapter 10 for more detailed discussion of clear space, turning radius and access.

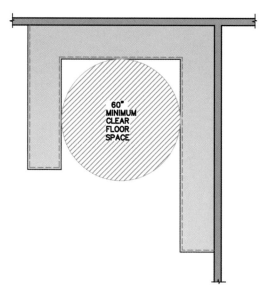

60"
MINIMUM
CLEAR
FLOOR
SPACE

Figure 7.23 Planning for a 60-inch work aisle allows space for a wheelchair to turn around and is especially needed in an accessible U-shaped kitchen. (Kitchen Access Standard 6)

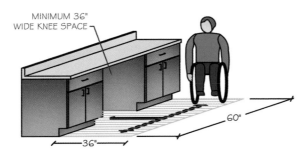

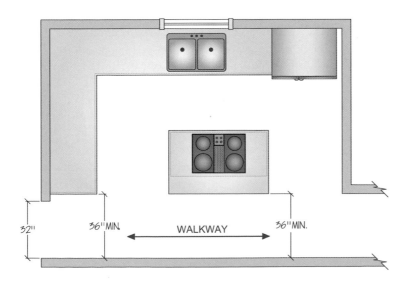

Figure 7.24 An alternative method for achieving access in a kitchen design uses clear space to create room for a T-turn. (Kitchen Access Standard 6)

CIRCULATION

Traffic may move through the kitchen in order to access entries and other parts of the room. A walkway or traffic aisle that is used only for walking should be a minimum 36 inches wide to allow for passage by one person. This will allow for the width of the person carrying a tray or other similar object. This width is also acceptable to a person using a mobility aid. If two people will be passing each other in the walkway frequently, then consider a walkway that is 48 to 60 inches wide. A 36-inch walkway that turns at a right angle should have one part that is a minimum 42 inches wide to allow a person using a mobility aid easier maneuvering.

The Kitchen Planning Guidelines and Access Standards that are particularly relevant to traffic, circulation and work aisles are Guidelines 1, 2, 6 and 7. They can be found in Chapter 12.

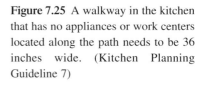

Figure 7.25 A walkway in the kitchen that has no appliances or work centers located along the path needs to be 36 inches wide. (Kitchen Planning Guideline 7)

SINK CENTER

The sink center is the most used center in the kitchen because it is the place of both food preparation and cleanup. It is also likely that other household activities will occur at or around the sink. While the requirements for food preparation and clean up are different, the water source and sink are essential elements for both types of activities resulting in a sink center that typically accommodates both. In larger kitchens or kitchens that are frequently used by multiple cooks, an auxiliary sink may be planned to reduce the congestion that can occur at the sink when all of these activities are being carried out at the same time.

Food Preparation Activities

- Washing and drying hands before and during food preparation is important for food safety. Locate hand soap (bar or liquid) and hand towels at the sink.

- Washing fruits, vegetables and other food items under water at the sink is also important for food safety and quality. The food must be retrieved from its storage (often the refrigerator), brought to the sink, rinsed and possibly dried with paper or cloth towels. Some foods will be rinsed using a colander or strainer.

- Some of these fruits and vegetables will be cut or chopped and this will likely occur near the sink. Paring knives, peelers, cutting boards and bowls or dishes will be needed during this process. Peels and waste will need to be put in the trash, compost container or garbage disposer.

- All types of food and beverage preparation require water and will involve the sink. Tea kettles, coffee pots, a pasta pot, sauce pans and several small appliances will be brought to the sink to be filled with water. A pot filler faucet at a range or cooktop may reduce the need to complete these tasks at the sink.

- Mixing and combining ingredients that will be served or cooked is a basic food preparation task that should occur near the sink. Ingredients need to be retrieved from where they are stored in cabinets or the refrigerator. Mixing bowls, casserole dishes or other pots, pans and utensils must be brought to the food preparation area. A recipe (often in a cookbook) might be used. Water is often used as an ingredient and will be measured at the sink and brought to where food items are being prepared.

Used boxes and cans will need to go in the trash or recycling. Besides all the storage that is needed near this area, a large work surface or counter area will be needed for all of the equipment and ingredients for this task.

- After some foods have been cooked using water, the water will be drained from the pot or pan into the sink. A colander or strainer may be used in this process.

Cleanup Activities

- Stacking dirty pots and pans often occurs during the food preparation process. Some cooks wash or put dirty items in the dishwasher as they are preparing the food, but others will get the dirty dishes close to or in the sink and go on to the next task. If they make it to the sink, dirty pots and pans can soak, if needed.

- In the cleanup process, several steps are likely to occur. Food is usually scraped off of dirty dishes (including pots and pans) into the trash, garage disposer and/or compost container.

- After scraping, dishes go into the dishwasher. Most dishwashers are designed so that the dishes should not be rinsed before being cleaned, but rinsing is a fairly ingrained habit in many households. Dishwashers come in a variety of sizes (18, 24 and 30 inches) and have cycles for a variety of cleaning situations. The dishwasher will require detergent and other additives.

- Once the dishes are cleaned, they may stay in the dishwasher for awhile, but eventually the dishwasher is unloaded and the dishes are put away. Storing dishes, glassware and flatware close to the dishwasher can make putting things away more convenient.

- Some items will require hand washing rather than being placed in the dishwasher. Small households may find it more convenient to hand wash dishes. Hand dishwashing will require detergents, a drain board, dish towels and other items, such as scrubbers.

Other Activities

- Getting a glass of water is a common activity that occurs at the kitchen sink. Water filters and hot water dispensers might be added conveniences for preparing beverages. Glasses, mugs and drink mixes probably need to be stored close by.

- Taking medications in the kitchen was an activity of over 70% of the households surveyed in the Virginia Tech research. Often this will occur at the sink, so planning for medicine storage in this center might be important if this is the pattern in the client's household.

- Sometimes the sink center might be used for other household activities like arranging flowers, repotting and watering plants. The sink might be the water source for some hobby and craft projects. The sink can sometime become important for household cleaning projects like hand laundry, mopping floors and other scrubbing. While we might like separate areas for these activities, often they occur at the kitchen sink.

Recommendations

Placement. Because the sink center is the most used space in the kitchen, place it in a central and accessible spot. Plan to locate the sink in between or across from the major cooking area and the refrigeration storage area.

In traditional kitchens, a window was often planned at the sink so that a view to the outdoors was available while the cook worked at the sink. This made sense in kitchens before dishwashers when a lot of time was spent standing at the sink during clean up. And it can also be appropriate in today's kitchens if a view to the outdoors is desired, or when the cook is supervising children in outdoor play.

A sink placed so that the cook can look into the social areas of an open kitchen may also be appropriate. Sinks placed on an island or peninsula encourage the cook to interact with family and guests, supervise homework or watch television.

The sink drain line must be vented in order to work properly and meet building code requirements. Information on venting options is presented in *Kitchen & Bath Systems*.

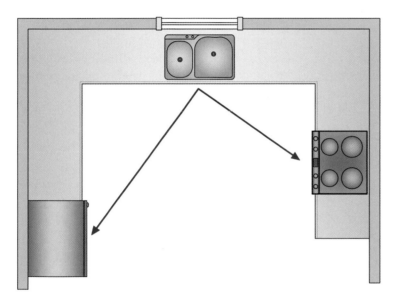

Figure 7.26 If a kitchen has only one sink, it should be adjacent to, or across from, the cooking surface and the refrigerator. (Kitchen Planning Guideline 10)

Landing Area. A certain amount of counter space is needed within each center to serve as a place to put some of the things used there. This is called a landing area.

By definition, a landing area will need to be at least 16 inches deep and between 28 inches and 48 inches above the finished floor. It is measured along the front edge of the countertop. Because base cabinets are usually about 24 inches deep, the back 8 inches will be available for storing items that are regularly or temporarily kept at the center, but this area is not needed for the counter area to count as a landing area. Clearance will be needed above the landing area to fully access it and to complete tasks. At least 15 inches of clearance will be needed above the landing area for it to count as useable countertop frontage.

The minimum landing area requirements at the sink are 24 inches on one side and 18 inches on the other. It is not important which side of the sink the areas are on, as long as they are immediately adjacent and on the left and right side of the sink.

The landing area will be used for some of the food preparation tasks mentioned above: a place to sit the pot while the water is being turned on, or where the washed vegetables will be placed or peeled. The landing area will also be important during clean up since the dirty dishes might be located to one side, or the drain board has to be set on the counter. More generous landing areas might be required to meet the cooking needs for some clients.

Figure 7.27 Plan 24 inches of landing area to one side of the primary sink and 18 inches on the other side. (Kitchen Planning Guideline 11)

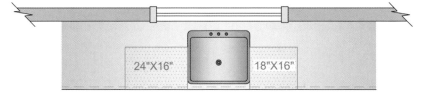

24"X16"   18"X16"

If the sink is placed near the corner of the kitchen arrangement, then the 24 inches landing area can be located on the adjacent arm of the counter. Plan 3 inches of countertop frontage between the sink and the corner and then plan at least 21 inches of countertop frontage beside the corner. A sink in or near a corner may restrict access to the sink to just one person at a time and may not be a good choice for a two-cook kitchen, unless a second sink is also planned.

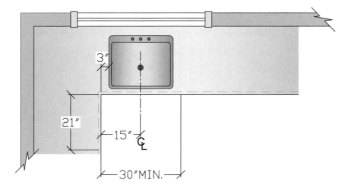

Figure 7.28 The 24 inches of recommended landing area can be met by planning 3 inches of countertop frontage from the edge of the sink to the inside corner of the countertop if more than 21 inches of countertop frontage is available on the return.

If the countertop areas adjacent to the sink are at different heights, then there should be a minimum 24 inches to one side of the sink and 3 inches on the other at the same height as the sink. For example, if a raised dishwasher is being planned next to the sink on a lowered work area to include the sink, then there should be at least 3 inches between the sink and the raised area. The raised area will have to serve as the other landing area. Having only 3 inches between the sink and a vertical surface might cause some problems with water spray and splash, so the designer should consider finishing this surface with water-resistant materials.

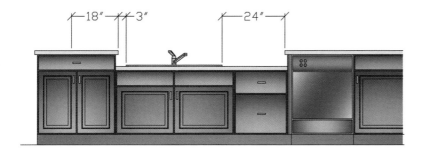

Figure 7.29 When raising the countertop at the primary sink, allow for 24 inches of landing area adjacent to the sink and at the same height. Allow 3 inches on the other side of the sink, before the countertop height changes. (Kitchen Planning Guideline 11)

Preparation Area. Counter space will be needed immediately next to the sink for mixing and other preparation activities. This will serve as the primary preparation/work area.

The recommended size is at least 36 inches measured along the countertop frontage and 24 inches deep. Figure 7.30 illustrates the typical area required for a preparation area. The cook will primarily work within the smaller arc of 16 inches, but will be able to reach the larger arc of 24 inches. Therefore the requirement for the preparation area is deeper than the landing area requirements because a cook will use the complete depth of the counter for assembled ingredients and work in the front area.

Figure 7.30 At least one preparation area should be planned in the kitchen. It must be 36 inches wide and 24 inches deep to allow 16 inches for a clear work area and 8 inches for storage.

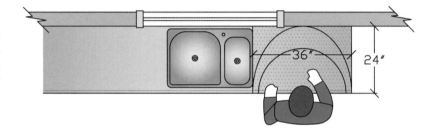

When planning a kitchen for two cooks, consider how they might use the preparation area. Research has shown that at least two different cooking patterns occur with two cooks. With the student-teacher cooking pattern, one cook helps another. This might occur when a mom helps children bake cookies or one roommate shows the other how to bake lasagna. A preparation area of 60 to 72 inches is needed for two persons to stand together to work on one task.

Independent cooks work on separate recipes or foods at the same time. Two separate preparation areas, each at least 36 inches, need to be planned for these cooks. When multiple preparation areas are planned, consider varying the heights and providing a knee space to accommodate different cooks.

Special Preparation Areas. Sometimes a client may request special features to help in a particular task. In each of these cases, the designer must use the information gained from client interviews to shape the design solution.

• **Baking.** A baking area is the dream of any cook who likes to regularly prepare breads, rolls, cakes, pastries, pies and tarts. A specialized baking center is a secondary center and should include storage and 36 inches to 54 inches of counter space for mixing and baking tasks. Store specialized equipment, including mixing bowls, measuring cups and utensils, pans, rolling pins and ingredients close by.

Small appliances like blenders and stand mixers are needed here and could be stored on the counter or in an appliance garage. An appliance garage or fold-up mixer stand might add to the convenience of this area. Kneading dough or rolling out pastries requires extended arm movement, so a 32-inch high counter is more ergonomically correct for average-sized users. If the baking center is not located next to the sink, then an auxiliary sink should be considered for this area. An undercounter refrigerator would be a nice addition to the baking center if the primary refrigerator is not close by.

Figure 7.31 A pop-up mixer stand is an added convenience in a baking center. (Courtesy of KraftMaid Cabinetry)

• **Seated Work Area.** Cooks may enjoy sitting to work on some
food preparation tasks, such as snapping beans or stirring a
cooked pastry cream. Cooks who use a mobility aid or have
weak legs may require areas for sitting throughout the kitchen.
A typical counter height that allows the cook to sit to work
is 32 inches. A 30-inch high table height is also appropriate.
Space beneath the counter should be provided so that legs can
pull under the counter and good posture can be maintained.
A knee space 30 inches wide minimum, 24 inches deep and 27
inches high provides room for a person in a wheelchair to
pull under the counter.

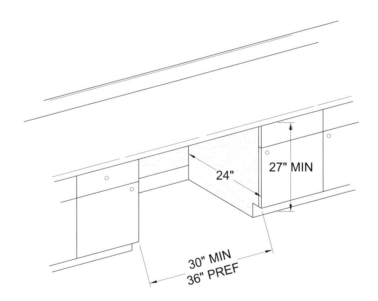

Figure 7.32 A knee space at a counter
should be at least 30 inches wide (36
inches preferred), 24 inches deep and
27 inches high.

• **Food Preservation.** Some households may conduct food
preservation tasks, such as canning, freezing and drying. Often
large quantities of fresh food are brought into the kitchen and
prepared by rinsing, chopping, peeling and shelling. Some food
is blanched, drained and cooled before being put into jars or
freezer containers. The preparation area for these tasks, at least
36 to 48 inches wide, should be located between a sink and
cooktop. Consider a surface that is acid and stain resistant.
A deep sink might be desirable and a pull-out spray or
specialized faucet for filling large pots will be needed.

Dishwasher Placement. The primary dishwasher should be placed within 36 inches of the cleanup sink. Placing the dishwasher immediately adjacent to the sink has some advantages:

- If dishes are rinsed, water is less likely to drip on the floor;

- The person can stand in one place and reach dishes stacked in or near the sink and the dishwasher; and

- The 24-inch width of the typical dishwasher assures a 24-inch countertop area above which will serve as the sink landing area.

Despite these advantages, the dishwasher may need to be moved away from the sink, but there should be no more than 36 inches from the edge of the sink to the edge of the dishwasher.

Figure 7.33 The cleanup sink and the dishwasher should be within 36 inches of each other. (Courtesy of Joyce Cessar – Gibsonia, Pennsylvania)

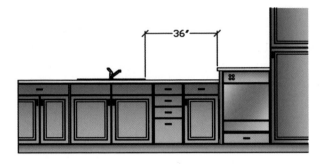

Figure 7.34 Locate nearest edge of the primary dishwasher within 36 inches of the nearest edge of a cleanup/prep sink. (Kitchen Planning Guideline 13)

Placing the dishwasher some distance from the sink might happen when the sink and dishwasher are being placed at an angle. If a right angle arrangement is being planned, the designer must allow at least 21 inches for a person to be able to stand at the dishwasher to load and unload the appliance. The standing space between the dishwasher and a perpendicular counter or wall is also needed if the dishwasher is next to the sink. The standing space is measured from the edge of the dishwasher to the countertop, cabinet or other appliance.

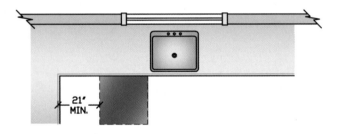

Figure 7.35 Allow 21 inches for standing space between the edge of the dishwasher and an adjacent perpendicular counter or wall. (Kitchen Planning Guideline 13)

If the sink and dishwasher are placed at an angle other than 90°, the 21 inches is measured from the middle of the sink to the edge of the dishwasher door with the door in the open position. In an installation where the sink is in the corner at a 45° angle to the dishwasher, a small cabinet will need to be specified between the sink and the dishwasher to provide for this space.

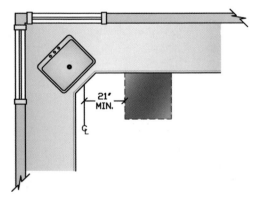

Figure 7.36 When a sink and dishwasher are placed at an angle to one another, plan a 21-inch standing space between them by measuring 21 inches from the centerline of the sink to the edge of the dishwasher. (Kitchen Planning Guideline 13)

Trash. The trash receptacle is such an ordinary thing that designers might tend to forget about it. However, it is a critical element in both food preparation and clean up and should be effectively planned into the kitchen. Recycling has also become an important activity in many homes and communities. How effective households are in their recycling behaviors can be influenced by how the designer plans for this activity (See discussion in Chapter 4). Many older kitchens were planned before this activity became common and recycling containers may be found in a closet or the garage. Today, several storage devices have been designed to handle the trash and recycling activities (See Figure 7.37).

It is recommended that the kitchen contain two waste receptacles: one for trash and one for recycling. The trash receptacle should be located near the sink and, while the recycling receptacle can be placed near the sink, it can also be planned elsewhere.

Carefully consider the client's recycling activities and patterns in order to plan the best container design and location.

A trash compactor might be desirable for some clients with large amounts of trash or without local trash collection. Some clients may also compost food waste and the designer should explore ways to plan for this activity near the sink and preparation areas.

A

B

Figure 7.37 Base cabinet pull-out bins provide effective waste and recycling storage. (a-Courtesy of Crystal Keyline, b-Courtesy of Rev-A-Shelf)

Figure 7.38 A second or auxiliary sink is handy for a variety of purposes. It should have at least an 18-inch landing area to one side and 3-inch clear space on the other. (Courtesy of Sandra L. Steiner-Houck, CKD – Columbia, Pennsylvania)

Auxiliary Sink. A second sink is often desired in today's kitchens. The auxiliary sink can be useful when more than one cook is working in the kitchen. It might be used as part of a secondary preparation area, a place to make salads or to provide water in a baking area. An auxiliary sink might also serve as part of a beverage center, where family members can get a drink of water, tea or coffee without interfering with the cook's activities.

An auxiliary sink might also be used as a cleanup sink. If placed close to the serving and dining areas and combined with a dishwasher, a second sink can keep some preparation and cleanup activities separate or provide greater convenience in the cleanup process.

An auxiliary sink can be at a lowered height to accommodate varied users. Provide a knee space below the auxiliary sink and it becomes suitable for sitting to work.

Landing areas are also necessary at the auxiliary sink. NKBA recommends at least 18 inches to one side of the sink and 3 inches of clearance on the other side. This may not be enough space for some activities that are planned at a second sink, such as major cleanup. It allows a minimum number of items to be placed next to the sink area, so plan for more space if major activities will occur at the auxiliary sink. Often, available landing area is limited at an auxiliary sink. When this is the case, moving the sink to 8 inches from one end of the landing space will improve the overall function of the landing space on the other side.

The Kitchen Planning Guidelines and Access Standards that are particularly relevant to the sink area are Guidelines 11, 12, 13, 14 and 15. They can be found in Chapter 12.

REFRIGERATION CENTER

The refrigeration center can be considered a somewhat passive center. The main activity is storing food items in the refrigerator and freezer. An organized cook may only go to the refrigerator one or two times while preparing a food item, taking out all of the ingredients needed for preparation at one time. A chaotic cook will likely go to the refrigerator several times to take out items one-by-one as needed. It is probably true that having the refrigerator close to food preparation areas is much more important to the chaotic cook than the organized cook, because the trips to the refrigerator may be numerous and tiring if it is placed too far away.

The refrigerator will also be used when ingredients and leftovers are stored. Again this may require several trips or only a few, depending on the cooking style and number of items. Often storage containers for leftovers are kept near the refrigerator, which is a logical place for them. Somehow those plastic freezer cups and containers seem to multiply and can overrun allocated space fairly quickly. Plan accordingly.

Recommendations

Placement. The refrigeration center is often placed at one end of a kitchen work arrangement. The typically tall unit will not interfere with other work areas if it is placed at the end of the workflow, and often this will make it more accessible to family members getting beverages or preparing to serve the table. However, avoid placing the refrigerator directly beside a wall. There may not be room to open the refrigerator door beyond 90°, making it difficult to access the interior for storage and cleaning. If a refrigerator must be placed adjacent to a wall, plan additional space between the refrigerator and the wall to provide room for the door swing.

Make sure there is adequate floor space in front of the refrigerator for the door to swing open and for a user to maneuver in front of, and around, it. In some wider built-in units this could be as much as 48 inches of clear floor space.

Because the refrigerator is most often used in food preparation, it is a good idea to place a preparation area next to the refrigerator. Remember, the 36-inch primary preparation area could be placed between the sink and the refrigerator, or a secondary preparation area could be planned there.

Undercounter style refrigerators allow for placing multiple refrigerators in multiple locations, adding flexibility and improving access. A refrigeration unit might be placed in an area where salads and vegetables are regularly prepared. Or a small unit for beverages might be placed close to the serving area of the kitchen and completely out of the food preparation areas. Wine coolers and beer kegs can help make entertaining convenient. Refrigerator drawers may be particularly useful for placing cold food storage at a height that does not require bending.

The style of refrigerator should be selected based on volume and access needs of the household, as well as the general parameters of the space.

Figure 7.39 Undercounter refrigerators are conveniently located in a prep area in this kitchen. (Courtesy of Tom Trzcinski, CMKBD – Pittsburgh, Pennsylvania)

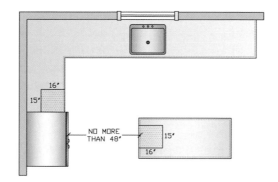

Figure 7.40 A 15-inch landing area can be located beside the refrigerator or on a counter no more than 48 inches across from the refrigerator. (Kitchen Planning Guideline 16)

Landing Area. The landing area at the refrigerator should be a minimum 15 inches wide, measured as countertop frontage. (Remember a landing area is at least 16 inches deep.) The placement of the landing area can vary depending on the style of refrigerator used. It should be on the door handle side of a top or bottom mount refrigerator-freezer, so that when the refrigerator door is open, an item can be transferred from the refrigerator to the landing area without interference of an open door. In a side-by-side refrigerator, the 15-inch landing area can be located on either (or both) side(s), since both refrigerator and freezer doors are narrow. Because most food will be removed from the refrigerator side of the unit, it is probably best if a landing area is on the freezer side, but other planning considerations may indicate the opposite.

NKBA guidelines allow a landing area to be placed on a counter or island across from the refrigerator. The landing area must be within 48 inches measured from the front of the appliance to the edge of the landing area. This will allow the user to remove an item and turn to place it on the landing area. It is probably not as convenient as a landing area next to the refrigerator, but it is manageable for most users.

If undercounter refrigerators are used, a landing space 15 inches wide by 16 inches deep should be planned above the refrigeration unit.

The Kitchen Planning Guideline and Access Standard that is particularly relevant to the refrigeration center is Guideline 16 which can be found in Chapter 12.

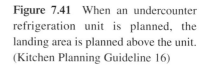

Figure 7.41 When an undercounter refrigeration unit is planned, the landing area is planned above the unit. (Kitchen Planning Guideline 16)

243

COOKING CENTERS

While the sink center may be the most frequently used area in the kitchen, the cooking center or centers may be the true heart of the kitchen. People who love to cook will be very particular about the types and features of cooking appliances. They find true self-expression in their cooking techniques, and the quality of the final outcome of the food product and planning for this task is important. How do we cook?

- **Surface Cooking** – This refers to cooking that is taking place on the top of the range or on the cooktop. Frying, sautéing, steaming and boiling are typical methods of surface cooking. This type of cooking often requires high user interaction. Foods need to be turned and stirred. Ingredients need to be added. Often people check on the progress of the cooking and increase or decrease the amount of heat used. Pots, frying pans, spoons and spatulas are all needed at this area.

- **Oven Cooking** – Typical cooking in the oven includes baking, roasting and broiling. This may occur in the oven cavity of a range, or in a separate oven placed in a tall cabinet or under the counter. Ovens may include convection, microwave, speed or steam options. Often oven cooking is a passive activity, with the cook pre-heating the oven, putting the food in the oven, setting a timer and periodically checking on progress before it is done and removed from the oven. Various roasting and baking pans, casserole dishes and cookie sheets are used here. Hot pads, basters, meat forks and other utensils are needed.

- **Microwave Cooking** – Over 96% of households have a microwave and use it in a variety of ways. Some use it as part of the food preparation process—melting butter or boiling water. Others use it to prepare frozen foods for eating or to re-heat leftovers. Still others use it as a major cooking appliance, following microwave recipes for casseroles or other dishes.

  The way the microwave is used will determine where it should be located, what types of items are used with it and whether a second microwave is appropriate. There may be special cookware used to cook in the microwave or the same glass dishes used in the oven might be appropriate. Plates, mugs and measuring cups all might be used in microwave cooking.

- **Speed Cooking** – Several new appliances offer higher speed cooking that combines microwave with convection or light. These ovens may be used like a separate oven or a microwave.

- **Small Appliances** – Numerous small appliances perform some specialized cooking and may be important to the client. Toaster ovens are frequently used in small households to bake rolls or other items. Countertop grills may be used to prepare a hamburger or steak. Toasters, waffle irons and electric frying pans or griddles may also provide some specialized cooking. Most of the small appliances are placed on the countertop when they are in use, and various types of equipment will be needed, depending on the cooking tasks.

Recommendations

Planning the cooking center is more complicated today than in the past when the range was the only cooking appliance. With one appliance to anchor the center, it was relatively easy to plan work surfaces and storage that would surround the place of all cooking activities. Today it is typical to have several cooking appliances, so some of the recommendations must apply to several cooking areas. The recommendations for this center have been arranged according to the type of cooking.

Surface Cooking. Because of the interaction between the surface cooking appliance and food preparation tasks, this area is often considered the primary cooking center.

- **Placement.** It should be located with consideration to the other centers, particularly the sink center. Cooks will move most frequently between the sink and the cooktop, and there should be a clear uninterrupted path between these two areas. This means that the cooking surface will often be placed beside, or across from, the sink.

  Safety is a major concern at the cooking surface because there is danger of scalds, burns and fire. Several recommendations have been developed to keep this a safe area.

  Consider the location and design of appliance controls. Controls placed at the back of the appliance may mean that the cook must reach over hot and steaming pots to adjust cooking temperatures, and should be avoided when possible. Controls placed at the front edge of the range provide easy access to seated cooks, but might tempt small children to manipulate them, if they are easily manipulated. Controls on the top of the appliance and/or to the side, improve access to most users. Designers and clients are responsible for selecting products that consider the safety needs of all users.

Figure 7.42 The cooktop and sink are placed at a right angle to one another in this kitchen arrangement. A preparation area separates the two. (Courtesy of Aristokraft)

If the sink is on an island, there may be a desire to place the cooktop beneath the window, the traditional sink placement area. If this is done, the window should not be operable. Trying to open a window by reaching over hot pots is not safe and drafts from the window can affect cooking performance and safety. Fixed windows or a glass block area might be a solution, but consider how hard this area will be to clean. Your client may not thank you. If an inoperable window area is used, then any window treatment should not be of a flammable material, which could be a fire hazard.

Figure 7.43 The controls on this cooktop are located in the center, making them easy to reach, and convenient for two cooks to use at one time. (Courtesy of GE)

UNACCEPTABLE   ACCEPTABLE

Finally, plan a fire extinguisher in or near the kitchen. It should not be placed next to the cooking surface or oven because it may not be accessible if there is a fire. Place it close to an exit, in an accessible place and within the 15- to 48-inch reach range.

- **Landing area.** There should be a landing area on both sides of a cooking surface. Not only does the landing area allow for a place to put spoons, pot lids and ingredients to be added, it also provides a space to turn pot handles so that they are not hit by passing traffic. Unless the countertop is a heat resistant material, the landing area is not a place to put hot pots, unless it is an emergency.

There should be a minimum of 15 inches of counter frontage on one side of the range and 12 inches on the other. If there are various counter heights at the range, the 12- and 15-inch landing areas should be the same height as the cooking surface.

If the cooking surface is on an island or a peninsula that is the same height as the cooking surface, then there should also be 9 inches of counter space behind the cooking surface to prevent handles being hit and hot spatters getting onto people standing or sitting behind the cooking surface.

Occasionally, in a small kitchen, a cooking surface will be placed next to a wall or tall obstacle. This should only be done if it is in accordance with manufacturer's instructions for clearances. This closed configuration will not provide an adequate landing area on one side of the cooking center and can restrict the size of pots that will fit on the cooking surface. If no other configuration can be used, then fire retardant and easy-to-clean wall materials will be necessary.

Figure 7.44 Placing a window behind a cooking surface may mean it is difficult to clean, but it is acceptable to put a non-operable window behind the cooking surface. An operable window and/or a flammable window treatment are dangerous (Kitchen Planning Guideline 20).

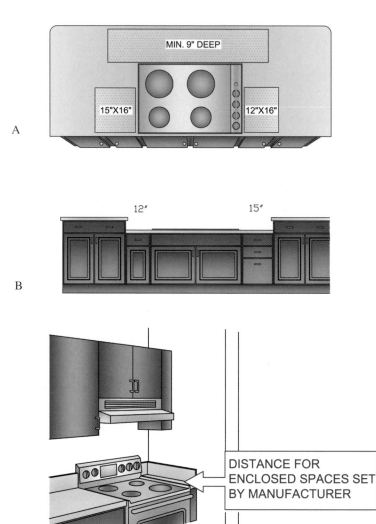

Figure 7.45 A 12- and 15-inch landing area should be planned beside the cooking surface. a) If the cooking surface is on an open island or peninsula at the same height then 9 inches of counter area should be planned behind it. b) If the cooking surface is at a height different from the other counter heights, the 12- and 15-inch landing areas should be planned at the same height as the cooking surface. (Kitchen Planning Guideline 17)

Figure 7.46 If a range or cooktop is placed close to a wall, make sure manufacturer's specifications for clearances are followed (Kitchen Planning Guideline 17)

- **Ventilation and Clearances.** A ventilation system is required for surface cooking. There are several different types of systems available. It is important that the designer match the ventilation system with the features of the surface cooking appliance. More information about ventilation systems is detailed in Chapter 8.

  Besides planning the size and style of ventilation, the designer must plan the placement of the ventilation system. Different cooking and ventilation appliance systems may have different requirements and manufacturer's specifications should always be followed.

A typical arrangement calls for placing the range hood over the cooking surface. Ideally, the hood should extend at least 3 inches beyond the cooking surface on both sides. A range hood is made of non-flammable materials and is fireproof. It should be placed at least 24 inches above the cooking surface. For a typical application, this would place the bottom of the hood at 60 inches. The eye height for a small woman is about 53 inches and for a tall man it is 69 inches. Consider the client's eye height and overall height when planning the hood placement, so that it does not interfere with the user's view and access to the cooking surface. If a microwave with built-in ventilation is placed above the range, follow manufacturer's instructions for correct clearance.

A proximity ventilation system is located either as part of the cooking appliance or within the counter next to, or behind, the cooking appliance. This type of system allows for a clear open space above the cooking appliance and might be used on an island or peninsula. Check cooktop and ventilation system manufacturer's specifications for placement and to determine counter depth. A telescoping system placed behind the cooktop may affect the specifications of base cabinets in this area. A cabinet or other flammable object placed above the cooking surface with proximity ventilation should be at least 30 inches above the cooking surface, while a protected or fireproof surface can be at 24 inches.

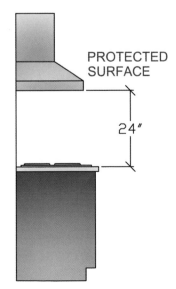

PROTECTED SURFACE

24"

Figure 7.47 A protected surface should be at least 24 inches above the cooking surface (Kitchen Planning Guideline 18). This would accommodate a range hood that is 18 inches deep or more without interfering with the average standing cook's line of vision.

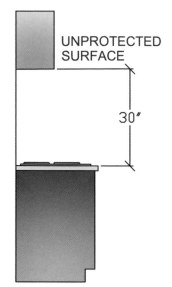

UNPROTECTED
SURFACE

30″

Figure 7.48 Cabinets placed over a range with proximity ventilation must be at least 30 inches above the cooking surface (Kitchen Planning Guideline 18).

Microwave Cooking. As mentioned previously, people use the microwave for a variety of cooking tasks, which can determine where the microwave should be placed in the kitchen.

- **Placement.** It might be suitable to place the microwave next to the refrigerator if it will primarily be used to defrost food and reheat leftovers. It could also be placed within a preparation area that is between the sink and refrigerator. This would be convenient for defrosting, reheating and some food preparation tasks.

  Other locations are more suitable for a microwave, microwave/convection combination or speed cooking appliance used for major cooking tasks. In this case, the microwave should be part of the primary cooking center. Placing the microwave in a preparation area that is between the sink and surface cooking appliance might be suitable for creating a primary cooking center with food preparation activities.

  A microwave combined with a ventilation system is sometimes placed over a cooking surface, placing both appliances at the anchor point of the primary cooking center. This can be efficient in a small kitchen, since the microwave is not taking up counter space or cabinet storage. However, the microwave will not be at a height that is safe and convenient for some users, and the ventilation system may not be adequate. There is one range designed with the microwave in a drawer above the range oven. This locates the microwave in the primary cooking center, but at a safer height.

  A microwave may be located with the wall oven in a cabinet, creating a secondary cooking center and in this case, the cook's height should be carefully considered. This might be appropriate if the microwave is used in ways similar to the oven. If the microwave cooking process will require frequent checking by the cook, the appliance should not be located outside of the cook's work area.

  If the microwave is used for preparing snacks and is not part of the regular food preparation or cooking activities, it might be placed outside of the cook's work area and convenient to users who prepare snacks.

Figure 7.49 Microwaves can be placed in several locations in the kitchen. a) The microwave is on the counter, concealed in a cabinet with a flip-up door. b) The microwave pulls out like a drawer. c) The microwave is placed below the countertop and is concealed with flipper doors. (a-Courtesy of Tom Trzcinski, CMKBD, Pittsburgh, Pennsylvania; b-Courtesy of Sharp and c-Courtesy of Amana.)

A

B

C

• **Placement Height.** Research has indicated the best body mechanics for using the microwave is for the bottom of the microwave oven to be placed no lower than 2 inches below a primary user's elbow and no higher than 3 inches below the primary user's shoulder height. This will allow the user to see into the microwave to observe food cooking, to see the controls (which often require a visual confirmation of settings) and it will provide for appropriate leverage when taking hot food out of the oven. NKBA recommends that the bottom of the microwave be placed no higher than 3 inches below the user's shoulder height.

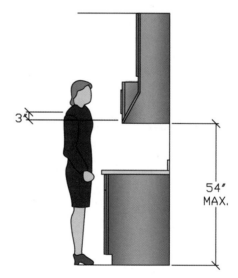

Figure 7.50 The bottom of the microwave oven should be placed no higher than 3 inches below the user's shoulder height (Kitchen Planning Guideline 21).

As a general interpretation of this recommendation, the NKBA guideline states that the bottom of the microwave should be placed no more than 54 inches off the floor. This will allow a microwave to be placed on the bottom shelf of a wall cabinet. However, this is not a good location if the user's shoulder height is below 57 inches or if the user has any problem with upper body strength.

If placing the microwave over the cooking surface, follow the manufacturer's instructions for clearances. Keep in mind that 24 inches between the cooking surface and a protected surface is recommended by NKBA, putting the bottom of the microwave at 60 inches, which is 6 inches above the maximum shoulder height recommendation.

However, more important than either of these recommended distances are the safety concerns of this application. Reaching over hot and steaming food on the cooktop can be dangerous for anyone, but especially if someone cannot see what they are getting. Also, there is not a convenient counter space below the microwave to place a hot food item.

Sometimes a microwave is placed below a raised or even a standard height counter. This might be appropriate for children or people working from a seated position, again improving access but requiring added attention to safety for toddlers. However, this application may require others to stoop and bend to read controls and to take food out of the oven. NKBA allows for this type of installation, but the bottom of the oven should not be below 15 inches off the floor.

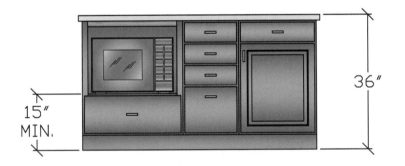

Figure 7.51 A microwave can be placed below a 36-inch high counter, when the bottom of the shelf is at least 15 inches off the floor. This may be suitable placement for a seated user or for children (Kitchen Planning Guideline 21).

Who the users of the microwave are and how they use the microwave will really determine the appropriate placement of the appliance. Make sure you understand the clients' functional requirements (shoulder height, upper body strength, eye height) and their use of the microwave (preparing snacks, cooking casseroles, prepping ingredients) when you plan the placement of the microwave. An arrangement that works for a family with teenage boys might not work for an older couple with physical limitations or a young family with toddlers.

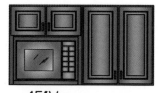

15"W
X
16"D

A

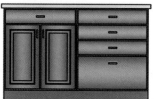
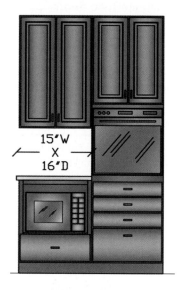

15"W
X
16"D

B

15"W
X
16"D

Figure 7.52 The landing area for the microwave should be at least 15 inches wide and planned a) below, b) above or c) beside, the unit. (Kitchen Planning Guideline 22)

C

- **Landing Area.** Wherever the microwave is placed, a 15-inch landing area should be provided above, below or adjacent to the microwave oven. Most microwaves have handles on the right and, ideally, the landing area should be on that side, but it is not always possible to do that. If a landing area is located across from the microwave, it should be within 48 inches of the front of the appliance. Remember all landing areas are between 28 and 45 inches above the finished floor, so evaluate where the landing area will be when a microwave is placed in a 48-inch high cabinet.

Oven Cooking. Oven cooking is a somewhat passive cooking activity, meaning the food is generally prepared in a preparation area and then placed in the oven. Often a timer is set and the cook might come back when the timer goes off. Of course, some foods and cooking techniques, such as broiling, should be more closely watched and the cook will return to check on progress.

- **Placement.** With a range, the oven will be in the primary cooking center and easy for the cook to observe. It is often the client's preference and the only choice for a small kitchen. Some separate ovens are also placed beneath the surface cooking appliance, in the same location as the range oven or below a counter. These applications place the bottom of the oven at an inconvenient height for many people, making bending and lifting difficult.

  A separate oven can be placed outside of the primary cooking center, because the cook is not constantly going to the appliance. This might be at one end of the work area or on a separate wall. Be sure to evaluate traffic in this secondary area, to avoid creating a hazardous situation. The oven door should not open into a traffic path.

  A separate oven can be placed at a height that is more convenient to the user. A single oven placed with the bottom of the oven at 30 to 36 inches above the floor allows food to be transferred between the oven and a counter at a similar height. Double ovens typically will have the lower oven at a similar height to a range oven. Today, we are seeing two separate ovens designed at comfortable heights, when space allows. The result is that both ovens can be at a height that places controls no higher than 48 inches and yet high enough to reduce bending.

• **Landing Area.** The landing area for an oven is 15 inches and can be placed on either side of the oven. This can coincide with the landing area required for a cooking surface if a range or oven beneath a cooking surface is used. The landing area can be located across from the oven as long as it is within 48 inches of the front of the oven. A major traffic path should not pass in front of the oven if the landing area is across from oven.

The Kitchen Planning Guidelines and Access Standards that are particularly relevant to the cooking center are Guidelines 17, 21, 22 and 23 which appear in Chapter 12.

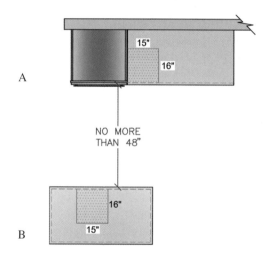

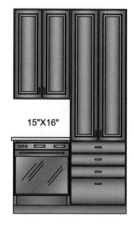

Figure 7.53 The landing area for a separate oven should be 15 inches wide and placed a) beside the oven, b) on a counter across from the oven, as long as this is not a major traffic path or c) on a counter above the oven.

Arranging the Centers

As the designer lays out the kitchen, the work flow of the client should be a major consideration in deciding where to place the work centers. An obvious and simple work flow is as follows:

Gather $\rightarrow$ Prepare $\rightarrow$ Cook $\rightarrow$ Serve $\rightarrow$ Cleanup

Of course, putting a meal together is a series of these steps with back steps, but this basic work flow has been instrumental in our thinking about how to arrange the work centers in kitchens. The work starts by gathering food from the refrigeration center, then moves to a preparation area near the sink center, and then moves to the cooking center. A serving area and eating space (covered in more detail in the next section) should be next and then, after the meal, it all goes back to the main sink center or an additional sink/cleanup zone.

A convenient way to incorporate the basic work flow is to remember the work triangle. The work triangle refers to the placement of the refrigerator, sink and range in a three-point arrangement. The idea has been around for many years and the consumer seems familiar and comfortable with the concept.

The introduction of additional major appliances, multiple cooks, and other activities has compounded the work triangle. Where does a separate oven or microwave go in the triangle? What about a kitchen with two sinks or two dishwashers? What happens when multiple refrigeration units are placed within centers? We can have multiple work centers or even multiple triangles often referred to as activity zones.

Because work patterns in the kitchen continue in the traditional order, NKBA continues to recommend using the three primary centers as points for the work triangle. As previously mentioned, the primary sink center should be in between the refrigeration center and the primary cooking center (surface cooking).

Planning for Two Cooks. The work triangle was originally conceived and applied to one cook, but in many households more than one cook works in the kitchen. Research has shown that in two-thirds of households, one cook still prepares most of the meals. In the other third, two cooks take turns cooking or cook together most of the time. Even when there is only one cook, entertaining and special occasions may bring in additional people to help with some tasks.

When two cooks prepare food together, the work triangle is affected and special consideration should be given to the concept of multiple zones. This is particularly true with independent cooks preparing separate food items at the same time. An auxiliary sink will be an important feature to have, since it will reduce congestion that would occur if there is only a single, primary sink.

If the auxiliary sink is one point on a second triangle, then other points might be the refrigerator and a secondary cooking center, such as the microwave, oven or grill. When two triangles are planned, examine the relationships carefully in order to avoid as much overlapping traffic as possible.

Distance. One of the most beneficial aspects of the work triangle concept is that it provides guidelines for the distance between the various centers. Each leg of the triangle should be no less than 4 feet and no more than 9 feet long. These distances assure that there will be some storage and counter space between each center, but that the distance is not so great that roller skates are needed to move from one center to the other. The sum of the three legs of the triangle should not total more than 26 feet. A work triangle leg should not intersect an island or peninsula by more than 12 inches. The distances of the leg should be measured from the center of the refrigerator, sink, range or other affected appliance.

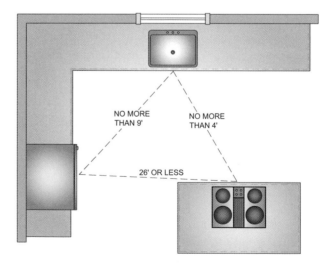

Figure 7.54 Plan the primary work centers in the kitchen so that each center is only 4 to 9 feet away from another center (Kitchen Planning Guideline 3).

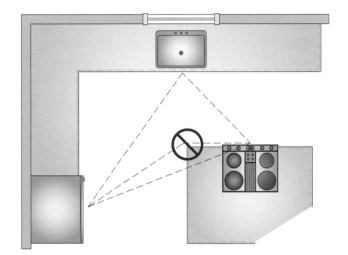

Figure 7.55 Measure the work triangle from the middle of the appliance or fixture located in the center. Measure around a counter, if the triangle leg will intersect with the counter by more than 12 inches. (Kitchen Planning Guideline 3)

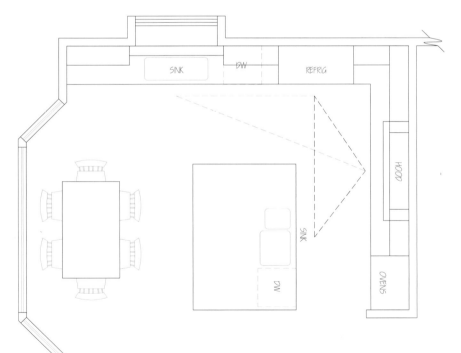

Figure 7.56 This kitchen incorporates a large preparation sink and dishwasher into the primary work triangle, and also includes a cleanup sink area with dishwasher. This fourth primary center separates the two major tasks that occur at the sink.

Separation of Centers. No tall cabinets or appliances should interfere with the work flow between any two primary work centers. The cook should be able to move items along the countertop without having to pull back and around tall features. For example, a pantry or wall oven should be placed outside the work area, not within the work triangle that connects the primary centers.

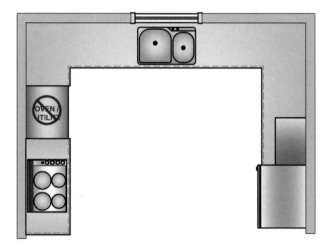

Figure 7.57 Place tall obstacles, such as a pantry or wall oven, outside the work triangle (Kitchen Planning Guideline 4).

If a wall cabinet is brought down to the counter, it is not considered a tall unit and it would not interfere with the work flow. Corner applications of tall units also are permissible if the corner cabinet is recessed back from the counter area. These applications still provide for clear movement of the work flow.

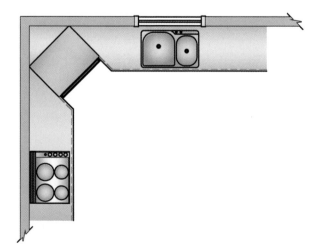

Figure 7.58 Tall corner cabinets within the work triangle are acceptable if they are recessed back from the counter edge (Kitchen Planning Guideline 4).

Traffic Interference. No traffic should interfere with the basic work triangle. Traffic interrupts the movements of the cook(s) and is dangerous if cooks are moving with hot pots and pans. Careful consideration should be given if two cooks will be working in the kitchen at the same time, so that major traffic between primary centers is not frequently interrupted. Remember to plan work aisles of 48 inches or greater to ease circulation.

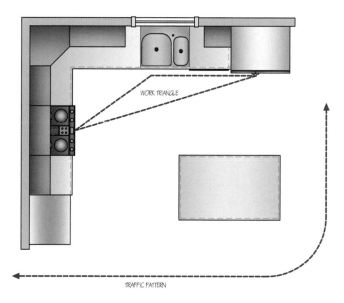

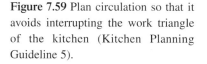

Figure 7.59 Plan circulation so that it avoids interrupting the work triangle of the kitchen (Kitchen Planning Guideline 5).

Counter Areas

The counter area is a critical element for working in the kitchen. Insufficient counter space is a common complaint for many people who have not yet remodeled their kitchen. Counter areas are used for landing space, preparation/work and storage. Carefully review the client's needs for counter space and storage.

Combining Landing Areas. Each center has minimum landing area requirements. Remember a landing area specification is given as countertop frontage—at least 16 inches deep and between 28 and 45 inches high.

- Sink – 24 inches and 18 inches

- Refrigerator – 15 inches

- Cooking surface – 15 inches and 12 inches

- Microwave – 15 inches

- Wall oven – 15 inches

Landing areas located beside each other can be combined. To calculate the minimum distance in a combined arrangement, take the longest specified landing area in the two centers and add 12 inches. For example, if a sink center and refrigeration center are next to each other, a minimum amount of landing area for the two centers is calculated by adding the 24-inch landing area of the sink (the longest one) and 12 inches (rather than 15 inches). Therefore, a 36-inch area should be planned. If the landing areas from the sink and range are combined on the other side of the sink, the combination would again use the 24-inch landing area from the sink as the longest landing area and 12 inches would be added.

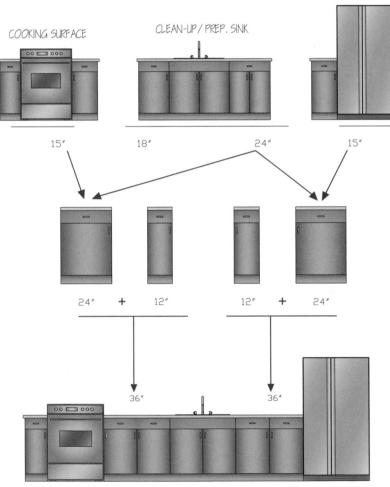

Figure 7.60 When combining two landing areas side-by-side, use the measurement from the largest landing area and add 12 inches (Kitchen Planning Guideline 24).

Total Counter Area. While the landing areas give the cook some space to place items temporarily and to complete a few tasks, they do not fulfill all of the requirements of the counter area. A preparation area should be provided near the sink, and it should be a minimum 36 inches wide by 24 inches deep, so that at least one useable work area is provided. This area could overlay the landing areas of the sink and refrigerator centers, if the landing areas are 24 inches deep.

Counter area is also used for storage in nearly all kitchens. For example, the counter area provided 10% of the total storage in the small kitchens in the Virginia Tech research. The number of items kept on the counter decreased in larger kitchens, since more cabinet and drawer storage was available. Although the idea of a clean counter appeals to many, in reality households keep a lot of frequently used things out on the counter, where they are easy to see and reach. Often items like heavy appliances or canisters stay on the counter. The back 8 inches of a 24-inch deep counter provides space that can be used for permanent and temporary storage.

NKBA recommends that at least 158 inches of countertop frontage be provided in the kitchen work area to accommodate landing areas, preparation areas and storage. This frontage should be 24 inches deep, so if any landing areas were planned at only 16 inches, such as with mantles at the cooking surface, those areas can not count toward the countertop frontage. There should also be at least a 15-inch clear space above the counter so that a cook can work there.

- **Appliance Garage.** When an appliance garage is placed so that it is parallel to countertop frontage, it can be counted within the total counter frontage, because it is storage. It can not be placed where landing areas and preparation areas are specified, because it would interfere with the depth of counter space needed for these areas. An appliance garage in the corner would not be affected by this calculation because it does not parallel countertop frontage, and none of the corner counter area counts as countertop frontage.

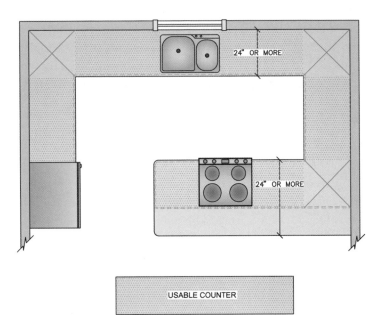

24" OR MORE

24" OR MORE

USABLE COUNTER

Figure 7.61 Plan 158 inches of counter area to accommodate landing areas, a preparation area and storage (Kitchen Planning Guideline 25).

Figure 7.62 An appliance garage can be placed on the counter within the 158 inches of counter space, as long as it does not interfere with landings and preparation areas (Kitchen Planning Guideline 25).

Counter Design. Consider several factors when planning the counter surface. Specify heat-resistant materials at the cooking surface and oven landing areas. Non-glare materials will make the work surface easier to see. Materials that provide a color contrast at the counter edge, or between the counter and the floor, may be easier for people with vision problems to see. Task lighting at the counter area will make it easier for everyone to see their work. See Chapter 8 for more information on lighting requirements and recommendations. Counter edges should be rounded or clipped so that there are not sharp edges to bump into.

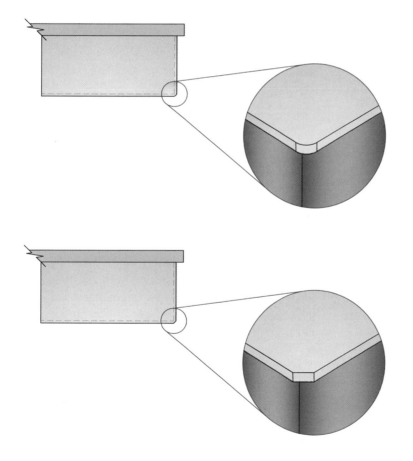

Figure 7.63 Counter edges should be rounded or clipped for safety (Kitchen Planning Guideline 26).

Storage

All of the food preparation tasks discussed thus far have required "things"—fresh, canned and boxed foods; equipment and utensils; pots and pans; mixing bowls and baking dishes; dishwashing detergent and dish drainers and many, many more. All of these things (and the things we need for dining and entertaining and managing the home) need a place to stay. The following storage principles should help the designer plan where, and what types of, storage should be provided in the kitchen to meet a client's needs.

- **Store items at point of first or last use.** Glassware could be stored close to the refrigerator and coffee mugs near the coffee pot. Or they could both be stored near the dishwasher, the point of last use in the cleanup process.

- **Store items in duplicate locations, if needed.** Hot pads should be stored next to the cooktop and the wall oven.

- **Items that are used together should be stored together.** Measuring cups and measuring spoons should be in the same drawer.

- **Items should be stored so they are easy to see.** Placing spices in a rack at eye level will make it easier to find the right one.

- **Frequently used items should be stored so they are easy to reach.** Leaving the coffeepot on the counter may be a good idea, if coffee is prepared every morning and sometimes in the afternoon. The comfortable reach range for the average standing cook is 25 to 59 inches, which is where most frequently used items should be stored. The universal reach range is 15 to 48 inches above the finished floor.

- **Like items should be stored or grouped together.** Dishes, bowls, flatware or canned goods are often grouped together by stacking.

- **Store hazardous items out of the reach of children or others who might be harmed by them.** Placing knives in a knife block on the counter could keep them inaccessible to small children. Often kitchen cabinets are retrofitted with childproof closures to keep small ones out of the cleaning supplies and breakables.

- **Store items in the appropriate environment.** Items like potatoes and onions are best stored in a dry place with good air circulation, so a basket might be used.

Amount of Storage. The research conducted at Virginia Tech has led to a new way for the designer to calculate and provide for the storage needs of a client. Base, wall, drawer and pantry storage are still the main elements of a storage system in the kitchen. However, storage recommendations are given as a total amount of storage capacity for the kitchen, instead of totals for wall, base and drawer units as in the past. Storage recommendations are based on shelf/drawer frontage, not just cabinet size. Different amounts of shelf/drawer frontage are recommended for small, medium and large kitchens:

a. 1400 inches for a small kitchen (less than 150 square feet);

b. 1700 inches for a medium kitchen (151 to 350 square feet); and

c. 2000 inches for a large kitchen (greater than 350 square feet).

The research indicated that newly designed kitchens had this amount of storage distributed in the following ways, and the NKBA recommendations suggest that you use these guidelines as a means to calculate the location of storage:

	Small	Medium	Large
Wall	300 inches	360 inches	360 inches
Base	520 inches	615 inches	660 inches
Drawer	360 inches	400 inches	525 inches
Pantry	180 inches	230 inches	310 inches
Misc.	40 inches	95 inches	145 inches

The chart indicates the following trends:

- Wall storage needs peak at 360 inches of shelf/drawer frontage. No more is needed in the large kitchen than in the medium-sized kitchen.

- Base and drawer storage needs increase as the kitchen size increases.

- Pantry storage is an important element in the storage system. Even in small kitchens, a pantry can provide needed and accessible storage.

- Miscellaneous storage is included in every size of kitchen. Miscellaneous storage is storage more than 84 inches above the floor. It is also furniture pieces, pot racks, as well as other types of storage that is not wall, base, drawer or pantry cabinets.

The chart recommends the allocation for different types of storage in each size kitchen. However, these specific recommendations do not have to be met as long as the appropriate total shelf/drawer storage is met for kitchen size. For example, it is not necessary for a small kitchen to have 180 inches of pantry storage. The kitchen may have no pantry storage and instead have more base, wall and drawer storage than indicated on the chart. The guidelines do indicate that only the amount specified as miscellaneous storage can count toward the totals. Since this is pretty inconvenient storage, it would not be a good idea to substitute lots of storage above 84 inches for base storage.

Since all but one of the categories of storage can vary, the designer has great flexibility in planning storage. This flexibility is important in open-plan kitchens that have few walls. It may be impossible to have wall cabinet storage in a room with large windows and island work areas, and it may be undesireable as so much of it is above the reach of shorter or seated cooks.

Fortunately, storage components are changing. Drawers can hold dishes. Open shelves can be placed in front of windows. Peg boards and pot racks can hold utensils and equipment. A narrow, but deep pantry can hold more than a wide, shallow wall cabinet. Calculating shelf/drawer frontage, rather than cabinet frontage, opens up the possibilities for creative and innovative storage solutions.

Figure 7.64 In this kitchen, base cabinets in the island help fulfill storage requirements. (Courtesy of Lance Arnold – Jarrettsville, Maryland)

Formula for Calculating the Amount of Storage in Cabinets. Cabinets have various shelf and drawer configurations that affect the amount of shelf/drawer frontage the cabinet offers. For example, a wall cabinet with three shelves offers more storage area than a two-shelf cabinet. A base cabinet with two 24-inch shelves holds more than one with one 24-inch shelf and one 12-inch shelf. Use the following formula to calculate the amount of shelf/drawer storage provided per cabinet:

Cabinet size X number of shelf/drawers X cabinet depth in feet
=Total Shelf/Drawer Frontage

Cabinet size: Standard cabinet width dimensions are usually given in 3-inch increments, i.e., 12, 15, 18 inches.

Number of shelf/drawers: Each cabinet will have a number of shelves and/or drawers specified. Check the cabinet catalog.

Cabinet depth in feet: Different cabinets have different shelf depths and designs that affect how much space is actually available for storage. Use the following measurement in feet (or fraction of feet) to calculate the actual amount of storage space provided in each cabinet. Wall cabinets of 12 inches have a depth of 1 (12" = 1'). In most base cabinets, the depth would be 2 (24" = 2'). Drawer frontage is calculated using the depth measurement as well.

Various cabinet depths provide different capacities for storage and a multiplier based on 1 = 12 inches is used to calculate the depth. For example, a 12-inch deep wall cabinet is 1, a 15-inch deep wall cabinet is 1.25, an 18-inch deep pantry cabinet is 1.5, a 21-inch deep wall cabinet is 1.75, a 24-inch deep base cabinet is 2, a 12-inch deep drawer is 1 and a 24-inch deep drawer is 2.

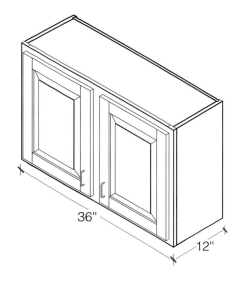

Figure 7.65 A 12-inch deep, 36-inch wide wall cabinet with three shelves provides 108 inches of actual wall cabinet shelf frontage.

Example of Storage Calculations. To explain the calculation process, we will calculate the storage available in the kitchen illustrated in Figure 7.73. First, let's examine how to calculate the amount of shelf/drawer frontage in a wall cabinet, a base cabinet, a drawer cabinet and a tall utility/pantry cabinet.

- **Wall cabinet calculation.** The following example provides an application of the formula for the W3630 cabinet:

  Multiply the cabinet frontage size (36 inches) by the number of shelves in the cabinet (3) and by the cabinet depth (12 inches = 1):

  $$36 \text{ inches } x \text{ } 3 \text{ } x \text{ } 1 = 108 \text{ inches}$$

  Thus, a 36-inch cabinet with three shelves would provide 108 inches of actual shelf frontage.

Figure 7.66 A 27-inch base cabinet with two 24-inch deep shelves provides 108 inches of base cabinet shelf frontage. Note that a standard base cabinet also provides drawer storage, which is calculated separately.

- **Base cabinet calculation.** The following calculation is for the B27 base cabinet with two 24–inch deep shelves. The cabinet also has one drawer. Multiply the cabinet frontage size (27 inches) by the number of shelves in the cabinet (2) and by the cabinet depth (24 inches=2). Calculate the drawer by multiplying the frontage (27 inches) by the number of drawers (1) by the depth (24 inches = 2).

  Cabinet: 27 inches x 2 x 2 = 108 inches

  Drawer: 27 inches x 1 x 2 =54 inches

  The 27–inch base cabinet has 108 inches inches of shelf frontage and 54 inches inches of drawer frontage storage.

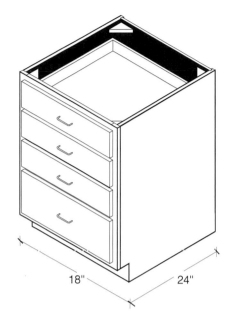

18"   24"

Figure 7.67 An 18-inch cabinet with four 24-inch deep drawers provides 144 inches of drawer frontage.

- **Drawer cabinet calculation.** The following calculation is for the BD18D4 with four drawers. Multiply the cabinet frontage (18 inches) by the number of drawers (4) by the depth of the cabinet (24 inches=2)

  18 inches x 4 x 2 = 144 inches

  This is the same formula used when calculating a single drawer in a base cabinet.

273

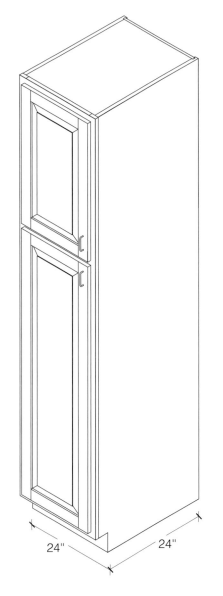

Figure 7.68 A 24-inch tall utility cabinet with three 24-inch deep shelves provides 144 inches of pantry cabinet shelf frontage.

24"   24"

- **Pantry cabinet calculation.** A tall utility cabinet is specified in the plan – U242484R. It has three fixed shelves. The following calculation would be used. Multiply the cabinet frontage (24 inches) by the number of shelves (3) and by the cabinet depth (24 inches = 2).

  24 inches x 3 x 2 = 144 inches

  If pull-out shelves were added, they could be calculated as drawer storage.

Corner cabinet calculations. Corner cabinet storage can have various configurations that affect the calculation of shelf frontage provided. To calculate the storage provided by the various types of corner cabinets consider the following:

- **Blind Corner** – Count the visible cabinet frontage as the cabinet size, then calculate the same as a standard wall or base cabinet. See Figure 7.69.

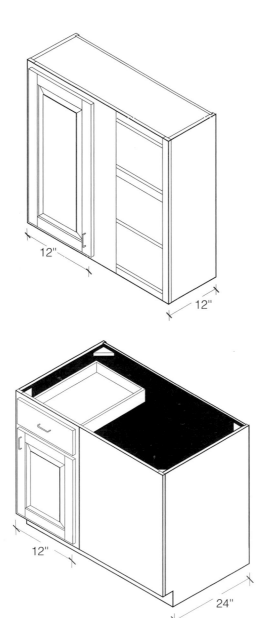

Figure 7.69 The blind corner wall cabinet (top) has 12 inches of visible cabinet frontage with three shelves 12 inches deep, for a total of 36 inches of total shelf frontage. The blind corner base cabinet (bottom) has 12 inches of visible frontage, and two shelves 24 inches deep, for a total of 48 inches of base cabinet shelf frontage. The drawer storage provided by the base cabinet is calculated separately.

275

- **L Corner** – For an L-shaped wall or base cabinet use the visible cabinet frontage and a shelf/depth multiplier of 1.5. See Figure 7.70.

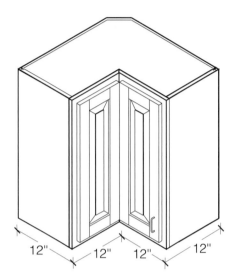

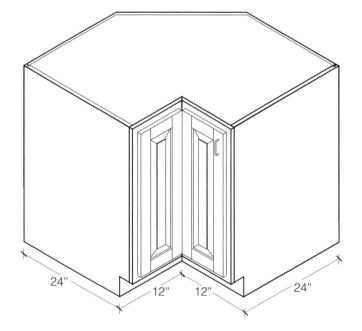

Figure 7.70 For an L-shaped wall cabinet use the visible cabinet frontage and a shelf/depth multiplier of 1.5. The wall cabinet would use 24 inches as the cabinet size, 3 shelves and a multiplier of 1.5 for a total of 108 inches. The base cabinet would use 24 inches as the cabinet size, 2 shelves and a multiplier of 1.5 for a total of 72 inches of base shelf frontage.

• **L Corner with Lazy Susan** – For an L-shaped wall or base
cabinet with a Lazy Susan, the shelf configurations are usually
similar to three quarters of a circle within the L shape of the
oversized cabinet. Use the wall side dimension as the cabinet
frontage measurement (24 inches or 27 inches for a wall
cabinet and 36 inches for a base cabinet) and 1.5 as the shelf
dimension, then follow the formula. See Figure 7.71.

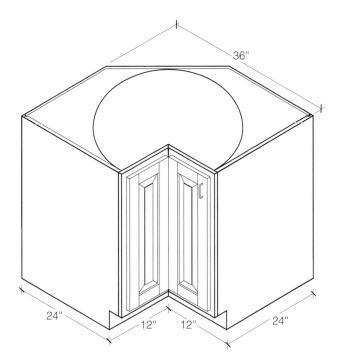

Figure 7.71 The L corner base cabinet
with Lazy Susan has a wall side
dimension of 36 inches that is used as
the cabinet frontage measurement. It has
two shelves and a multiplier of 1.5. This
cabinet will provide 108 inches of base
shelf frontage. (36 x 2 x 1.5 = 108)

• **Diagonal Corner with Lazy Susan** – In these cabinets, a full circle shelf is fitted within the cabinet. For a wall cabinet, use the wall side dimension (24 inches, 27 inches) and 1.5 as the shelf depth, then follow the formula. For a base cabinet, use the wall side dimension (36 inches) and 1.5 as the shelf dimension, then follow the formula. See Figure 7.72.

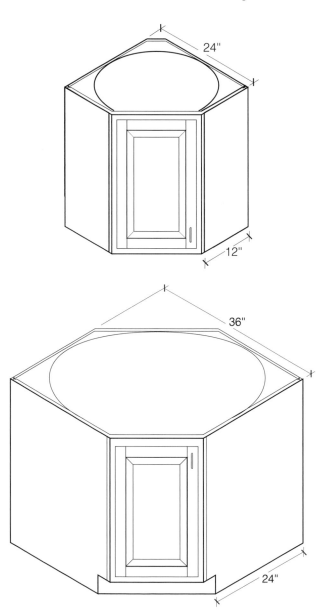

Figure 7.72 The diagonal wall cabinet has a side dimension of 24 inches and three round rotating shelves with a shelf depth multiplier of 1.5, for a total of 108 inches of wall cabinet shelf frontage. The diagonal base cabinet has a 36-inch side dimension and 2 round rotating shelves that use a multiplier of 1.5. The total base cabinet shelf frontage is also 108 inches.

Calculating Total Storage. We will use the kitchen in Figure 7.73 to illustrate how to check if enough storage has been provided. First, the size of the kitchen must be calculated. This kitchen is approximately 147 square feet and would be classified as a small kitchen. According to the previous recommendations, 1400 inches of shelf/drawer frontage is needed throughout the small kitchen. Further, we should consider the recommended distribution of this storage in different types of cabinets: 300 inches of shelf frontage in wall cabinets, 520 inches of shelf frontage in base cabinets, 360 inches of drawer frontage in drawers, 180 inches of shelf frontage in pantry cabinets and 40 inches in miscellaneous storage. Calculations in Figure 7.74 indicate how much storage is provided by each category of cabinetry.

Figure 7.73 A variety of cabinets and storage is planned in this small kitchen.

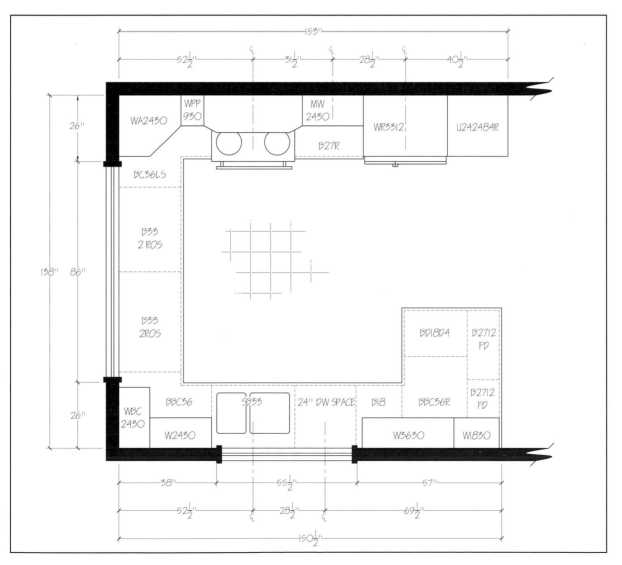

WALL

WR3312	33 X 1 X 1	=	33
MW2430	24 X 2 X 1	=	48
MPP930	9 X 3 X 1	=	27
WA2430	24 X 3 X 1.5	=	108
WBC2430	12 X 3 X 1	=	36
W2430	24 X 3 X 1	=	72
W3630	36 X 3 X 1	=	108
W1830R	18 X 3 X 1	=	54
			486

BASE

B27R	27 X 2 X 2	=	108
BC36LS	36 X 2 X 1.5	=	108
BBC361	12 X 2 X 2	=	48
B181	18 X 2 X 2	=	72
SB33	33 X 1 X 2	=	66
BC36D	36 X 2 X 1.5	=	108
B2712FD	27 X 3 X 1	=	81
B2712FD	27 X 3 X 1	=	81
			672

DRAWER

B27	27 X 1 X 2	=	54
BC36L	12 X 1 X 2	=	24
B33/2ROS	33 X 3 X 2	=	198
B33/2ROS	33 X 3 X 2	=	198
BD18D4	18 X 4 X 2	=	144
B18	18 X 1 X 2	=	36
			654

PANTRY

U242484R	24 X 3 X 2	=	144

Total	**1,956**

Figure 7.74 As this chart shows, the kitchen in figure 7.73 has more than the recommended amount of wall cabinets, base cabinets and drawer storage, but less than the recommended amount of pantry cabinet storage. Overall, the storage exceeds the total recommendation of 1400 inches shelf/drawer frontage for a small kitchen.

The calculations indicate that this kitchen has 486 inches of wall cabinet shelf frontage, 672 inches of base cabinet shelf frontage and 654 inches of drawer frontage, which are all more than the recommended amount. There is only 144 inches of pantry shelf frontage, which is less than the recommended amount and no miscellaneous shelf frontage. The total amount of shelf/drawer frontage is 1,956 inches of total shelf/drawer frontage, which is more than 1400 inches that is recommended.

Charts to use in calculating the shelf/drawer frontage of a kitchen plan are presented in Figure 7.75 and are available on the CD that comes with this book.

Cabinet Calculations

The chart below can help organize information from cabinet specifications needed to calculate the amount of shelf/drawer frontage in a kitchen. Enter the cabinet sizes and check specification for the number of shelves and depth of the shelves in each cabinet. Use the following formula to calculate the amount of shelf/drawer frontage provided by the cabinet.

Cabinet size x Number of shelves x Shelf/drawer depth multiplier
= Total shelf/drawer frontage per cabinet.

Multiply this by the number of cabinets of each size to determine the total amount of shelf/drawer frontage provided by all of the cabinets of a certain size. Add the totals together to determine the Total Shelf/Drawer Frontage for the Kitchen.

Standard Wall Cabinets Shelf Frontage — All shelves must be below 84 inches						
Cabinet Type	Cabinet Size	Number of Shelves	Shelf/Depth Multiplier	Total Shelf/Drawer Storage Per Cabinet	Number of Cabinets	Total
30 inches, 36 inches, 42 inches high/ 12 inches deep		3	1			
30 inches, 36 inches, 42 inches high/ 15 inches deep		3	1.25			
30 inches, 36 inches, 42 inches high/ 18 inches deep		3	1.5			
21 inches – 27 inches high/ 12 inches deep		2	1			
21 inches – 27 inches high/ 15 inches deep		2	1.25			
21 inches – 27 inches high/ 18 inches deep		2	1.5			
21 inches – 27 inches high/ 24 inches deep		2	2			

Figure 7.75 Calculating shelf/drawing frontage.

Cabinet Type	Cabinet Size	Number of Shelves	Shelf/Depth Multiplier	Total Shelf/Drawer Storage Per Cabinet	Number of Cabinets	Total
Standard Wall Cabinets Shelf Frontage, continued — All shelves must be below 84 inches						
12 inches – 18 inches high 12 inches deep		1	1			
12 inches – 18 inches high 15 inches deep		1	1.25			
12 inches – 18 inches high 18 inches deep		1	1.5			
12 inches – 18 inches high 21 inches deep		1	1.75			
12 inches – 18 inches high 24 inches deep		1	2			
Blind Corner	Visible cabinet frontage	3	1			
L Corner	Visible cabinet frontage	3	1.5			
Diagonal	Wall side dimension	3	1.5			
Other						
Total Wall Cabinet Shelf Frontage						

Base Cabinet Shelf Frontage

Cabinet Type	Cabinet Size	Number of Shelves	Shelf/Depth Multiplier	Total Shelf/Drawer Storage Per Cabinet	Number of Cabinets	Total
32 – 36 inches high x 24 inches deep w/ 12 inches deep shelf		1.5	2			
32 – 36 inches high x 24 inches deep w/ 24 inches deep shelf		2	2			
32 – 36 inches high x 24 inches deep sink base		1	2			
32 – 36 inches high x 21 inches deep w/ 12 inches deep shelf		1.5	1.75			
32 – 36 inches high x 21 inches deep w/ 21 inches deep shelf		2	1.75			
32 – 36 inches high x 18 inches deep w/ 18 inches deep shelf		2	1.5			
32 – 36 inches high x 12 inches deep w/ 12 inches deep shelf		2	1			
Blind corner w/ 12 inches shelf	Visible cabinet frontage	1.5				
Blind corner w/ 24 inches shelf	Visible cabinet frontage	2	2			
L Corner	Visible cabinet frontage	2	1.5			
L Corner Lazy Susan	Wall side dimension					
Diagonal	Wall side dimension	2	1.5			
Other						
Total Base Cabinet Shelf Frontage						

Drawer Frontage						
Cabinet Type	Cabinet Size	Number of Drawers	Drawer Depth Multiplier	Total Shelf/Drawer Storage Per Cabinet	Number of Cabinets	Total
24 inches deep base cabinet drawer		1	2			
3 drawer base cabinet (24 inches deep)		3	2			
4 drawer base cabinet (24 inches deep)		4	2			
Base Cabinet roll-out shelves/ Pull out trays (24 inches deep)		2	2			
21 inches deep drawer		1	1.75			
18 inches deep drawer		1	1.5			
12 inches deep drawer		1	1			
Other						
Other						
Total Drawer Frontage						

Tall/Utility/Pantry Cabinets Shelf Frontage – All shelves must be below 84 inches

Cabinet Type	Cabinet Size	Number of Shelves/ Drawers	Drawer Depth Multiplier	Total Shelf/Drawer Storage Per Cabinet	Number of Cabinets	Total
12 inches deep			1			
15 inches deep			1.25			
18 inches deep			1.5			
21 inches deep			1.75			
24 inches deep			2			
Oven – 24 inches deep			2			
Other						
Other						
Total Pantry Shelf Frontage						

Miscellaneous Shelf/ Drawer Frontage

Cabinet Type	Cabinet Size	Number of Shelves/ Drawers	Shelf/Drawer Multiplier	Shelf/Drawer Frontage Per Item	Number of Cabinets	Total
Furniture Piece						
Pot Rack						
Shelves higher than 84 inches						
Other						
Other						
Total Miscellaneous Shelf/ Drawer Frontage						

Total Wall Cabinet Shelf Frontage	
Total Base Cabinet Shelf Frontage	
Total Pantry Shelf Frontage	
Total Drawer Frontage	
Total Miscellaneous Shelf/Drawer Frontage	
Total Shelf/Drawer Storage for Kitchen	

Check against these recommendations:

Kitchen Size: _____

Small kitchen ≤ 150 square feet

Medium kitchen 151-350 square feet

Large kitchen > 351 square feet

Recommended Distribution of Shelf/Drawer Frontage			
	Small	**Medium**	**Large**
Wall	300 inches	360 inches	360 inches
Base	520 inches	615 inches	660 inches
Drawer	360 inches	400 inches	525 inches
Pantry	180 inches	230 inches	310 inches
Misc.	40 inches	95 inches	145 inches
Total	1400 inches	1700 inches	2000 inches

Storage at the Sink. Because so much activity occurs at the sink, it is important that ample amounts of storage be located there. The Kitchen Planning Guidelines recommend certain amounts of storage be located within 72 inches of the center of the sink front. At least 400 inches of shelf/drawer frontage is needed for a small kitchen; at least 480 inches for a medium kitchen; and at least 560 inches for a large kitchen. This storage can be wall, base, drawer or tall/pantry storage and can be located beside or across from the sink, although placing it beside the sink will be most convenient.

The kitchen we have been analyzing includes three wall cabinets and five base cabinets with shelf/drawer frontage within 72 inches of the sink center. The wall cabinets do not provide the needed storage (216 inches), but the base cabinets can also be included in calculating the total amount of shelf/drawer frontage needed at the sink. The total amount of shelf/drawer frontage provided by all of these cabinets is 732 inches, which is more than the 400 inches required in a small kitchen.

Figure 7.76 For storage at the sink, a small kitchen requires 400 inches of shelf/drawer frontage within 72 inches of the sink. A medium kitchen requires 480 inches; and a large kitchen, 560 inches. This small kitchen has only 216 inches of wall cabinets within the 72-inch radius. But 552 inches of base cabinet shelf/drawer frontage is within that radius and counts toward the required 400 inches. (Kitchen Planning Guideline 28)

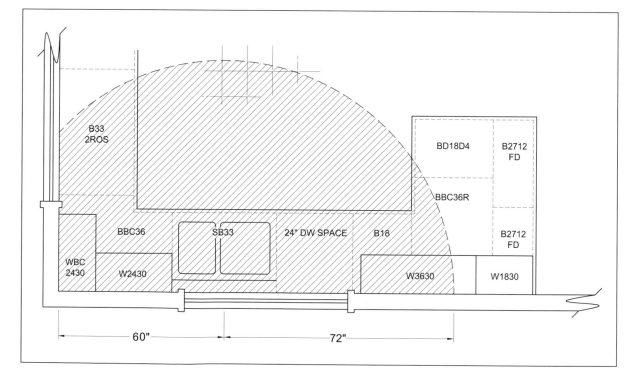

Corner Cabinet Storage. Corner areas may require some special considerations. In a basic arrangement, two cabinets are perpendicular to each other and there is empty and unusable space in the corner. A blind corner cabinet provides some accessible space, but the user may need to be a contortionist to get to the back areas.

Various Lazy Susan and pull-out designs provide corner storage that is easier to access. If the kitchen will have corner cabinet areas, it is recommended that at least one of the corners include some type of specialized corner cabinet.

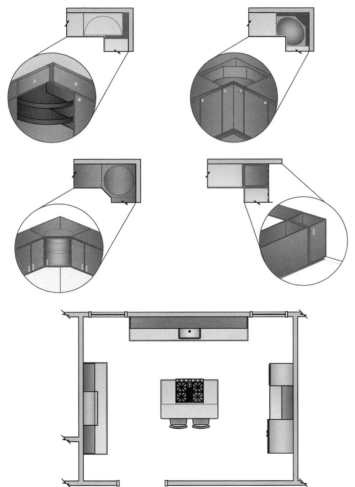

Figure 7.77 In a kitchen that features corner cabinets, plan at least one corner cabinet with functional storage. An unfitted kitchen may have no corner cabinets and is not subject to this guideline. (Kitchen Planning Guideline 29)

An "unfitted" kitchen with separate counters and furniture pieces may not have any corner units and is not subject to this recommendation.

Storage Organizers. Storage accessories or organizers enhance the efficiency of cabinetry by increasing access to items. Pull-out shelves and turntables allow the user to fully use a deep cabinet. Pull-out cutting boards add an extra work area and put it at a lower height that is convenient for chopping. Open shelves and backsplash storage make items easy to see and reach. Drawer dividers help keep utensils sorted into an arrangement that keeps them easy to locate. NKBA recommends that storage accessories be used to enhance storage based on the user's requirements.

A

Figure 7.78 A variety of storage organizers are available to help make items easy to see and reach: a) Customizable drawer for dishes and condiments, b) Backsplash rail systems hold spices as well as small utensils, c) Roll-out tray and lid dividers, d) Tilt-out sink front storage. (Courtesy a & b–Hafele; c–Diamond; and d–Rev-A-Shelf)

B

C

D

Figure 7.79 A variety of shelf configurations are available to increase access to pantry storage such as these pull-out adjustable wire baskets. (Courtesy of Rev-A-Shelf)

Pantry Storage. A pantry is a great storage feature. There are many different styles of pantries, including tall cabinets, closets and small rooms. Generally, a pantry should be placed outside of the work triangle so that the tall unit does not interfere with the flow of food preparation. Standard tall cabinets sizes are 12, 18 and 24 inches deep, but custom cabinets can be made at any depth. Different accessories (pull-out shelves and racks, turn tables) can be added to increase the effectiveness of the storage unit. Unlike wall and base cabinets, pantry cabinets allow for a large portion of stored items to be within the reach range of users, offering a universal option.

Some clients may really appreciate a walk-in pantry that has open shelving within a small room. This type of storage can accommodate items bought in bulk as well as oversized pots and serving pieces. Plan shelf depth, which can range from 6 to 30 inches, to accommodate the items being stored. Ideally, the door to a walk-in pantry will allow for a 32-inch clear opening, which will enhance the access to the space and allow for a useable clear floor space in the pantry.

The Kitchen Planning Guidelines and Access Standards that are particularly relevant to work arrangements, counter areas and storage are Guidelines 3, 4, 5, 24, 25, 26 27, 28 and 29. They all appear in Chapter 12.

SERVING AND DINING GUIDELINES

Hopefully, after the food is prepared, it is eaten. There are many ways to serve a meal and dine. The designer should determine the most frequent way the household dines and the special ways they dine and entertain. Probably each household will serve and eat meals in a variety of ways depending on the time of day, their schedules, their ages and the dining situation. Many lifestyles have become much more informal, but people still like to dress up a table and enjoy using the good china on special occasions.

Serving involves getting the food from the preparation area to the dining area. Some of the ways this might be done are:

- Food is moved from pots and pans into serving bowls and platters and brought to the dining table or buffet area.

- Food could be placed on individual plates and brought to each diner in the dining area.

- For some households with erratic schedules, food might be left in the pots and pans or in warming drawers and diners help themselves to it when they have time or are hungry.

- Beverages have to be prepared also. Each glass could be prepared and brought to the dining area. Ice could be provided and pitchers brought to the table or buffet. Or everyone could fix his/her own drink before sitting down.

Serving also involves preparing the table and necessary items for the meal. This could include:

- Retrieving dishes, glassware and flatware for the meal and setting the table or arranging it for a buffet.

- Arranging table linens or paper napkins so the diners can use them during the meal.

- Locating and arranging condiments that will be served with the meal, including salt and pepper.

- Flowers, candles and special lighting might also be included in a meal.

RECOMMENDATIONS

There are a lot of items needed to serve a meal and, although it is desirable, a special serving area is not required for a well-designed kitchen. However, the components of a serving area should be considered, even if a special area is not planned. The main components are storage and counter space.

Storage. Storage is needed for dishes, glassware, flatware, serving pieces, linens and accessories. Often this storage is provided in other centers. For example, dishes, glassware and flatware are stored in the sink center as part of the cleanup activities. This is the last place these items are used, so it is a convenient and suitable storage option. However, the designer should consider the ease of retrieving these items while food preparation is occurring. Ideally, these items should be stored so that they can be accessed without interfering in the work area.

Counter space. Counter space may be found in all parts of the kitchen and used as part of the serving process. Counter space beside the refrigerator may hold glasses while beverages are being prepared. That same space may be needed to hold items that have been refrigerated, but also needed for the meal (butter, pickles, etc.). Counter space next to the cooking surface and oven will be needed to hold serving platters and bowls.

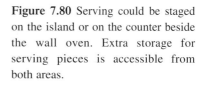

Figure 7.80 Serving could be staged on the island or on the counter beside the wall oven. Extra storage for serving pieces is accessible from both areas.

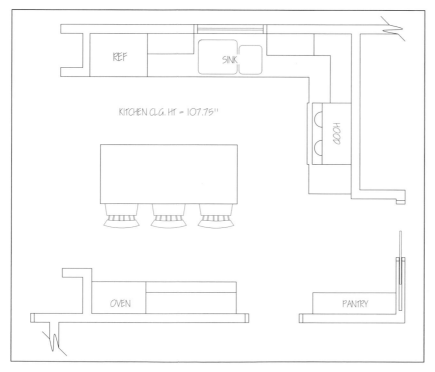

Past recommendations for a serving area range from 15 to 36 inches of counter space. Some of this can be combined with the recommended landing area at the cooking surface, oven and refrigerator. Increasing these areas beyond the minimum landing area requirements would help make any of these areas better suited for serving.

Placement. Whether a special serving area is provided or serving activities occur throughout the kitchen, consider the traffic flow from these areas to the dining area. As mentioned previously, serving should be able to occur without interfering with food preparation work flow. Placing the serving area outside the work triangle would be suitable. If serving is part of the kitchen, consider increasing both the refrigeration center and the cooking center in order to get extra storage and counter area.

Beverage Station or Bar. Planning a beverage station or bar might be a suitable option in some larger kitchens or entertaining areas. The beverage station or bar might include the following: a small auxiliary sink, undercounter refrigerator, ice machine and/or wine cooler, counter area and storage for glassware and beverages. This separate area allows family members to get beverages anytime, including mealtime, without interfering with the cook. It can be set up and stocked for guests who serve themselves or are served by a host.

The beverage station might be located in a kitchen area, outside the work triangle, but near the dining and social areas. If it will be primarily used to serve guests during entertaining, it could be located in a different room, such as a living or dining area.

Butler's Pantry. A butler's pantry was frequently planned into large homes of the past. It was a staging area between the kitchen and the formal dining room, where food was placed before it was served (by a butler). Typically it contained storage for dishes, serving pieces and silver, and counter area for the food and dishes to be placed both before and after the meal.

A similar area is planned into some homes today. It includes storage and counter space, but it might also include a warming drawer, auxiliary sink, wine cooler and other items associated with a beverage station. Some also have a second dishwasher so that clean up can occur as the dishes are being removed from the table.

Another configuration might be to provide only counter space and display storage. This area could be used as a space to serve a buffet or to set out dessert for a meal. Any area used as a buffet area should have between 48 and 60 inches of clear floor space to allow for one person to stand at the buffet line and another to walk behind carrying a plate full of food.

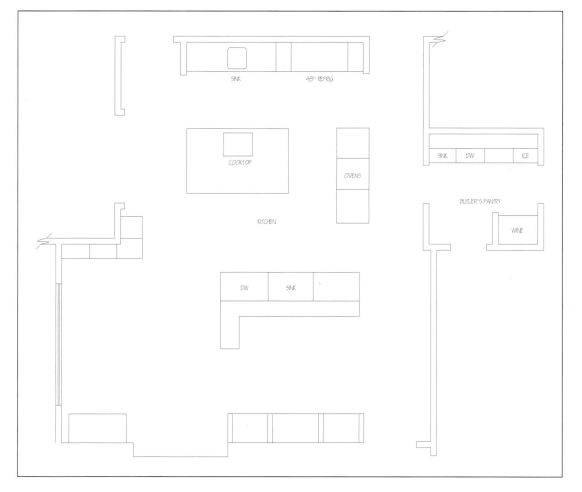

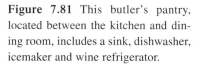

Figure 7.81 This butler's pantry, located between the kitchen and dining room, includes a sink, dishwasher, icemaker and wine refrigerator.

Dining

Households may eat in many different locations and ways. Whether it is sit-down dining or eating in front of the TV, the designer should try to plan the kitchen space so that it considers the dining habits and desires of the client.

RECOMMENDATIONS

Placement. As mentioned in previous sections, the kitchen location should be planned with considerations to the formal and informal dining areas, if the house includes both. Location is important to make serving convenient and to have the meal go smoothly.

Consider the view to other parts of the house and to the outdoors while in the dining area. If the cook is the chaotic type who has managed to get everything on the table at the right temperature, but not gotten all the pots in the dishwasher, it may be best to shield the view from the dining area to the work part of the kitchen. Pleasant views to a garden or play space may be more enjoyable.

Clearances for Dining. The required floor space needed for seating depends on the type of chair and the height of the table or counter. A typical table is 30 inches high and a person seated in a chair at this height table requires 18 to 24 inches of clear floor space beyond the table edge, depending on the size of the person and the type of chair used. A eating counter used for dining could be 36 inches high, which is the same as a typical work surface counter, or 42 inches. Seating height should be sized to match the counter height. A knee space depth of 12 to 18 inches is needed, decreasing as the height increases.

In order for the person to get up out of the chair, a 32-inch space is required from the edge of the table to a wall or other obstruction. If a person must edge past a seated diner or move behind a chair parallel to the table, then 36 inches of space will be needed between the edge of the table and the wall or obstruction. Allow at least 44 inches if a person needs to walk behind the seated diner. This would allow the person to walk perpendicular to the table and would be the most convenient clearance. A distance of 60 to 72 inches would be generous and allow for a server to serve the table or for a person with a mobility aid to maneuver around the table space.

Seating. Most people enjoy sitting down to eat, although standing up to finish off a bowl of cereal during the morning rush may be common in some households. Several different seating arrangements are common and require minimum clearances for the dining area and the diner.

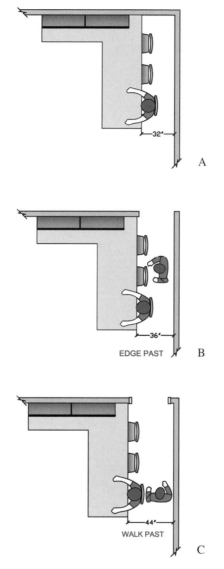

Figure 7.82 Traffic clearance at dining. Caption: a.) Allow 32 inches of clearance behind a table or counter, if there is no traffic, b.) Allow 36 inches behind the table or counter for someone to edge past and c.) Allow 44 inches behind the table or counter for someone to walk past (Kitchen Planning Guideline 8).

The minimum space needed for a place setting is 24 inches wide. This allows space for a plate, flatware and glassware arranged in the typical setting. A more generous space would be 30 inches wide. This would allow for a little more arm space while eating and would allow for a more formal table setting. The 30-inch width would also allow for a person in a wheelchair to sit.

The size and shape of the table will determine how many place settings and people can be served. A banquette, with some bench seating, can be planned in a corner or bay window area. Figure 7.83 illustrates various sizes of tables and the number of seats that can comfortably fit at the table.

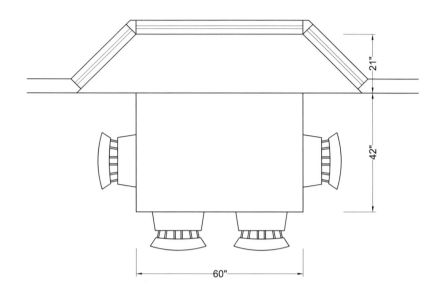

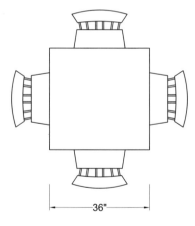

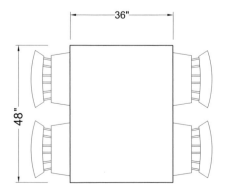

Figure 7.83 Various seating and table arrangements come in a range of sizes and shapes.

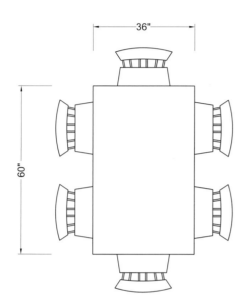

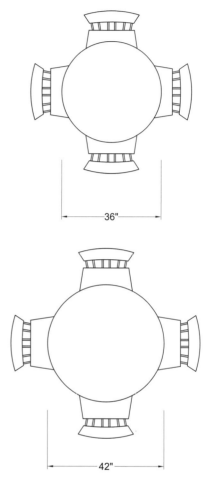

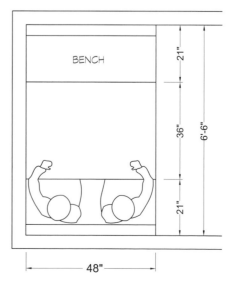

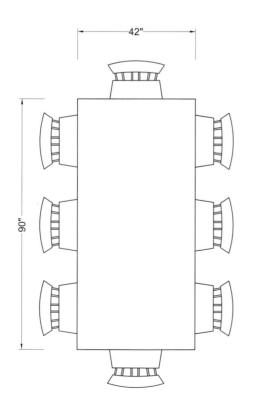

The depth of the place setting depends on the height of the table. For a table height at 30 inches, allow 18 inches depth for a seated diner. This depth below the table will provide the knee space to allow the diner to sit comfortably and the top area will provide a generous space for a place setting or serving pieces.

When seating is at a raised counter, allow 15 inches of depth at a 36-inch high counter and 12 inches at a 42-inch high counter. Clearances below the counter will allow leg room for the tall chairs and stools used at these counter height. They will not be deep enough to accommodate a typical place setting, but can serve snacks and small meals.

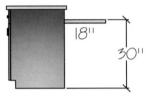

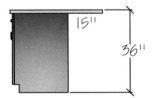

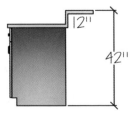

Figure 7.84 This chart diagrams the height and depth of different seating options (Kitchen Planning Guideline 9).

The Kitchen Planning Guidelines and Access Standards that apply to dining areas are Guidelines 8 and 9, which can be found in Chapter 12.

THAT'S ENTERTAINING

Entertaining is an important part of many lifestyles today and the kitchen is a crucial element. The aim is to provide good food and conversation in a pleasant setting. Informal entertaining often means the hosts, and, sometimes, the guests prepare and serve the food. Kitchens that are open to social spaces facilitate interaction and encourage the guests to participate in the preparations.

Two entertaining trends require some special consideration in kitchen design—using a caterer and outdoor entertaining. When a caterer is used frequently for entertaining, the kitchen might include some special features that can accommodate the caterer's requirements. When preparing food and dining outdoors is a preferred way of informal entertaining, then the outdoor kitchen can add to the convenience and ambiance of the event.

Kitchens For Caterers

Caterers provide several different types of services that can help take the worry out of having a party. They typically provide the food, table service and servers to make sure the event is successful. Often the caterer will prepare much of the food in their facilities and bring it to the home. In other cases, some or all food will be prepared in the host's kitchen. The menu and quantity of food help to determine where and how the food is prepared.

Here are some ideas for a kitchen that a caterer can work in:

- The kitchen should be located with easy access to an outside entrance that can be used for unloading and loading food and supplies.

- A kitchen that is separate from the social areas allows caterers to work in the kitchen without interfering with guests and entertaining. The sight lines and sound insulation need to be considered.

- Wide work aisles, at least 48 inches, help the catering crew circulate and work at different centers simultaneously.

- Larger appliances handle some of the caterers' trays and equipment. Check the interior size of refrigerators and ovens to make sure they can accommodate larger pans and trays.

- A warming drawer holds prepared food at a serving temperature.

- Expanded counter space may be needed for larger preparation tasks.

- A separate beverage station, including an ice machine and extra refrigeration, allows beverages to be prepared outside any food preparation areas.

- A large serving area may be needed for a set-up space.

- The caterer may need additional space to store coats, boxes and supplies.

Outdoor Kitchens

Cooking outdoors is a great way to entertain and serve a wide variety of meals. Grilling foods is an important food preparation method today and many people prefer to do this outside, to reduce smoke and odors indoors. We can cook outside with just a grill, but there are so many more possibilities that a designer can use to create an exciting cooking experience. The food preparation in an outdoor kitchen may be modified from the typical food preparation sequence and many of the Kitchen Planning Guidelines we have just examined can be modified to suit the requirements of the client.

LOCATION

An outdoor kitchen is often planned next to or close to the kitchen of the house. This will increase the efficiency of extending water, gas and electrical utilities to the area. It will also be efficient for a cook who prepares part of the meal in the indoor kitchen and brings it to the outdoor eating area.

Examine the overall design of the private outdoor areas to consider how to integrate the kitchen with other outdoor living areas, such as a pool or other landscape feature. Patio or deck areas will be needed for dining and conversation areas if the outdoor kitchen is part of the outdoor entertaining area.

The inclusion of shelter over an outdoor kitchen may depend on the climate and location of the house. How often does it rain? How hot does it get? Is shade needed? Will the clients be using the outdoor kitchen all year long or will they need to winterize the kitchen? Are strong winds an issue that might affect the placement of the outdoor kitchen or the grilling unit?

EQUIPMENT

The gas grill is an essential element in the outdoor kitchen. The size and features of the grill are varied. Many appliance manufacturers have developed outdoor grill units that have the capacity to act as an expanded cooking center. They have a grill and limited counter areas and warming areas. Other cooking equipment might be warming drawers, smokers and wood burning ovens or grills. Historically, often no mechanical ventilation was planned, so we have learned to consider how the smoke from the grill will be dispersed. An enclosed outdoor kitchen can capture the smoke or even funnel it back into the house. A UL-rated ventilation system for outdoor use should be specified.

An undercounter refrigeration unit is a possibility in an expanded outdoor kitchen. The unit should be UL-rated for outdoor use, well insulated and made of a weather resistant material, such as stainless steel.

While a sink might be desirable, it requires connection to water and sewer lines. Plumbing connections should be easily accessible. One option that does not require a complete plumbing installation is a sink with a connection to the outdoor hose system. If the sink is insulated and covered, it can double as a cooler. Make sure any sink that is used is made of a material that can endure outdoor conditions and is easy to maintain. A heavy gauge stainless steel is often recommended.

Specify cabinets and counters that are weather-resistant. Cabinets might be made of a light concrete material, stainless steel, solid surface or teak. Borrowing from the boating industry, cabinetry is available made from resins that resist weather. Among the countertop choices are granite, slate, concrete, stainless steel, solid surface or tile. Consider storage for carts that can help in transporting food. Leveling the ground, deck or patio surface before the installation of cabinets or allowing for the natural irregularities of the outdoor flooring becomes critical.

Figure 7.85 This outdoor kitchen includes a large rotisserie grill, sink, cooktop, small grill, stainless cabinetry and open shelving. (Courtesy of Viking Range Corp.)

Heating units might be desirable in some regions. Portable patio heaters that use gas or propane are available, and fireplaces and fire pits might provide a focal point as well as heat to the area. All of these should be designed so that guests are not in danger of being burned. Check local codes to determine if these heating devices are permitted in your client's area.

Figure 7.86 Portable patio heaters can extend the season and add to the functionality of outdoor kitchens. (Courtesy of Fisher & Paykel)

SPACE PLANNING

Typically, the grill is located at the center of the work flow in an outdoor kitchen. Landing areas should be planned on both sides of any cooking appliance and on both sides of the sink. If food preparation will actually occur in the outdoor kitchen, provide a 36-inch preparation space.

Because some outdoor kitchens are compact, following the guidelines for a work triangle may not be feasible. But clear floor space should be provided in front of all of the major appliances and fixtures. Often, more than one person is working in an outdoor kitchen and work centers or zones may actually be safer and more functional if they are separated. Follow recommended clearances for work aisles, walkways and seating. When outdoor decks and patios are planned on several levels, make sure extra wide traffic space is planned near level changes without rails. Also, give careful consideration to how the level changes are executed for the various abilities and mobilities of clients and their guests.

A KITCHEN WHERE YOU NEED IT

The modern kitchen continues to represent the heart of the home, but lifestyle considerations and house design have created a need for kitchen components to be planned throughout the house. There are outpost kitchens in areas like the bedroom, bathroom, home office or studio. If a client is interested in having the convenience of one of these kitchens, carefully consider what specific features are needed. Review local zoning requirements and building codes before planning any outpost kitchen to determine if it will constitute a second kitchen, and if that is permissible or will impact the classification of the home as a single-family house.

Morning Kitchen

A morning kitchen in the bedroom and/or bathroom area provides a place to prepare the first coffee of the day or perhaps an evening snack. Especially if the private area is located a significant distance from the main kitchen, a morning kitchen can add convenience. Coffee, juice, toast, bagels or pastries might be prepared right in the bedroom while completing the morning routine and without having to go to the kitchen. For some, medicines need to be taken first thing in the morning or at night and with food or beverages that could be stored in a morning kitchen. A morning kitchen is often part of a master suite, but it could also be convenient in a guest suite used by a caregiver or a relative staying for an extended time. A juice bar would provide cold refreshments and could be planned close to an exercise space or home spa.

Mini Kitchen

Other outpost or mini kitchens might be located near semi-private or public spaces in the home. Locating a kitchen at point-of-use in a family or game room adds flexibility and improves access to users of various sizes and abilities. A home office or studio space located in a basement, attic or in an accessory unit could benefit from a small kitchen space to prepare snacks and beverages for someone frequently working at home. Home recreational areas, like spaces planned for pool or cards, can benefit from a small, convenient kitchen area that makes entertaining go smoothly.

Considerations

A variety of equipment could be included in an outpost kitchen and the designer should choose items needed for the planned activities. An undercounter refrigerator can fit into a small space and provide enough capacity to accommodate the needs of the outpost kitchen. In some settings, an icemaker might also be needed.

A small sink can provide water for drinking, limited food preparation and help with clean up. Water filters and hot water dispensers might add to the convenience of having a sink, and a small dishwasher could help with clean up. A small microwave can fit into some spaces and provide a way to prepare some snacks. If a one- or two-unit burner is needed, then ventilation should also be provided.

Small appliances may be the best way to accomplish food preparation in an outpost kitchen. A coffeemaker, toaster, toaster oven, blender or juicer might be used in certain areas. Extra electrical receptacles should be planned for the kitchen area to accommodate the small appliances that might be used.

Storage will be needed for cups, glassware, dishes, silverware and utensils. Often cabinets, open shelving and counter space are provided to accommodate storage and work areas. The amount of storage and work space needed will depend on the activities planned.

Figure 7.87 A mini kitchen might be located in a family room, game room, home studio or office. (Courtesy of U-Line Appliances)

Particular attention should be given to isolating the noise and odors of an outpost kitchen. Extra lighting may be needed and ventilation and insulation may be required.

SUMMARY

As you have seen, there are many decisions and details involved in creating a space plan for a kitchen that is functional and useable. Not only must you consider your client's needs and the physical space you are working in, you must consider the selection of product in relation to some of the spatial requirements. You may find that you have to use a certain style of sink, cooktop or refrigerator, because of space and planning restrictions. On the other hand, you may have to arrange space to accommodate the appliance or activity desired by the client. There may be several ways that the kitchen could be planned depending on the choices.

Previous chapters presented assessment tools and background information to help you understand your client's needs and desires. In this chapter, you have been presented with numerous NKBA planning guidelines that will further influence your design decisions. The guidelines provide key criteria for effective space planning. However, you may not always be able to meet every guideline. Budget, time and space restrictions will influence how you incorporate the guidelines within the parameters of each job. Remember to meet any requirements specified in local building codes.

Throughout this chapter and the rest of the book, improved universal access has been incorporated into recommendations and considerations. As a designer, you will work with clients whose needs are individualized. Refer to Chapter 8 for a more extensive list of universal and accessible design concepts arranged according to user groups. This is a great place to look for ideas that might be useful if your client is older, has children, a unique mobility or handedness requirement, or has sensory or cognitive impairments.

Remember that infrastructure requirements also must be considered in planning the kitchen. There are several decisions related to the mechanical systems that must be made in the design of a kitchen. Lighting, ventilation and placement of receptacles have been referred to in this chapter, but there are more details (and guidelines) related to these areas in Chapter 8 that will affect the planning of the kitchen. Be sure you are familiar with these recommendations and requirements when you start to design a space.

More information about the design process and steps for the final layout of the kitchen are discussed in detail in Chapter 11. Until you have mastered the planning criteria, be prepared to refer to the guidelines and information presented in this chapter throughout the design and planning process. NKBA's Kitchen Planning Guidelines and the applicable Access Standards can be found in Chapter 12.

CHAPTER 8: Mechanical Planning

Planning for electrical and mechanical equipment is more essential than ever. Changing lifestyles, an insurgence of technology, and an increase in the number of activities, fixtures and electronic devices in the kitchen result in a space that demands attention to the systems that form the structure for this equipment. Without a clear and detailed plan, necessary components of such a system can be overlooked, leading to disappointment on the part of the client, or added costs if features need to be redone. Consider these early in the project in order to assure that they are in place before the installation of cabinetry, fixtures and finishes is completed.

The technicalities of these systems are covered in depth in the NKBA's *Residential Construction* and *Kitchen & Bath Systems* books. This chapter describes the mechanical factors from a kitchen design and planning perspective.

WIRING/ELECTRICAL

Be sure to familiarize yourself with the applicable codes for your area. However, the kitchen wiring and electrical system should be designed to not only meet current codes, but also the needs of the individuals using the home. Whether building or remodeling, use the forms in Chapter 6 – Needs Assessment, to evaluate the electrical needs of the client. Then consult current codes to see what must be implemented and suggest additional ideas for improving the electrical system to address the future needs of the client. Then, review the wiring plan before the walls are enclosed.

Wiring

One component of older homes that is typically outdated, especially homes built before 1973, is the electrical wiring. Home wiring added from 1965 – 1973 could most likely be aluminum, which has been found to develop fire hazards. Copper wire is the wire of choice today, so if aluminum wire is present, the entire home must be rewired as part of the remodeling project. Updating the wiring will ensure that the electrical system is safe and meets current electrical codes.

Signs of inadequate or outdated wiring include

- The home is over 30 years old.

- A fuse box is present instead of a circuit breaker panel box.

- The system has only two wires and therefore is not grounded.

- Aluminum wire is present.

- No ground fault circuit interrupters are present.

- Lights flicker when another appliance is turned on.

- Motors overheat or sound like they are bogged down.

- Appliances heat slowly.

- Fuses blow or circuit breakers trip often.

- Too few switches, receptacles or lights are present.

- Extension cords must be used.

- The electrical supply is 100 amps or less.

Wiring requires careful planning because its placement affects both functional and aesthetic qualities of the home. Adequate wiring also includes a sufficient electrical supply to meet the household's needs. Even fairly new homes may need a substantial update to the wiring and electrical system.

Two terms used when discussing electrical service are voltage and amperes. Voltage (volts) is the force that moves the electrons along the wire. Amperes (amps) is the quantity or amount of current flowing.

Begin by determining the size of the electrical service and the number of circuits that service will support. Many existing homes have between 60- and 100-amp service. For today's homes, a 200-amp service is more appropriate. An electrician can evaluate the service for you, and the level of service should also be stamped on the fuse box or circuit breaker panel.

The circuit breaker panel (or fuse box in older homes) is where the electric service is divided into circuits that supply electricity throughout the home. Each breaker is rated for either 120-volt or 240-volt service or a certain amperage. Each room of the home may include a number of different types of circuits and some receptacles may even be serviced by two different circuits. The use of two different circuits, or split wiring, allows you to continue using an outlet even if a problem occurs with one of the circuits. Circuits can be of three different types:

General or Lighting Circuits. Handle lighting and most wall receptacles in the home.

LIGHTING CIRCUITS

Code requires 3 watts of light per square foot of living space.

- one 15-amp circuit for each 600 square feet of living space, or

- one 20-amp circuit per 800 square feet of living space

RECEPTACLE CIRCUITS

Rule of thumb for including receptacles.

- 12 receptacles for a 15-amp circuit

- 16 receptacles for a 30-amp circuit

Small Appliance Circuits. Designed to accommodate small appliances.

Recommendation:

- two 20-amp circuits or what the code requires for the kitchen counter area

- One or more circuits in the pantry, dining room or family room.

Individual or Dedicated Circuits. Designated for an individual appliance, with either 120-volt or 240-volt requirement.

Examples of individual circuits:

- 240-volt circuit: Range, cooktop, on-demand water heaters, wall ovens

- 120-volt circuit: Disposer, dishwasher, microwave oven, refrigerator, exhaust fan

Not only are consumers bringing more electrical devices into the kitchen, but also replacement appliances may have different electrical requirements than the previous ones. Newer models of appliances that previously used 120 volts may now require 240 volts. For example, clothes washers that heat water to higher temperatures or small ovens that have large power requirements now need 240 volts. Be sure these new circuits are in place before the finishing work is completed.

Receptacles

Consumers often find that rooms in the home do not have an adequate number of receptacles. In addition to the standard kitchen appliances, like toasters and coffee makers, many families now have a collection of other small appliances they use for food preparation.

The International Residential Code (IRC) specifies that receptacle outlets should be installed at each wall counter space that is 12 inches or wider, and receptacles should be installed such that no place along the counter will be more than 24 inches from a receptacle. For islands and peninsula counter spaces, most receptacles are located below the countertop or work surface. The universal design reach range recommendation places receptacles below 44 inches, which would place the top of the receptacle only 8 inches above the standard 36-inch counter height.

If you are specifying an appliance garage or other cabinets, such as a cabinet with a lift for a large mixer, installing receptacles within those cabinets will make it possible to plug in appliances where they are stored. Receptacles may also be needed in upper cabinets if you are planning to add such items as a built-in television or a microwave shelf.

Ground Fault Circuit Interrupters

Anytime water and electricity are in close proximity, electrical safety is an issue. To improve kitchen electrical safety, the International Residential Code requires ground fault circuit interrupter (GFCI) receptacles on counter walls as well as near a water source. Check local codes for proper placement. They reduce the hazards of electrical shock by breaking the circuit when the device senses the slightest disruption in the electrical flow. GFCI receptacles fit in the same space as the standard receptacles, but need to be appropriately wired.

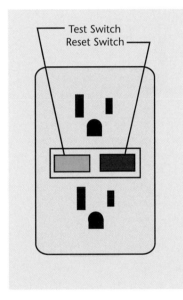

Figure 8.1 Codes require GFCIs in kitchens.

Special Wiring Needs

With the addition of more equipment in the kitchen, plan for the wiring needs before walls are finished. Here are a few examples:

- Under cabinet, soffit and floor lighting

- Built-in appliances

- Toekick heaters

- Communications equipment

- Computer or laptop

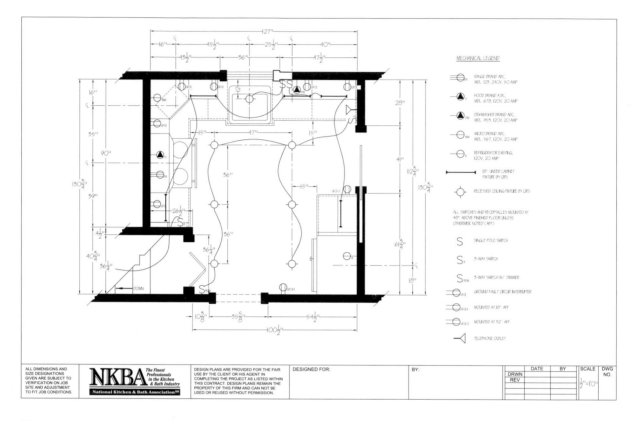

Figure 8.2 An accurate mechanical plan ensures that all mechanical connections are included.

Communications

Communication systems are becoming a standard component in the kitchen, so consider the wiring needed for these components early in the project. Linking the kitchen to the outside world and other parts of the house requires special wiring and planning. New structured or bundled wiring packages provide all the wiring needed for home communications and entertainment together. It makes installation easier because only one wire bundle needs to be installed rather than installing each wire individually.

Home intercom networks are becoming common, and the kitchen is a logical location. Consider the users when deciding on the most appropriate type and placement of the intercom unit. It should be accessible by all family members.

A telephone in the kitchen is standard today, so wiring for the telephone may already be available. The new kitchen plan, however, may require moving the phone line, along with the necessary electrical line, to a new location. Your client may wish to have a computer in the kitchen, which will probably need an Internet connection, either through the telephone line or a high-speed, broadband connection, such as a cable modem, Ethernet, or DSL service. A base station for wireless Internet capability may be requested. In addition, more appliances are including the capability of being Internet ready, so wiring for the Internet now is advisable.

As families include more activities in the kitchen, the television becomes a familiar feature. Linking the kitchen to the home cable or satellite system allows family members to keep up with the news while involved with other kitchen activities. Connections for a VCR, DVD player and speakers or sound system are also part of the entertainment package. If the client does not want electronic equipment located in the kitchen space, installing speakers in the ceiling or wall that connect to home electronics located elsewhere will allow the sound to be projected into the kitchen. Speakers may be recessed or wall mounted.

Kitchen Planning Guideline 30 relates to electrical receptacles and can be found in Chapter 12.

GAS

Gas is used for many home heating systems and is also a popular cooking fuel in the kitchen. Gas is delivered to homes in one of two forms: natural gas, which is piped into the home and not available to all residences, and propane gas, which requires a storage tank on the site that must to be filled on a periodic basis. If your client desires to have gas cooking equipment in the kitchen, keep the following considerations in mind:

- If you are installing gas into the kitchen for the first time, make sure gas lines are installed before the finish work on the floors and walls is completed.

- Current gas lines can be adjusted or relocated without too much difficulty due to the use of flexible pipe. A gas range can generally be relocated up to six feet from the old range connection. These changes should be decided early in the remodeling process if you would like the connector concealed behind a wall or under the floor.

- Check to make sure the gas appliances you specify fit the type of gas delivered to the home. Gas ranges and cooktops must be equipped with different orifices depending on the type of gas used.

- When using a gas range or cooktop, install an outside exhaust ventilation system with the equipment. See the section on Ventilation in this chapter for more details.

HEATING

While there are many ways in which to add heat to a kitchen, if necessary, the first step is to take measures to reduce heat loss by sealing leaks, improving insulation in exterior walls, and upgrading the windows.

Types of Heaters

Heating systems for the kitchen come in a wide variety of types. They vary as to installation needs, space requirements, energy sources, responsiveness, comfort and heating mode. Some of the most common choices of systems for a kitchen are listed below. Heaters are described in more detail in the book *Kitchen & Bath Systems*.

- **Central heating systems**. Many homes have a central heating system that also services the kitchen space. Central heating ducts are often used for the cooling ducts as well. Some vent location possibilities are shown in Figure 8.3.

- **Electric toekick heater.** A small electric or hydronic heater installed in the toekick space below the cabinets can provide comfortable supplemental heat to the feet and floor area. Locate these heaters where a little extra heat is needed. Select a heater with a variable temperature setting and on/off switch so that it can be adjusted to the user's comfort level. A provision for this type of heater needs to be made when the cabinet is installed.

- **Individual baseboard heaters.** As one of the choices for electric heating, these heaters are inexpensive to install and allow zonal control, but they take up valuable floor space. If the current space makes use of baseboard heating, other types of electric heating could take their place.

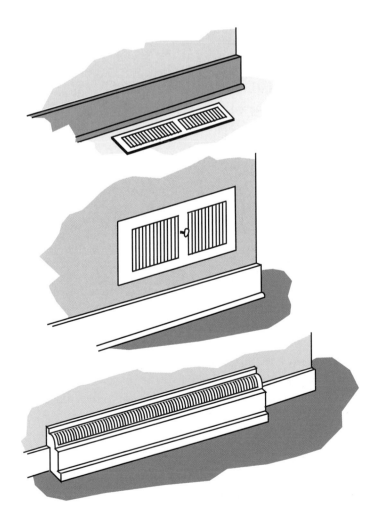

Figure 8.3 Locations for central heating and cooling vents.

- **Hot water (hydronic) heating.** Hot-water heating systems make use of a radiator, baseboard convectors or floor system. These systems may not be as conducive to zoning, and if you are adding heat to a new or renovated space, it may be difficult to find similar units to use. These radiators also become very hot and take up valuable floor space. Steam heating is another type of hot water system, and these systems are not used much today but may be found in some older construction.

- **Floor heaters.** Floor heating systems place heating units under the entire floor space and can be of either the electric or hydronic type. Both deliver a very even and quiet heat without drafts. Heat from these systems is very steady because they do not lose heat as quickly as other systems. Heated floors are comfortable to walk on, especially for anyone who needs a late night snack or drink of water. When the feet are warm, the whole body feels warm. Young children also like the warm floors because that is where they end up most of the time. This type of system is a desirable option for the kitchen because it does not interfere with cabinet or furniture placement. These systems can also be zoned, allowing flexibility in the temperature in each room. Because this system does not use ductwork, often a cooling system with ductwork will still need to be added to the home.

Electric floor heating systems consist of a series of heated wires placed just below the floor surface. These systems are easy to install during construction, but can also be retrofitted during a remodeling project. Because of the high cost of electricity, this system could be more expensive to operate.

A hydronic system would be a good choice if there is hot water heat in other parts of the home. It would be a little more difficult to retrofit into an existing home because you would need to add a boiler or other type of water heating system. These systems place piping through which hot water is pumped, either within or under the flooring material. This floor heating system delivers hot water to the floor and returns cooled water to the boiler (Figure 8.5). The cost to install is high, but they are typically very efficient.

Keep in mind that both the electric and hydronic units may raise the height of the floor, so door clearances may need to be adjusted. If cabinets are not going to be replaced, they may need to be adjusted to accommodate the added floor height. When selecting a floor covering to place over floor heaters, remember that some manufacturers do not advise installing wood floors that could be damaged by the excess heat. Tile, stone or poured surfaces are good options. The massive types of flooring materials take a longer time to heat up, but retain the heat for extended periods of time.

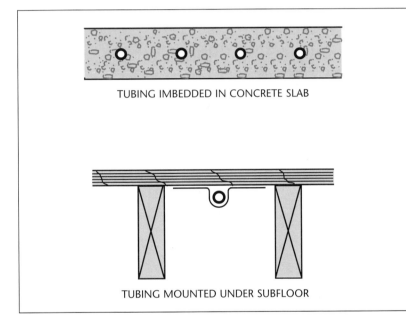

TUBING IMBEDDED IN CONCRETE SLAB

TUBING MOUNTED UNDER SUBFLOOR

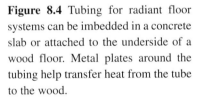

Figure 8.4 Tubing for radiant floor systems can be imbedded in a concrete slab or attached to the underside of a wood floor. Metal plates around the tubing help transfer heat from the tube to the wood.

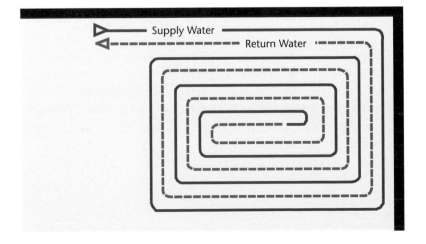

Supply Water

Return Water

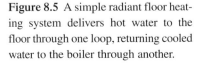

Figure 8.5 A simple radiant floor heating system delivers hot water to the floor through one loop, returning cooled water to the boiler through another.

CONSIDERATIONS
FOR THE KITCHEN

When selecting a heating system for the kitchen, keep the following in mind:

- Even if the kitchen is part of the central heating system duct network, consider adding some supplemental heat in colder climates to provide flexibility. This is especially important if the kitchen is at the end of the duct run, on the north side of the house, or if the client tends to keep the rest of the house cooler than they would like the kitchen.

- When ducting a central heating system into the kitchen, carefully plan in the location of the vents. Floor vents may be difficult to position away from where people will be walking or where food items and dirt will collect. Floor vents may also make it difficult to arrange cabinetry and other kitchen furniture, especially in a small kitchen. Consider the toe-kick areas for a duct or register location.

- Registers installed low on the wall will provide heat where cold air collects, but they consume wall space, which is premium in a small kitchen.

- Do not locate the heating vent too close to the kitchen ventilation system as this will reduce the efficiency of both systems.

- Locating vents in the ceiling removes them from the floor, but not all heating systems allow this option. If ceiling vents are used, locate them so they do not have a negative effect on the space. For example, do not include vents that direct air down onto a dining table.

- Do not place a heating vent directly over a refrigerator. This adds to the heating load that the refrigerator is trying to disperse.

- If your design incorporates a previously unheated area into part of the kitchen, be sure the central heating system can handle the additional load. If this new space is too far from a central heating system, a supplemental heater may be necessary.

COOLING

Climate will have a substantial impact on which cooling measures are necessary in a kitchen. In cool climates, little, if any, mechanical cooling may be necessary because summertime temperatures may not be extreme enough. In warmer climates, mechanical cooling is, for the most part, an essential component. In addition to cooling, some mechanical units can help remove excess humidity. Cooling systems are not, however, a replacement for good ventilation, as discussed further in this chapter.

Home orientation is another factor that can affect cooling needs. If the kitchen is located on the east or west side of the home, windows, especially large windows or those unprotected by landscaping, can allow excess heat into the space. Therefore, more cooling will be necessary during certain times of the day. Northern windows and southern windows with adequate overhangs should not have the heat gain problems from direct sunlight.

The amount of wall insulation also affects cooling needs. Just as an elevated level of insulation will help keep a home warmer in the winter, it will also keep the entire home cooler and require less mechanical cooling in summer.

Appliances also affect cooling needs. Although cooking may add welcome warmth to the house during cooler weather, it can add to the discomfort in warmer weather. The impact of these cooking appliances can be minimized, however, using an exhaust ventilation system to carry away some of the added heat. In addition, other appliances, such as the dishwasher and refrigerator, emit heat that needs to be handled by cooling equipment. Specify well-insulated and efficient appliances to minimize the amount of added heat in a room.

The choice and amount of lighting can also impact heat gain in the kitchen.

There are two main types of cooling methods for the kitchen: natural cooling and mechanical cooling. Depending upon the climate, one or both methods may need to be incorporated into the plan.

Natural Cooling

The most basic method for natural cooling is to open windows. Heat generated in the home can many times be cooled to a comfortable level just by opening a window to let in fresh air. Even on fairly warm days, allowing in cool night air and then closing windows during the heat of the day may be enough to keep a home comfortable. If it is possible to set up cross ventilation, opening windows on two walls of a room or two ends of the home increases circulation. A kitchen often could include a door to a patio or deck to open the space to the outdoors.

Windows with low-e coatings can also assist with keeping out the heat waves from direct sunshine. More information on window choices is discussed in Chapter 3 and is available in the NKBA book *Residential Construction*.

Your choice of surface materials can also assist with cooling. Ceramic tile, stone, concrete and other materials can provide a cool touch to the room. Keep in mind that these materials will also feel cool in colder weather so need to be warmed during that time of year.

Mechanical Cooling

If natural cooling methods cannot give the comfort levels desired, then mechanical means are necessary. The most basic is the fan. Although portable and window fans are available, they are typically not attractive and take up space. A ceiling fan is a better option if the ceiling is tall enough to accommodate one. Ceiling hugger fans are available for standard height ceilings, but above average height clients may have an issue with whirling blades just a short distance above their heads. A lighting fixture below the fan will lower the clearance further. Keep in mind that ceiling fans create breezes that will help cool occupants of the room, but the air can also cool food on a table or counter. Avoid placing recessed lighting fixtures above the blades of the fan, because the movement of the blades will create a flickering effect.

Mechanical cooling methods include refrigerated cooling and evaporative cooling. Refrigerated cooling is the most commonly used type of air conditioning in North America. This type of system dehumidifies the air as it cools, which is important for summertime moisture control. For more on moisture problems in kitchens see Chapter 4. Evaporative coolers actually cool by adding moisture to the air and are effective in hot, dry climates. For more on cooling systems, refer to *Kitchen & Bath Systems*.

When incorporating either type of cooling system, be aware of how the vent placement may affect the installation of fixtures, cabinetry and other components. Also evaluate how the vent location will affect the occupants. Cool air blowing directly on people in the rooms will not be very comfortable and cool air blowing on a dining table or counter will quickly chill hot food.

VENTILATION

Cooking, cleanup and other kitchen activities can generate moisture, odors, grease, and even smoke. Uncontrolled, these potential air pollutants can lead to both air quality problems as well as maintenance issues. Chapter 4 discusses moisture problems in kitchens and other air quality issues—and the importance of a mechanical ventilation system in the kitchen.

The kitchen designer is responsible for planning a balanced and efficient ventilation system that does not compromise user comfort and works with the existing mechanical systems in the home. Importantly, the designer needs to provide a ventilation system that will be used.

Residential ventilation systems are generally designed with the assumption that inside air is improved by mixing or replacing it with outside air. Air from outdoors is perceived to be fresher. Depending on the location of the home, this may not always be true. If the outside air is polluted, special ventilation systems may be needed that provide additional air filtration. In addition, in very cold climates, a heat recovery or energy recovery ventilation system may be recommended to provide more energy efficient ventilation.

In today's kitchens, there are two common choices in ventilation systems. The first is a fan mounted above the cooktop or range, usually with a hood (updraft). The second is a proximity system, installed in the cooktop or adjacent to the cooking surface (downdraft). Some kitchens may have a ceiling or wall-mounted exhaust fan, but that is generally not considered as effective as the updraft or downdraft systems. A house with a whole-house ventilation system will typically include an exhaust vent in the kitchen.

A

B

C

Figure 8.6 A variety of hood styles provide ventilation while adding a design element to the kitchen. (Photo a-Courtesy of Blue Arnold IV, CKD – Jarrettsville, Maryland, b-Courtesy of Rebecca G. Lindquist, CMKBD – Duluth, Minnesota, c-Courtesy of Scott Gregor – Portland, Oregon.)

Figure 8.7 In this open plan kitchen, a proximity ventilation system is provided with the island cooktop. (Courtesy of Sandra Steiner-Houck, CKD – Columbia, Pennsylvania)

Kitchen ventilation systems are usually located near the cooking surface, considered the primary source of odors, grease and moisture. However, other appliances contribute to kitchen air pollution. An oven in a range typically vents through a burner on the cook top, putting moisture and odors in the vicinity of the ventilation system. A built-in or wall oven typically vents to the front of the appliance, into the room air, which may or may not be near the ventilation system. A microwave oven, which may vent to the front, side, or back, is often not placed near the kitchen ventilation system. Dishwashers also vent warm moist air.

Canopy or updraft ventilation systems can be either a recirculating (ductless) system or an exhaust system. Downdraft ventilation systems are all exhaust systems. A recirculating system pulls the air through a filter then returns the air to the room. The filter may be a simple grease filter screen or include an activated carbon type filter to remove odors. Moisture and heat are not removed. Combustion pollutants from gas cooking, including carbon monoxide and water vapor, are also not removed. Recirculating systems are less expensive and easier to install, but less effective. Exhaust systems, on the other hand, remove air as well as heat, moisture, odors, combustion pollutants and grease, from the kitchen to the outside. Generally, a recirculating ventilation system should only be used when it is impossible to install the duct work for an exhaust system.

There are many variables involved in designing an effective exhaust ventilation system for the cooking area in a kitchen, including:

- Type of cooking

- Type of cooking appliance

- Type of cooking fuel

- Location of the range and/or cooktop within the kitchen

- Size and location of the hood, if used

- Size, length and number of turns in the ducts needed to connect the fan to the exterior vent

- Type and size of fan used in the system

- Make-up or replacement air available to the fan

Updraft Ventilation Systems

Generally, a range hood with an exhaust fan vented to the outside (updraft) is considered the most effective system. The hood helps capture the pollutants, such as moisture and grease, before they disperse in the air in the kitchen. There are many styles and designs of hoods available. Some are a focal point in the room; others, such as retractable models, are barely noticeable. The placement of the fan above the cooking area takes advantage of the natural rise of the heated air.

A well-designed and properly placed hood can improve the efficiency of the ventilation system and can reduce the fan size needed. A hood should be at least the size of the cooking surface, and preferably 3 to 6 inches larger than the cooking surface, in all directions. Although ideal, this may be hard to achieve. Hoods are typically available in widths of 24 inches to 54 inches (in 6-inch increments), so a hood wider than the cooking surface may be selected. However, few hoods have a depth greater than 17 to 21 inches. Hoods with greater interior height have a larger capture area, which increases efficiency.

The bottom of the hood should be 24 to 36 inches above the cooking surface. Kitchen Planning Guideline 18 recommends a minimum 24-inch clearance between the cooking surface and a protected non-combustible surface, such as a hood, above it. (See Chapter 7 for further information on this Planning Guideline.) A larger hood can be mounted higher on the wall than a smaller hood, with comparable efficiency. If the same sized hood is mounted higher on the wall, the fan size may need to be increased to maintain efficiency. Mounting the hood higher on the wall can provide better visibility to the cooking surface, access to large pots, especially on the back burners, and prevents bumped heads.

When selecting a hood, it is important to know how the ducts will need to be installed to exhaust air outside. Some ducts will run vertically and some will run horizontally. Not all hoods can accept ducts in both directions.

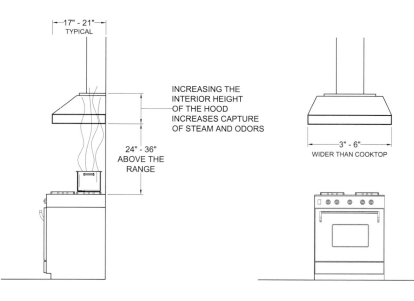

Figure 8.8 The size and placement of the hood are important to provide effective ventilation.

Microwave Ovens and Ventilation System Combinations

Some microwave ovens are integrated with a ventilation system, so that they can be installed over a cooking surface. This type of ventilation is not likely to be as effective because the flat bottom of the microwave lacks the canopy shape of a hood, which helps to trap pollutants. In addition, the microwave tends to be shallower than a hood (12 to 13 inches is typical), giving less coverage of the cooking surface.

For the most ventilation efficiency, yet greatest safety, the combination microwave oven and ventilation system should be installed at the 24-inch minimum clearance above the cooking surface (recommended in Planning Guideline 18), typically 60 inches above the floor (36-inch counter height + 24 inch clearance). However, this does not meet the recommendations in Kitchen Planning Guideline 21 (See Chapter 7), which recommends a microwave be installed with the bottom 3 inches below the shoulder of the principle user (which will be less than 60 inches for many cooks) and no more than 54 inches above the floor. Most microwave oven ventilation system combination appliances are installed 15 to 18 inches over the cooktop or range, to visually align with wall cabinets and for ease of reach.

If your client is interested in a combination microwave oven and ventilation system, consider the type of cooking surface, height of the cooking surface, need for ventilation and the type of cookware. Then, be sure to follow all manufacturers' instructions for placement and installation.

Downdraft Ventilation Systems

A downdraft or proximity ventilation system can be an effective alternative for grilling, frying and other cooking from shallow pots and pans. The downdraft system, including those with "pop-up" vents captures pollutants near their source (see figure 8.9). A larger fan is required in a downdraft system because there is no hood to help capture the cooking by-products and because the fan must work against the natural tendency for warm air to rise. Before specifying a downdraft ventilation system, determine that there is space for the ductwork.

Ventilation Efficiency

When a cooking appliance is located against a wall, ventilation is more effective. Ventilation systems for ranges and cooktops that are in open islands or peninsulas require larger fans and/or hoods to compensate for cross-drafts.

Effective ventilation is more critical with a gas cooking system. With gas cooking, there are by-products of combustion, such as carbon monoxide. In addition, gas combustion produces water vapor, so moisture is more of an issue.

Professional-style gas ranges with higher Btu output and gas grills need larger capacity ventilation systems. One general guideline, used by many manufacturers, is that you need 1 cubic feet per minute (cfm) for each 100 Btu of output. It is important to follow manufacturers' recommendations, as well as local codes, when selecting ventilation systems for larger ranges and grills. It is possible to put in a system that is too large and create an alternate set of problems.

If your kitchen design includes a gas cooking appliance, it is important to recommend that the home have a carbon monoxide detector. This is a safety feature that may be required by code.

Figure 8.9 A "pop-up" or telescoping ventilation fan is almost invisible when not in use and lowered. Such proximity ventilation systems are particularly useful in island applications. (Courtesy of GE)

Ducts

Ductwork can alter the efficiency of a ventilation system. A design decision about the location of the cooktop, and thus the ventilation system, will influence the ductwork needed to install the system. Longer duct runs or more turns or angles, reduce efficiency in the system.

- **Length of duct run.** Generally, if the duct run is more than five feet from the intake vent in the kitchen to the exhaust vent in the wall or roof, the size of the fan should be increased to compensate for the resistance of a longer duct run.

- **Elbows or bends in the ducts.** Generally, if there is more than one elbow or bend in the duct, the size of the fan should be increased to compensate for the greater resistance. Three 90-degree elbows are considered the maximum.

Smooth ducts with sealed joints offer less resistance to air movement and provide quieter, more efficient operation. Any duct that must go through spaces that are not heated or cooled should be insulated to help prevent moisture condensation. The ducts should not terminate in the attic or basement but continue to the outside. Warm, moist air exhausted into the attic can lead to condensation and eventual structural problems.

A back-draft flap on the exhaust vent is important to the fan system. This prevents infiltration of outside air, or loss of conditioned air from inside the home, when the fan is not operating. Also, the flap can prevent insects, birds and other animals from getting into the fan duct.

Fan Size

Ventilation fans are sized in cfm or L/s (Liters per second). These terms both describe the volume of air the fan can move in a period of time.

In addition to NKBA, there are several sources for sizing kitchen ventilations fans, including the Home Ventilating Institute, the American Society of Heating, Refrigeration and Air-conditioning Engineers (ASHRAE), and the 2006 International Residential Code. Although the ventilation requirements are determined somewhat differently, the resulting recommendations are similar in practice.

Kitchen Planning Guideline 19 recommends a minimum size fan of 150 cfm. The code requirement, from the model 2006 International Residential Code (IRC), is 100 cfm ducted to the outside, in addition to following the manufacturers' specifications. A similar recommendation of 100 cfm minimum is found in the ASHRAE Standard 62.

If a home has a whole house ventilation system, a separate ventilation system over the cooking surface is not used, because an exhaust vent is provided in the kitchen. The standard for the exhaust vent in the kitchen, according to the model 2006 IRC, is 25 cfm of continuous ventilation. If a high Btu cooking appliance is added to a home with an existing whole house ventilation system, be sure to consult the project's heating and cooling contractor to determine if any system adjustments are needed.

The ventilation recommendations of the Home Ventilating Institute, an industry organization, are shown in the table below. Fan sizes are increased for cooking surfaces in an open island. In a combination cooktop and grill, a multi-speed or two-fan system is recommended to provide low and high ventilation for different types of cooking.

	Recommendation	Fan needed for a typical 30-inch range with a 36-inch hood
Hood placed along a wall	Minimum: 40 cfm per lineal foot	120 cfm
	Recommended: 100 cfm per lineal foot	300 cfm
Hood above an island or peninsula (no wall)	Minimum: 50 cfm per lineal foot	300 cfm
	Recommended: 150 cfm per lineal foot	450 cfm

Source: Home Ventilating Institute (www.hvi.org)

Finally, consult the cooking appliance manufacturer's recommendation for the recommended fan size and CFM capacity to properly vent the appliance.

Replacement Air

A final, often overlooked factor in kitchen ventilation system efficiency is make-up or replacement air. Exhaust ventilation systems remove air from the kitchen, and this air must be replaced. If replacement air is not provided, the fan will not operate effectively. In addition, a negative pressure in the home could be created. With a larger ventilation fan, such as might be paired with a professional-style range, there is a greater possibility of depressurizing the home.

If the home has negative pressure, there will be problems with other combustion appliances that need to exhaust to the outside, such as a gas furnace or water heater. Combustion by-products will not be able to exhaust from the home through the chimney or flue. Instead, these by-products will spill back into the interior of the home. This situation is referred to as back-drafting. When back-drafting occurs, dangerous combustion pollutants, such as carbon monoxide, as well as excess moisture will be pulled into the home. In extreme cases, back-drafting could lead to fatal carbon monoxide poisoning of the residents.

In older homes, make-up air would usually come from natural air leakage. In newer or renovated, more tightly constructed and energy efficient homes, this replacement air must be provided. A simple solution could be opening a window slightly when operating the kitchen exhaust fan. A supply vent could be installed in the soffit or toe-kick, to provide make-up air. In this type of vent, an in-line heater could be included to preheat the incoming air as needed. Other solutions include a mechanical ventilation system that balances airflow in the home.

Some jurisdictions in the United States and Canada have addressed the concern for negative pressurization of the home through codes. In some cases, there may be a requirement to have the ventilation system performance tested.

Noise

Although the noise of a kitchen ventilation system is not a factor in efficiency, it is a major concern of the users. Noise is a frequent reason for not using kitchen exhaust fans.

The noise level of fans is rated in sones. Ventilation fans will vary in their sone rating. The fewer the sones, the quieter the fan. Larger fans and longer or more convoluted duct runs can increase noise. Axial or propeller fans are noisier than centrifugal or "squirrel-cage" fans, although the axial fans are usually cheaper.

Installing the fan in a remote location, such as the attic, instead of the kitchen, reduces noise. Installing the fan on rubber gaskets or similar cushioning will reduce vibration, and the fan will operate more quietly.

Controls and Features

A multi-speed fan is a desirable feature. The fan can be used at a high setting if needed for quick or powerful ventilation, but the lower, quieter setting will encourage regular use. Some fans feature heat sensors that will increase fan speed automatically if there is extra heat.

The ventilation fan filter should be easily removed for cleaning. A convenient feature is a filter that can be washed in the dishwasher. The smaller the diameter of the filter mesh, the more effective it is in catching grease.

Most ventilation hoods come with lights, typically incandescent or halogen lamps. Some feature dual lamps or high/low settings. Make sure that the hood lighting is consistent with the overall plan for kitchen lighting.

The Kitchen Planning Guideline and Access Standard that applies to ventilation, Guideline 19, can be found in Chapter 12. In summary, a kitchen ventilation system needs to be carefully designed to provide good control of moisture, heat, grease, odors and other by-products of cooking. However, ventilation systems are only as effective as their frequency of use. Therefore, quiet, convenient ventilation systems are most desirable.

LIGHTING

Many tasks take place in the kitchen, all requiring the appropriate lighting. As more activities move into the kitchen area, lighting must be more varied and flexible to accommodate them.

The technical properties of lighting are discussed in NKBA's book *Kitchen & Bath Systems*. The focus here is on planning considerations.

Your client will be the main source of information for determining lighting needs. Once you have determined the client's kitchen activities in Chapter 6 – Assessing Needs and made note of any special vision needs, you will have a better idea of the required light sources and types. Also, investigate the client's likes and dislikes regarding lighting and light fixtures.

You will be incorporating various levels of the basic types of lighting—daylighting, general, task and accent lighting.

Natural or Daylighting

Daylighting makes use of windows, glass doors and skylights to add natural light to a space. When planning daylighting, first determine when the kitchen is most used. Emphasizing natural light when the kitchen is only used in the evening or very early morning may not be logical or cost-effective. Use these ideas to help plan daylighting in a kitchen:

- Too much natural light can lead to glare. If the window area faces a sunny direction, incorporate window treatments that can help control the bright sunlight.

- Large windows can provide adequate daytime lighting needs, plus visually open the room to the outdoors. Select windows that have a high insulating value to keep the kitchen more comfortable year around.

- Skylights can provide about five times as much light as comparably sized windows on a wall, without sacrificing wall space. If the ceiling is not at the roof line, a shaft will need to be added. The shaft can be straight, angled, or wider at the ceiling line. Select high-quality skylights and have them installed properly to avoid leaks or condensation. When positioning a skylight, decide where the direct light will enter the space. Avoid adding extra heat to a dining area or the refrigerator, or creating glare onto a glossy surface.

- Privacy may be another consideration when incorporating a large amount of glass. Privacy measures such as glass block on the exterior or adequate window treatments may be necessary.

Types of Artificial Lighting

Natural lighting often does not provide enough illumination for the kitchen's activities, so artificial means must be incorporated. When sizing artificial light, decide what is needed to supplement the natural light during the day and then consider the needs in the room after dark. Artificial lighting can be included in a number of ways.

General or Ambient Lighting

When daylighting is not adequate, artificial lighting is needed to illuminated traffic paths, see into cabinetry and prevent accidents. Provisions for general lighting can be accomplished through a variety of sources including ceiling fixtures, lamps, track lighting, pendants, wall fixtures, recessed lights and indirect or cove lighting.

How many light fixtures it will take to achieve this level depends on many factors. The height of the ceiling impacts how much light a fixture delivers to the area. Dark and more textured surfaces absorb more light than light and smooth surfaces and therefore need to be considered in the formula. A kitchen with dark surfaces will need about one-third more light than a kitchen with light surfaces. The recommended footcandle level for general lighting is 30-40 depending on the reflective value of the kitchen surfaces.

Figure 8.10 Adequate general or ambient lighting is provided by the large window area and recessed ceiling fixtures. (Courtesy of Blue Arnold IV, CKD – Jarrettsville, Maryland)

Kitchen Area	Fixture Placement	Incandescent Lamping	Fluorescent Lamping
Counter	Mount incandescent or fluorescent fixtures under cabinets, as close to the front of the cabinet as possible	Use low voltage halogen or xenon light strips (bulbs 2" apart) or puck lights (18" apart). Some require a transformer.	Tubes long enough to extend 2/3 length of counter
	Counters with no overhead cabinets, hang pendants 24"–27" above the counter	60-75W for every 20" of counter	
	OR		
	Recessed or surface mounted units: 16"–24" apart, centered over the counter	75W reflector lamp	
At the Range	Built-in hood light	60W bulb	
	With no hood, place recessed or surface mounted units 15"–18" apart over the center of the range	Minimum of two 75W reflector floods	Two 36" 30W or three 24" 20W
At the Sink	Same as for range	Same as for range	Same as for range
Eating Area	Pendant centered 30" above table or counter, multiple pendants over counter 4' or longer	One 100 W or two 60W or three 40 W or 50/100/150W	

Source: American Home Lighting Institute

It is possible to add too much light to a space. Multiple light-colored surfaces and excessive amounts of light can produce glare, which makes the space uncomfortable for work. Also keep in mind that some light sources are high-heat producers.

Task Lighting

Based on how the family uses the kitchen, plan lighting for each task or activity. At a minimum, plan to incorporate task lighting for the cooking surface, at the sink, over the counters and over any table or other work surface. A lighting level of 75-100 footcandles on work areas is recommended for kitchens. Task lighting may be in the form of a pendant over a table, a hood light over a cooktop, or a recessed light positioned over a sink.

Low voltage systems are widely used for undercabinet lights that illuminate the counter work surface. Some undercabinet lights can be simply attached to the bottom of the cabinet and plugged into the wall. But this application features dangling cords that look unattractive and can get in the way of kitchen activities. A preferred application is to hard wire the lighting into the electrical system so that all cords are hidden. Although these lights can usually be hard wired as a retrofit, it is much easier to conceal the wiring during the kitchen construction or renovation project. Be careful of using undercabinet lights with plastic diffusers above a toaster or toaster oven. They may be damaged by heat from the appliances.

Accent Lighting

The purpose of accent lighting is to highlight various features of the kitchen (Figure 8.11). Your client may wish to illuminate a soffit area above the wall cabinetry where a collection of items can be displayed, open shelves filled with decorative items, or glass-door cabinets holding special dishes. Use light to highlight wall art, surface textures and architectural features. If there is deeply carved cabinetry you would like to emphasize, situate the accent lighting to create shadows. Track lighting, recessed lights or wall-mounted lights can all be used to provide the lighting coverage you want for an area, but be careful that the lights do not shine into occupants' eyes. Accent lights can vary from small intense spot lights to the soft glow of a rope light. Select the light that gives the desired effect.

Lighting Fixtures

Lighting fixtures come in a wide variety of styles, mounting types and sizes. When deciding which type to use, consider the size of the space you are lighting, the type of light you want, the design theme of the space and the tasks that must be illuminated. Following are a few important points to consider concerning light fixtures.

Figure 8.11 Accent lighting highlights vases displayed on open shelves and in a storage unit. (Courtesy of Toshie Lim, CKD, CBD – Alameda, California)

Location

Locate the light fixtures where they can deliver the maximum amount of light for their purpose. Think through the needs for each area and decide how the lighting should be positioned to achieve the effect you want. Some location considerations are as follows:

- **General Lighting.** General lighting might involve one or two lights in the center of the room, or a number of recessed lights around the perimeter. Provide enough light to cover the floor area so that dark corners do not form. Be aware of fixtures that can get in the way of the users. For example, wall sconces in the walkways of very small kitchens or central ceiling fan lights in average height ceilings.

- **Dining Tables.** A pendant light or chandelier over the dining table should be no lower than 25 to 30 inches above the table and 7 feet to 7 feet 6 inches above the floor. These lights can also be in the way if they do not allow for location flexibility. Table fixtures may be a problem when the client decides to move the table, for example.

- **Recessed Lighting.** Recessed lights, sometimes called cans, come in a variety of styles. Some have the lamp located a few inches up inside the cylinder, which may have a white, black or reflective coating. Other recessed fixtures are closed and flush with the ceiling, while still others have an eyeball design for adjusting direction. Place recessed lights about 12 to 16 inches apart and 6 to 8 inches out into the room. These lights are described by how they distribute light—wide, medium or narrow beam, so choose the style that fits your needs. Recessed lights are often positioned above islands, peninsulas or countertops.

If you are using recessed lighting to illuminate a work or counter area, the fixtures should be mounted so that they cast light onto the task area without causing glare or shadows from people working at the task area. For example, a pot rack should not interfere with the functional lighting, often recessed, of the island or work surface over which it hangs. Many times it's difficult to avoid this type of interference which is why undercabinet lighting is a better choice for work surfaces.

Figure 8.12 This kitchen uses lighting fixtures, as well as natural light, in a variety of types and locations to provide general, task and accent lighting. (Courtesy of Peter Ross Salerno, CMKBD – Wyckoff, New Jersey)

Recessed fixtures must be selected and installed so that they do not pose a fire hazard. The housing or covering of some recessed fixtures must not have insulation in contact with the fixture. However, others, type IC (insulation contact) housing, can be covered with insulation. Select the type that is most appropriate for the job and check local codes. Some jurisdictions require that all recessed fixtures are the IC type, but not all fixtures are available with IC housing.

- **Other Uses.** Do not forget to place some general lighting in all compartments of the kitchen, including large pantries and laundry areas. Consider illuminating the ceiling to expand the feel of the room.

- **Accent Lighting.** Accent lighting should be positioned to achieve the effect your client desires. Many variations exist. The soffit is a good example. Decorative items can be highlighted from the front, back or both. The light can be continuous or in the form of spot lights. Accent lighting can also take the form of a night light near the floor. Placed in the toekick area of the cabinetry, this soft glow is just the right level light for nighttime visitors to the kitchen.

Controls

Controls for general lighting should be located where users enter the room so they do not walk into a dark room. If the kitchen has multiple entries, such as from a deck, hall, dining room, garage and perhaps a living area, use a combination of three- or four-way switches to control lights from multiple locations. Additional rooms within or near the kitchen, such as a pantry, wet bar or laundry room typically have their light controls at the room entrance rather than the main kitchen entrance.

Other lighting controls need to be close to where the light is used. In addition to the controls for general light fixtures that illuminate the space, help your client decide which other lights should be controlled individually. As an example, it is probably not desirable to have one switch for turning on all of the task and accessory lighting in the room. Instead, you may wish to have separate switches at the point of use for the undercabinet lighting, soffit lighting, shelf and glassed cabinet lighting, and floor lighting.

Because every kitchen has many lights to control, try, as much as possible to consolidate the controls into banks of switches to avoid having the wall dotted with switches. When grouping controls, some professionals recommend only two switches in one location. If more need to be grouped together, four switches is the maximum in one location. When arranging the switches, try to make it easy for your client to remember which switch controls which fixture(s). This may be difficult, but devise a logical order so that a light switch is nearest the corresponding light fixture. The general surface lighting should be the first accessible switch for the room. The recommended universal reach is for controls to be placed less than 48 inches from the floor or 44 inches when over a counter.

Many different types of controls are now available for lighting. Select the type your client could use easily, as well as the style they prefer. The flip switches are perhaps the most common. You may also choose a toggle or rocker switch, a motion sensor switch, or even a remote control switch for adjusting light levels on an elevated ceiling. The remote control switches are especially nice for ceiling fans that also include lights.

Controlling the amount of light is important in some areas of the kitchen. For lighting over a table or bar area, consider adding a dimmer. Be aware that different types of light sources such as fluorescent, halogen and xenon can be dimmed, but each requires a different type of dimming device or ballast, in the case of fluorescent.

Low Voltage Lighting

Low voltage lighting systems have many uses in a kitchen lighting plan. These light sources can be in the form of a small strip that easily disappears behind the moulding above or below a cabinet. Other low voltage design options are the round puck light that can be placed under the cabinets or inside cabinets, and the smaller track lighting units with self-contained transformers for a minimal visual effect. In addition to small track and recessed lights for general lighting, low voltage units can light cabinets, counters, shelves, soffit areas, floors and art work. Low voltage lights also make good night lights.

These lighting systems use a transformer, either as a separate unit or built into the lighting fixture, to transform the 120-volt service to the lower voltage (usually 24, 12 or 6 volts). Larger capacity transformers are used to control multiple applications of low voltage lights installed in one area. These transformers can be fairly large (5 x 5 x 9 inches), so you need to decide where they will be hidden, which may be in or above a cabinet or in the ceiling. Transformers incorporated into a fixture make the fixture a little larger and more difficult to conceal.

Low voltage lights come with either halogen or xenon bulbs, which give off a crisp, clear light. Halogen lights burn at a high temperature, and even though the low voltage bulbs are small, added together they can still produce a significant amount of heat. Therefore, keep them out of reach of users and flammable objects.

Safety

All lighting fixtures and components should have a safety approval label by a recognized testing laboratory, which most codes require. Although most lighting systems are generally tested and safe to use, follow proper installation instructions and place fixtures in locations away from contact with people to prevent light fixture hazards. If a recessed light is installed too close to combustible materials, the heat from the light could ignite the materials around it. Guidelines for installation are given in the NKBA book *Kitchen & Bath Systems*. Many recessed fixtures are designed with built-in air spaces to help cool the bulbs.

Installing the incorrect bulb into a fixture can also increase the chances of a fire. When a fixture is selected, it may be difficult to tell how much light it will emit into a room. The size of the room, the colors and textures used, can all affect the available light. If your clients find the fixture is not producing the amount of light they desired, they may increase the wattage of the bulbs. This will provide more light, but at the same time, the larger bulbs will give off more heat than the fixture can handle. The fixture becomes hot to the point where it could crack or ignite. Many types of light bulbs, like incandescent and halogen, produce a significant amount of heat. Be careful to locate these where your client cannot easily come into contact with the bulbs, such as while walking through the room or reaching for something. Think through your client's lighting needs carefully to avoid this mistake.

The Kitchen Planning Guideline and Access Standard regarding lighting, Guideline 31, can be found in Chapter 12.

CHAPTER 9: More Than a Kitchen

Today's kitchen is more than just a place to cook and to eat. In fact, the kitchen may function like command central for the household. Sometimes it's a gathering place that allows busy family members to work and play near each other. Oftentimes activities merge here, allowing one or more household members to perform multiple tasks, like laundry, cooking, homework and bill paying, all at the same time. The kitchen may be the place where household members come and go and keep their lives organized.

As a kitchen designer, you may be called on to design activity spaces in or adjacent to the kitchen that include social, home management or hobby activities. In this chapter, we discuss designing these auxiliary spaces to integrate with the primary food preparation and eating areas of the kitchen. Specifically, we will discuss a family foyer or mudroom, a home planning center, a laundry area, a craft/hobby area, a gardening area and social spaces. It is unlikely that you will design all these spaces into one kitchen project, but hopefully, you will find many suggestions and ideas that will be beneficial to your clients.

THE FAMILY FOYER OR MUDROOM

Many American homes have beautiful foyers or front entrance areas. These ceremonial entrance areas may be grand, vaulted spaces or simple but defined designs. However, many of them share an important characteristic—the members of the household seldom use them on a regular basis. Instead, most homes have another, more casual entrance to the back, side or rear of the home that is used for the daily comings and goings of household members. Typically, this entrance is off the garage or parking area, and often opens directly into the kitchen or an area adjacent to the kitchen. Therefore, a busy household has people coming and going through the kitchen, not to prepare and eat food, but to enter and exit the home.

As part of the design of the kitchen, it may be important to think in terms of a family foyer or a mudroom. These terms are both applied to an informal entrance to the home, used by members of the household and perhaps close friends. This is where groceries come into the house and the trash and other materials are removed. It might be where backpacks and briefcases wait in readiness for a quick morning departure. Winter coats and boots, sun hats and gardening gloves might find temporary homes in such a space. Perhaps the baby's stroller or a snow shovel is kept in this space.

The family foyer or mudroom is also a communication space. Messages and reminders might be left there. Outgoing mail, recycling or dry cleaning may wait in the space for the next person to take it out. Depending on the household, some of the functions of the home planning center may overlap with the family foyer or mudroom. Be sure to read the section on the home planning center for further ideas about designing a communication center for the home.

A family foyer is likely a simple space, a transition between outside and inside. A mudroom is usually a more detailed space, including storage and activity spaces, and may be a separate room. Part of the decision as to what is appropriate to a particular home will depend on what other spaces are available, such as a garage, laundry or hobby area. A family foyer might include:

- Passageway in and out of the house, without interfering with kitchen work areas.

- Space to put on and remove outer clothing, such as coats, boots or hats.

- A bench or other seated area to use when putting on or removing boots or shoes.

- Storage space for items carried in and out of the house, such as backpacks, briefcases, purses and packages.

- An idea from the pre-school classroom: individual "cubby-holes" for household members. Things can be left for picking up before leaving, or to be put away later.

- Storage space on shelves, hooks or bins for items frequently used outside, such as an herb gathering basket or snow shovel.

- Tack space for messages, reminders, notes or coupons.

- Hooks for frequently used items such as keys, flashlights, the dog's leash or umbrellas.

- Hanging space for outer wear, such as coats, scarves or hats.

- Baskets or bins for mittens, gloves, scarves or other small items.

Figure 9.1 A family foyer can include a bench with storage underneath and pegs for hanging hats and other garments. (Courtesy of American Woodmark)

- Storage space to leave wet coats, boots, shoes, or umbrellas until they dry.

- A mirror for a quick check of appearance before leaving the house.

- Easy-to-clean materials that are not damaged by water, mud or sand.

A mudroom might include many of the same features of the family foyer and one or more of the following:

- A wall- or floor-mounted utility sink that might be used for activities such as washing garden produce, washing up after working in the yard, or cleaning muddy shoes.

- A laundry area (more about laundry areas later in this chapter).

- An indoor gardening, house plant, or potting area (more about indoor gardening areas later in this chapter).

- A pet washing, feeding or sleeping area.

- Storage for outdoor tools, gardening equipment or outdoor recreation equipment.

- A shower, lavatory and/or toilet facilities, so that someone working or playing outside could use the toilet or cleanup without going into the the house.

- Overflow storage from the kitchen, such as bulk paper goods storage, a pantry for home preserved foods, a beverage or snack refrigerator, or a separate freezer.

- Collection area for recycled items (See Chapter 4, Environmental Considerations).

Figure 9.2 A mudroom incorporated into the informal entrance includes storage, a sink and work area, hang-up space for hats and coats, a place for shoes and boots and durable, easy clean materials. (Courtesy of American Standard)

Designing the Family Foyer/Mudroom

There are many possible configurations for a family foyer or mudroom, depending on the flow of people through the space and its relation to the kitchen. Is this a separate space, closed off from the kitchen? Or, is it integrated with the kitchen? Does the space match the kitchen stylistically?

First, think about the space as a circulation area. Here are some important dimensions for you to keep in mind.

- Any doorway should have a minimum of a 32-inch clear opening (refer to Kitchen Planning Guideline 1 in Chapter 12).

- A minimum of 36 inches is needed for a walkway (refer to Kitchen Planning Guideline 7 in Chapter 12). This is adequate for one person. Additional space is needed if several people will be passing through the area at the same time.

- A wheel chair requires a 60-inch circle to turn around (refer to the Kitchen Planning Access Standards in Chapter 12). Providing a clear area will help make the space accessible for current and future household members and guests who might use mobility aids.

COATS, JACKETS, HATS, AND OTHER OUTERWEAR

A typical family foyer or mudroom will include space to store coats, jackets, rain slickers, boots, hats, scarves, mittens and other items of outerwear. This is also the space where these items are likely to be put on or taken off. What exactly is kept in this area will depend on the climate as well as other storage areas in the home. A house in a cold climate is likely to need more space for bulky winter clothes, while a house in a warm climate may need space for items like rain wear and sun hats.

If a coat closet is planned, here are some useful dimensions:

- A typical closet is 24 inches deep, with the rod placed 12 inches from the wall. However, coats and jackets are bulkier, and need 26 inches to 28 inches to hang perpendicular to the rod. Bulky outerwear, such as parkas or ski jackets, may need 30 inches of depth. If closet rod depth is inadequate, clothes will hang at an angle, and additional rod storage length will be needed.

• Heavy coats may take up 4 to 5 inches wide or more on a rod. The amount of rod length needed will depend on the number of coats and jackets to be stored.

• The height of the rod needs to be reachable by the user, but high enough that the garments clear the floor (Figure 9.4).

If the household for which you are designing includes a person who uses a wheelchair or mobility aid, a person with limited reach, or a shorter person, lower rods will be appropriate. Although 48 inches is considered the upper limit of the universal reach range for a seated person, this may vary with individual abilities. Refer to **Form 1: Getting to Know Your Client** in Chapter 6 for specific information about your client. See Chapter 5 for general information on reach ranges for different people.

Children cannot reach a full height closet rod. However, every parent wants to teach their children to hang up their own clothes. The solution might be adjustable rods that can be increased as children grow, their clothes get bigger and they can reach higher.

If boots or shoes will be kept on the closet floor, be sure that the rod is high enough for adequate clearance. A drip pan or rack for boots and shoes can be useful.

Figure 9.3 Plan adequate space to accommodate bulky coats and jackets. (Courtesy of Closet Maid)

Figure 9.4 Functional rod heights will depend on who uses the closet and what type of coats and garments will be stored.

Age and Type of Garment	Suggested Rod Height
Children, ages 2–6	30"–40"
Children, ages 6–12	40"–54"
Teens, ages 12–16	54"–63"
Adults, jackets & parkas	45"–48"
Adults, top coats & dress coats	54"–63"

- Adequate space to access hanging clothes is important to a well-planned coat closet. A clearance of 33 to 38 inches is recommended in front of the hangers in order to remove hangers (Figure 9.5). This clearance gives space for activities such as turning, holding up coats and jackets or removing items from a hanger.

It takes an area equal to about a 42-inch circle to put on or remove a coat. Therefore, increasing the clearance or access space in front of the closet to 42 inches is preferable.

If a shelf is placed above the rod, a clearance of 2 to 3 inches is needed to allow space to remove the hangers from the rod.

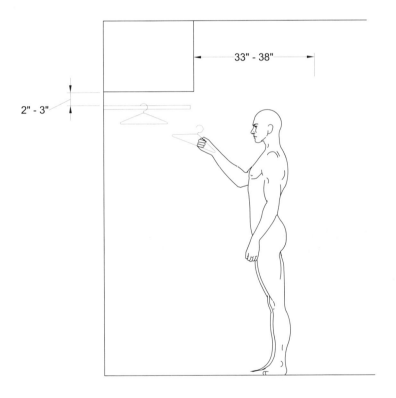

Figure 9.5 Adequate clearance space allows access to hangers.

Hook Storage. Instead of a coat closet, hooks can store coats and jackets for easy access. This might be desirable for frequently used garments, in season. Hooks are also easy to use for children, provided they are at a height they can reach. Use large and sturdy hooks or pegs that can hold bulky outer garments.

- A minimum height for a hook would be the length of the garment or item to store, plus 6 inches of clearance beneath. For multiple hooks, space them about 12 inches apart, to allow for the bulk of coats and jackets.

- Make sure that hooks are clear of passageways so that there is no danger of people walking into them when not in use.

- Provide 33 to 36 inches of clear space in front of the hook (for removing or hanging up items on the hook), or preferably, 42 inches (for putting on or removing a coat or jacket).

SEATING AREA

A seating area in the family foyer or mudroom is helpful for putting on or removing boots and shoes. This can help prevent tracking dirt into other areas of the home and save time on maintenance.

- A typical chair seat is 16 to 20 inches high. However, when designing seating for people to put on or remove shoes or boots, you may want to lower the height. The lower height will also be better for children.

- Consider putting a handrail or handle near the seating area to aid in getting up and down from the seat.

- Allow at least 24 inches in width and 18 inches in depth for a person to sit on a bench seat.

- An oversized seating area could double as a bench or shelf area to hold packages, backpacks, or briefcases while putting on or taking off coats.

- An open area underneath a seating bench can be used to temporarily store boots and shoes. Alternatively, a box bench can open up to provide storage inside.

Design Details

The design for the family foyer or mudroom is not complete until you have selected materials and planned for mechanical systems. Although these details are not the focus of this book, they should be mentioned here. By definition, this is a busy space in the home, and one that will get a lot of wear and tear.

MATERIALS

Whether designing a family foyer that is just an area off the kitchen, or a separate mudroom, choose materials that are durable and easy to maintain. Think about the traffic through the space. Select materials that can withstand the bumping and scraping of backpacks, briefcases, packages and assorted items.

The flooring materials will be particularly important in this space. As a designer, you may not often think about what type of soil is in an area. However, for the floor of a mudroom, this can be important. Depending on the location of the home, you may need to select flooring that is resistant to the grit of sand, the staining of iron-rich soil or the corrosion of salt used to melt icy sidewalks. In some climates, the floor of the entry area may often be wet, and this is an important design challenge for both safety and maintenance. In some cases, such as a beach or farm home, or in a snowy climate, consider a floor with a drain system.

MECHANICAL SYSTEMS

The electrical and lighting requirements of the family foyer or mudroom will be dependent on the activities that will take place there. In general, make sure that there is adequate lighting for people coming in and out of the space. Be generous with receptacles and circuits to allow future additions of electrical equipment.

Pay special attention to the placement of switches. Since this is a transition space between inside and outside, there are likely to be multiple switches for both interior and exterior lights. Group switches logically so that it will be easy to remember which switch goes with what light.

Since the family foyer or mudroom is an entrance to the home, consider planning for security or automatic lighting, both inside and outside the entrance. Lights can be on timers, photocells or motion detectors, and be set to turn on and off, according to the client's preferences. A low level "night light" might be appreciated.

In addition to security lighting, your client might have a home alarm system, fire monitoring, weather monitoring or other security systems. These may need to be included in your plans as well.

HOME PLANNING CENTER

Many activities that are important to the management of a busy household are conducted from the kitchen. With the kitchen as a central gathering place in the home, it follows that management and planning activities—the business of the household—are also handled in this space. Therefore, it becomes important that a planning or management center be part of the kitchen, separate from the food preparation area but integrated into the overall design.

A home planning center can be a communication center for the household members. The mail may be collected, a calendar posted and reminders or messages left. Perhaps a telephone is located in the area.

At the other end of the spectrum is the home planning center that functions like a home office. There is likely a computer and possibly other electronic equipment. Files may be needed to store household papers and records. Space may be needed for bill paying, making out grocery lists or completing correspondence.

Most likely, the home planning center will include elements of both a communication center and a home office. Start with an understanding of how your client will use the space. Refer to Chapter 6 for **Form 3: Checklist for Kitchen Activities**, especially the section on "Other Kitchen Activities," for ideas about the types of activities to be accommodated in a home planning center. In addition, refer to **Form 4: Kitchen Storage Inventory**, and the sections on "Management/Home Office" and "Miscellaneous" items, for information on what your client may want to store in the home planning center.

Locating the Home Planning Center

The home planning center is not part of the flow of food preparation activities and thus, should be located outside of the primary work triangle. In addition, the planning center is usually not part of the traffic flow from the food preparation to serving or eating area.

In many households, while one person is cooking, another member of the household might be using the desk or work area of the home planning center for reading the newspaper, school work or paying bills. These people like to be able to easily communicate, so the planning center should be convenient to the food preparation areas. The home planning center is commonly where the kitchen telephone is located and cookbooks are stored—another reason there should be convenient access from the food preparation areas to the home planning center.

Figure 9.6 A small home planning center has enough space for a laptop and is located near the secondary sink center so that the user can converse with the primary cook. (Courtesy of American Woodmark)

355

Often, the home planning center is a collection area for things like the day's mail, school papers, house or car keys and messages. Therefore, the center should be convenient to entrances/exits to the home, especially those used most frequently by household members. In some homes, the planning center may be part of the family foyer or mudroom and these spaces may overlap in function.

Later in this chapter, we will discuss a kitchen sitting area as part of a social space. In some homes, a planning center, especially the planning desk, may be located in a casual sitting area that is part of, or adjacent to, the kitchen.

The Desk Area

A typical home planning center is anchored around a desk or work surface area with a chair. The size of the desk area will vary, depending on the type of activities. For example, meal planning may require work surface space to open several cookbooks at the same time, while bill paying may only require space for the checkbook and a few pieces of paper.

Figure 9.7 A compact planning center desk, just off the kitchen work area, provides file and cubby storage. (Courtesy of American Woodmark)

Often, a planning center desk is 24 inches deep because this matches the depth of the kitchen counters. However, a 30-inch depth would be preferable for a desk (Figure 9.8). The full 30-inch depth provides space for office supplies and equipment without compromising the work area. Likewise, a width of 60 to 72 inches is recommended for the desktop to provide both work area plus convenient surface storage.

Some of the area under the desk may be used for storage, but adequate space for sitting at the desk must be allowed. Following the recommendations used in Kitchen Planning Guideline 9 (See Chapter 12), for seated areas at a 30-inch high counter or table (similar to a desk height), maintain clear knee space under the desk that is at least 18 inches deep and 24 inches wide.

The recommended height of a desk is 29 to 30 inches (Figure 9.9). An adjustable height chair is recommended, with a seat that varies in height from 14 to 20 inches above the floor. This type of chair will adapt to different users, but will still allow at least 7 inches of clearance under the desk for the user's thighs. A footrest may be needed to accommodate users with shorter legs.

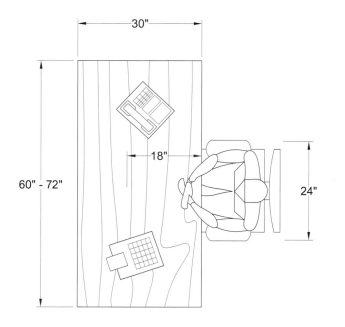

Figure 9.8 A minimum 30-inch by 60-inch desk top allows a generous work area and provides space for supplies and equipment. Clear knee space, 24 inches wide by 18 inches deep, is needed under the desk.

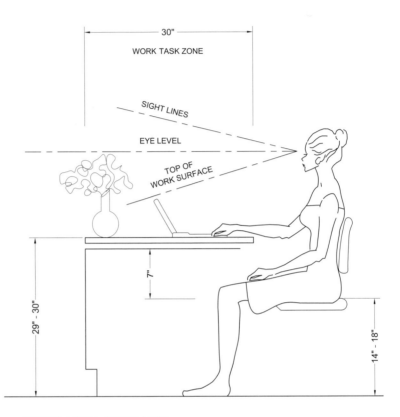

Figure 9.9 A chair with adjustable height allows different-sized people to use a standard height desk.

DESK AREA STORAGE

In addition to the work surface, a desk area usually includes storage. As suggested, refer to Chapter 6 and **Form 4: Kitchen Storage Inventory**, for the kinds of items your client will want to store in the desk area. Keep in mind the principles of storage as you plan storage in the desk area. Make items easily accessible, visible and near the point of use.

Items stored in the desk area are likely to include the usual office supplies, such as paper, tablets, pens, pencils, markers, paperclips, rubber bands, scissors, tape, stapler and hole punch. Shelf space may be needed for items such as cookbooks, phone books, directories, address books and a dictionary. File space may be needed for items such as appliance instruction booklets, warranty information and recipes.

Some people may want to have display space in the home planning center to show personal items such as mementos, family pictures, antiques, collections or decorative items. Shelf space or wall space can provide options for these special pieces. Glass door cabinets are another option for display.

In today's electronic age, you can expect that the desk area may include several different pieces of equipment. Typically, the planning center will include a telephone, but this might be a charger base for a portable phone or a cell phone and an answering machine. A fax machine may be connected to the phone system. Other items might include an electric pencil sharpener, electric stapler, clock, CD player, television and radio. Perhaps charger bases for items like flash lights or the base station for wireless Internet connections are kept in the planning center. Determine what items will be kept on the desk and which items need to be permanently connected to a power supply. Check to see if any items have special utility requirements, such as connections for cable or satellite communications.

Some households have laptop computers that are used in different parts of the home. Those clients might want the convenience of using a laptop in the planning center. This might include work surface space at a convenient height, easy access to a power supply connection and perhaps an Internet connection.

CLEARANCE AROUND THE DESK AREA

Kitchen Planning Guideline 8 in Chapter 12 recommends that 44 inches be allowed from the edge of counter/table to a wall or obstruction, in order to walk behind someone seated at that counter or table. However, if there is a file in the desk, the user often wants to move in front of an open file drawer for more convenient access. Therefore, the clearance behind the desk should be increased by the depth of the file drawer, which can be from 12 to 24 inches (Figure 9.10). If there is no traffic or passage behind the person seated at the desk, Kitchen Planning Guideline 8 recommends 32 inches clearance from the edge of the counter/table to a wall or obstruction. This allows enough space to sit at the desk and to get up or down from the chair. Although 18 to 24 inches of that space is needed for the seated person, 32 inches would not allow enough room to access most file drawers, except from the side (Figure 9.10).

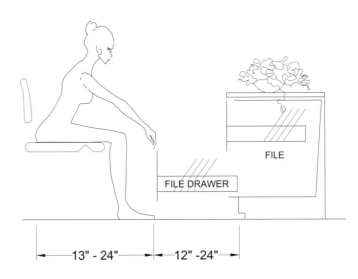

Figure 9.10 A file drawer will add 12 to 24 inches to the clearance needed in front of the desk.

13" - 24" 12" -24"

FILE

FILE DRAWER

LIGHTING

Good lighting is important in the home planning center, especially when it is used for desk work. Task lighting should be provided at the desk area and be shielded from the eye level of a seated user. Lighting in the planning center should be on separate switches from other kitchen lighting. For more information on kitchen lighting, see Chapter 8.

A STANDING DESK

Not every household wants a sitdown desk area in the home planning center. For some households, perhaps the center is more of a communication area. Maybe a counter that works well at a standing or podium height, such as 36 to 42 inches, is a better choice. Great for jotting down messages and giving the mail a quick read, this type of counter would allow space for files, bins, or drawers underneath. Wall space above the counter provides vertical storage and display space. A standing desk could be designed to be as shallow as 12 inches, to take advantage of an otherwise unused, narrow space.

Household Communications

The home planning center is often "communication central" for the household. Often, the planning center may be the spot that everyone passes going in and out of the house. Therefore, car keys, briefcases, backpacks, school books, messages and reminder notes may be there to be picked up or dropped off as people come and go. The day's mail may be deposited until someone has time to review and sort it. Phone messages may wait to be claimed. Perhaps the home has an intercom system or audio system with controls in the planning center. This may also be the place where the monitor for the alarm or security system— or the readout for the electronic weather monitoring system—is located.

All of the items that contribute to the activity of the household and its communications activities can become a clutter problem if not organized properly. Here are some ideas you can incorporate into the planning center to help manage the "stuff" that moves through it on a daily basis:

- Provide a message board. Include a tack surface to pin notes and messages as well as special school papers. Magnetic surfaces work well for the same purpose. A dry erase or chalk board can be used to write messages or reminders. Hang message boards on walls or integrate them into the doors of cabinets, pantries, closets or the refrigerator.

- A flat writing surface, such as a small counter area or pullout board, is useful for making notes.

- Provide hooks. Small hooks hold car and house keys; heavy-duty hooks hold bags and backpacks. Make sure that hooks do not protrude into passageways.

- Think of the old-fashioned pigeon-holed desk and provide places to sort items such as mail, bills, coupons, recipes and messages.

- Use glass door cabinets to store items, which are then easy to find when needed.

- Pullout bins and drawers can be divided into sections to sort items for easy access.

Computer Workstation

In the household where the planning center functions as the home office, it usually includes a computer workstation. If a computer will be added to the planning center desk area, there are additional design considerations. Is this the only computer in the home? How will the computer be used? Are recipes saved and grocery lists accumulated? Are family bills and records managed on spreadsheet software? Are school work essays written and class assignments completed on word processing programs? Do people play games and shop on-line? The frequency and type of use, as well as the number of users are important in designing the computer workstation. It is even possible that the client will want more than one computer workstation in the home planning center.

First, determine what type of computer will be used. Will there be a table or console model computer located permanently in the desk area? Or, will there be a laptop computer that is sometimes moved someplace else? Will there be a laptop docking station left on the desk?

As you design for a computer area, here are some factors to consider:

- Measure all components of the computer system. There are no standardized sizes in the computer industry. You may choose to custom design the space to fit particular computer components or to be flexible to adapt to different components, if a new computer is selected in the future.

- In addition to a computer, your client may have, or plan to add, peripheral equipment, such as a printer, scanner, speakers or digital camera dock. Plan space to accommodate these items.

- Think carefully about the placement of computer components with respect to switches, disk bays, CD trays, USB ports or other parts of the computer components that need to be accessed during use of the computer.

- The computer keyboard should be placed so that the hands, wrists and forearms are level and parallel to the floor (Figure 9.11). This is usually achieved through a combination of an adjustable height chair (with foot rest, if needed) and lowered keyboard surface. A keyboard height of 26 to 27 inches is often recommended for typing surfaces.

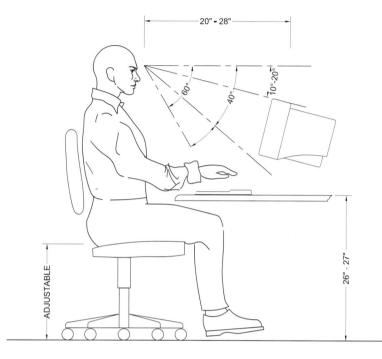

Figure 9.11 Adjust the computer workstation so that the forearm, wrist and hand are parallel to the floor and the monitor is below eye level.

- The mouse is usually placed next to the keyboard, on the right or left, depending on user preference. The surface height of the mouse is comparable to the keyboard.

- The monitor or viewing screen should be 20 to 28 inches in front of the user, or about an arm's length away. The location should be 10 to 60 degrees below horizontal eye level.

- If the computer station will include a printer, consider how the printer will be placed in relation to the rest of the equipment. Usually, the printer is used after the primary computer work is completed, so the printer may not need to occupy immediate work space. However, it must be connected to the computer. Plan enough space to load printer trays, retrieve printed papers and change ink cartridges.

- In addition to the space for the computer equipment, most people need some work surface space adjacent to, in front of, or beside the computer equipment to accommodate notes, papers, books and other reference materials.

- Storage space is needed in a computer work area to accommodate items such as disks, CDs, computer instruction manuals, printer paper, cartridges and files of projects in progress.

- Most households that have a computer workstation in the home planning center will want an Internet connection. Discuss with your client whether this will be a modem connection through a telephone line or a broadband connection, such as an Ethernet or DSL service. If the home has wireless Internet capability, determine whether the base station will be located in the home planning center or elsewhere.

- Computer components need to be well ventilated during use. Avoid enclosing computer components in cabinets or drawers that limit air circulation.

- Typically, a computer system requires a lot of electrical cords. Consider how you will manage these so that the system is functional but the cords will not be problematic. Cable channels or raceways can be used to hide cords at the back of desktops, underneath counters or in other inconspicuous places.

- The electrical requirements for a computer station depend on the requirements of the computer equipment. Typically, one or more dedicated circuits with surge protection will be necessary. Determine which components of the computer system, or peripheral pieces of equipment, need their own power supply. Consider planning extra receptacles for future expansion.

A LAUNDRY AREA

A laundry area in or near the kitchen is a convenience. Laundry can be sorted, washed, and dried while doing other activities in the kitchen. Mechanical connections for plumbing, electricity, and perhaps gas, are readily available in the kitchen area, which can reduce construction costs. The challenge to the designer is to consider how to design a functional laundry area, providing adequate space and needed storage, that is compatible with the other kitchen activities, including cooking and eating.

What Type of Laundry?

Some people like the idea of having a complete laundry area centrally located near the kitchen. This may be the only laundry area in the home, or the household may have another "mini-laundry" near the bathroom or bedroom for washing towels or doing quick loads of laundry while bathing, grooming, or dressing. Some people may only want to use the kitchen to rinse out or hand wash single items, and then hang them up to drip-dry, in the kitchen or elsewhere in the home.

Your client needs assessment (Chapter 6) should reveal what type of laundry area your client might like, in or near the kitchen. In addition, the checklists and questionnaires in the assessment will help you determine what type of laundry activities, equipment, and supplies will need to be accommodated in your design. This section will give you some specific information about planning a laundry area.

A laundry area in or near the kitchen can be convenient, but there are some factors to consider first:

- Who will use the laundry area?

  A laundry area used by different members of the household needs to be centrally located, for easy access.

- Is there adequate space for laundry equipment?

  A laundry area is more than a washing machine. A well-designed laundry includes storage, hanging, and folding space, a sink, and adequate clearance to move and complete tasks. Will laundry area space interfere with other activities and space needs associated with the kitchen?

- What about access to the laundry?

  Door and hall width clearance for carrying laundry baskets and hanging clothes needs to be considered. If an outside clothesline is used, there needs to be a direct route to the outdoors. Access to the laundry should not interfere with cooking activities.

- What about noise associated with laundry equipment?

  A busy kitchen may already be a noisy place, with food sizzling, water running and people talking. The sound of laundry equipment, located near the kitchen for convenience, should not be an annoyance.

- Is it feasible to provide the infrastructure for a laundry area in or near the kitchen?

  Water supply and drainage for the washing machine and electrical or gas connections, as well as exhaust ventilation for the dryer, need to be considered in planning. The floor structure may need reinforcing for the weight or vibration of the laundry equipment. A floor drain is good protection in event of a leak or other water problem. These features may be easy to provide in new construction, but more of a problem in a remodeling project.

- A laundry area can be messy.

Laundry areas seem to collect clothes waiting for special treatment, or to be washed, folded, ironed or repaired. This is a utility area of the home, and may not be the most aesthetically pleasing. Will the laundry area be closed or open, especially when not in actual use?

Laundry Equipment

A washing machine and automatic dryer anchor most laundry areas. A typical washer or dryer is 28 to 30 inches across the front and 25 to 30 inches deep. Most are about 36 inches high, although a back control panel will typically be 4 to 8 inches higher. Always check the exact size of the equipment in the manufacturer's specifications, or by measuring the actual equipment. Keep in mind that the installed depth of the appliance will usually be greater, due to the utility hook-ups at the back.

A washer can either be a top-loading or a front-loading model. Most dryers are front-loading, although there are top-loading models on the market. Washer doors can be hinged on either side, depending on the model. Some top-loading models may have a door hinged at the back. Dryer doors can also be hinged on either side and some models are hinged on the bottom.

Front-loading laundry appliances are usually the easiest to use for people using mobility aids or with limited reach range. The location of the appliance controls, typically on a back control panel, is also important to consider for universal access.

Some front-loading models may be appropriate to install under a counter, depending on the location of the controls. The counter will provide landing and work space for laundry. Access for servicing of the equipment should be considered.

Knowing the location and swing of the door is important for efficient placement of laundry equipment. It should be convenient to remove wet laundry from the washer and place it in the dryer without interference from the open door of either piece of equipment. This movement of laundry between appliances determines how the appliances are placed in relationship to each other.

Front-loading washers and dryers require the user to bend down to load and unload. This is a problem for some people. An alternative is to install the equipment on a raised platform so that the door is easier to access. If the equipment is raised, be sure that the user can still reach and read the controls.

Stacked Washer and Dryer. If space is limited, a stacked washer and dryer can be a good choice. A stacked washer and dryer takes up about the same floor space as a single washing machine (approximately 30 inches by 30 inches), yet provides the capacity for full loads of laundry. While stacked equipment saves floor space, the height of the equipment precludes locating any accessible storage above it. If a stacked washer and dryer are selected, be sure that the user can access all controls and door openings.

Smaller sized stacked washers and dryers with reduced capacity are available. These machines are good choices for a secondary laundry area or a smaller household.

Figure 9.12 Raising a front-loading washer or dryer, up to about 12 inches reduces bending and makes access easier, but still allows most people to reach the controls. Some washer and dryer manufacturers sell a pedestal to raise the appliance, as an accessory. (Courtesy of Whirlpool Corp.)

UTILITY SERVICE

Utility service requirements for laundry equipment are specified by the manufacturer and may be controlled by local building codes. Listed below are typical requirements.

Washing Machine

- $1/2$ inch hot and cold water supply

- 2 inch vented drain

- 120 volt, 20 ampere dedicated electrical circuit

Electric Dryer

- 240 volt, 50 ampere dedicated electrical circuit

- Exterior ventilation within 20 to 25 feet of dryer exhaust outlet

Gas Dryer

- $3/4$ inch natural or LP gas connection

- 120 volt, 20 ampere dedicated electrical circuit (may be able to share electrical circuit with the washer if a 30 ampere circuit is used)

- Exterior ventilation within 20 to 25 feet of dryer exhaust outlet

One or more additional electrical circuits are recommended in the laundry area, to use additional clothes care equipment, such as irons, sewing machines or clothes steamers. An electrical circuit for lighting is also needed. A sink in the laundry area is common, and water supply and drains are needed for this. Alternatively, the laundry area may not need a separate sink, if the primary or secondary kitchen sink is convenient to use.

Exterior ventilation of the dryer is important, even though there is sometimes consideration of venting dryers to the inside. The thought behind venting a dryer to the inside is that heat is retained, which is seen as an advantage in cold climates in the winter. However, the problems with this practice far outweigh the energy savings. The excess moisture can lead to serious condensation and mold problems in the home (see Chapter 4, Environmental Considerations). Odors from laundry products can be a problem. Lint in the exhaust air presents maintenance problems. Gadgets are available to add to the dryer exhaust vent to filter lint. However, these filters require regular maintenance, and failure to do so clogs the exhaust vent, leading to a fire hazard.

Building codes typically require vinyl, rubber, or other moisture-resistant flooring under laundry equipment. A floor drain near the washing machine is a desirable feature, to minimize the problems with water leaks. If this cannot be provided, the washer can be installed in a floor pan that would contain leaks and overflows.

Space Planning in the Laundry Area

Adequate space is needed in the laundry area to move, turn, bend, and twist while moving laundry in and out of the equipment. Space for a laundry basket or cart is also needed. A clearance of 42 inches in front of a washer, dryer, or stacked washer and dryer is recommended (Figure 9.13a). This will give adequate space to access either front or top loading machines, allowing space for door swings and a person to kneel or bend. Whether this 42-inch clearance can overlap with other workspace clearances in the kitchen will depend on how your client envisions laundry activities overlapping with food preparation, serving, and cleanup activities.

When the washer and dryer are placed side by side, the 42-inch clearance space should be 66 inches wide (Figure 9.13b). If front-loading appliances are being used, check to see that this dimension allows adequate clearance for a door swing. If appliances are placed at right angles or across from each other, the clearance space for each machine overlaps (Figures 9.13c and 9.13d).

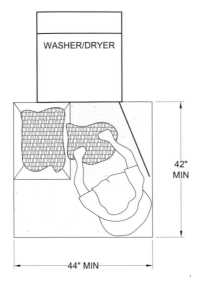

Figure 9.13a Clearance in front of laundry equipment provides space for bending and kneeling as well as for door swings and a laundry basket or cart. This illustration shows clearances for a single washer or dryer or a stacked washer and dryer.

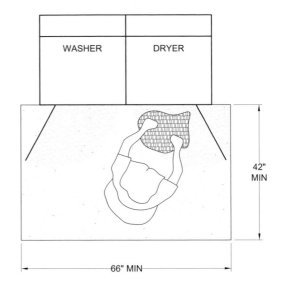

Figure 9.13b shows clearances for a side-by-side washer and dryer.

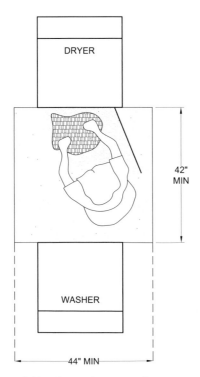

Figure 9.13c shows clearances for a washer and dryer arranged on opposite sides.

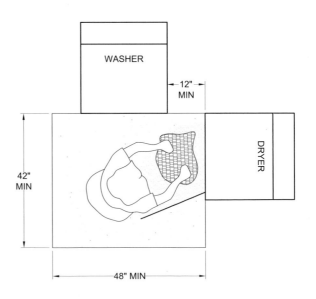

Figure 9.13d shows clearances for a washer and dryer at right angles.

If the person doing the laundry uses a mobility aid, such as a wheelchair or cane, these clearances will need to be increased. Refer back to **Form 1: Getting to Know Your Client**, in Chapter 6, for information on collecting clearances for mobility aids your client might use.

LAUNDRY IN TRANSITION

Designing a laundry area is more than installing equipment with clearance space. The flow of laundry in and out of the space needs to be considered. Dirty laundry is brought into the area; clean laundry is moved out. During the transition, clothes, towels, bed linens, and other items may spend time "hanging out" in the laundry area. To help organize the laundry area, and minimize clutter, consider the following ideas.

- Dirty laundry needs to be collected. Hampers, bins, or baskets in the laundry area can be used for short-term storage of dirty laundry. Good ventilation of the dirty laundry containers is necessary to dispel dampness and odors.

  Several containers might be used to pre-sort laundry. For example, white socks, t-shirts, and underwear might go into one container, jeans into another. (The effectiveness of this system depends on cooperation of everyone in the household.) Or, if several members of the household do laundry separately, each person can have their own container, using it to accumulate enough laundry for a washer load.

- Because dirty laundry needs to be sorted before washing, a table or counter surface works well for this task and then can later be used for folding and sorting clean laundry. A work surface 24 to 36 inches deep and 32 to 36 inches high would work for most people. The length of work surface depends on how much laundry is typically sorted and how much space is available. If laundry and cooking are not done at the same time, the prep counter area might work well for this task.

  Several bins or baskets might be used to sort laundry. These items might rest on a work counter, or pull out from underneath a counter or from inside a cabinet.

  Avoid using the kitchen or laundry room floor for sorting dirty laundry, which can create congestion and clutter.

- Hanging up items removed from the dryer minimizes wrinkles. Provide a space to hang shirts, blouses, skirts, dresses and similar items. This hanging space should be convenient to the dryer. Garments on hangers should not block work areas or passages. Good ventilation is needed to allow garments to cool without wrinkling.

  Refer to the section on "Clothes Storage" in Chapter 9 in the NKBA book *Bath Planning* for information on planning space and clearances for hanging clothes storage.

- Not everything goes into the dryer. Some items, like sweaters, need to lay flat, on a clean, smooth surface to dry. Other items are hung up to drip-dry—and they may drip while drying—so a waterproof area is needed. Delicate items, like lingerie, may be put over a drying rack. The amount of space devoted to these activities will depend on your client.

  If your client frequently air-dries laundry items, be sure that the area is adequately ventilated to prevent moisture problems.

  An air-dry area may be elsewhere in the house, but consider how wet clothes are moved to this area without dripping. A laundry cart might be desirable, but consider where the cart will be kept when not in use.

- Clean laundry needs to be folded. A table or counter work surface, such as used for sorting dirty laundry, will provide a space to fold clean laundry. If laundry is folded fresh from the dryer, wrinkles are minimized. Many people want space to sort clean laundry, by type of garment or item, or by its owner. Clean laundry may be stacked into a basket or cart for transport to storage areas in the home.

  Several bins or baskets might be used to sort laundry by its owner. Household members can then come claim their own laundry.

- A sink in the laundry area is a desirable feature. Some laundry products need to be diluted. Pre-rinsing may be helpful in removing stains. The sink can also be used for hand washing items or soaking soiled items.

A laundry sink is typically placed next to the washer to facilitate plumbing connections, and for convenience of workflow. Unless your client does a lot of hand laundry, an extra deep utility or laundry type sink is not necessary. A small bar-type sink can work well. Select a gooseneck or pullout faucet for fitting bulky items under the water flow. Look for controls that are easy to operate with one hand.

Depending on the kitchen layout and its proximity to the laundry, a secondary sink in the kitchen can double as the laundry area sink.

• A laundry needs adequate lighting that is conveniently switched. Good color rendition in the light sources is important for noting stains and other problems on fabrics—and for matching socks. See Chapter 8 for more information about lighting.

STORAGE

Easily accessible storage is needed for laundry supplies. Items such as detergent and fabric softener are used almost every time something is washed and need to be easily reached. Other laundry supplies, such as stain removers, special detergents, bleaches, wrinkle removers and fabric fresheners, may be used less frequently, but still need to be convenient to the laundry equipment. Most of these items will fit on 8-inch to 9-inch deep shelves.

Storage in laundry areas is often placed over the laundry equipment. However, the depth of the washer or dryer reduces the height of the user's reach. Bringing a shelf forward makes items more accessible, as long as they will not get "lost" at the back of extra-deep shelves. Keep in mind that some laundry products, such as detergent, come in large, heavy containers that are awkward to lift, especially for people with limited strength. These items should not be stored above shoulder height (52 to 57 inches for most people) and are best stored within the universal reach range of 15 to 48 inches. Finally, shelves above laundry equipment should not interfere with door openings for top-loading equipment or access to controls. For all these reasons, storage areas adjacent to laundry equipment may be more desirable for the most frequently used items.

Other items may be stored in the laundry area including hangers, clothespins, measuring cups for laundry products, stain removal guides, sponges, brushes, rags and cleaning supplies. A divided drawer or small bins work well to collect items found in garment pockets or buttons that pop off. Some people keep basic sewing supplies in the laundry area so repairs can be made on the spot.

Open storage in the laundry area increases accessibility by making it easier to see stored items and eliminating cabinet doors that might not swing out of the way. However, the desirability of this depends on how open the laundry area is to view from the kitchen and other spaces in the home.

Laundry storage can be messy. Containers of detergents and other laundry products may drip when being used. Spills are inevitable. Storage areas, in fact all of the laundry area, should be made of durable, easily cleaned materials that are not damaged by exposure to water, detergents and other laundry products. Vinyl, ceramic tiles, and plastic laminates are popular materials used in laundry areas. For more about materials used in laundry areas, see the NKBA book *Kitchen & Bath Products*.

IRONING

Despite permanent-press fabrics and finishes, many people still want a place to iron clothes and household linens. The laundry area is a logical place to put an ironing area. Built-in ironing boards fold down from wall cupboards or pullout from underneath a countertop, yet are out of the way when not in use. Many of these include storage space for the iron as well. Racks are available to hang freestanding ironing boards, or ironing boards can fold up to store in utility closets.

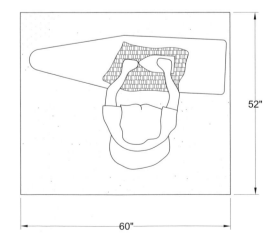

Figure 9.14 A typical ironing area requires a space that is 60 inches by 52 inches.

Include adequate space in the laundry area to use the iron and ironing board. The amount of space may need to be increased if the user requires a mobility aid. Because an iron is hot and the cord could be a tripping hazard, the ironing area should not be in a passage or walkway. Most ironing boards adjust in height to allow a person to sit or stand to work.

Figure 9.15 An ironing board and iron can be hidden in a kitchen cabinet when not in use, but be convenient when the need arises. (Courtesy of Whirlpool Corp.)

A CRAFT/HOBBY AREA

Hobbies and crafts encompass many different activities as varied as scrapbook making, sewing, stamp collecting, building models, making jewelry or solving crossword puzzles. These activities can be done by adults or children. Hobbies and crafts can be done on a regular basis, such as children's school projects, or they can be occasional activities, such as a family get together to make holiday decorations.

In Chapter 6 Assessing Needs, your client may have indicated "crafts" on **Form 3: Checklist for Kitchen Activities**. If they checked this as a frequent activity, you might want to get more detail. What type of craft activities? Who participates? How often do they do these crafts? How much space is needed? What supplies and equipment do they use? There may be specialized space needs for a particular craft activity.

Consider the other auxiliary areas that we have discussed in this chapter as possible areas for hobby and craft activities. For example, the laundry area may be a convenient place to add a sewing space. The mudroom may be a good place for messy activities, such as painting, working with clay, or indoor gardening as discussed later in this chapter. The planning desk can also be used as a writing surface for hobbies. Even the kitchen counter can get called into service as a good surface for wrapping packages or making a collage. Later in this chapter, we will discuss a kitchen sitting area, which might include a table and chairs, that would make a great place for school projects, jigsaw puzzles or scrapbook assembly.

For the household that wants to use the kitchen or related space for general hobby or craft activities on an occasional basis here are some design suggestions:

- Kitchen counters make an excellent area for many hobby activities because they provide a level surface and adapt to both seated and standing activities. Durable, nonporous materials that are easily cleaned help assure that food residues and craft materials will not likely get mixed.

- If a counter area will be used for standing activities, make sure that there is adequate toekick space on all open sides.

- Plan for a seated work counter in or near the kitchen to be used for craft activities. This can also double as the eating counter, prep area or serving bar.

- If the household includes children, be sure that there are chairs or stools that have adjustable height seats, with foot rests, so that the children can use the work counters comfortably along with the rest of the household.

- Many craft and hobby activities need a water source, or are messy enough to require hand washing and water for cleanup. A sink near the area used for crafts or hobbies will be convenient. If chemicals are used in the hobby activity, make sure that the sink material is resistant to that chemical.

Figure 9.16 A planning desk can double as a craft area and nearby storage can hold supplies. (Courtesy of *Country Home* – Meredith Corp.)

- Make sure that the craft or hobby area is well lit with adjustable light levels. Many hobby activities can require a lighting level that is brighter than would usually be used for eating or social activities.

  Chose light sources with good color rendition, especially important for art activities.

- Plan electrical receptacles or power strips convenient to the hobby or craft area. Ask your client about specialized equipment or electrical needs. For example, many craft patterns are now available in digital form, so a person may want a laptop available. Electric scissors, soldering irons and hot glue guns are just a few examples of tools requiring electrical connections.

- Plan storage for craft or hobby supplies, tools, and equipment in or near the kitchen. This storage area can be cupboards, drawers or shelves, depending on what will be stored. This storage area should be out of the primary work triangle and separate from food storage.

  In some cases, hobby supplies may need to be stored in childproof cabinets. In other situations, hobby supplies will be stored so that young children can independently access them.

- Temporary storage may be needed in or near the kitchen. For example, newly crafted items may need to be hung up or laid out flat to dry. Equipment may need to be set aside to cool before being put away. This type of storage may be in the kitchen, or in an auxiliary area, such as the mudroom.

- Consider planning some display space for finished craft projects in or near the kitchen. Depending on the activity, this might be a tack board, magnetic board, hooks, a plate rack, open shelves or a glass door cabinet.

- Make sure that the kitchen has an exhaust ventilation system with adjustable fan speeds. Many hobby activities involve glue, paint and other chemicals that could contribute to indoor air pollution. The kitchen ventilation system can help remove the vapors from the air. See Chapter 8 for more information about kitchen ventilation systems.

A GARDENING AREA

Indoor gardening may be a desirable activity in a kitchen or nearby area. Typically, the space will be used for potting plants, trimming house plants, watering and fertilizing potted plants, arranging flowers and similar tasks. An area for growing herbs and starting cuttings or seeds may be included. Storage will be needed for pots and vases of various sizes, potting soil, fertilizer, scissors, spades and assorted tools for indoor gardening.

A gardening area may be included in the kitchen proper, but usually not in the primary work triangle. Or a garden area may be incorporated into other areas that are adjacent to the kitchen, such as the family foyer, mudroom, laundry area or a sunroom. The gardening area may be a defined space. Or, you may design a multi-purpose space, such as a laundry area, recycling center, or pet washing area that can also work for indoor gardening. The amount of space, and the complexity of the gardening area, will depend on how important gardening is to your client.

Planning the Indoor Garden Area

One approach to planning an indoor garden area is to think of it as another prep area—but this time it is for plants. Using this approach, the garden area would include work counter area, a sink and storage for tools and supplies.

WORK COUNTER AREA

Most garden activities will occur with the person standing. Therefore, a comfortable height at, or slightly below, the gardener's elbow is recommended. The standard 36-inch height of a kitchen counter is a good compromise, but may not work as effectively for a tall or short person, or someone in a wheelchair.

As in the prep center in the kitchen, approximately 16 inches of counter depth is used as work area. Additional depth becomes storage or landing area for tools and supplies. Therefore, a standard 24-inch counter would work well for a gardening area. If the work counter is also used to hold pots with growing plants, a deeper counter may be desired.

The amount of counter space will vary with the type of gardening activities and the size of pots used most frequently. Counter frontage of 36 inches would likely be considered a minimum.

Figure 9.16 A gardener's dream is adjacent to the laundry in this mudroom, convenient to both the outside door and the kitchen. There is even a place for washing muddy boots. (Courtesy of Kohler Company)

The counter needs to be durable and easy to clean. Choose a non-absorbent material that will resist garden chemicals as well as abrasion from rough pots. Glazed tile, solid surface, engineered stone, sealed concrete or sealed masonry are possible choices.

Even the most careful gardeners will sometimes get potting soil, plant cuttings or debris on the floor instead of the work counter. Durable, easy-to-maintain flooring—much like the mudroom—is important in the gardening area.

A GARDEN SINK

Water is used on plants, to mix fertilizer and other plant chemicals and to cleanup. A water source is needed for the gardening area. If at all possible, provide a separate sink.

A single-bowl sink will serve most garden area needs. When repotting, many gardeners like to water a plant and then let it drain in the sink, so make sure the sink is large enough to handle the pots the gardener will use. A large sink will actually become a work area for most gardeners (Figure 9.17). Also, choose a sink of a durable material that is not easily scratched by rough pots.

A clever idea is to fit the garden sink with a slatted insert, so that pots rest on the insert for draining, and the sink is protected from scratching (Figure 9.18). A slatted drain board over the sink is an alternative idea.

Think about the relationship of the faucet to the sink, and plan for room for pots and large containers, such as watering cans. Consider a gooseneck faucet or a wall-mounted faucet to provide adequate clearance. A faucet with a spray attachment makes it easier to water plants, especially in large pots.

Figure 9.17 A large garden sink, surrounded by a ledge, becomes a potting area in a rustic enclosed porch. (Courtesy of American Standard)

Figure 9.18 A slatted sink insert makes a great place to drain plants or fill pots. (Courtesy of Kohler Company)

STORAGE

Start planning storage in the garden area with simple open shelves to accommodate pots, baskets, vases, trays and similar items. Provide some storage for heavier or bulkier items that does not require the gardener to lift the item above shoulder level. Book shelf space can be used for garden books and reference manuals.

Drawer storage is desirable for small items, such as scissors, spades and twist ties. Pull-out baskets or bins can also be used to store pots and oddly shaped items. If the gardener buys or mixes potting soil in large amounts, a tilt-out bin for ready access to the soil would be a great convenience.

In a household with small children, there needs to be secure storage in the gardening area for garden chemicals such as fertilizer and insecticides, as well as sharp tools, such as scissors. A locked cabinet or a drawer with a childproof latch is recommended.

A Growing Area

Many gardeners also want an area in the kitchen or nearby where they can grow indoor plants, especially herbs. Most herbs need a window area that gets full sunlight at least five hours a day (or up to 15 hours a day of fluorescent/grow light artificial light). Usually this means a southern or western exposure, although in some climates, the western exposure may be too hot. Most herbs prefer cooler temperatures (60 to 65 degrees F) and need to be protected from strong drafts. Before planning a growing area, be sure that these ambient conditions can be provided.

There are many ways to provide a growing area in a kitchen, such as a greenhouse style window that "bumps out". Another idea is to pull the cabinets out from the wall, creating a deeper countertop, and use the extra depth as a plant area. Hanging baskets can provide plant space, but must be clear of passageways and "head space" for people working in the kitchen. Sometimes, extra deep window sills are available. Or in homes with high ceilings, plants on top of partial height partitions can thrive under well-placed skylights.

SOCIAL SPACES

Throughout this book, we have talked about the kitchen as a gathering space. How many times have you heard a client say, "no matter what is planned, guests always seem to gravitate to the kitchen?" How many clients want to design their kitchen so that being in the kitchen is part of the entertainment? In Chapter 7, we discussed many aspects of kitchen design related to guests, entertaining, and socializing in the kitchen: serving centers, dining areas, butler's pantries, beverage bars and caterer's kitchens. So why, in a chapter that is about "more than a kitchen," are we talking about social spaces?

First, let's think about how the kitchen is part of the social or community area of the home. How does the kitchen, as a unit, relate to other social spaces of the home, such as a family room, den or great room? Many homes today are designed or remodeled with the kitchen as central and open to the living or social areas of the home. Some homes may have another separate, more formal, social and/or dining space, but these are typically not used on a daily basis.

Some kitchens may have a small sitting area adjacent to the primary kitchen work area. This area might function as a casual eating area, a place for morning coffee or afternoon tea. Maybe it is a place for one household member to sit and read the newspaper or share the day's events while another person takes their turn to cook. Perhaps this area includes a fireplace, a sunroom, or an enclosed porch. Sometimes these areas are expanded to a breakfast room, or they may be called a hearth room, country kitchen or inglenook. People in these social spaces usually feel part of the kitchen, but are out of the primary work area.

Another arrangement is a kitchen that is adjacent to the family living area. The kitchen space has one or more sides in common with the family living area. There may be a partial barrier between the kitchen and living area, such as a counter or bar. There is a visual and usually an auditory link between the spaces. This type of arrangement is designed so that the two spaces flow into each other, but there is a sense of separate areas. Activities occur simultaneously in the kitchen and living areas, and people can communicate, but people in the living areas are not in the kitchen.

Thus, the kitchen that is open to a social or community area of the home can both be defined as a separate space and unified with the larger area. The amount of integration and separation depends on your design choices. Visual definition or separation of the kitchen comes by:

- Change in flooring material between the kitchen and the social space.

- Change in ceiling material or height between the two spaces. The kitchen space could be defined by a lowered soffit as well.

- Separate lighting system for the kitchen, especially the lighting that defines the food preparation areas or an eating area within the kitchen.

- A counter, bar or partial wall that physically defines the parameters of the kitchen.

- Backsplash color, design or material that is unique to the kitchen area.

Figure 9.19 Although the eating counter separates the food preparation area, many design features work to integrate the living and bar/serving area into the kitchen area. (Courtesy of Sandra Ahearn – Jacksonville Beach, Florida)

Figure 9.20a In this kitchen open to a social space, the two areas are unified by using the same flooring, cabinet style and upholstery fabric, as well as a similar color scheme. (Courtesy of KraftMaid Cabinetry)

Alternatively, unity of the larger space, integrating the social area with the kitchen, can be achieved by:

• Using the same or coordinating flooring materials throughout.

• Using the same ceiling finish or height.

• Coordinating wall finishes in color, texture or material.

- Using the same cabinetry style and material as in the kitchen for features, such as a computer desk area, games storage or media center, in the social area.

- Coordinated window styles and treatments throughout the space.

Figure 9.20b The different finishes on the cabinetry and the orientation of the living area furniture to the focal point of the fireplace all establish the social area as a separate space. (Courtesy of KraftMaid Cabinetry)

The Kitchen Sitting Area

An adjacent sitting area is usually stylistically coordinated and integrated with the kitchen. There is usually a sense of a single space. However, people need to be able to walk into and out of the sitting area without interrupting the work triangle in the food preparation area.

Start planning the kitchen sitting area by considering the following questions:

- What is the capacity of the sitting area? Will just members of the household use it or will this also be an area for entertaining?

- Will the sitting area be used for eating meals? Often a sitting area and casual eating or breakfast area are integrated together. What about lap-meals or snacks?

- What type of seating will be included—couches, love seats, easy chairs or rockers? Figure 9.22 gives the typical dimensions, in plan, of common types of furniture.

- What will be the focal point of the area—a fireplace, a view to the outside, a television or media center—or into the kitchen?

- How will the seating arrangement be oriented—toward the kitchen or away from it?

- How will the kitchen be oriented to the seating area—across the sink, the cooktop, the prep area or an eating counter?

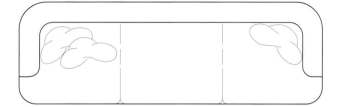

COUCH
30"-36" x 72"-90"

CHAIR
18" x 18"

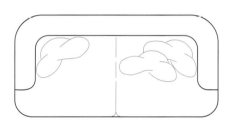

LOVESEAT
30"-36" x 60"

END TABLE
18" x 26"-30"

EASY CHAIR
30"-32" x 34"-36"

COFFEE TABLE
18" x 48"

Figure 9.21 Furniture sizes are not standardized, but these examples will give you an idea of the approximate size of common pieces of furniture that might be used in a sitting area.

Here are some suggestions to consider when designing a kitchen sitting area:

- Pay very close attention to sight lines and eye height.

  Most people in the kitchen will be looking into the sitting area from a standing eye level. Be aware of cabinetry and other structures that might interfere with sight lines into the seating area. Wall cabinetry that is installed at the usual height of 15 to 18 inches above the counter will be 51 to 54 inches above the finished floor and block most people's sight lines.

  People in the sitting area will more likely be at a seated eye level. This can be used to advantage if you wish to partially screen kitchen work areas. However, remember to consider seated eye level for placement of other features, such as mullions on window.

- Keep the conversation circle in mind. Group furniture for easy conversation by keeping distances less than 10 feet. Plan traffic so that it goes around the conversation circle rather than through it. Also, people find it easier to converse when someone is at a right angle, or across, from them, rather than directly beside them.

- Since this sitting area is part of the kitchen, assume that people using it will often have drinks or snacks. Plan landing space convenient to each seat, such as a side or coffee table.

- A sitting area may include a table and straight-back chairs, even if there is another eating area. These can be used for casual meals, snacks, homework, menu planning or any number of activities that are facilitated by sitting at a table surface. Refer to Chapter 7 for guidelines on seated table space and clearances.

- A planning desk, as described previously in this chapter, may be part of the kitchen sitting area.

- If a television will be located in the sitting area, determine who will be watching it. Will it be located for prime viewing by someone working in the kitchen, or someone sitting in an easy chair? An adjustable viewing location may be desirable.

  Viewing distance for a television is related to the size of the screen. The 10-foot distance for conversation is often used as a guide for television viewing, but a large screen television can be viewed from a greater distance.

  Volume can be an issue with the television. A television speaker in the sitting area may not be loud enough to be heard in the kitchen area. Consider a system with multiple speakers for the most flexibility. A sound specialist may need to be consulted to assure effective placement of speakers.

- Plan for storage in the sitting area. Often, cabinetry matching or coordinating with the cabinetry in the kitchen work area is used. Shelves for books, mementos, decorative items and plants are often desired. Games, CDs, videos, puzzles, magazines, and craft and hobby supplies are examples of additional items that might be stored in the sitting area. Depending on the relationship of the sitting area to the dining area, china, silver and linens may also be kept there.

- Control of noise from kitchen activities will be important so that it does not interfere with conversation and other activities in the sitting area. Carefully consider whether hard surface materials that reflect sound are appropriate. Review the information in Chapter 4 on noise.

- Good ventilation will be important in the kitchen so that grease, smoke and odors are removed effectively from the cooking area and do not linger in the sitting area. Review the information on ventilation in Chapter 8.

- The kitchen sitting area is an everyday space, a gathering place for members of the household. Plan to use durable, easy-to-maintain materials that resist the wear and tear of frequent use and spills from drinks and food.

SUMMARY

The kitchen, and the auxiliary spaces adjacent it to it, are truly the heart of a home. Many activities—from managing the home to socializing with family and friends, from keeping track of busy lives to engaging in pleasurable hobbies—all take place in these spaces. As a designer, your expertise and creativity can help assure that the auxiliary areas of the kitchen are well planned to accommodate and support these activities as effectively and efficiently as the food preparation and eating activities of the primary kitchen area.

CHAPTER 10: A Closer Look at Your Client

To the greatest extent possible, incorporate universal design into the kitchen in order to meet the needs of clients throughout their lifespan and the changes in their physical condition. In some cases, you may be asked to design a kitchen that functions for a client with a particular need or disability, and this chapter is an information source for those situations. While universal design concepts have been included throughout the book, in this chapter, user characteristics and appropriate design concepts are grouped together to serve as an aid to the design process. Where appropriate, concepts will be explored in more depth to broaden your understanding, or additional resources may be listed to enable you to go further in solving client problems. In short, if you are designing for a client whose needs are in common with any of the identified user groups, check here for ideas to help with the design of their kitchen.

The tools presented in Chapter 6, Assessing Needs, give you a great way to gather information that can help you identify and plan for each client's needs. When a specific chronic condition or disability is involved, the client will often be your best source of information regarding unique needs and solutions. In addition, health professionals involved with your client, such as occupational or physical therapists, make great team members. Their expertise is the body and its workings, whereas yours is the space and its function and components. Keep in mind that when specific medical equipment is involved, your role as designer may be to provide appropriate space planning and to involve the equipment expert to execute the plan.

ADDRESSING DIFFERENCES

In any client/designer relationship, a mutual respect and a comfort level must be established. A considerate approach to a client who has different abilities than yours requires that you pay careful attention to your attitude and that you work harder at dropping your own assumptions and listening to your client's needs and priorities. Raising one's voice does not help a person who speaks another language or one who is blind understand you, yet we often experience this. Assuming that a client who uses a wheelchair must have a cooktop with a knee space could be incorrect if that client does not want or need to use the cooktop.

When speaking or referring to a person with a disability, refer to the person first and avoid negative descriptions—not "confined to a wheelchair," but, "a person who uses a wheelchair." For many of us, the word "handicapped" conjures up negative images of institutional settings and today the word is used with care to avoid any suggestion of "less than." If you are not sure how to refer to a disability, ask your client and if you feel you've misspoken, apologize—in other words use positive references and honest conversation.

The following suggestions are fairly evident and universal. Position yourself to speak at the client's eye level. Respect a client's assistive devices and do not interfere with their use by moving them or positioning yourself between the person and his aide. Respect your client's privacy by accepting what the client may choose not to discuss with you. Keep in mind that these suggestions are intended to help you focus on the person and the space, and not the disability, to achieve the most positive results.

DESIGN CONSIDERATIONS FOR USERS

Kitchen space planning considers the given parameters of the job, the NKBA Guidelines and Access Standards in Chapter 12, and a client's preferences and budget. Included in this, space planning must consider clear floor space and knee spaces based on the client's needs and abilities. The following information should help you to accomplish this. In finishing the space, lighting and contrast, product and control specifications, surfaces, and all aspects of the room can impact the success of the space, in relation to the client's needs and abilities. The user groups and design concepts listed here are not in any way complete, but they provide a good start in your effort. There is much overlap. For example, the knee space that allows access at a sink or cooktop for a person using a wheelchair also provides for seated use by a pregnant woman experiencing fatigue. It also can function as a storage place for a step stool for a child. For some use considerations, information is repeated and for others, different sections of the chapter and book are referenced. Many of the design implications are similar for various types of users.

Across The Lifespan

From childhood to old age, we are growing and changing. While many of our needs as young children are similar to our needs as aging adults, there are also differences.

CHILDREN

A child's body is constantly changing and growing, their senses finding new discoveries everyday. Their language and reasoning skills are only just beginning to develop. Children see the world differently than adults and often do not understand danger or the consequences of their actions. They are small in stature, have limited reach, stamina, balance, strength, and dexterity, coupled with huge spurts of energy. In addition they have a short attention span and occasionally, a lack of body function or control. It is critical to acknowledge their limited awareness of risk/safety factors, and lack of understanding, in designing spaces they will inhabit.

A child's stature at age six is closer to that of a seated adult than it is to even the shortest of standing adult females.

General design considerations include:

- Lower or adjustable heights for fixtures, fittings, storage, and controls, or other accommodation to smaller stature.

- Work center that includes frequently used items within a comfortable reach range.

- Assistance in accessing appliances, fixtures, fittings, storage, and controls.

- Safety measures regarding water, cooking appliances, medicines or poisons, and sharp objects.

- Lower sight lines.

- Cabinet doors with locks.

- Flexible equipment and assistive devices that can change as a child grows.

Kitchen Design Implications. If children are encouraged to use the kitchen to make their own drinks and snacks, storage items and appliances should be placed within reach so they can function independently without help from a parent or climbing on counters. Concern arises when placing items within reach of an older child, which are still off-limits to a younger child or toddler. Detailed conversation with the supervising adult is needed to determine at what age the children in that household are encouraged to use the kitchen independently, and what responsible safety precautions must be taken.

Sink Center. Small children will be learning to wash hands and to help themselves to a glass of drinking water, so it is important that the water center be planned to assist with these activities. The following are some ways to make this area convenient:

- A step stool at the sink eliminates the need to climb on the counter to use the sink or access storage.

- An open knee space provides storage for the stepstool.

- Any design for faucet controls other than smooth round knobs improves function.

- A single control faucet is easier to use than separate hot and cold controls.

- Hot and cold controls should be easily identified with red and blue indicators.

- Instant hot water faucets eliminate use of cooktop or microwave for some food and beverage preparation.

- An anti-scald, temperature limiting device can prevent burning.

- A filtered drinking water faucet within child's reach will encourage the child to get their own drink.

- The option of a height-adjustable sink area might work in some households.

- Eased counter edges avoid a potential hazard for an unstable toddler's head or busy child's shoulder or hip.

- The location of a child's "stuff" should be well within easy reach, which would be at the lower end of the universal reach range.

- A dishwasher with a shutoff switch or a model that has programmable lockout prevents a child from accidentally turning on the appliance.

- A batch feed disposer or a continuous disposer with a clearly marked switch to eliminate confusion with other switches, placed out of the reach range of younger children, will be more difficult for a child to accidentally turn on.

- A trash compactor with a lock will keep children out. Some manufacturers offer removable key lock.

Cooking Center. Preventative measures should be taken in the cooking center to avoid burning the skin or starting a fire. For this reason, the microwave can be an ideal cooking appliance for older children.

- A microwave 15 inches to 48 inches above the floor allows use by older children without climbing.

- Microwaveable and shatter-proof items should be stored near the microwave where children can easily find and access them.

- Take advantage of technology with easy programming options, such as microwaves with one-step/instant-on touch controls for popcorn, beverages, and reheating, which will encourage older children to use the appliance.

- To avoid reaching over burners, select range or cooktop appliances with controls that are placed at the front for use by older children, yet are removable or can be covered to avoid use by toddlers.

- Cooktops with a control lock-out program keep children from accidentally turning on the appliance.

- Electronic cooktops with a heat indicator light help older children recognize that the cooktop is hot.

- Electronic or induction cooktops that sense the presence of a pan and automatically shut-off if left on are safer.

- Ovens with automatic shut-offs reduce the dangers of a hot oven accidentally left on.

Figure 10.1 A microwave placed under the counter is convenient for use by children. (Courtsey of KraftMaid Cabinetry)

- An oven with a central lock-out program can keep children from accidentally turning it on.

Refrigeration Center and Preparation Area. Safety concerns in the preparation area are not as potentially dangerous as the water and cooking centers, but preventative measures should be taken to avoid consumption of adult food and beverages.

- A side-by-side refrigerator with handles that extend the full length of the doors allows operation by anyone, regardless of height.

- Consider refrigerators with lightweight and easy to open doors.

- Ice and water dispensers on the refrigerator door are convenient features because they direct children away from the cleanup water center and avoid the need for a step stool to access the faucet.

- In addition to the main refrigerator, consider an undercounter unit which is easily accessible.

Storage. Controlling access to storage areas can be an important way to discourage inappropriate and dangerous behavior. Making the storage of items that are needed for the child's activities accessible encourages their involvement.

- Temporary or permanent locks on cabinets should be considered.

- Storage for medications, sharp objects, and poisonous cleaning supplies should be planned out of the child's reach.

- Dangerous items, like knives and adult beverages, should be in locked storage.

- A storage accessory, such as a mechanical pull-down unit to lower wall cabinet storage, can make it easier for the child to reach some items.

Figure 10.2 A pull-down storage accessory can make it easier for children to reach items in wall cabinets. (Courtesy of Rev-a-Shelf)

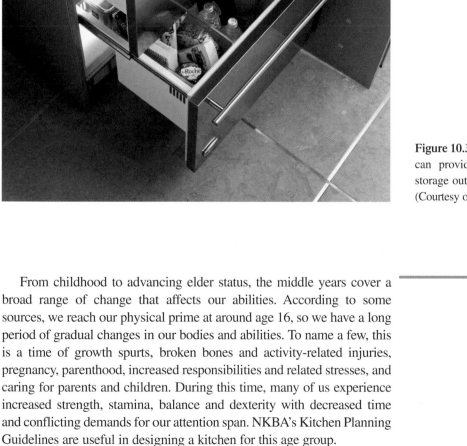

Figure 10.3 Undercounter refrigeration can provide accessible chilled food storage outside of the main work area. (Courtesy of Sub-Zero Freezer Co.)

MIDDLE YEARS

From childhood to advancing elder status, the middle years cover a broad range of change that affects our abilities. According to some sources, we reach our physical prime at around age 16, so we have a long period of gradual changes in our bodies and abilities. To name a few, this is a time of growth spurts, broken bones and activity-related injuries, pregnancy, parenthood, increased responsibilities and related stresses, and caring for parents and children. During this time, many of us experience increased strength, stamina, balance and dexterity with decreased time and conflicting demands for our attention span. NKBA's Kitchen Planning Guidelines are useful in designing a kitchen for this age group.

AGING

We reach a point in the growth process where a number of our abilities again begin to change. Although this begins very early, we adapt ourselves to the changes as we age and may not notice any difference until our environment is not supporting us. Being able to use the kitchen to prepare one's meals is a part of daily life and the design of the space and selection of appliances can make a difference.

Physical Changes

- **Mental Changes.** Some memory loss or occasional forgetfulness, as opposed to overall mental decline, is very common. The ability to learn does not decrease with age, but stereotypes cause many of us to fear the loss of mental ability as we age. Reaction time generally is longer. Reduced physical and reaction abilities cause many to prefer home, where things are familiar, allowing for a sense of security.

- **Vision Changes.** Physical changes in the eyes increase with age and can lead to vision impairment, such as difficulty seeing in dim light, increased light sensitivity, difficulty focusing on moving objects, and a decrease in peripheral vision. More time is needed for the eyes to adjust when transitioning between light and dark areas. Reading glasses become a common need beginning in the 40s, and our lenses begin to yellow, causing difficulty in distinguishing some colors. The section "Vision" on page 417 has additional information.

- **Hearing Changes.** Another common occurrence is some level of hearing loss, usually beginning with difficulties with high frequencies and progressing to lower frequencies. Ringing in the ears is common. Hearing loss and the inability to communicate can cause significant emotional stress but potential negative effects can be reduced through design. The section "Hearing and Speech" on page 422 has additional information.

- **Other Sensory Changes.** We may experience a general and gradual decline in our other senses. People may have a change in their ability to taste, including a decline in the recognition of sweet, sour, and salty foods, and often complain about a bitter taste in the mouth or of food tasting bland. Some experience a decline in ability to smell such odors as smoke and leaking gas. Sensitivity to touch may decline as well. Some people have increased (but less conscious) thresholds of pain, and a decreased sensitivity to internal body temperature.

- **Bone and Muscle Changes.** We experience a decrease in strength due to bone and muscle loss, causing an increase in accidents and fractures. Decreased mobility can be caused by changes in joints, stooped posture, and/or decrease in height, and common disorders such as arthritis, osteoarthritis, and osteoporosis. See the "Mobility" section for additional information. As we shrink in height, our reach ranges are shorter than those of middle aged people, moving closer to the reach range we had as children.

- **Internal Functions.** Changes in the nervous system result in slower movements, and decreased balance and coordination due to inefficiency of the nervous system and central brain processes. Many people experience a sleeping pattern change, requiring less sleep and/or experiencing less sound sleep.

General design considerations include:

- Flexibility in the space that can change as the client ages.

- Adjusted heights of appliances, fixtures, fittings, storage, and controls, for an accommodation to shortened stature and reduced balance.

- Intuitive controls, visible storage, and organization to compensate for memory losses.

- Optional seating at the major kitchen centers.

- Dual cueing on appliances and safety devices, such as a smoke alarm that flashes and sounds its warning.

- Increased and adjustable lighting.

- Protection from scalding.

Kitchen Design Implications. Sufficient clear floor space for functional passage is a design challenge when planning for this age group. As our strength, stamina, and balance decrease, minimal passage clearances, such as a galley kitchen or island configuration, give us support as we move through a space, but when we add a mobility aid, more generous spaces are mandatory. The flexibility of a rolling cart is one possible solution. Single lever, easy-to-operate controls at faucets and doors, and use of controls that are easy to reach and operate for windows, lighting, and fixtures are additional solutions. Also, the kitchen of an older adult that is used day to day to cook for one or two is also used for occasional large family gatherings.

When possible, a smaller concentrated work triangle within a larger more flexible workflow area can be effective.

Sink Center. Beside single-lever faucet controls, some ideas specific to the sink include:

- Plan the main sink or secondary prep sink with the option of flexible knee space. Remember to incorporate support for the sink and counter at a knee space and to cover the plumbing for protection. (see "Mobility" section)

- Storage should be placed at the point of use and within easy reach.

- A dishwasher with adjustable racks offers flexibility.

- When the space allows, elevate the dishwasher for less bending and improved access from a seated or standing position.

Cooking Center. The cooking center should be planned to minimize bending, lifting, and carrying. It should avoid the risks involved in reaching over burners.

- Take advantage of technology with easy programming options, such as microwaves with one-step/instant-on touch controls for popcorn, beverages, and reheating, which will make it easier to use.

- Induction cooktops sense the presence of a pan and will automatically shut-off.

- A separate cooktop and oven places both appliances at convenient heights and avoids the bending associated with a range oven.

- Oven heights should be planned to reduce the need to bend or lift.

- Heavy and commonly used pots should be stored close to the cooking surface.

- A water source or a sink near the cooktop reduces the need for carrying heavy pots of water across the kitchen.

- Lowering the work surface that includes the cooktop can accommodate shorter or seated cooks, making it easier to see into the pots on the cooktop.

- An angled mirror above the cooktop can make it easier for shorter or seated cooks to see into the pots, but it offers a maintenance challenge.

- A knee space can accommodate easier use of the cooktop and oven, particularly with heat-proof work surfaces.

- The knee space below the cooktop can be used for storage of a rolling cart, a rolling waste container unit or a stool, adding to the flexiblity.

Preparation Area. The preparation area should include continuous work counters for occasional large quantities of food that are convenient to the other work centers for efficient everyday use and limited carrying.

- Open storage, such as a rail system on the backsplash, is easy to view and access.

- Increased lighting from varied sources, natural and artificial, with adjustable controls, will accommodate variations in visual needs.

Figure 10.4 Separating the cooktop and oven allows both to be placed at user friendly heights as well as allowing for the option of a knee space. (Courtesy of KraftMaid Cabinetry)

- Glare can be minimized by careful selection of materials and attention to light sources including windows.

- Rolling storage or pull-out counters can provide additional work surfaces at proper heights.

Other Areas. Some extra features to enhance safety and security:

- Install a phone and/or an intercom in the kitchen for added security.

- Dual cueing, both audio and visual, should be used for door bell, security, and smoke alarms.

- Make sure the fire extinguisher is visible and easily reached.

- Consider the relationship of the kitchen door to an express exit route to allow for longer reaction times.

MOBILITY

Have you ever tried to walk a straight line on a moving airplane or train, or use steps that are slippery with water or ice? Have you ever tried to pass through a space not big enough to accommodate you? Do you remember, as a child, trying to reach the faucet at the sink?

Changes in our mobility include body stiffness and rigidity, as well as diminished strength, stamina, balance, and range of motion, usually in our spine, legs, and/or lower body. This includes those who use a wheelchair, scooter, walker, crutches, braces, or other mobility aid. Less obvious, this group also includes those whose mobility is challenged, sometimes temporarily, by pregnancy, excess weight, cardio-vascular or respiratory problems, injury, or fatigue. It also includes people who have difficulty bending or stooping.

Measurements used to plan the kitchen should include any assistive device the client uses. The wheelchair or mobility aid should be measured, just as you would document a client's height or body breadth. Standard dimensions for a person using a mobility aid are listed in Chapter 5 Human Factors and Universal Design, but in fact, each client and each mobility aid is unique. In the assessment tools in Chapter 6, particularly **Form 1 Needs**, you will find several diagrams to use when measuring clients who use mobility aids.

General design considerations include:

- Increased clear floor space to maneuver.

- Space to store and recharge mobility aid.

- Space at entry from garage or outdoors to clean mobility aid.

- Space and support for approach and use of a sink, cooktop, or work surface, including a knee space.

- Organized storage and function with minimal movement.

- Attention to sight lines, especially if the client is seated.

- Attention to adjustments in functional reach range.

- Safety.

Kitchen Design Implications

General. The use of mobility aids often increases the space needed to maneuver. Again, each mobility aid will have different requirements, but often the maneuvering requirements for a wheelchair would provide adequate clearance for other aids. Consider the following general areas:

- **Doorways.** The following recommendations can be used for doors from the kitchen to adjacent spaces including garages, laundry rooms, pantries, and outside. If feasible, remove the door between spaces to avoid conflict with the door swing.

  Although a 32-inch clear door opening is the size recommended in the Kitchen Planning Guidelines and is allowed in access standards, NKBA's Access Standard recommends that entry doors into the kitchen should maintain a clearance of 34 inches which is the typical clearance of a 36-inch door minus the thickness of the door and doorstop. When you consider the space taken by a person in a wheelchair is 30-inches wide, this seems a bare minimum.

  Swing-away hinges allow the door to swing out of the door opening and increase the clear space by 1 to $1^1/2$ inches, the thickness of the door.

  A clear floor space 18- to 24-inches wide on the pull side of a standard door is necessary to permit a person using a mobility aid to position themselves next to the door, beside the handle/lever, and out of the way of the door swing in order to pull it open. This clear space is detailed in Chapter 7. This dimension varies based on the type of door and the approach, as detailed in Figure 10.5.

  In older homes, hallways will sometimes be less than the 42 inches desired. When the width of the hallway can not be changed, sometimes a creative solution can come from alternative door designs (Figure 10.5).

- **Clear Floor Space.** The 48- x 30-inch area, a standard clear floor space for a person using a wheelchair, is a minimum at each appliance. This can be parallel or perpendicular to the appliance.

  A space that requires few turns provides easier maneuvering for a person using a wheelchair or other mobility aid.

  A 60-inch turning space is the diameter needed for a 360 degree circular turn in a wheelchair.

  A T-turn 36- x 36- x 60-inches works well and is sometimes easier to plan into a space, particularly with a knee space under the sink or cooktop (detailed in the Access Standard for Guideline 6).

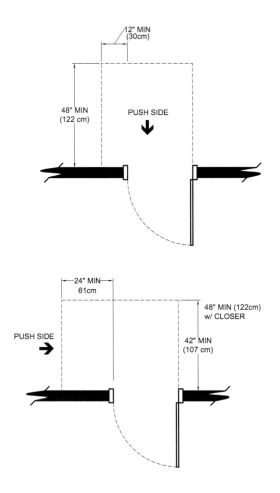

Figure 10.5 Clear Floor Space
Beyond the basic clearances listed in the NKBA's Access Standards, these recommendations help clarify space needed, based on door style and approach.

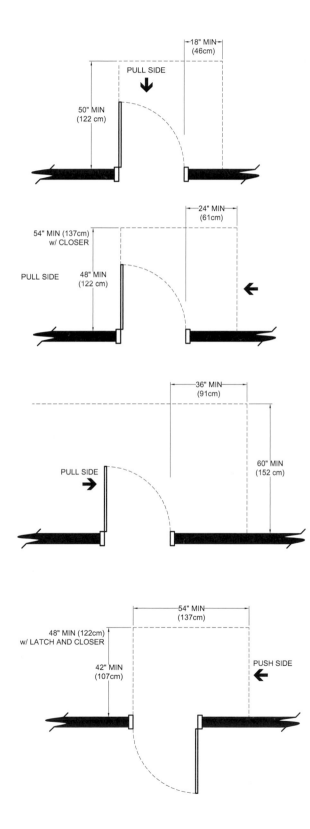

18" MIN
(46cm)

PULL SIDE

50" MIN
(122 cm)

24" MIN
(61cm)

54" MIN (137cm)
w/ CLOSER

PULL SIDE

48" MIN
(122 cm)

36" MIN
(91cm)

PULL SIDE

60" MIN
(152 cm)

54" MIN
(137cm)

48" MIN (122cm)
w/ LATCH AND CLOSER

PUSH SIDE

42" MIN
(107cm)

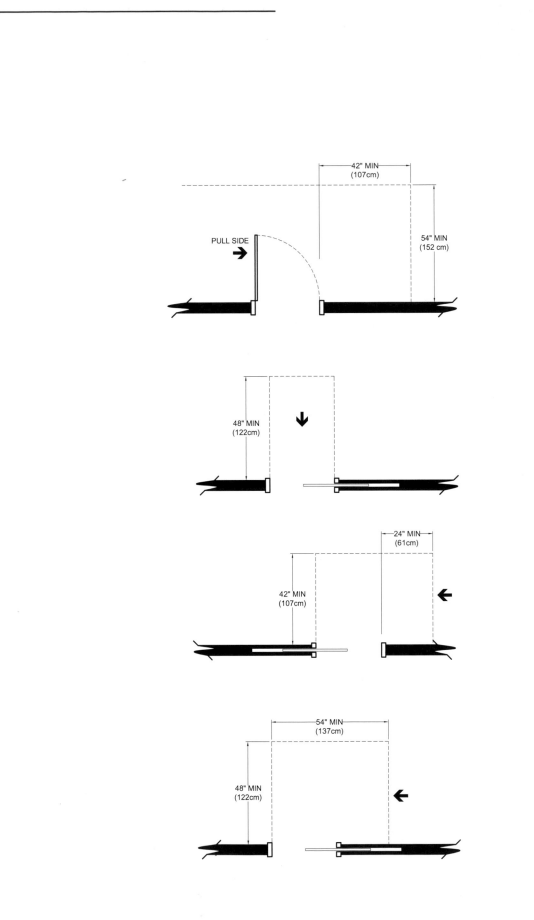

Kitchen Planning

Figure 10.6 Raised Dishwasher
This raised dishwasher reduces bending. (Courtesy of Poggenpohl US, Inc.)

Sink Center. The sink center is an ideal location for a knee space because it is the primary work center in most kitchens, and is often the center of the kitchen, literally.

- Sink controls offset to one side reduces reaching.

- Raising the dishwasher 6 inches to 9 inches reduces bending.

- A dishwasher with adjustable racks may make loading more convenient.

- A waste container unit on a rolling shelf can be removed by sliding it off, rather than lifting it up.

- **Knee space.** When planning a knee space, the minimum dimensions are 30 inches wide by 27 inches high by 19 inches deep under the counter as mentioned in Chapter 7. The exact counter height for a specific client will be determined by the height of their wheelchair arm, or their knees if the wheelchair arms are not an issue.

A preferred knee space minimum width is at least 36 inches as this allows the knee space to function as one leg of a T-turn and it allows for easier maneuvering. When planning for retractable doors, be careful to deduct the space they will use when calculating the kneespace width.

Remember to include sufficient support for the sink and counter at a knee space as the front edge of that counter may be leaned on for support as one approaches the sink.

A maximum sink depth of 6 1/2 inches is recommended in order to keep the work surface above the knee space no higher than 34 inches (28 to 34 inches preferred) and still clear the cook's knees.

Also, remember to cover the plumbing or otherwise block contact between the sink and the user. Protective coverings include material to match surrounding cabinetry or the sink, or they may be designed from custom railing systems to coordinate with the fittings or accessories.

Cooking Center. When possible, separate cooktop and oven appliances to provide more flexibility in their position and location.

- The cooktop counter can be lowered to accommodate a knee space or to improve the view into tall pots for a seated user.

- Cooktops with smooth glass top or continuous grates allow items to slide across the surface.

Figure 10.7 This knee space at 45 inches wide makes maneuvering and turning easier. (Courtesy of Mary Jo Peterson, Inc.)

Figure 10.8 The controls on this oven offer digital and pictorial communication. (Courtesy of GE)

- To avoid reaching over burners, select a range or cooktop appliance with controls placed at the front.

- A separate oven can be placed so that the door opens at a comfortable height.

- Side swing oven doors allow the cook to get closer to the interior and are less of an obstacle.

- A microwave hung immediately below a wall cabinet may be outside the user's reach range, and placing the microwave on the counter or below the counter may be a more comfortable height.

- A drawer microwave may improve access, provided the cook has the ability to lift things out of the oven.

- Side swing oven doors and new oven configurations can reduce challenges created by the open hot oven door.

- Smaller ovens can sometimes better accommodate the seated or shorter cook by reducing the size of the oven door.

- Ventilation controls should be located within reach of the user.

- A faucet with retractable spray head planned in a main or secondary sink near the cooking surface allows pots to be filled outside the sink with less lifting.

- Heat resistant landing counters planned adjacent to cooking appliances allow hot items to be transferred directly from the heat source.

Refrigeration Center

- A refrigerator recessed into the wall or a built-in style refrigerator with 24 inches case depth is easy to reach into and increases clear floor space in front of unit.

411

- A side-by-side refrigerator with handles that extend the full length of the doors allows operation by anyone, regardless of height.

- Side-by-side refrigerator doors are narrower and easier to maneuver around.

- French door refrigerators improve access to freezer and refrigerator space for most users.

- When space allows, separate refrigerator and freezer units provide complete and equal access to the refrigerator and freezer.

- Refrigerators with light and temperature controls located in the front portion of the interior improve access and view.

- Specifying 180° door swing on the hinge of the refrigerator improves access to the interior.

Storage. Plan the maximum amount of storage within the 15 inches to 48 inches universal reach range.

- Shallow hutch storage 12 inches deep will accommodate most kitchen glassware and dishes and will minimize obstruction of clear floor space while providing storage at the point of use.

- Raising toekicks on sink and storage cabinets 9 inches to 12 inches provides clearance for wheelchair footrests and other mobility aids, increasing clear floor space. When planning for a particular client, measure their footrest clearance to confirm height.

- Rolling storage carts can be moved out of an area to increase clear floor space.

- Many pantry items used in the kitchen fit in a small space and wall cabinets or storage systems 12 inches deep or less will increase the reach range and meet many needs.

- Open storage, such as rail systems on the backsplash, is easy to view and access.

Flooring

- Like ceramic tile, stone can be uncomfortable to stand on for long periods of time, and a rug or padding placed at frequently used work areas can relieve discomfort, provided it is recessed so it maintains a level floor.

- Resilient flooring is dense, non-abrasive flooring capable of shock absorption and is more comfortable for standing.

Have you ever tried to lift a mixer out from the back of a base cabinet or to balance and lift a stack of china above your head?

Included in this group of clients are those who are fatigued or frail from illness or age, and the multitudes of us with limited upper body strength. Also included are individuals with pain or limited joint or muscle motion due to temporary or minor injuries and illness. Specific conditions include arthritis, carpel tunnel syndrome, asthma, allergies, chemical sensitivities, post-polio syndrome, stroke, Parkinson's disease, multiple sclerosis, ALS, cerebral palsy, and numerous additional unique physical conditions.

Typical design considerations include:

- Placement of appliances, storage, controls, and work spaces within a limited reach range.

- Organization of space for limited movement and reduced strength and bending.

- Use of lighter weight objects that are easier to move, lift, use, and store.

- Easy to use appliance handles and doors, controls, and fixtures.

- Flexibility to allow for seating or standing at work centers.

Kitchen Design Implications

GENERAL

- Controls, handles, and door/drawer pulls should be operable with one hand, require only a minimal amount of strength for operation, and not require tight grasping, pinching, or twisting of the wrist.

- Pulls are preferred because they allow a person to pass an assistive device through the opening, or they at least allow use of the whole hand and not just the fingers.

- If knobs are selected, they should be large, asymmetrical, or textured to make grasping easier.

- Motion-sensor light switches eliminate the use of hands in operation.

Figure 10.9 Door and drawer pulls should be easy to grasp with one hand, and allow use of the whole hand, not just the fingers. (Courtesy of MNG)

Figure 10.10 Lever or loop handles on faucets are easiest to use. (Courtesy of Kohler Company)

SINK CENTER

The selection of the sink and fittings can improve function.

- Lever or loop handles on faucets are the easiest to use. Smooth round handles should be avoided.

- An electronic or battery-operated motion sensor faucet eliminates the use of hands in operation.

- Foot controls for water flow or disposer reduces the use of hands in operation.

- Select a sink with integrated accessories, like chopping blocks and strainers/colanders, so both hands can be used to cut or pour.

- Dishwashers raised 6 inches to 9 inches reduce bending, provided they enhance the design.

- Dishwashers with adjustable racks offer flexibility in loading the appliance.

- Dishwashers with automatic soap dispensing eliminate the need to add soap in every wash.

- Soap dispensers, installed within reach of the user, reduce needed strength and dexterity.

- A waste container unit on a rolling shelf can be removed by sliding it off, rather than lifting it up.

COOKING CENTER

- An appliance with a smooth cooking surface allows pots and pans to slide across the surface.

- Heat resistant landing counters should be adjacent to cooking appliances.

- A faucet with retractable spray head in a main sink, secondary sink, or a pot filler faucet near the cooking surface, allows pots to be filled outside the sink with less lifting.

- A sink that one can cook in eliminates the need to lift pots that are heavy with water.

- Side swinging or retractable oven doors allow the cook to get close to the interior and are less of an obstacle.

- Technology with one-touch easy programming options, such as microwaves with one-step/instant-on touch controls for popcorn, beverages, and reheating, require less hand manipulation.

- Heavier pots and equipment stored near work surface height helps avoid lifting.

- A space that can be used as a knee space enables a user to sit while cooking.

- Gas cooking elements with wok support accessories help stabilize a wok.

Figure 10.11 Smooth cooking surface allows pots to be easily slid. (Courtesy of Whirlpool Corp.)

REFRIGERATION CENTER

- To enhance use, plan for a refrigerator with lightweight and easy to open doors or ask manufacturers about vacuum breaker options.

- Refrigerators with light and temperature controls located in the front portion of interior provide for improved access and view.

- Web-connected refrigerators that "maintain themselves" reduce user maintanence tasks.

- Ice and water dispensers on the refrigerator door are convenient features that require use of one hand and less movement/maneuvering.

STORAGE

- Drawers on full-extension slides, open shelves, or extra countertop surface improve access to stored items.

- Rolling storage is flexible, allowing stored items to be moved into place easily or transferred to other work centers.

- Pull-out work surfaces add flexibility to countertop heights.

- Open storage, such as a backsplash rail system, is easy to view and access.

Figure 10.12 With a rolling storage unit, items can be easily moved to their point of use. (Courtesy of NY Loft)

- Storage should be placed at the point of use and within easy reach, organized for minimum required movement, including storage of heaviest items at no-bend and minimal lifting heights.

- Accessories, such as a mechanical pull-down unit, can be used to lower cabinet storage and must be planned within the cook's reach range.

- Generous counter depth and/or appliance garages can hold frequently used small appliances that assist with mixing, chopping or blending.

- Leaving small appliances on the counter eliminates the need to lift and carry items to storage.

VISION

Have you ever driven west into a setting sun, or struggled to focus when entering a dark theater from a bright lobby, or experienced uncertainty as a guest in a home or hotel trying to find the faucet and pour a glass of water in the dark because you don't want to disturb others?

Because vision changes are a natural part of the aging process, many of us would not consider ourselves disabled, but we would benefit from responsive design. People with vision impairments include those who are blind or who have partial vision loss due to cataracts, glaucoma, retinitis, macular degeneration, or eye injuries, as well as those with congenital vision impairments or ones caused by other conditions. Depending on the condition, the user's needs will be different.

Typical design considerations include:

- Increased lighting.

- Ability to adjust lighting levels (ambient down and task up).

- Increased tactile and audio cueing for way-finding, function, and warnings.

- Passage or maneuvering space clear of clutter and obstructions.

- Allowance for a four-legged companion trained to assist the client.

- Careful uses of color, contrast, and pattern.

- Selection of materials and lighting to reduce glare.

Kitchen Design Implications

LIGHTING

- Non-glare lighting minimizes the direct sight line to the light source.

- In addition to overhead ambient lighting, task lighting best illuminates the work surface and cuts down on shadows.

- Responsive lighting concepts for nocturnal visits to the kitchen include such features as motion sensor lighting, night lights, and glow-in-the-dark grout.

- Switches that are lighted in the off position assure that controls can be seen in the dark.

Figure 10.13 Increased lighting such as this interior cabinet lighting helps to accommodate users' vision changes. (Courtesy of KraftMaid Cabinetry)

COLOR AND CUEING

- As eyes age, it becomes difficult to differentiate colors that do not contrast, such as navy, black, and brown, or pastel colors. Placing light objects against darker backgrounds, or vice versa, helps them stand out, and can be useful on controls, work surfaces, and storage.

- Color contrast can be used to highlight edges or borders, such as the edge of a counter or a border around the floor.

- Eased counter edges and rounded corners are helpful, since they may be used as a tactile guide.

- Colors and patterns should be chosen with consideration of the total room in terms of contrast and light.

- Use tactile cueing to identify hot or cold water, and to aid in way finding, such as on the edge of a counter, or a frequently used setting on the microwave.

- Matte or low-sheen surfaces reduce glare.

Figure 10.14 Controls raised from the surface of the cooktop can provide a tactile sense for the user. (Courtesy of Viking Range Corp.)

Figure 10.15 There is a trend towards sliding and tambour doors. These door types reduce risk of injury by staying out of the way. (Courtesy of Vernon Applegate – San Francisco, California)

STORAGE

- Plan storage in a linear way to make memorizing of frequently used items easier.

- Reduce the number and depth of obstructions by planning shallow storage areas with open shelves.

- Tambour, sliding, and up-lifting doors will not project into a passage space.

- Lighting storage interiors will improve visibility.

- Self closing door/drawers reduce obstructions.

CONTROLS

- Audio and tactile cueing will provide dual messaging.

- Controls raised from the surface will provide a tactile sense.

- Glass touch controls do not provide a tactile cue.

- Contrast the surface around a control to help it visibly stand out.

- Electronic backlit controls or glow-in-the-dark controls provide better contrast.

- Refrigerators with controls located in front portion of interior improve access and view.

- Dual cueing, both audio and visual, should be used for door bell, security, and smoke alarms.

SINK CENTER

- A soap dispenser installed in the sink center will help eliminate items falling or being rearranged in an unknown order.

- A remote drain stopping mechanism will reduce the risk of reaching into a sink blindly.

COOKING CENTER

- Appliances with auditory indicators will provide an indication of settings.

- Appliances with large, easy-to-read controls facilitate use.

- Proximity or downdraft ventilation or shallow, retractable overhead ventilation systems with eased or radius edges do not obstruct the cook and avoid possible contact with the cook's head.

- Electronic cooktops with heat indicator lights can help people with limited vision.

- Interior oven lighting should be near the front of the cavity.

HEARING AND SPEECH

Have you ever tried to have a conversation on a cell phone with background noise? Or tried to have a conversation in a noisy bar or restaurant?

Many of us experience some loss of hearing as we age, often beginning with high frequencies or ringing in the ears. Also there are those who are deaf or who have a loss of hearing as a result of illness, disease, blockages in the inner ear, damage from prolonged exposure to excessive noise, head injuries or stroke, or other causes. Again, we may not identify a change in hearing as a disability, but a space can be designed to be more accommodating if we examine common needs and possible responses.

Typical design considerations include:

- Reduced ambient noise.

- Visual cueing in function and warnings.

- Clear sight lines.

- Safety.

Figure 10.16 If an overhead ventilation unit is used, eased edges will reduce risk of injury to the head. (Courtesy of Sub-Zero Freezer Company)

Kitchen Design Implications

GENERAL

- Design good lighting, and provide clear sight lines throughout the space so a person who cannot hear will be able to see throughout the space.

- When appropriate, place sink, cooking appliances, and/or preparation centers facing out to a snack counter or table to encourage face-to-face contact.

- In multiple cook kitchens, plan adjacent or facing preparation counters and avoid back-to-back interaction.

- Seating should encourage face-to-face conversation.

Figure 10.17 The sink center opposite the eating area encourages face-to-face conversation. (Courtesy of Merrie Fredericks, CMKBD – Newtown Square, Pennsylvania)

NOISE CONTROL

- Select quiet appliances, especially the dishwasher and ventilation unit, to minimize background noise distortion for someone with partial hearing.

- Reverberation of noise off hard surfaces makes it more difficult for persons with limited hearing to perceive sound, so incorporation of sound absorbing materials in the kitchen can improve acoustics.

- Wall, floor, and window treatments, such as cork, carpet, and fabrics, can absorb some of the room's noise

VISUAL CUEING

- Appliances and controls incorporating indicator lights provide an additional way to determine the end of a cycle, on/off, or hot/cold.

- A smoke detector with a visual or flashing alarm, as well as an auditory signal, should be used.

- Volume control can increase the effectiveness of audio cueing on appliances.

COGNITION

Have you ever been in a foreign country and tried to use the phone? Or driven through the day and night and then tried to follow oral directions to the nearest motel or gas station?

People with cognitive impairments include those with limited comprehension or memory, some confusion, and/or reduced reasoning. A few of the contributing factors include injury, illness, learning disability, stroke, general aging, using a foreign language exclusively, or youth/limited vocabulary and reasoning skills. The primary focus with a client who has cognitive impairments should be safety. Involving caregivers in the design process is critical.

Typical design considerations include:

- Safety and security concerns.

- Organization and patterning to help interpret function.

- Repetition and reminders for completing tasks.

- Simple one-step operations.

- Creating familiar spaces.

- Visual cueing.

Kitchen Design Implications

GENERAL

- Overuse of contrast, particularly on walls and floor borders, can prohibit a person from functioning normally and must be carefully planned.

- An entry door into the kitchen provides the option of closing off the kitchen entirely.

- Pictures or symbols might provide better communication than words.

- Appliances with the option of bilingual communication can be helpful to some.

- Cabinet panels on integrated appliances can cause confusion and should be avoided.

Sink Center. Concerns in the water center are scalding and leaving the water on.

- Electronic sensor faucet controls help ensure that the water is not left running.

- Intuitive cueing uses a blue color for cold and a red color for hot.

- An anti-scald faucet device should be specified.

- Instant hot water faucets eliminate the use of cooktop or microwave for some food and beverage preparation.

- A dishwasher installed with a shutoff switch can prevent accidentally turning on the appliance.

- A trash compactor with lock will help control access to this appliance. Some manufactures offer removable key lock.

- Continuous feed disposers should have a clearly marked switch to eliminate confusion with other switches.

Cooking Center. Preventative measures should be taken in the cooking center to avoid burning the skin or starting a fire.

- Cooktops with control lock feature prevent someone from using the appliance.

- Electric cooktops with heat indicator lights help warn about a hot surface.

- Redundant cueing can indicate the end of a cycle with sound and light.

- Induction cooktops or electric cooktops that sense the presence of a pan automatically shut-off if left on.

- Ovens with automatic shut-off and controls that can be removed are recommended.

- Take advantage of technology with easy programming options, such as microwaves with one-step/instant-on, touch controls for popcorn, beverages, and reheating

Figure 10.18 Electric cooktop safety features include a universal off switch that lets the user shut down all the cooktop elements at once, a lock key that child-proofs the unit, and an integral hot surface indicator for each element, which stays lit until the element has cooled. (Courtesy of Wolf)

REFRIGERATION CENTER

- Refrigerator with doors that close automatically when left slightly open help assure that the door is not accidentally left open.

STORAGE

- Temporary or permanent locks on cabinets should be considered.

- Storage for medications, sharp objects, and poisonous cleaning supplies should be locked.

- Open shelves and other open storage, such as a backsplash railing system or generous counters, allow for easy viewing and ordering of stored items, which may be helpful when memory fails.

- Glass cabinet doors also allow for viewing contents to aid memory.

SUMMARY

In this chapter, you have been presented with groups of physical characteristics and related design concepts to help stimulate and streamline your process when working on a space that is to accommodate a client with a specific disability. It is worth repeating that just as there is no average person, no two people with disabilities are alike. These general client groups have been created simply to help pull together and further explore the design concepts discussed throughout the book and particularly in Chapter 7. Hopefully, you will continue to build on the lists and grow your library of access-related design. As you do, you'll discover that most of the access "solutions" are better for everyone and you'll be experiencing that "Ah ha!" of universal design.

CHAPTER 11: Putting It All Together

Design is a process—but not a neat, tidy, linear process. Moving from the idea, or the wish, for a new kitchen to the finished product involves a lot of going back and forth, checking and rechecking. Developing a kitchen design involves a dose of inspiration, a spark of creativity, but mostly a lot of hard work.

Throughout this book, we presented a considerable amount of information about kitchens, what to include and how to arrange the space. We talked about appliances, cooking styles, where to eat and the many activities that take place in a kitchen. We even talked about designing auxiliary spaces around a kitchen. We emphasized how to gather client information to help focus your design to meet their needs and desires.

In this chapter, we show you how to organize this wealth of information and translate it into an actual kitchen design. First we discuss the overall design process and how to move from an idea to a complete design. Next we focus on the design program, the part of the process where you organize all your information and ideas into a plan for the kitchen design. And finally we address the design drawing and present a method to move from a concept to an actual layout. Throughout the chapter, we will supplement the text with an example of a basic kitchen design, from the design program to the design drawing.

In this chapter, we develop a single design drawing through the use of the design process. In reality, you will probably use this design process to develop several alternative plans to present to your client and then these plans will be evaluated by you and your client before making the final selections for the kitchen design.

THE DESIGN PROCESS

There are many different ways to approach design, probably as many as there are designers. As designers gain more experience, they develop a method and unique style that is personally successful.

If you are a new designer, you can benefit by following a formal structure for the design process. This will help you become adept at sequencing the steps in developing a kitchen design and assure that no parts of the process are forgotten.

If you are an experienced designer, reviewing a formal design process may give you a fresh approach and spark new creativity in your designs. What follows is a brief discussion of the design process as we will present it in this book.

SUMMARY OF THE DESIGN PROCESS

- Identify the client.
- Organize the information.
- Identify the activity spaces.
- Visualize the activity spaces.
- Develop the visual diagram.
- Refine the visual diagram.
- Think in three dimensions.
- Evaluate the plan.
- Think about details, details, details.

A review of the formal design process can be useful to make sure all parts of the process are included.

- **Identify the client.** Gather information about the client. This is both the tangible, such as anthropometric information and a list of items for storage, and the intangible, such as ambience desired in the space or style preferences. Chapter 6 of this book is a detailed guide to gathering information and assessing client needs, and provides forms and checklists to facilitate the process. You may also need additional research, learning about things such as appliances, products or materials that the client wants.

- **Organize the information.** Develop the first part of your design program by determining the goals and objectives for the design. Prioritize the needs and wants of the client and identify the limitations of the project. (Design programming will be discussed in more detail later in this chapter.)

- **Identify the activity spaces.** Develop the second part of the design program by preparing the User Analysis, which groups design requirements by the major activities that will take place in the kitchen space. (See Figure 11.1 for an example of a User Analysis.) In most cases, this will mean that you are organizing information by the activity centers that were described in Chapter 7.

  Check your User Analysis against the client needs assessment information (Chapter 6) to make sure that you have accommodated the client's priority needs. You may even want to share the User Analysis with the client, as a double check.

- **Visualize the activity spaces.** This is the stage when you are moving from verbal and quantitative information to visual ideas. Many designers use bubble diagrams to represent activity spaces or various centers and to explore the relationships of the different spaces. For example, you may have one bubble for the cooking center (representing a cook top and the surrounding cabinetry and counter space), another bubble for the refrigerator area, and so on. (See Figure 11.3 for an example of a bubble diagram.)

- **Develop the visual diagram.** Select the best one or two bubble diagrams for refinement. Prepare a room outline, to scale (1/2 inch equals 1 foot), and note project parameters, such as windows or doors, that are fixed in location. Start using templates for each center or activity space and place them on your room outline, using the bubble diagrams as your guide. A design template is a scale drawing representing the appliances, cabinetry and clearances for a center or activity space. (See Figures 11.4 for an example of a design template.) Templates allow you to see how spaces fit together and how your design ideas will work in the actual kitchen space.

  Check your visual diagram against the User Analysis.

- **Refine the visual diagram.** You will be moving from the bubble diagram to the arrangement of templates to a sketch of a floor plan. Work in scale. Evaluate your visual diagram against the project parameters.

- **Think in three dimensions.** Use elevation or perspective sketches to develop the vertical elements for your design. Changes in the floor plan may be required.

- **Evaluate the plan.** Check the preliminary design against the design program. Review the relationship of the centers. Evaluate zoning and circulation within the kitchen as well as in relationship to adjacent rooms. Evaluate your plan against the Kitchen Planning Guidelines (see Figure 11.16 on page 494) and if appropriate, the Kitchen Access Standards (see Figure 11.17 on page 496). Both of these checklists are also on the CD included with this book.

- **Think about details, details, details.** Lay out the design of the kitchen in dimensioned drawings. Specify the actual appliances, cabinetry, materials, fixtures and other items in the space, so that you can verify sizes, installation requirements, clearances and other details. Check dimensions to make sure that everything will fit as you envision.

THE DESIGN PROGRAM

Let's imagine that you have just completed an exciting meeting with your client. Lots of ideas were shared back and forth. Enticing possibilities for a unique kitchen design were explored. You are eager to sketch, pull out material samples and develop your thoughts into a new design. Ready to go? What? Write a design program? No, you say, let's just go straight to the design. You can incorporate your client's needs as you go along.

If you skip the design program, how will you know what to design?

Design programming is an important and necessary part of successful designing. When we discussed the design process, did you note how often we recommended you check your developing design against the design program? Think of the design program as the contract between you and your client. It is an organized directory of all the client's needs, wants and wishes for the kitchen design, plus the important parameters of the total design.

In Chapter 6, we talked about the design program as the next step in the needs assessment process. Developing the design program allows you to make sure you have—and understand—all the information necessary for the kitchen design. A typical design program is in three parts:

- Goals or purpose

- Objectives and priorities

- Activities and relationships

Goals and Purpose

Can you briefly describe the goals of the design project? Think of this part of the design program as the overview. It should include a description of the client(s), the type and scope of the project, the budget and your role and responsibilities in the project. Include the major criteria for the kitchen design and any unique aspects of the project.

You might want to share your goal statements with your client to determine that you have interpreted the project correctly. The statements could also be included in your contract.

Objectives

Objectives are used to operationalize your goals. If goals tell what you want to do, objectives tell how you are going to do it. Objectives are written with active verbs and the outcomes can be measured.

- Goal: The kitchen will be a social space.

- Objectives: Install a raised counter area across from the cook-top with seating for three. Design two prep areas. Provide an open view from the sink area into the family room.

Write objectives to identify the client's major wants and needs. Use the development of the objectives to sort out priorities—must have, should or want to have, and desire or would like to have.

Activities and Relationships

This section is the crux of the design program. Focus on the various activities that will take place in the kitchen and what is needed in the design to support the activities. You may want to group activities together into centers. For example, kneading bread, assembling pies, packing a lunch box and preparing vegetables for a stir-fry, all have similar workspace requirements, and could be grouped together as part of the food preparation center. **Form 3: Checklist for Kitchen Activities** and **Form 4: Kitchen Storage Inventory**, found in Chapter 6, are arranged in sections by center, so you can collect activity and storage information in an organized fashion.

Since the focus is on the activities taking place in the space, the emphasis is on who is doing what. Organize the activity information into a User Analysis chart (Figure 11.1). You might want to prepare a User Analysis for each center in the kitchen or group of related activities. The User Analysis includes the following information:

- Activities that take place in the space

- Who will be doing the activities; the users

- Frequency of activities

- Appliances, fixtures, fittings, furnishings, accessories and any other physical items needed to support the activities, including special sizes or characteristics

- Storage needed to support the activities

- Amount of space needed for the activities, including clearances; and relationships to other spaces

- Ambience requirements

- Special requirements, such as safety features

- Future changes to be accommodated

- Summary of Planning Guidelines or Access Standards relevant to the activities and requirements of the client and their kitchen

Preparing the User Analysis as a chart or table helps to organize the information into an easily referenced format to which you can refer during the development of your design. Using a spreadsheet program or the table function in a word-processing program on your computer makes it easy to prepare a User Analysis. However, it is a good idea to leave some open space for extra notes if changes are needed.

Activity Space	Users	Frequency	Appliances, Fixtures, Fittings, Furniture, Etc.		Storage
Sink Center: automatic dishwasher; hand wash large items; produce prep; primary water source for kitchen	Vincent, Rose	Daily	• Dishwasher, 24" energy efficient, quiet • Garbage disposer • Two-bowl sink, 33", 18 gauge stainless steel • Pull-out spray faucet, single lever • Hot water dispenser		• Drawer storage • Cleaning supplies • Vegetable prep tools • Tea & mugs • Ice tea maker • Coffee pot & supplies • Everyday dishes • Waste receptacle

Space Relationships	Ambience	Special Needs	Future Needs	Guidelines and Access Standards
• 42" work aisle, 48" preferred • Adjacent to prep center • 21" minimum clearance by dishwasher • 18" & 24" landing space by sink, more preferable	Night light at sink	• Sink below window • 36" window to be added • Pull-out cutting board • Toekick step by sink	None noted	Kitchen Planning Guidelines: 2, 3, 6, 10, 11, 13 14, 26, 28, 30, 31

As you develop your User Analysis, you will be relying on the client interview and needs assessment to determine what activities will take place in the kitchen. Using a prepared assessment form, like Form 3: Checklist for Kitchen Activities, can help assure that all activities are considered. However, you will want to review your User Analysis to make sure that it is inclusive. Some activities are so common and routine that we might not think about them. For example, your clients might tell you that they frequently chop and dice vegetables for salads and stir-fry (requiring a cutting surface at an appropriate height, counter space for assembling ingredients and convenient storage for knives) but assume that you know that they also wash and drain the vegetables first (requiring a water source near the cutting surface, an area to drain the vegetables and storage for a colander). Further, did you think about refrigerated and non-refrigerated storage for these vegetables?

As you develop the User Analysis it is a good time to review the Kitchen Planning Guidelines and Access Standards that apply to the spaces you are designing. You can note the number of the Guidelines that apply, as we did in our example, or note detail, such as "increase light level".

Figure 11.1 This is an example of a User Analysis chart, showing information for a sink center. This could be used in the design template shown in Figure 11.4, and in the sample kitchen design shown in Figures 11.5 through 11.15.

RELATIONSHIP MATRIX

The detail you include in your User Analysis will depend on the complexity of the project. For a larger project, especially if it involves multiple spaces, you may want to use a matrix to graph the relationship among the activity areas. The matrix can help you more easily see the relationships among activity spaces and assist in determining how to group and separate activities into different centers and spaces. You can also use a matrix to graph relationships between the kitchen and other spaces in the home.

Sink			
1	Prep		
2	1	Cook	
2	2	2	Refrigerator/Storage

1 = Direct access needed

2 = Partial or indirect access desirable

3 = No access necessary

To read the matrix: read down a column and across a row from the right to the cell where the column and row meet. For example, the orange highlighted cell is in the Sink column and the Cook row. There is a number 2 in the cell. That tells us that partial or indirect access is desirable. However, if we look at the blue highlighted cell, in the Prep column and the Cook row, we see that there is a 1, which means that direct access is needed. Using the matrix can help you prioritize relationships between centers or other areas within your design.

Figure 11.2 This is an example of a matrix showing physical access between centers and other areas in the kitchen. Similar matrices could be developed for visual access or auditory access. Or, the same matrix approach could be used to study access between the kitchen and other spaces within the home. This matrix was used in developing the bubble diagram (Figure 11.3) and the visual diagram (Figure 11.6) for the sample kitchen design.

BUBBLE DIAGRAM

When you have completed the information gathering and analysis stages of the design process, you are ready to begin moving to visualization. It is time to start with a bubble diagram, which lets you begin to think about space relationships.

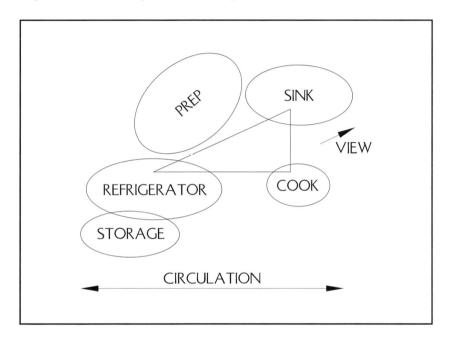

Figure 11.3 A bubble diagram is a simple sketch to show how different activity areas can be arranged in a kitchen space. Each "bubble" is an activity area. This is an example of a bubble diagram for a remodeled kitchen. We will be using this as the basis for our design and drawing examples throughout this chapter.

THE DESIGN DRAWING

Moving from the design program to the completed design solution is an exciting and creative process. It is also a process that requires accuracy and verification.

In this section, we discuss how to move from the design program to a dimensioned design drawing of your solution. We will emphasize the importance of checking and rechecking dimensions to verify that your design solution will work in "real space." This section tells you how to manage the technical details—you supply the creativity.

Templates

As you begin refining your conceptual ideas, the bubble diagrams, it is important to begin working to scale. First, this gives you a realistic picture of space relationships and possibilities—very important in the complex spaces of a kitchen. Second, it helps prevent you from making mistakes. If you work with the right proportions and sizes from the beginning, you tend to "see" the space relationships more clearly and you are less likely to misjudge clearances and space needs.

A helpful way to develop your visual diagram is to use design templates. A design template is used to represent an activity space or a center, and includes any appliances, fixtures or equipment, plus the clearances needed. For example, you can have a sink center template, which would show the sink in its cabinet, associated counter space, the dishwasher and the clearances needed for door swings and access. Or a refrigerator center template would include the appliance, landing space countertop, door swings and clearances, and perhaps note where water and electrical connections are required.

It is a good idea to prepare design templates in both plan and elevation view. This can be very useful as you evaluate your design in three-dimensions. You may want to prepare several elevation views, as you experiment with different arrangements of wall cabinets, or to be prepared to work with different ceiling heights.

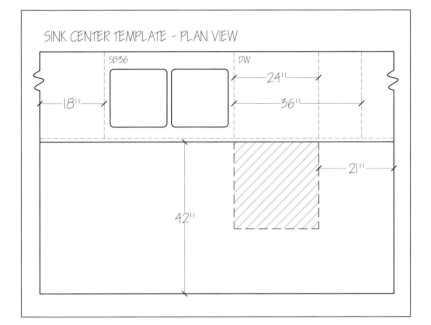

Figure 11.4a A design template for a plan view of a sink center, including a sink cabinet (36 inch) and dishwasher (24 inch) to the right of the sink. Landing areas of 18 inches and 24 inches and preparation area of 36 inches are included next to the sink, according to Planning Guidelines 11 and 12. Clearances are based on the guideline recommendations for dishwasher placement (Planning Guideline 13) and work aisle clearances (Planning Guideline 6). Additional clearances to meet the Access Standards could be added.

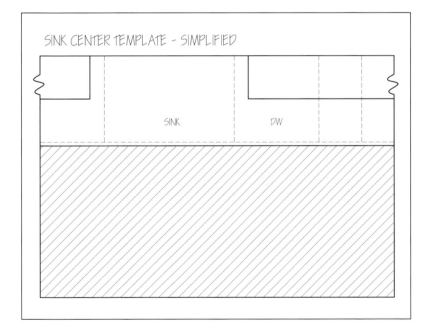

Figure 11.4b A simplified template of the sink center, with wall cabinets blocked, would be useful in experimenting with different design layouts.

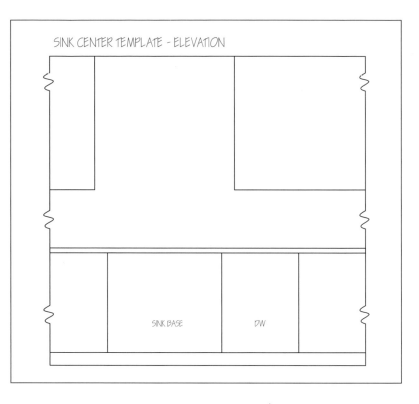

SINK CENTER TEMPLATE - ELEVATION

SINK BASE   DW

Figure 11.4c A simplified elevation view of the sink center template, using a 96-inch ceiling.

Draw your design templates in a scale of $^1/2$ inch to 1 foot. Since this is the typical scale for kitchen drawings, starting in this scale will be a time saver.

Based on your design program, you will need to develop a number of design templates for a particular kitchen design. Consider special needs and requests of your client. You may develop alternative templates for the same activity space. For example, you may develop two design templates for different sized refrigerators and then determine which size refrigerator will fit best in the final design.

Label your design templates. This will facilitate using them to develop the kitchen plan. It will also help you develop a timesaving file of design templates for future use. For example, if you have design templates for 33-inch, 36-inch and 39-inch refrigerators with clearance, from one project, you can likely use them on many other kitchen designs. Depending on your preferred style of working, design templates can be saved in computer files or on sturdy paper.

Room Outline

An important foundation for producing your visual diagram, and eventually your design drawing, is the room outline. The room outline is a scaled drawing of the perimeter of the kitchen space. Prepare a drawing of all walls and fixed structural or architectural features, such as windows and doors. The information you need to complete the room outline should be found on the following needs assessment forms from Chapter 6: **Form 8: Dimensions of the Kitchen – Floor Plan**; **Form 9: Dimensions of the Kitchen – Elevations**; **Form 10: Dimensions of Mechanical Devices**; **Form 11: Window Measurements**; **Form 12: Door Measurements**; and **Form 13: Fixture and Appliance Measurements**.

In some kitchen design projects, walls, windows, doors, and other structural features are fixed, and cannot be moved or altered. For example, moving windows affects the exterior design of the home, and the client may not want to change this. In other projects, you may have some options to relocate some features or even expand the space. Perhaps a doorway can be moved or an interior wall removed. This is the type of information recorded on **Form 7: Job Site Inspection**.

You may find it useful to prepare two room outlines. One room outline shows the existing room space as it is. The second drawing removes features that can be changed but retains the fixed features. The second drawing will help you see the possibilities of the space (Figure 11.5).

You may have other limitations on your design that should be noted on your room outline. All mechanical, electrical and plumbing parameters need to be noted. For example, the location of one or more plumbing fixtures or appliances may be predetermined. Or, the location of heating and cooling vents may be fixed.

Add any additional information to your drawing that will help in design decisions. Note what types of spaces surround the kitchen. Note interior and exterior walls. The height of windows or any fixed structural features will be useful to know. Important interior or exterior views can be noted.

It is important to note all constraints and options on your room outline. Noting these features on your room outline helps assure that your design will remain within the parameters of your project.

Verify all room measurements and check your room drawing. The room outline must accurately represent the space of the kitchen.

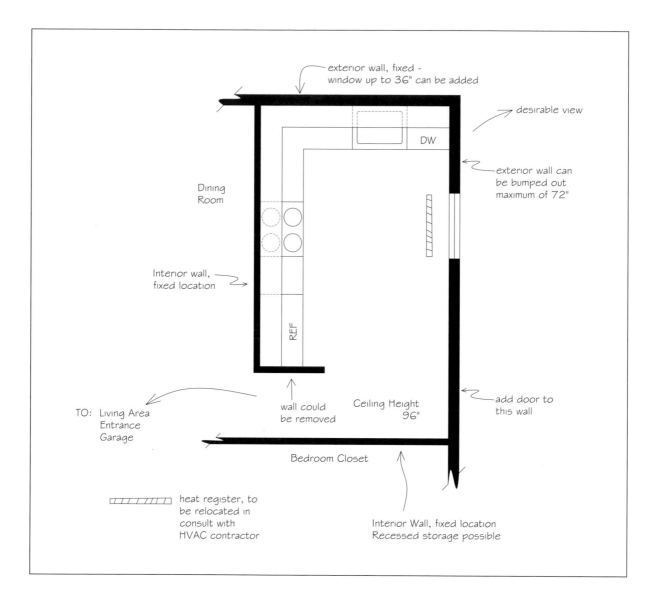

exterior wall, fixed -
window up to 36" can be added

desirable view

exterior wall can
be bumped out
maximum of 72"

Dining
Room

Interior wall,
fixed location

DW

REF

TO: Living Area
Entrance
Garage

wall could
be removed

Ceiling Height
96"

add door to
this wall

Bedroom Closet

heat register, to
be relocated in
consult with
HVAC contractor

Interior Wall, fixed location
Recessed storage possible

Figure 11.5a The existing kitchen
space with project parameters.

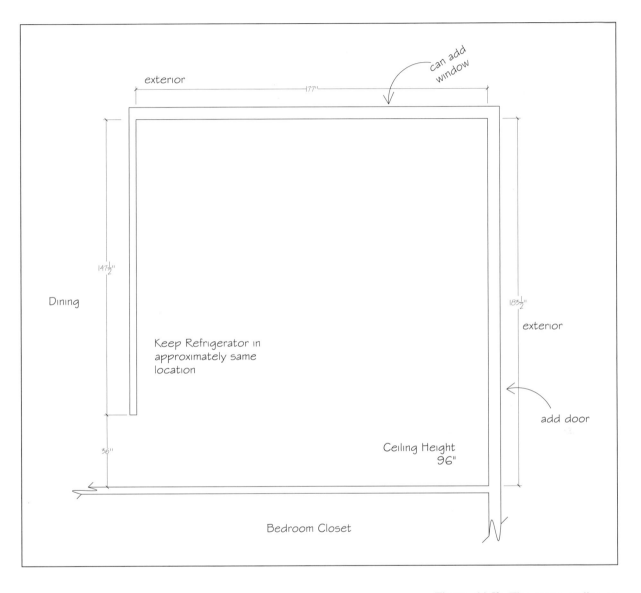

exterior

177"

can add window

Dining

147½"

183½"

exterior

Keep Refrigerator in approximately same location

add door

Ceiling Height 96"

36"

Bedroom Closet

Figure 11.5b The room outline as altered. Non-fixed features are removed, the exterior wall is bumped out, fixed features are included and dimensions are shown.

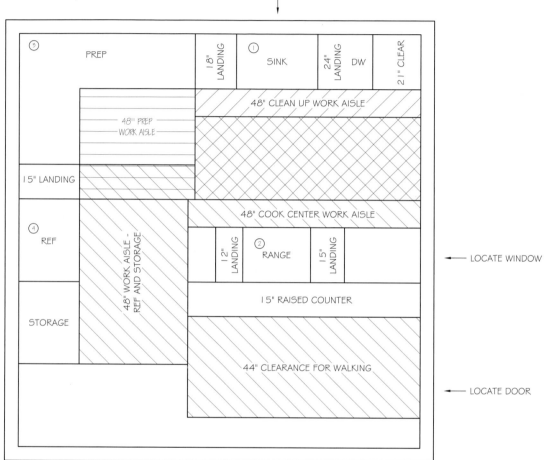

LOCATE WINDOW

⑤ PREP

18" LANDING

① SINK

24" LANDING

DW

21" CLEAR

48" CLEAN UP WORK AISLE

48" PREP WORK AISLE

15" LANDING

48" COOK CENTER WORK AISLE

④ REF

48" WORK AISLE - REF AND STORAGE

12" LANDING

② RANGE

15" LANDING

15" RAISED COUNTER

STORAGE

44" CLEARANCE FOR WALKING

LOCATE WINDOW

LOCATE DOOR

① SINK STORAGE (DESIGN TEMPLATE)
* SINK IN 36" CABINET
* 24" DISHWASHWER
* 18" LANDING SPACE TO LEFT & 24" LANDING SPACE TO RIGHT OF SINK
* 21" CLEARANCE BETWEEN DISHWASHWER AND WALL
* 48" WORK AISLE

② COOK CENTER (DESIGN TEMPLATE)
* 30" RANGE
* 12" LANDING SPCE TOR IGHT AND 15" LANDING SPACE TO LEFT
* 15" RAISED COUNTER
* 48" WORK AISLE AND 44" CLEARANCE FOR WALKING

⑤ PREP AREA (DESIGN TEMPLATE)
* COUNTER SPACE ADJACENT TO SINK
* 48" WORK AISLE

④ REFRIGERATOR CENTER
* 36" REFRIGERATOR
* 15" LANDING AREA
* 48" WORK AISLE

Figure 11.6 The visual diagram uses the room outline from Figure 11.5 and bubble diagram from Figure 11.3. Four design templates were used to develop the visual diagram, with landing space and clearances determined by Kitchen Planning Guideline recommendations.

Visual Diagrams

Your bubble diagrams suggested ways to arrange the spaces in the kitchen. Now it is time to see if these ideas can be translated into a design that will work in the actual space. This is the development of the visual diagram.

Using the design templates that you developed, place them in the room outline. Use the ideas generated by the bubble diagrams to guide your work. Refer to the information on the room outline to see if your design ideas are possible within the existing space.

You will want to try a number of different layouts before you achieve the best solution. As you consider a possible layout, review the information on your room outline that details project parameters. Refer back to the design program, especially the User Analysis, to remind yourself of what the design layout needs to accomplish.

If you are having trouble getting everything into the space, reconsider the templates you are using. Could space clearances overlap without compromising function or safety? Could a smaller fixture be used and still meet client needs?

Three Dimensions and Vertical Relationships

Very early in the design process, think in three dimensions. For example, placing the wall oven next to the refrigerator may work fine in plan, but how will it look vertically? We experience space in multiple dimensions, so we must design for all perspectives.

After you have developed one or more visual diagrams that appear to work in plan, develop some three-dimensional sketches. Elevation sketches of a wall, to scale, are useful to evaluate spatial relationships of appliances, fixtures, cabinetry and structural features. Design templates of elevation views can speed the process.

Many computer programs used in developing designs will generate perspective views of a design. This technology is an excellent way to view your design from different angles and evaluate its effectiveness.

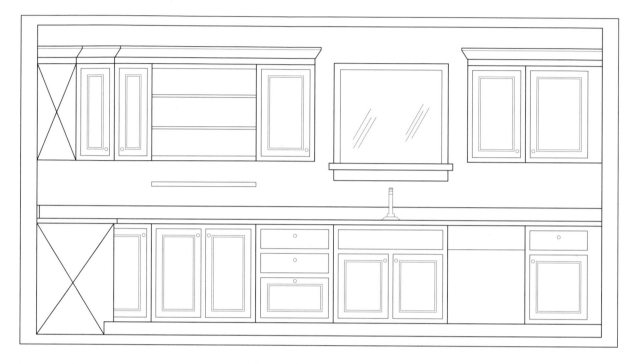

Figure 11.7 A rough elevation sketch of the wall with the sink center, taken from the visual diagram in Figure 11.6, shows vertical relationships and encourages you to begin thinking about details such as the placement of specific cabinets and drawers.

After reviewing your visual diagrams, in plan and vertical views, select the best design layout. Review your design program to determine that the layout meets the goals and objectives. Verify that the design layout is appropriate to the structural and mechanical parameters of the project. Refer back to the jobsite inspection forms in Chapter 6 to verify information. Or, if you are working with new construction, consult project documents.

Now you are ready to detail your design solution in a complete dimensioned drawing.

Priority Areas

Start your dimensioned design drawing with the priority areas of the plan. These are the elements of your plan that are not moveable, demand the most space, or are most important to the client. For example, you might start your dimensioned drawing with the sink center because plumbing connections or a window dictate the location. Or you might start with the placement of a commercial-style range because of its large size and because it is going to be a focal element of the kitchen design.

A SAMPLE DESIGN DRAWING

To best explain how to use priority areas to layout a design drawing, we will take you through an example. The visual diagram in Figure 11.6 and elevation sketch in Figure 11.7 got us started on the kitchen design that is being used throughout this chapter.

For our example, we are going to start with the sink center wall. The client wants to add a window to that wall and the location of the sink will determine the placement of the window. First, we draw the room walls to scale. We lightly add the wall thicknesses and overall dimensions (Figure 11.8). We may need to modify walls as we add windows and doors, or move dimensions to complete the drawing. However, it is important to start with an accurate drawing of the space. (For further details on drawing according to NKBA Graphic & Presentation Standards refer to the NKBA book *Kitchen & Bath Drawing*, part of the Professional Resource Library.)

We will start detailing our drawing at the corner, where the two exterior walls meet, to the right of where we expect to place the sink. Referring to the design template and the visual diagram, we know that we want to have at least 21 inches of clearance before we place the dishwasher, and that we have generous wall space to fit in the cleanup center. We choose to place a 21-inch base cabinet with a 3-inch extended stile on the right and label the cabinet with appropriate nomenclature (Figure 11.8a).

Next, we draw the centerline, to place a 24-inch dishwasher next to the base cabinet. Continuing, we place a 36-inch sink base cabinet next to the dishwasher, label it with correct nomenclature, and draw the centerline for the sink (Figure 11.8b).

Now, we have a decision to make. We know that we need at least 18 inches of landing space next to the sink. However, from our visual diagram, we know that we have room for a generous amount of counter space for the prep area to the left of the sink. So, we choose to put a 24-inch drawer base next to the sink, which will balance the dishwasher on the other side of the sink (Figure 11.8c).

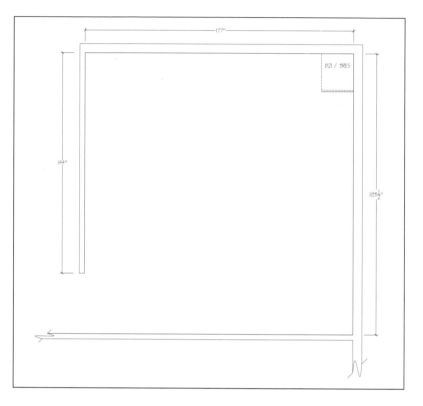

Figure 11.8a

Figure 11.8b

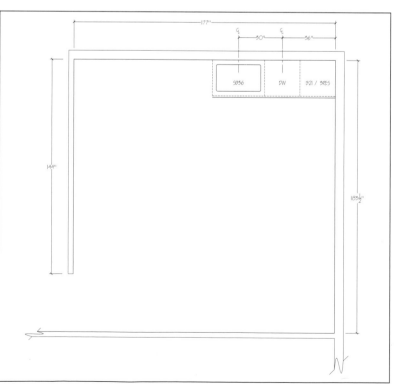

Figures 11.8a, b & c These show the sequence of placing the base cabinets and dishwasher in the sink center. Figure 11.8a shows the whole room, while 11.8b and 11.8c focus on the sink center. These are the first steps in developing the design drawing based on the visual diagram of Figure 11.6.

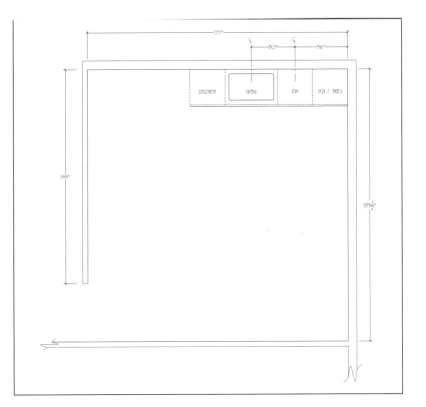

Figure 11.8c

The base cabinets and counters of the cleanup center are now placed. There are several options to continue working on our design drawing. We may choose to place all the base cabinets in the kitchen and then work on wall cabinets. We could layout the peninsula with the range next, so that its design will relate to the cleanup center.

The best advice is to work on priority areas. The next priority, in our example, is to place a corner cabinet with a lazy Susan in the prep area. This corner cabinet will determine the remaining cabinetry placement and sizes on both kitchen walls, so it should be placed next. Therefore, we will draw a 36-inch base corner cabinet in the prep area, and label it with nomenclature (Figure 11.9).

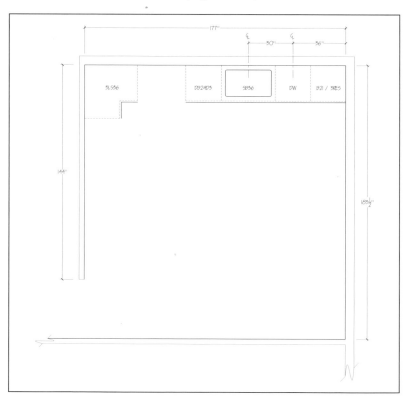

Figure 11.9 To continue the design drawing begun in Figure 11.8 we add a base corner cabinet.

The next priority area in our design drawing is most likely the placement of the refrigerator. This is a large appliance and has a strong vertical presence. In addition, the client has expressed a desire that the refrigerator remain in approximately the same location as in the original kitchen. For function and a compact work triangle, we decide to put the refrigerator a little closer to the prep area and sink center, yet still along the same wall. On the wall shared with the dining room, we decide to place open shelves (turned 90 degrees to face the walkway) at the end of the wall, a 24-inch pantry, and a 36-inch refrigerator. We label the pantry with nomenclature and draw the centerline for the refrigerator (Figure 11.10).

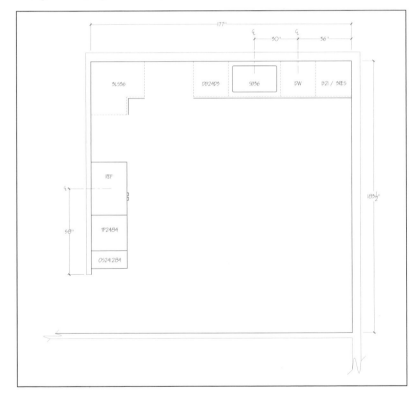

Figure 11.10 With the addition of the pantry storage and refrigerator to our design drawing, the L-shape of the kitchen plan becomes apparent.

We know that we need to place a base cabinet next to the refrigerator and that we need to provide at least 15 inches of landing space. However, we are going to wait to place that cabinet until we can evaluate it in the design of the whole prep center and determine the best size and function of cabinet for the space.

As shown, we have the basic plan for the L-shape portion of the kitchen design. Before we go any farther, let's block in the location of the peninsula that will hold the range and raised eating counter (Figure 11.11). We may adjust the exact size when we detail the cabinets, but, for now, we will block the maximum dimension based on work aisle clearances. Our kitchen design is starting to take shape.

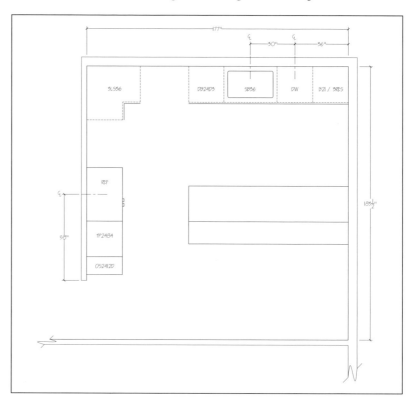

Figure 11.11 The next step in developing our design drawing is to block in the location of the peninsula that will include a range and eating counter.

It is time to look at some specific details of dimensions and cabinet sizes. As we make final decisions on placement of the remaining cabinets, we need to consider many things, such as: storage needs of the client; functional arrangements of work centers; types of storage, such as drawers or roll-out shelves, and the visual relationship of vertical and horizontal design elements. In this section, we will focus on making sure that everything fits in place.

Let's look at the window wall of the kitchen with the cleanup center. First, we will calculate the total amount of wall space used in the cabinets placed so far. Then we can determine what additional cabinetry can be placed. To help assure accuracy, we will start with the total wall length and subtract for each cabinet or appliance.

177 inches	Total wall length
− 24 inches	21-inch base cabinet with 3-inch extended stile
153 inches	
− 24 inches	Dishwasher
129 inches	
− 36 inches	36-inch sink base cabinet
93 inches	
− 24 inches	24-inch drawer base
69 inches	
− 36 inches	36-inch base corner cabinet
33 inches	

Using this method, we can determine that we have 33 inches remaining on the wall for base cabinetry. Given that the space is in the prep area, let's put a 33-inch base cabinet with rollout shelves, for easily accessible storage. Now, the base cabinets are complete on this wall (Figure 11.12). We can verify the accuracy of our calculations by adding the dimensions together.

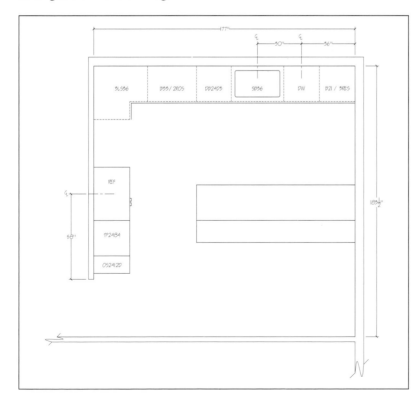

Figure 11.12 With the addition of a 33-inch base cabinet, the placement of base cabinetry on the sink center wall is complete.

The next step in completing our dimension drawing would most likely be to determine the wall cabinet placement for the same wall—the window or exterior wall where the sink center is located. This allows us to coordinate wall cabinets with base cabinets and determine if any changes are needed. We started by placing a 24-inch diagonal corner wall cabinet and then coordinating the remaining wall space with the base cabinets. Figure 11.13 shows the placement and nomenclature for wall cabinets along that wall.

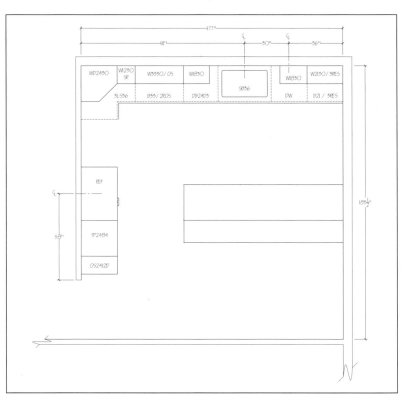

Figure 11.13 The wall cabinets are shown on the sink center wall.

We can now check the dimensions on the wall cabinets. Again, it is good to start with the total wall length and subtract the various measurements, in order. Then double check by adding them up working in the opposite direction.

177 inches	Total wall length
− 24 inches	21-inch wall cabinet with 3-inch extended stile
153 inches	
− 18 inches	18-inch wall cabinet
135 inches	
− 6 inches	Set back for window and allowance for window casing
129 inches	
− 36 inches	Clearance for 36-inch window
93 inches	
− 6 inches	Set back for window and allowance for window casing
87 inches	
− 18 inches	18-inch wall cabinet
69 inches	
− 33 inches	33-inch wall cabinet, no doors
36 inches	
− 12 inches	12-inch wall cabinet with spice rack
24 inches	
− 24 inches	24-inch diagonal corner wall cabinet
0 inches	

Finishing The Floor Plan

After the priority areas are placed and dimensioned, add the other centers, appliances, cabinetry, fixtures and features in the plan. Continue checking dimensions by subtracting the amount of space for each item placed in the plan from the remaining wall space. Be sure to verify dimensions in each direction.

As you check dimensions, allow for door swings and clearances for hardware. In some places, you might need to plan on fillers or extended stiles on cabinetry to provide the space to open doors or pull out shelves and drawers. In our example, we had originally planned to put 21 inches between the dishwasher and the wall, to provide the minimum clearance recommended in Kitchen Planning Guideline 13. However, we decided to increase that to 24 inches by using a 21-inch cabinet with an extended stile. The extended stile pulls the cabinet out of the corner, providing more space for the door swing and hardware.

Now that you have worked through some examples, finish the sample plan. Complete the placement of cabinetry along the wall with the refrigerator. Be sure to evaluate the design of the prep area—you may want to make some changes in the choice of cabinets that we have already made. Next, work on laying out the peninsula with the range and raised eating counter. Place the windows and doors that will be added in the remodeling. Remember to verify that everything will fit.

ADJUSTING THE DIMENSIONS

Sometimes, at this point, the dimensions do not work out. You may find that your total space for appliances, cabinetry and other features adds up to more or less than the length of a wall. If this is the case, you need to consider alternatives.

If you have extra space, you may decide to increase the size of selected cabinets or add additional cabinets. This is a good solution if you do not have a lot of extra space. For example, a 33-inch cabinet can be substituted for a 30-inch cabinet. Using one or more fillers or extended stiles may also solve the problem. Another alternative, if appropriate to the client's needs, would be to use a larger fixture, such as 36-inch sink instead of a 33-inch model.

Be sure to consider how these size changes affect the balance, visual impact and function of your design. If you have a large amount of additional space, you might want to reconsider your design to determine if you have chosen the best solution.

If you are short on space, the solution can be more challenging. As you consider each alternative, review your design program to make sure that changes in your design do not compromise important needs of the client. Some ideas for alternatives:

- Reduce the amount of cabinetry or countertop space in a center. If you have allowed generous space for landing areas or prep areas, you could reduce it a bit. For example, if you have planned a cooktop with 18 inches of landing area on both sides, you could reduce this to 16 or 17 inches on one or both sides. This would still meet the Kitchen Planning Guidelines recommendation for landing areas.

- Use smaller appliances or cabinetry. For example, instead of a 33-inch wall oven, use a 30-inch oven. Or substitute a 15-inch drawer base for an 18-inch drawer base. Again, make sure that you try to meet recommendations of the Kitchen Planning Guidelines.

- Choose alternative design elements. For example, a range that includes both cooktop and oven uses less space than a separate cooktop and wall oven. Specifying the single range may allow you to choose a larger appliance, yet conserve space, as compared to two separate appliances. Another example is to choose a full-height, pantry style cabinet to provide the same amount of storage as two base cabinets, but in less floor space.

- Choose cabinetry or appliances with smaller doors, to reduce door swings. This might mean going from a single door 24-inch cabinet to a two-door, 27-inch cabinet. Or choose a side-by-side refrigerator instead of a bottom-mount model. However, consider the functionality of the size of the door opening, the continuity of cabinet spacing, and client preferences when making size alterations.

You may need to try several alternatives to make sure your layout fits the actual space. As you are exploring alternatives, be sure that you are working with the actual dimensions of the various appliances, fixtures, cabinets and other items to be placed in the kitchen. Do not depend on the size shown on a drawing template or a generic example in a computer program.

Vertical Relationships

Dimensioned elevation drawings of each wall of the kitchen are needed to determine the vertical relationships of the design. You may choose to place all items on the floor plan and verify the dimensions before drawing the elevations and verifying vertical placement and dimensions. Or, you may choose to work with one wall at a time—place the cabinets, appliances, fixtures, clearances and other elements on the floor plan, and then draw the elevation. If you are developing your design using computer software, you will likely find it easy to develop elevations as you go along.

Begin drawing the elevation of a wall by drawing an outline of the wall, showing the length and height of the wall. Include any architectural and structural features. Dimension these basic elements of the elevation.

Just as you did with the dimensioned drawing of the floor plan, start with the priority areas. For example, if you started with the sink and cleanup center, project the centerline of the sink and dishwasher onto the elevation. Project the cabinets onto the elevation. Mark the height of the cabinets, countertop, appliances and other features—as determined from actual measurements or product specifications, and dimension this on the elevation. Show other details, such as the backsplash and toekicks.

Continue drawing the elevation by adding items from the floor plan, for which the height is known, such as cabinets and appliances. Dimension the heights of each item. Detail items that are important to the design and visual continuity of the elevation design, such as cabinet doors and hardware placement.

Now, place items that were not identified in your dimensioned drawing of the floor plan, such as cabinet hardware, light fixtures and mouldings. Make sure cabinetry details, such as placement of doors and drawers, size of doors and door style, are determined, considering client needs, function and design impact. Review the elevation for both the vertical and horizontal relationships of line and shape.

Consider the functional placement of items, such as switches, under-cabinet accessories, or towel racks. In some cases, you may need to do a detail drawing, such as an island.

Check all dimensions on the elevation drawing. Verify that individual items are dimensioned correctly and that all vertical dimensions are correctly added.

In our sample kitchen drawing, we started with the sink center. That is where we will start the elevation drawing (Figure 11.14). First, we block in the whole wall. Then, we locate the centerlines for the sink and dishwasher and draw the base cabinets. Next, we locate the wall cabinets. Next, we place the rest of the cabinetry along the wall. We also need to draw the window, verifying the specifications.

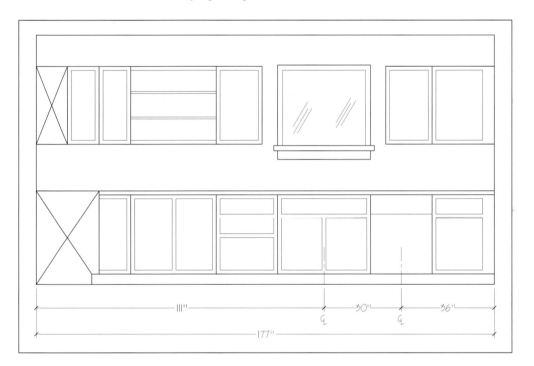

Now consider details and design decisions that were not in the floor plan. However, you may find it useful to block out elevations of all the walls in the kitchen before working on details. Thus, you get a better sense of the total design, before spending time on details. You may also choose to make some modifications in the cabinet arrangement or placement at this stage.

To complete the elevation of the cleanup center wall, consider details such as a valence over the sink area and moulding above the wall cabinets. We might draw hardware on the cabinetry to give our client an idea about style, scale and placement (Figure 11.15).

Figure 11.14 Begin drawing the elevation of the sink center wall by transferring information from the design drawing floor plan to an elevation view.

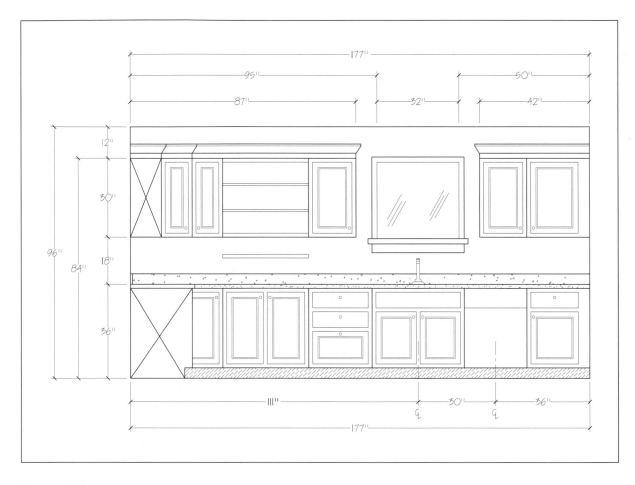

Figure 11.15 Complete the elevation drawing by adding details not found in the floor plan. In addition, the elevation is dimensioned to verify all the cabinet specifications.

It is useful to develop all the wall elevations and then compare them together. Consider how your eye will be drawn across the room and the horizontal relationships from one wall to the next. Is there a unity to your design? What type of rhythm is established by the vertical and horizontal elements in the space? Are all the functional requirements of the design program met? For details on acheiving rhythm, unity and other aesthetic aspects of kitchen design, consult the NKBA book *Design Principles*.

If you are working with computer-aided design software, you may also want to look at a perspective view at this stage of the design process. This can be helpful in giving a realistic view of the kitchen and a sense of the space. However, do not rely on these perspective drawings as your only review of vertical relationships in the space. Perspective views can be distorted, depending on where the view is taken. In addition, they cannot be used to verify dimensions.

Evaluating and Checking

Begin the evaluation of your plan by scoring your design against the Kitchen Planning Guidelines. This is an important step to make sure that you have developed a design that is functional as well as safe. On the following page is a checklist that you can use to score your plan against the Kitchen Planning Guidelines. Review your plan against each guideline on the checklist. Your design should meet all the "Must Haves," which are Planning Guidelines based on code requirements and are shown unshaded on the following checklists. Also, your design should meet the "Recommended" Planning Guidelines, unless there are extenuating circumstances that prevent this.

Depending on your clients and their needs, review your plan against the Access Standards. In your User Analysis, you will have noted the relevant Access Standards. On page 464 is a checklist to evaluate your plan using the Access Standards.

Kitchen Planning Guidelines Checklist	Must Have (meet or need)	Recommended
1. Door entry is 32" clear opening	■	
2. Door does not interfere with safe operation of appliance	■	
Appliance doors do not interfere with one another	■	
3. Distance between 3 primary work centers is no more than 26'	■	
No leg less than 4' or more than 9'	■	
Leg intersects island/peninsula or other obstacle by no more than 12"	■	
4. Tall obstacle does not separate two primary work centers	■	
5. No major traffic should cross through the work triangle	■	
6. Work aisle is 42" for one cook, 48" for two cooks	■	
7. Walkway width is 36"	■	
8. 32" behind seated diner if no traffic	■	
36" behind seated diner to edge past	■	
44" behind seated diner to walk past	■	
9. 30" high table/counter: allow 24" wide x 18" deep per diner	■	
36" high counter: allow 24" wide x 15" deep per diner	■	
42" high counter: allow 24" wide x 12" deep per diner	■	
10. One sink adjacent to or across from cooking surface and refrigerator	■	
11. Sink landing area if level counter height: 24" and 18"	■	
Sink landing area if varied counter height: 24" and 3"		
12. Continuous countertop 36" wide x 24" deep next to sink for prep area	■	
13. Dishwasher within 36" of sink edge	■	
21" standing space to side of dishwasher	■	
14. Two waste receptacles: one at sink; one for recycling	■	
15. Auxiliary sink countertop frontage: 18" and 3"	■	
16. Refrigerator landing area: 15" on handle side, or on either side of a side-by-side, or above, or within 48" across from the refrigerator	■	
17. Cooking surface landing area: 12" and 15" at height of cooking surface	■	
On island or peninsula include 9" behind the cooking surface	■	
18. 24" behind cooking surface and protected noncombustible surface	■	
30" between cooking surface and an unprotected/combustible surface		
Follow manufacturer's specifications for a microwave/hood application		
19. Correctly sized, ducted ventilation system, at least 150 cfm	■	
Minimum required exhaust rate for ducted hood: 100 cfm		

Kitchen Planning Guidelines Checklist, continued

	Must Have (meet or need)	Recommended
20. Cooking surface not under operable window		
No flammable window treatments over cooking surface		
Fire extinguisher located near exit of kitchen		
21. Microwave bottom 3" below user's shoulder, between 54" and 15" off the finished floor		
22. Microwave landing area: 15" above, below, or adjacent to handle side		
23. Oven landing area: 15" beside or within 48" across from oven		
24. Combine landing areas by using longest measure and adding 12"		
25. Total countertop frontage: 158" long, 24" deep, with 15" clearance above		
26. Counters have clipped or rounded edges		
27. Shelf/drawer frontage total: 1400" for small kitchen (150 sq. ft. or less)		
1700" for medium kitchen (151-350 sq. ft.)		
2000" for large kitchen (351 sq. ft. or more)		
28. Shelf/drawer frontage at sink: 400" for small kitchen (150 sq. ft. or less)		
480" for medium kitchen (151-350 sq. ft.)		
560" for large kitchen (351 sq. ft. or more)		
29. One corner cabinet includes a functional storage device		
30. GFCI outlets at countertop receptacles		
31. Task lighting at work surfaces		
General lighting with at least one switch at entry		
Window/skylight area equals 8% of kitchen square footage		

Figure 11.16 Kitchen Planning Guidelines Checklist

Kitchen Planning Access Standards Checklist	Must Have (meet or need)	Recommended
1. Door entry is 34" clear opening		
2. Door does not interfere with safe operation of appliance		
Appliance doors do not interfere with one another		
Clear floor space for maneuvering (pull side of door, width of door +18" x 60"; push side, width of door X 48")		
3. Distance between 3 primary work centers is no more than 26'		
No leg less than 4' or more than 9'		
Leg intersects island/peninsula or other obstacle by no more than 12"		
4. Tall obstacle does not separate two primary work centers		
5. No major traffic should cross through the work triangle		
6. Work aisle is 42" for one cook, 48" for two cooks		
Work aisle is minimum clear floor spaces: 30"x 48" at each appliance;		
60" turning diameter or T-turn space of 36" x 36" x 60";		
Knee space 36" wide x 27" high x 17" deep;		
60" between opposing counters in U-shaped kitchen		
7. Walkway width is 36"		
8. 60" behind seated diner if traffic; 36" behind seated diner if no traffic		
9. Allow 30"–36" wide x 28"-34" high x 19" deep per diner		
10. One sink adjacent to or across from cooking surface and refrigerator		
Sink 34" high, or adjustable 29"–36"		
Knee space 36" wide x 27" high x 17" deep at least one sink		
Sink bowl 6½" deep		
Exposed pipes covered		
11. Sink landing area if level counter height: 24" and 18"		
Sink landing area if varied counter height: 24" and 3"		
12. Continuous countertop 36" wide x 24" deep next to sink for prep area		
30" wide section of counter, 34" high with an adaptable or permanent knee space		
13. Dishwasher within 36" of sink edge		
When appropriate, install the dishwasher 6-12" above floor		
30" x 48" clear floor space adjacent to dishwasher door		
14. Two waste receptacles: one at sink; one for recycling		
15. Auxiliary sink countertop frontage: 18" and 3"		
16. Refrigerator landing area: 15" on handle side, or on either side of a side-by-side, or above, or within 48" across from the refrigerator		

Kitchen Planning Access Standards Checklist, continued

	Must Have (meet or need)	Recommended
30" x 48" clear floor space offset 24" from centerline of refrigerator.	▓	
17. Cooking surface landing area: 12" and 15" at height of cooking surface	▓	
Consider lowering the cooktop & adjacent counters to 34" maximum height and creating a knee space.	▓	
On island or peninsula include 9" behind the cooking surface	▓	
18. 24" behind cooking surface and protected noncombustible surface	▓	
30" between cooking surface and an unprotected/combustible surface		
Follow manufacturer's specifications for a microwave/hood application		
19. Correctly sized, ducted ventilation system, at least 150 cfm	▓	
Minimum required exhaust rate for ducted hood: 100 cfm		
Controls no higher than 44" if obstructed or 48" unobstructed and easy to use		
20. Cooking surface not under operable window	▓	
No flammable window treatments over cooking surface	▓	
Fire extinguisher located near exit of kitchen no higher than 48"	▓	
21. Microwave controls no higher than 48"	▓	
22. Microwave landing area: 15" above, below, or adjacent to handle side	▓	
23. Oven landing area: 15" beside or within 48" across from oven	▓	
24. Combine landing areas by using longest measure and adding 12"	▓	
25. Total countertop frontage: 158" long, 24" deep, with 15" clearance above	▓	
Include at least two counter heights, one 28-36" and one 36-45".	▓	
Include a minimum 30" wide, maximum 34" or variable in height, preferably with a knee space.	▓	
26. Counters have clipped or rounded edges	▓	
27. Shelf/drawer frontage total: 1400" for small kitchen (150 sq. ft. or less)	▓	
1700" for medium kitchen (151-350 sq. ft.)	▓	
2000" for large kitchen (351 sq. ft. or more)	▓	
28. Shelf/drawer frontage at sink: 400" for small kitchen (150 sq. ft. or less)	▓	
480" for medium kitchen (151-350 sq. ft.)	▓	
560" for large kitchen (351 sq. ft. or more)	▓	
29. One corner cabinet includes a functional storage device	▓	
30. GFCI outlets at countertop receptacles		
31. Task lighting at work surfaces	▓	
General lighting with at least one switch at entry		
Window/skylight area equals 8% of kitchen square footage		

Figure 11.17 Kitchen Planning Access Standards Checklist

The final step in developing the design drawing is to check all dimensions. Double-checking for accuracy is critical.

- Verify all jobsite dimensions. If necessary, return to the jobsite and re-measure. The success of your final design is dependent on working from accurate information.

- Verify the construction constraints. Review all mechanical, electrical and plumbing information for accuracy.

- Verify that the actual dimensions of the space were transferred to the room outline that was the starting point of your dimensioned drawing.

- Verify the placement of all centerlines of appliances and fixtures. First, verify the sizes of all appliances and fixtures from actual measurements or product specifications and determine that there is adequate space. Review the landing space and clearances that are recommended and/or required in the Kitchen Planning Guidelines and verify that you have met these.

- Verify the size of the cabinets, both vertically and horizontally. Check the dimensioned sizes on your drawing against the product literature or actual measurements.

- Verify all vertical relationships. Double-check the heights of appliances and other features and review that there will be adequate clearance above or below items.

Once your design has been finalized, you will create all the necessary project documents for your client and all tradespeople. These are explained in the NKBA book *Kitchen & Bath Drawing*.

PUTTING IT ALL TOGETHER — A SAMPLE PROJECT

Meet Leah and Matthew. Their kitchen remodeling project is being used as an example of how to prepare a design program. We interviewed Leah and Matthew at their home. We used the various forms and checklists from Chapter 6 to collect information for their design project. Then, we developed this design program.

After you read the design program, look at the design that was prepared for Leah and Matthew. Do you think the design meets their needs? Is the design solution functional, safe, and convenient? Use the Kitchen Planning Guideline and Access Standards Checklists (Figure 11.16 and Figure 11.17) to evaluate the plan.

Note: This sample design program will focus on space planning, the emphasis in this book. If you were developing a design program, you might want to give additional attention to color, style and visual impact.

A Sample Design Program

GOALS AND PURPOSE

Client description: Leah and Matthew are in their late 20s and have a 4-year-old son, Ethan. Both Leah and Matthew are employed in child advocacy professions. They live a family-centered lifestyle. Extended family, especially grandparents Rose and Vincent, are frequent visitors. The couple bought their first home about a year ago, knowing that the kitchen would require some work. Matthew hopes to do at least part of the renovation work himself.

Project description and goals: After years of tiny apartment kitchens, Matthew and Leah dreamed of an efficient and spacious kitchen in their own home. While their existing kitchen is light-filled and opens to the family living area, there is limited counter, storage and circulation space. It is difficult for two people to cook at the same time, and even harder to encourage Ethan's growing interest in helping with meals.

Figure 11.18 Leah and Matthew's existing kitchen is limited on counter space and storage.

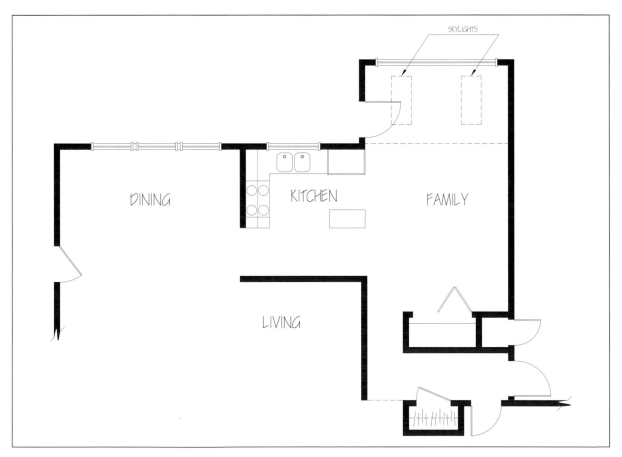

Leah and Matthew would like a kitchen with two prep areas. They would consider borrowing some space from the family and/or living room to expand the kitchen area. However, they want to keep the kitchen visually connected to the family living area. Adding a baking area would be desirable.

SCOPE OF THE PROJECT

- Develop a design that meets the client needs.

- Select all appliances, fixtures, fittings and finish materials.

- Prepare drawings and specifications for completion of the project.

- Supervise construction and installation of the project.

OBJECTIVES AND PRIORITIES

- Create room for at least two people to work in the kitchen at the same time.

- Create a baking area with easy access to the oven and sink.

- Relocate the wall between the living room and kitchen to expand the size of the kitchen.

- Reorient the kitchen sink so that it faces toward the family living area.

- Provide increased refrigerator storage, including space for produce, convenient to both cooking and family living spaces.

- Design a bar counter seating space for casual eating to seat 2-3 people.

- Provide a dual-fuel range with hood ventilation system.

- Expand window area in exterior wall.

ACTIVITIES AND RELATIONSHIPS

A User Analysis was prepared for Leah and Matthew's remodeling project. The User Analysis for the baking area is shown in Figure 11.19.

Activity Space	Users	Frequency	Appliances, Fixtures, Fittings, Furniture, Etc.	Storage
Bake Area: mix cookies & bread; make pies; cool baked goods	Leah, Ethan, Rose	2-3 times a week; Rose less often	• Large stand mixer • Food processor	• Counter storage for appliances • Vertical storage for cookie sheets & cooling racks • Spice rack • Drawer storage • Pie safe cabinet • Roll-out shelves for bowls, baking pans, etc.

Space Relationships	Ambience	Special Needs	Future Needs	Guidelines and Access Standards
• 42" work aisle, 48" preferred • Easy access to sink & oven • 42" counter frontage, more desirable	Good lighting	• Non-porous, heat-proof surface • Lower counter 2"–3" • Toekick step stool • Pull-out cutting board	None noted	Kitchen Planning Guidelines: 6, 26, 30, 31

The Design Solution

From Leah and Matthew's design program, we developed several bubble diagrams before choosing the one that seemed to work best (Figure 11.20). Then we drew design templates and a room outline. We explored borrowing some space from the family and living rooms to expand the kitchen—which fit with the design program. We laid out the templates within the expanded room outline. After choosing the best layout for the visual diagram (Figure 11.21), we tried some elevation sketches and then refined the dimensioned design drawing (Figure 11.22). Finally, we carefully checked all our dimensions and clearances. We developed elevations (Figure 11.23) and a perspective (Figure 11.24).

We evaluated the kitchen design against the Kitchen Planning Guidelines using the Checklist in Figure 11.16. As we developed our design, we checked for clearances and landing spaces. Looking at the plan, we can verify that there are over 158 inches of counter space (Guideline 25) and an effective work triangle (Guideline 3). Figure 11.25 explains the storage calculations (Guideline 27) and shows that the kitchen has more than the recommended minimum amount.

Figure 11.19 This User Analysis highlights the design requirements for the baking area.

Figure 11.20 The bubble diagram presents a workable plan for activity spaces in Leah and Matthew's remodeled kitchen.

Figure 11.21 The visual diagram shows the layout for Leah and Matthew's kitchen, using an expanded room outline. Clearances and landing areas are verified.

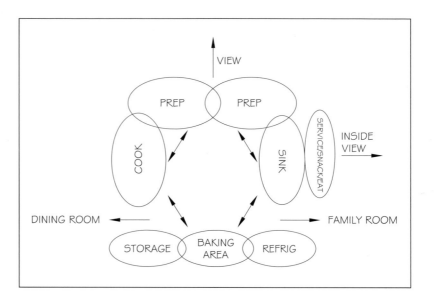

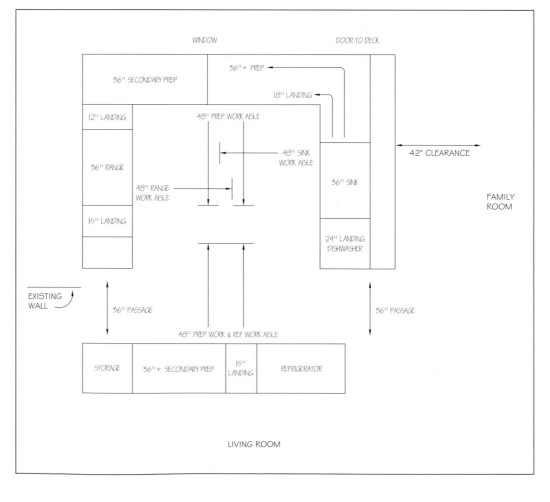

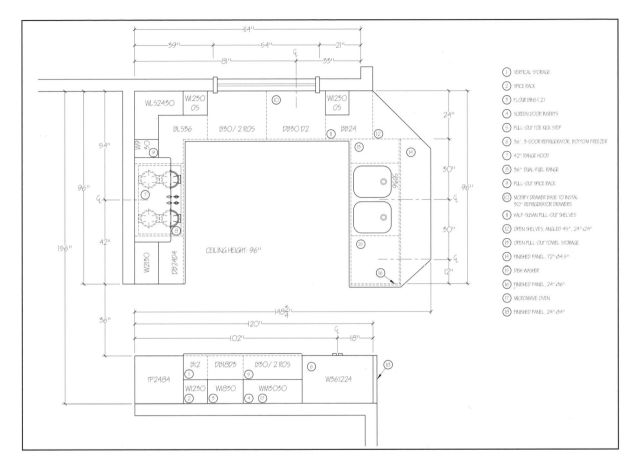

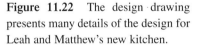

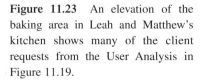

Figure 11.22 The design drawing presents many details of the design for Leah and Matthew's new kitchen.

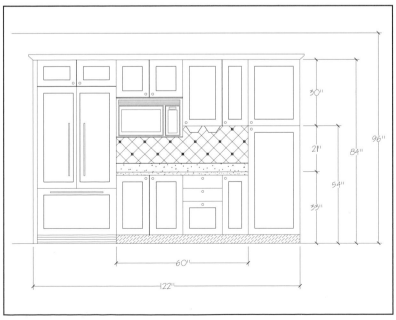

Figure 11.23 An elevation of the baking area in Leah and Matthew's kitchen shows many of the client requests from the User Analysis in Figure 11.19.

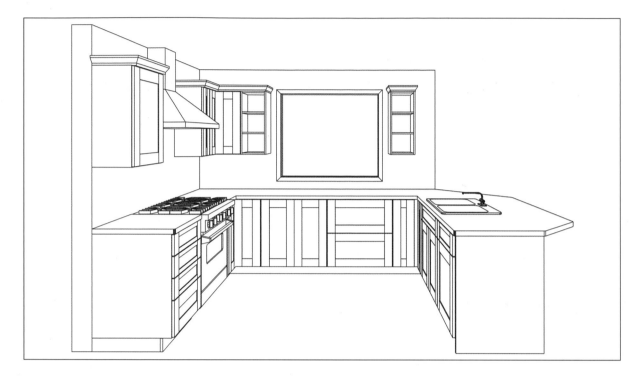

Figure 11.24 Perspective of Leah and Matthew's kitchen

LEAH AND MATTHEW'S KITCHEN

Leah and Matthew's new kitchen appears to meet their goals and objectives of the Design Program. Bumping a peninsula 24 inches into the family room and taking 48 inches along the living room wall gained additional space for the kitchen. The peninsula between the kitchen and the family living area contains the sink and dishwasher, as well as an eating counter. Family members can sit at the counter to chat with cooks in the kitchen or the counter can be used for serving snacks.

Generous counter area between the sink and range provides prep area for two cooks, a refrigerator drawer for additional produce storage, access to either the sink or the range, and a view to the deck. A baking area is located next to the refrigerator center, providing a lowered counter, microwave oven, specialized storage for baking pans and racks, flour and sugar bins, a ventilated cabinet and a pantry.

Critique. Throughout this chapter, we have emphasized that design is a process. At the beginning of the chapter, we discussed the back and forth nature of the design process: going forward, but returning to check ideas against the design program, for example. The same is true with a finished design. A critique can help you learn to improve and create better designs, each and every time.

Kitchen size = 156 square feet (156" x 148") medium

Calculation formula:
frontage (inches) x number of shelves/drawers x depth (feet) = storage inches

Drawer/Roll-out Shelf Storage

DB 2424	24 x 4 x 2 = 192
BS30/2ROS	30 x 3 x 2 = 180

(cabinet has 2 roll-out shelves + 1 drawer)

DB30D2	30 x 2 x 2 = 120
BS30/2ROS	30 x 3 x 2 = 180

(cabinet has 2 roll-out shelves and 1 drawer)

DB18D3	18 x 3 x 2 = 108
TP2484	24 x 4 x 2 = 192

(pantry has 4 roll-out shelves & 3 fixed shelves)

Total: 972

Base Cabinet Storage

BLS36	36 x 2 x 1.5 = 108
BB24	12 x 2 x 2 = 48
SB36	36 x 1 x 2 = 72
B12	12 x 2 x 2 = 48

Total: 276

Wall Cabinet Storage

W2130	21 x 3 x 1 = 63
W930	9 x 3 x 1 = 27
WLS2430	24 x 3 x 1.5 = 108
W12300S	12 x 3 x 1 = 36
W12300S	12 x 3 x 1 = 36
WM3030	30 x 2 x 1 = 60
W1830	18 x 2 x 1 = 36
W1230	12 x 3 x 1 = 36

Total: 402

Pantry Storage

TP2484	24 x 3 x 2 = **144**

Miscellaneous Storage

Open towel storage 12"	= 12
W361224	36 x 1 x 2 = 72

Total = 84

Summary

Summary	Kitchen	Guideline 27
Drawer/Roll-out	972"	400"
Base cabinet	276"	615"
Wall cabinet	402"	360"
Pantry	144"	230"
Miscellaneous	84"	95"
Total: 1,878"		**1,700"**

Figure 11.25 Leah and Matthew's kitchen is medium-sized and offers 1,878 inches of shelf/drawer frontage. Within this total, we have chosen to increase the amount of drawer/roll-out storage and decrease the amount allocated to the other types of storage.

Can you critique Leah and Matthew's kitchen? What are some weaknesses, or less than successful parts of the design? We have noted a few concerns, places where we made compromises between the ideal design and the reality of the existing space.

- There is a traffic pattern through the work triangle (Planning Guideline 5). Although this traffic pattern (not a primary path) only goes to the formal dining area, it does separate the sink/cleanup, prep and cooking areas from the refrigerator. This was necessary in order to enlarge the size of the kitchen, and maximize the size of the prep areas.

- Only part of the refrigerator has a full 48-inch work aisle in front of it (Planning Guideline 6). This resulted from positioning the refrigerator to maximize the size of the baking area. A French door model refrigerator, with narrower doors, was chosen.

- The U-shaped kitchen has two corners, which can be problematic and limit accessible storage. We put a Lazy-Susan (BLS36) in one corner. In the other corner, we installed a blind base cabinet (BB24), with half-Susan pullout shelves, and then used the backside of the corner to put angled shelves that open to the family room area.

- The microwave oven is installed above the counter, in the baking area, to be conveniently located yet give maximum work surface area. The height of the microwave shelf is in accordance with Planning Guideline 21 (no more than 54 inches above finished floor). However, the controls are above the universal reach range of 48 inches (Access Standard 21).

Can you suggest other improvements? Perhaps you have ideas that would better meet Leah and Matthew's needs, create a more functional space, be more economical to build, or be easier to maintain? After all, this is where the creativity is at work.

CHAPTER 12: Kitchen Planning Guidelines with Access Standards

The National Kitchen & Bath Association developed the Kitchen Planning Guidelines and Access Standards to provide designers with good planning practices that consider the needs of a range of users. In this chapter, Planning Guidelines are accompanied by Access Standards with illustrations to provide a complete listing.

The code references for the Kitchen Planning Guidelines are based on an analysis of the 2006 International Residential Code (IRC) or the International Plumbing Code.

The code references for the Access Standards are based on the ICC/ANSI 117.1 – 2003 Accessible and Useable Buildings and Facilities. Be sure to check local, state, and national laws that apply to your design and follow those legal requirements.

KITCHEN PLANNING GUIDELINE 1
DOOR/ENTRY

Recommended:

The clear opening of a doorway should be at least 32" wide. This would require a minimum 2'-10" door.

Code Requirement:

State or local codes may apply.

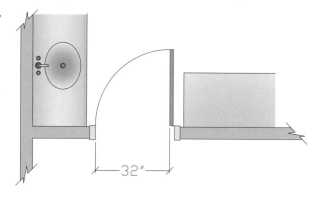

32"

ACCESS STANDARD

Recommended:

The clear opening of a doorway should be at least 34". This would require a minimum 3'-0" door.

Code Reference:

- Clear openings of doorways with swinging doors shall be measured between the face of door and stop, with the door open 90 degrees. (ANSI 404.2.3)

- When a passage exceeds 24" in depth, the minimum clearance increases to 36". (ANSI A117.1 404)

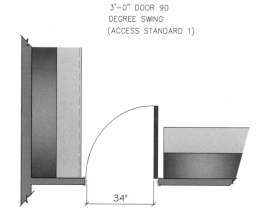

3'-0" DOOR 90
DEGREE SWING
(ACCESS STANDARD 1)

34"

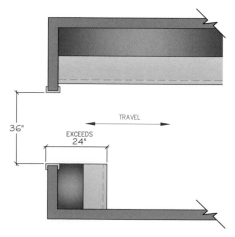

24" DEPTH CLEARANCE
(ACCESS STANDARD 1—ANSI)

TRAVEL

36"

EXCEEDS
24"

KITCHEN PLANNING GUIDELINE 2
DOOR INTERFERENCE

Recommended:

No entry door should interfere with the safe operation of appliances, nor should appliance doors interfere with one another.

Code Requirement:

State or local codes may apply.

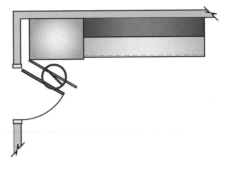

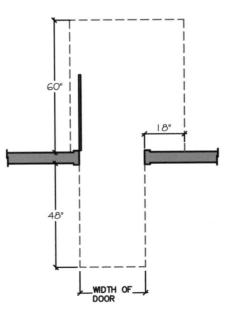

ACCESS STANDARD

Recommended:

In addition, the door area should include clear floor space for maneuvering which varies according to the type of door and direction of approach.

Code Reference:

- For a standard hinged or swinging door, the clearance on the pull side of the door should be the door width plus 18" by 60". (ANSI A 117.1 404.2.3.1)

- The clearance on the push side of the door should be the door width by 48". (ANSI A 117.1 404.2.3.1)

FRONT APPROACH TO SWING DOORS (ACCESS STANDARD 2)

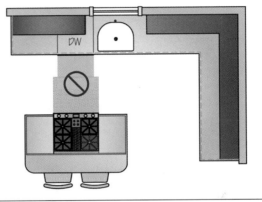

60"

18"

48"

WIDTH OF DOOR

KITCHEN PLANNING GUIDELINE 3
DISTANCE BETWEEN WORK CENTERS

Recommended:

In a kitchen with three work centers* the sum of the three traveled distances should total no more than 26' with no single leg of the triangle measuring less than 4' nor more than 9'.

When the kitchen plan includes more than three primary appliance/work centers, each additional travel distance to another appliance/work center should measure no less than 4' nor more than 9'.

Each leg is measured from the center-front of the appliance/sink.

No work triangle leg intersects an island/peninsula or other obstacle by more than 12".

A major appliance and its surrounding landing/work area form a work center. The distances between the three primary work centers (cooking surface, cleanup/prep sink and refrigeration storage) form a work triangle.

Code Requirement:

State or local codes may apply.

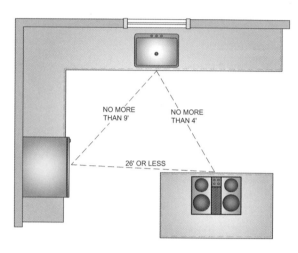

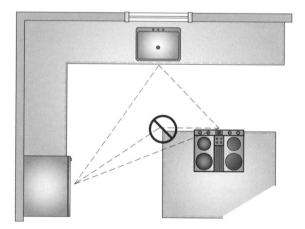

ACCESS STANDARD

Recommended:

Kitchen guideline recommendation meets Access Standard.

KITCHEN PLANNING GUIDELINE 4
SEPARATING WORK CENTERS

Recommended:

A full-height, full-depth, tall obstacle* should not separate two primary work centers.

A properly recessed tall corner unit will not interrupt the workflow and is acceptable.

*Examples of a full-height obstacle are a tall oven cabinet, tall pantry cabinet or refrigerator.

Code Requirement:

State or local codes may apply.

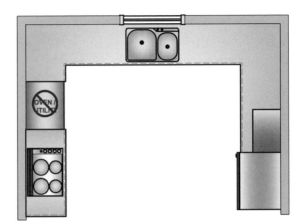

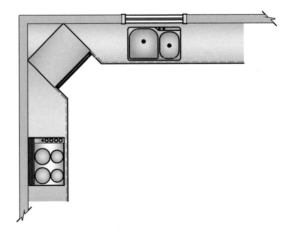

ACCESS STANDARD

Recommended:

Kitchen guideline recommendation meets Access Standard.

KITCHEN PLANNING GUIDELINE 5
WORK TRIANGLE TRAFFIC

Recommended:

No major traffic patterns should cross through the basic work triangle.

Code Requirement:

State or local codes may apply.

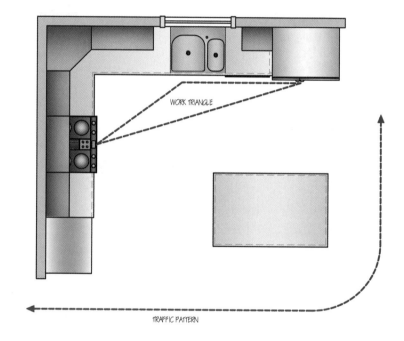

WORK TRIANGLE

TRAFFIC PATTERN

ACCESS STANDARD

Recommended:

Kitchen guideline recommendation meets Access Standard.

KITCHEN PLANNING GUIDELINE 6
WORK AISLE

Recommended:

The width of a work aisle should be at least 42" for one cook and at least 48" for multiple cooks. Measure between the counter frontage, tall cabinets and/or appliances.

Code Requirement:

State or local codes may apply.

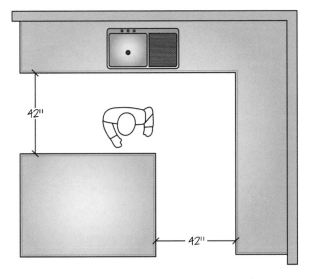

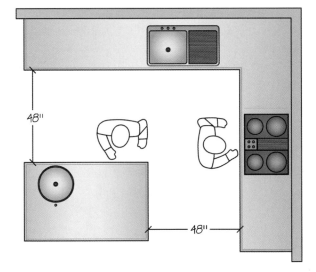

KITCHEN PLANNING GUIDELINE 6
WORK AISLE, CONTINUED

ACCESS STANDARD

Recommended:

Kitchen guideline recommendation meets Access Standard recommendation. See Code References for specific applications.

Code Requirement:

- A clear floor space of at least 30" by 48" should be provided at each kitchen appliance. Clear floor spaces can overlap.
  (ANSI A 117.1 305.3, 804.6.1)

- In a U-shaped kitchen, plan a minimum clearance of 60" between opposing arms.
  (ANSI A117.1 804.2.2, 1003.12.1.2)

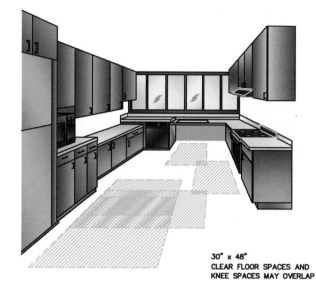

30" x 48"
CLEAR FLOOR SPACES AND
KNEE SPACES MAY OVERLAP

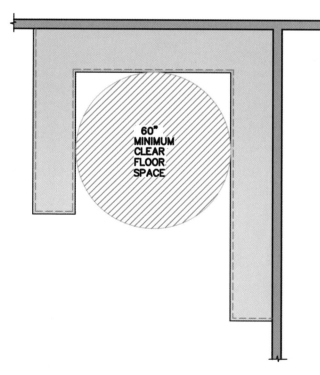

60"
MINIMUM
CLEAR
FLOOR
SPACE

KITCHEN PLANNING GUIDELINE 6
WORK AISLE, CONTINUED

- Include a wheelchair turning space with a diameter of at least 60", which can include knee* and toe* clearances.
  (ANSI A117.1 304.3.1).

- A wheelchair turning space could utilize a T-shaped clear space, which is a 60" square with two 12" wide x 24" deep areas removed from the corners of the square. This leaves a minimum 36" wide base and two 36" wide arms. T-shaped wheelchair turning spaces can include knee and toe clearances.
  (ANSI A117.1 304.3.2)

*Knee clearance must be 30" wide and maintain a 27" clear space under the cabinet, counter, or sink for a depth of 8". The next 11" of depth may slope down to a height of 9", with a clear space of at least 17" extending beneath the element.

*Toe clearance space under a cabinet or appliance is between the floor and 9" above the floor. Where toe clearance is required as part of a clear floor space, the toe clearance should extend 17" minimum beneath the element. (ANSI A117.1 306.2)

Code Requirement:

State or local codes may apply.

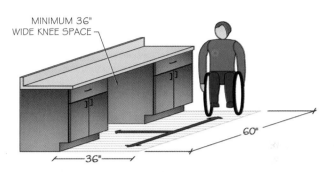

MINIMUM 36" WIDE KNEE SPACE

60"

36"

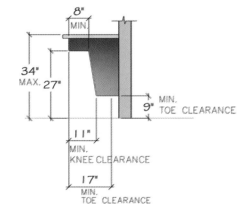

8" MIN.

34" MAX. 27"

9" MIN. TOE CLEARANCE

11" MIN. KNEE CLEARANCE

17" MIN. TOE CLEARANCE

KITCHEN PLANNING GUIDELINE 7
WALKWAY

Recommended:

The width of a walkway should be at least 36".

Code Requirement:

State or local codes may apply.

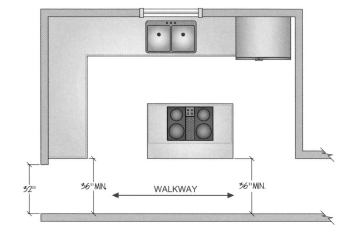

ACCESS STANDARD

Recommended:

If two walkways are perpendicular to each other, one walkway should be at least 42" wide.

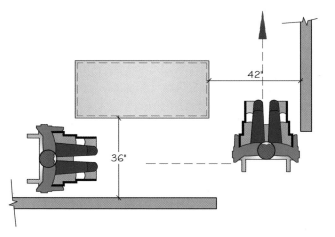

KITCHEN PLANNING GUIDELINE 8
TRAFFIC CLEARANCE AT SEATING

Recommended:

In a seating area where no traffic passes behind a seated diner, allow 32" of clearance from the counter/table edge to any wall or other obstruction behind the seating area.

a. If traffic passes behind the seated diner, allow at least 36" to edge past.

b. If traffic passes behind the seated diner, allow at least 44" to walk past.

Code Requirement:

State or local codes may apply.

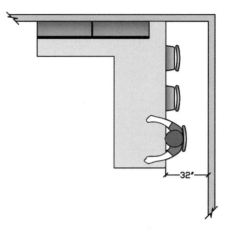

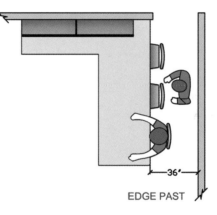

EDGE PAST

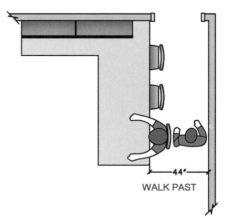

WALK PAST

KITCHEN PLANNING GUIDELINE 8
TRAFFIC CLEARANCE AT SEATING, CONTINUED

ACCESS STANDARD

Recommended:

In a seating area where no traffic passes behind a seated diner allow 36" of clearance from the counter/table edge to any wall or other obstruction behind the seating area.

If traffic passes behind the seated diner, plan a minimum of 60" to allow passage for a person in a wheelchair.

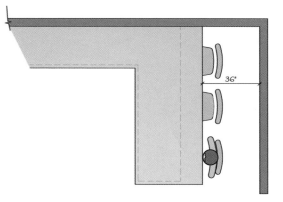

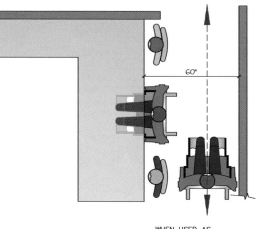

WHEN USED AS
WALKWAY SPACE

KITCHEN PLANNING GUIDELINE 9
SEATING CLEARANCE

Recommended:

Kitchen seating areas should incorporate at least the following clearances:

a. 30" high tables/counters:

   Allow a 24" wide x 18" deep knee space for each seated diner and at least 18" of clear knee space

b. 36" high counters:

   Allow a 24" wide x 15" deep knee space for each seated diner and at least 15" of clear knee space.

c. 42" high counters:

   Allow a 24" wide x 12" deep knee space for each seated diner and 12" of clear knee space.

Code Requirement:

State or local codes may apply.

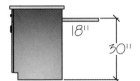
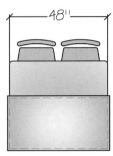

18"
KNEE SPACE

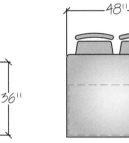

15"
KNEE SPACE

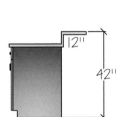
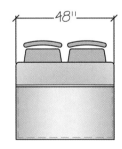

12"
KNEE SPACE

KITCHEN PLANNING GUIDELINE 9
SEATING CLEARANCE, CONTINUED

ACCESS STANDARD

Recommended:

Kitchen seating areas should be 28" – 34" high x 30" – 36" wide x 19" deep to better accommodate people of various sizes or those using a mobility aid.

Recommended minimum size for a knee space at a table or counter is 36" wide x 27" high x 19" deep.

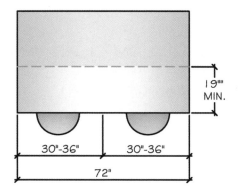

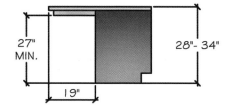

KITCHEN PLANNING GUIDELINE 10
CLEANUP/PREP SINK PLACEMENT

Recommended:

If a kitchen has only one sink, locate it adjacent to or across from the cooking surface and refrigerator.

Code Requirement:

State or local codes may apply.

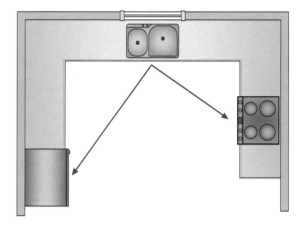

ACCESS STANDARD

Recommended:

Plan knee spaces at the sink to allow for a seated user. Recommended minimum size for a knee space is 36" wide x 27" high x 8" deep, increasing to 17" deep in the toe space, which extends 9" from the floor. Insulation for exposed pipes should be provided.

Code Reference:

- The sink should be no more than 34" high or adjustable between 29" and 36". (ANSI 117.1.1002.4.2)

- The sink bowl should be no more than $6^1/2$" deep (ANSI 117.1 1002.12.4.3)

- Exposed water supply and drainpipes under sinks should be insulated or otherwise configured to protect against contact. There should be no sharp or abrasive surfaces under sinks. (ANSI A117.1 606.6)

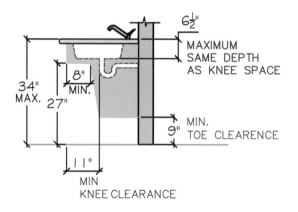

489

KITCHEN PLANNING GUIDELINE 11
CLEANUP/PREP SINK LANDING AREA

Recommended:

Include at least a 24" wide landing area* to one side of the sink and at least an 18" wide landing area on the other side.

If all of the countertop at the sink is not the same height, then plan a 24" landing area on one side of the sink and 3" of countertop frontage on the other side, both at the same height as the sink.

The 24" of recommended landing area can be met by 3" of countertop frontage from the edge of the sink to the inside corner of the countertop if no more than 21" of countertop frontage is available on the return.

*Landing area is measured as countertop frontage adjacent to a sink and/or an appliance. The countertop must be at least 16" deep and must be 28" to 45" above the finished floor to qualify.

Code Requirement:

State or local codes may apply.

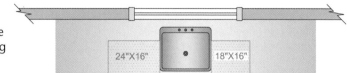

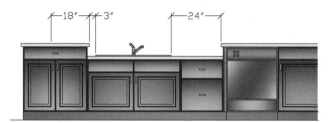

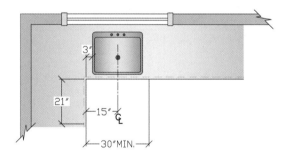

ACCESS STANDARD

Recommended:

Kitchen guideline recommendation meets Access Standard.

KITCHEN PLANNING GUIDELINE 12
PREPARATION/WORK AREA

Recommended:

Include a section of continuous countertop at least 36" wide x 24" deep immediately next to a sink for a primary preparation/work area.

Code Requirement:

State or local codes may apply.

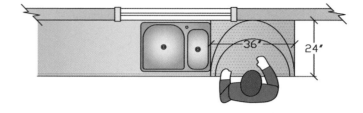

ACCESS STANDARD

Recommended:

A section of continuous countertop at least 30" wide with a permanent or adaptable knee space should be included somewhere in the kitchen.

See Access Guideline 6 for knee space specifications.

Code Reference:

• In a kitchen, there should be at least one 30" wide section of counter, 34" high maximum or adjustable from 29" to 36". Cabinetry can be added under the work surface, provided it can be removed or altered without removal or replacement of the work surface, and provided the finished floor extends under the cabinet. (ANSI A 117.1 8.04.6.3, 1003.12.6.3)

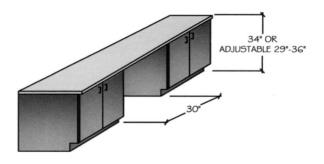

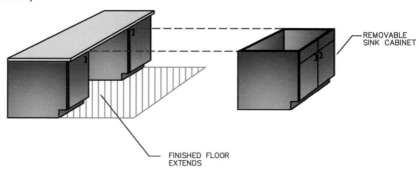

491

KITCHEN PLANNING GUIDELINE 13
DISHWASHER PLACEMENT

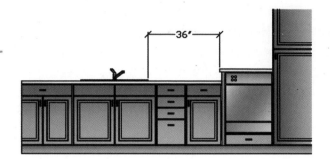

Recommended:

Locate nearest edge of the primary dishwasher within 36" of the nearest edge of a cleanup/prep sink.

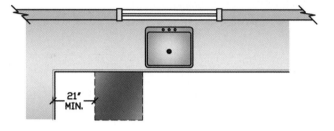

Provide at least 21"* of standing space between the edge of the dishwasher and countertop frontage, appliances and/or cabinets, which are placed at a right angle to the dishwasher.

*In a diagonal installation, the 21" is measured from the center of the sink to the edge of the dishwasher door in an open position.

Code Requirement:

State or local codes may apply.

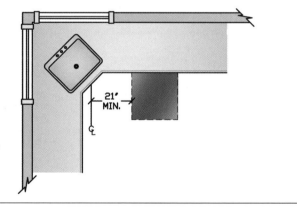

ACCESS STANDARD

Recommended:

Raise dishwasher 6" – 12" when it can be planned with appropriate landing areas at the same height as the sink.

Code Reference:

• A clear floor space of at least 30" x 48" should be positioned adjacent to the dishwasher door. The dishwasher door in the open position should not obstruct the clear floor space for the dishwasher or the sink. (ANSI A 117.1 804.6.3, 1003.12.6.3)

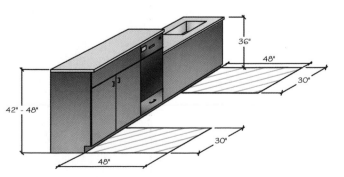

KITCHEN PLANNING GUIDELINE 14
WASTE RECEPTACLES

Recommended:

Include at least two waste receptacles. Locate one near each of the cleanup/prep sink(s) and a second for recycling either in the kitchen or nearby.

Code Requirement:

State or local codes may apply.

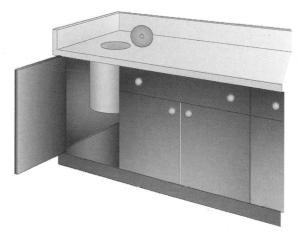

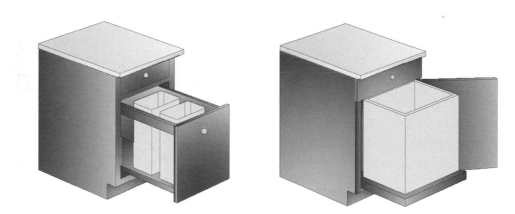

ACCESS STANDARD

Recommended:

Kitchen guideline recommendation meets Access Standard.

KITCHEN PLANNING GUIDELINE 15
AUXILIARY SINK

Recommended:

At least 3" of countertop frontage should be provided on one side of the auxiliary sink, and 18" of countertop frontage on the other side, both at the same height as the sink.

Code Requirement:

State or local codes may apply.

18" or MORE   3" MIN.

ACCESS STANDARD

Recommended:

Plan a knee space at, or adjacent to, the auxiliary sink.

See Access Standard 6 for knee space specifications.

KITCHEN PLANNING GUIDELINE 16
REFRIGERATOR LANDING AREA

Recommended:

Include at least:

a. 15" of landing area on the handle side of the refrigerator or

b. 15" of landing area on either side of a side-by-side refrigerator or

c. 15" of landing area which is no more than 48" across from the front of the refrigerator or

d. 15" of landing area above or adjacent to any undercounter style refrigeration appliance.

Code Requirement:

State or local codes may apply.

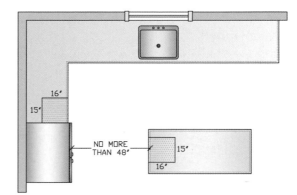

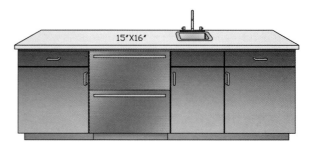

ACCESS STANDARD

Recommended:

See Code Reference

Code Reference:

• A clear floor space of 30" x 48" should be positioned for a parallel approach to the refrigerator/freezer with the centerline of the clear floor space offset 24" maximum from the centerline of the appliance. (ANSI A 117.1 804.6.6, 1003.12.6.6)

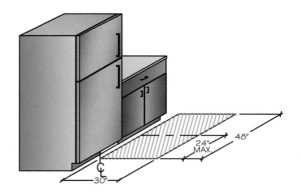

KITCHEN PLANNING GUIDELINE 17
COOKING SURFACE LANDING AREA

Recommended:

Include a minimum of 12" of landing area on one side of a cooking surface and 15" on the other side.

If the cooking surface is at a different countertop height than the rest of the kitchen then the 12" and 15" landing areas must be at the same height as the cooking surface.

For safety reasons, in an island or peninsula situation, the countertop should also extend a minimum of 9" behind the cooking surface if the counter height is the same as the surface-cooking appliance.

For an enclosed configuration, a reduction of clearances shall be in accordance with the appliance manufacturer's instructions or per local codes. (This may not provide adequate landing area.)

Code Requirement:

State or local codes may apply.

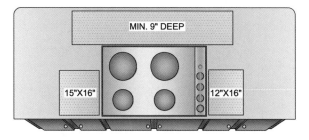

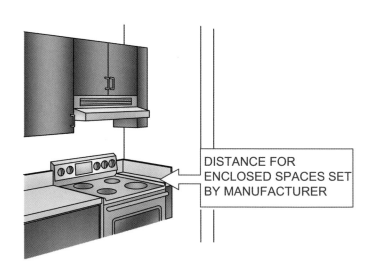

DISTANCE FOR ENCLOSED SPACES SET BY MANUFACTURER

KITCHEN PLANNING GUIDELINE 17
COOKING SURFACE LANDING AREA, CONTINUED

ACCESS STANDARD

Recommended:

Lower the cooktop to 34" maximum height and create a knee space beneath the appliance.

See Access Standard 6 for knee space specifications.

Code Reference:

• When a forward-approach clear floor space is provided at the cooktop, it should provide knee and toe clearance and the underside of the cooktop should be insulated or otherwise configured to prevent burns, abrasions, or electric shock. (ANSI 1002.12.6.4)

• The location of cooktop controls should not require reaching across burners. (ANSI 1003.12.6.4)

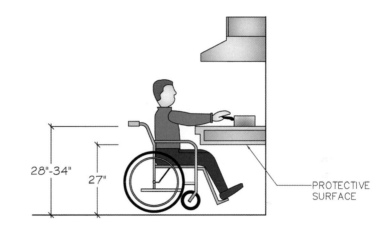

497

KITCHEN PLANNING GUIDELINE 18
COOKING SURFACE CLEARANCE

Recommended:

Allow 24" of clearance between the cooking surface and a protected noncombustible surface above it.

Code Requirement:

- At least 30" of clearance is required between the cooking surface and an unprotected/combustible surface above it.
  (IRC M 1901.1)

- If a microwave hood combination is used above the cooking surface, then the manufacturers' specifications should be followed.
  (IRC M 1504.1)

Refer to manufacturer's specifications or local building codes for other considerations.

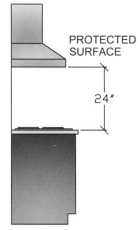

PROTECTED SURFACE

24"

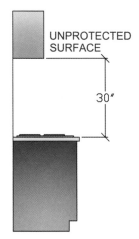

UNPROTECTED SURFACE

30"

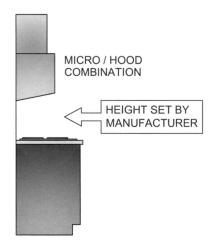

MICRO / HOOD COMBINATION

HEIGHT SET BY MANUFACTURER

ACCESS STANDARD

Recommended:

Kitchen guideline recommendation meets Access Standard.

KITCHEN PLANNING GUIDELINE 19
COOKING SURFACE VENTILATION

Recommended:

Provide a correctly sized, ducted ventilation system for all cooking surface appliances. The recommended minimum is 150 cfm.

Code Requirement:

- Manufacturer's specifications must be followed. (IRC G 2407.1, IRC G 2447.1)

- The minimum required exhaust rate for a ducted hood is 100 cfm and must be ducted to the outside. (IRC M 1507.3)

- Make-up air may need to be provided. Refer to local codes. (IRC G 2407.4)

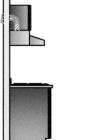
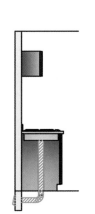
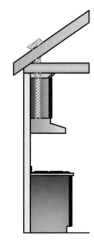

MINIMUM 150 CFM

ACCESS STANDARD

Recommended:

Ventilation controls should be placed 15" – 44" above the floor, operable with minimal effort, easy to read and with minimal noise pollution.

Code Reference:

- Operable parts should be operable with one hand and not require tight grasping, pitching or twisting of the wrist. The force required to activate operable parts should be 5 pounds maximum. (ANSI A117.1 309.4)

- Where a forward or side reach is unobstructed, the high reach should be 48" maximum and the low reach should be 15" minimum above the floor. (ANSI A117.1 308.2.1 and 308.3.1)

- Where a forward or side reach is obstructed by a 20" – 25" deep counter, the high reach should be 44" maximum. (ANSI A117.1 308.2.2)

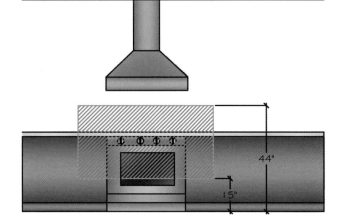

VENTILATION CONTROLS WITHIN 15" – 44"
WHEN REACH IS OBSTRUCTED BY COUNTER

KITCHEN PLANNING GUIDELINE 20
COOKING SURFACE SAFETY

Recommended:

a. Do not locate the cooking surface under an operable window.

b. Window treatments above the cooking surface should not use flammable materials.

c. A fire extinguisher should be located near the exit of the kitchen away from cooking equipment.

Code Requirement:

State or local codes may apply.

UNACCEPTABLE

ACCEPTABLE

ACCESS STANDARD

Recommended:

Place fire extinguisher between 15" and 48" off the finished floor.

KITCHEN PLANNING GUIDELINE 21
MICROWAVE OVEN PLACEMENT

Recommended:

Locate the microwave oven after considering the user's height and abilities. The ideal location for the bottom of the microwave is 3" below the principle user's shoulder but no more than 54" above the floor.

If the microwave oven is placed below the countertop the oven bottom must be at least 15" off the finished floor.

Code Requirement:

State or local codes may apply.

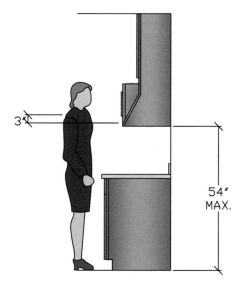

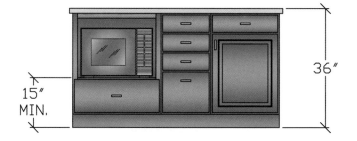

ACCESS STANDARD

Recommended:

Locate the microwave controls below 48."

KITCHEN PLANNING GUIDELINE 22
MICROWAVE LANDING AREA

Recommended:

Provide at least a 15" landing area above, below, or adjacent to the handle side of a microwave oven.

Code Requirement:

State or local codes may apply.

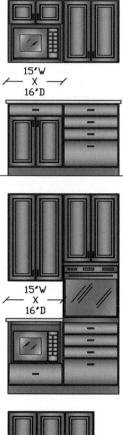

ACCESS STANDARD

Recommended:

Provide landing area in front of or immediately adjacent to the handle side of the microwave.

KITCHEN PLANNING GUIDELINE 23
OVEN LANDING AREA

Recommended:

Include at least a 15" landing area next to or above the oven.

At least a 15" landing area that is not more than 48" across from the oven is acceptable if the appliance does not open into a walkway.

Code Requirement:

State or local codes may apply.

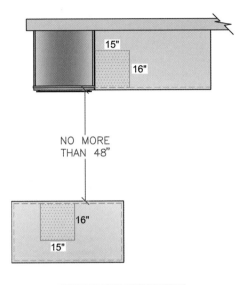

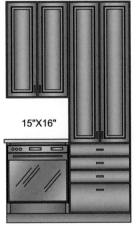

ACCESS STANDARD

Recommended:

See Code reference

Code Reference:

• For side-opening ovens, the door latch side should be next to a countertop (ANSI A 117.1 804.6.5.1)

KITCHEN PLANNING GUIDELINE 24
COMBINING LANDING AREAS

Recommended:

If two landing areas are adjacent to one another, determine a new minimum for the two adjoining spaces by taking the longer of the two landing area requirements and adding 12."

Code Requirement:

State or local codes may apply.

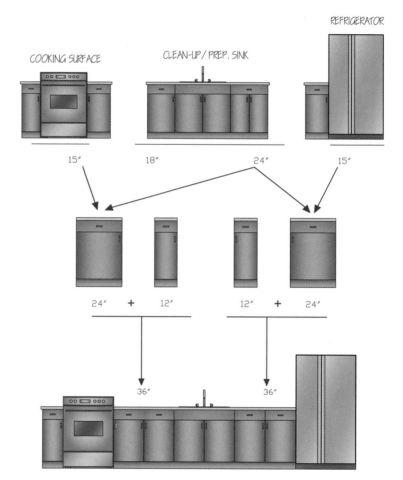

ACCESS STANDARD

Recommended:

Kitchen guideline recommendation meets Access Standard.

KITCHEN PLANNING GUIDELINE 25
COUNTERTOP SPACE

Recommended:

A total of 158" of countertop frontage, 24" deep, with at least 15" of clearance above, is needed to accommodate all uses, including landing area, preparation/work area, and storage.

Built-in appliance garages extending to the countertop can be counted towards the total countertop frontage recommendation, but they may interfere with the landing areas.

Code Requirement:

State or local codes may apply.

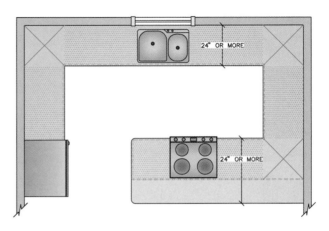

USABLE COUNTER

ACCESS STANDARD

Recommended:

At least two work-counter heights should be offered in the kitchen, with one 28"– 36" above the finished floor and the other 36"– 45" above the finished floor.

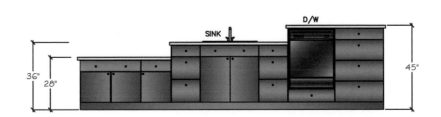

KITCHEN PLANNING GUIDELINE 26
COUNTERTOP EDGES

Recommended:

Specify clipped or round corners rather than sharp edges on all counters.

Code Requirement:

State or local codes may apply.

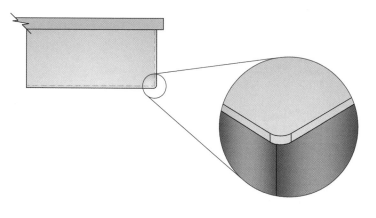

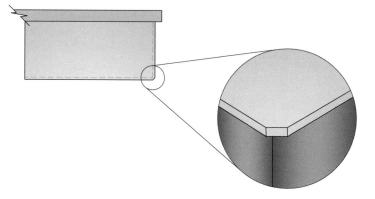

ACCESS STANDARD

Recommended:

Kitchen guideline recommendation meets Access Standard.

KITCHEN PLANNING GUIDELINE 27
STORAGE

Recommended:

The total shelf/drawer frontage* is:

a. 1400" for a small kitchen
   (less than 150 square feet);

b. 1700" for a medium kitchen
   (151 to 350 square feet); and

c. 2000" for a large kitchen
   (greater than 350 square feet).

The recommended distribution for the shelf/drawer frontage in inches is:

	Small	Medium	Large
Wall	300"	360"	360"
Base	520"	615"	660"
Drawer	360"	400"	525"
Pantry	180"	230"	310"
Misc.	40"	95"	145"

The totals for wall, base, drawer and pantry shelf/ drawer frontage can be adjusted upward or downward as long as the recommended total stays the same.

Do not apply more than the recommended amount of storage in the miscellaneous category to meet the total frontage recommendation.

Storage areas that are more than 84" above the floor must be counted in the miscellaneous category.

Shelf and drawer frontage is determined by multiplying the cabinet size by the number and depth of the shelves or drawers in the cabinet, using the following formula:

Cabinet width in inches x number of shelf/drawers x cabinet depth in feet (or fraction thereof) = **Shelf/Drawer Frontage**

Storage/organizing items can enhance the functional capacity of wall, base, drawer and pantry storage and should be selected to meet user needs.

|— 24" —|

1 drawer 24" x 2' = 48" drawer storage
+1 shelf 24" x 1' = 24" base storage
+1 shelf (bottom) 24" x 2' = 48" base storage

Total: 48" drawer storage and 72" base storage

|— 24" —|

1 drawer 24" x 2' = 48" drawer storage
+2 roll-outs 24" x 2' = 96" drawer storage

Total: 144" drawer storage

|— 21" —|

1 drawer 18" x 1³/4' = 31¹/2" drawer storage
+1 shelf 18" x 1' = 18" base storage
+1 shelf (bottom) 18" x 1³/4' = 31¹/2" base storage

Total: 31¹/2" drawer storage and 49¹/2" base storage

|— 21" —|

1 drawer 18" x 1³/4' = 31¹/2" drawer storage
+2 roll-outs 18" x 1³/4' = 63" drawer storage

Total: 94¹/2" drawer storage

|— 18" —|

3 drawers 18" x 1¹/2' = 81" drawer storage

Total: 81" drawer storage

|— 12" —|

3 shelves 24" x 1' = 72" wall storage

Total: 72" wall storage

|— 15" —|

3 drawers 24" x 1¹/4' = 90" wall storage

Total: 90" wall storage

|— 12" —|

6 shelves 24" x 1' = 144" pantry storage

Total: 144" wall storage

KITCHEN PLANNING GUIDELINE 27
STORAGE, *CONTINUED*

Code Requirement:

State or local codes may apply.

2 shelves 24" x 2' = 96"
pantry storage

+3 drawers 24" x 2' = 144"
drawer storage

Total: 144" drawer storage and
96" pantry storage

Tray dividers 30" x 2' = 60"
pantry storage

+3 drawers 30" x 2' = 180"
drawer storage

Total: 180" drawer storage and
60" pantry storage

ACCESS STANDARD

Recommended:

Plan storage of frequently used items 15" to 48"
above the floor.

Code Reference:

- Where a forward or side reach is unobstructed,
  the high reach should be 48" maximum and
  the low reach should be 15" minimum above
  the floor.
  (ANSI A117.1 308.2.1 and 308.3.1)

- Where a 20" – 25" deep counter obstructs
  a forward or side reach, the high reach
  should be 44" maximum.
  (ANSI A117.1 308.2.2)

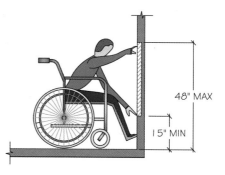

UNOBSTRUCTED FORWARD REACH

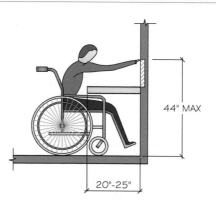

OBSTRUCTED HIGH FORWARD REACH

KITCHEN PLANNING GUIDELINE 28
STORAGE AT CLEANUP/PREP SINK

Recommended:

Of the total recommended wall, base, drawer and pantry shelf/drawer frontage, the following should be located within 72" of the centerline of the main cleanup/prep sink:

a. at least 400" for a small kitchen;

b. at least 480" for a medium kitchen;

c. at least 560" for a large kitchen.

Code Requirement:

State or local codes may apply.

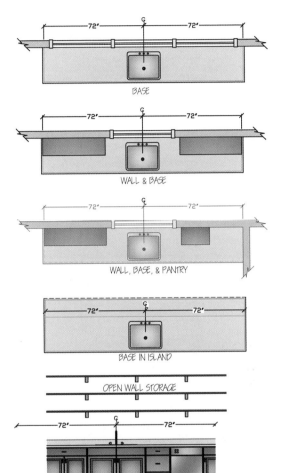

BASE

WALL & BASE

WALL, BASE, & PANTRY

BASE IN ISLAND

OPEN WALL STORAGE

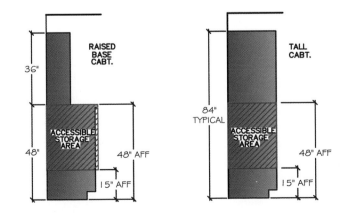

ACCESS STANDARD

Recommended:

Plan storage of frequently used items 15" to 48" above the floor.

Code Reference:

• See Access Guideline 27 for reach specifications.

KITCHEN PLANNING GUIDELINE 29
CORNER CABINET STORAGE

Recommended:

At least one corner cabinet should include a functional storage device.

This guideline does not apply if there are no corner cabinets.

Code Requirement:

State or local codes may apply.

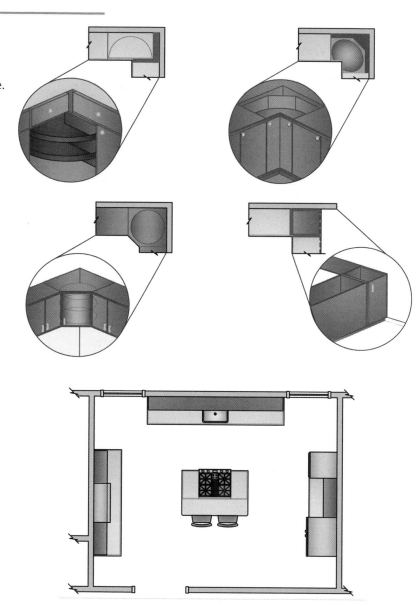

ACCESS STANDARD

Recommended:

Kitchen guideline recommendation meets Access Standard.

KITCHEN PLANNING GUIDELINE 30
ELECTRICAL RECEPTACLES

Code Requirement:

- GFCI (Ground-fault circuit-interrupter) protection is required on all receptacles servicing countertop surfaces within the kitchen.
  (IRC E 3802.6)

Refer to IRC E 3801.4.1 thru E 3801.4.5 for receptacle placement and locations.

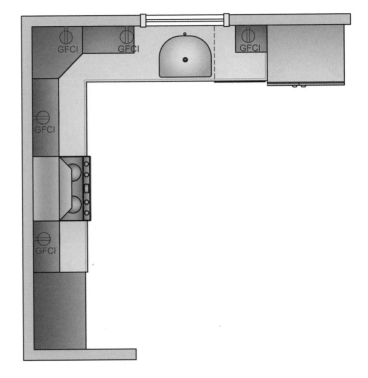

ACCESS STANDARD

Recommended:

See Code Reference.

Code Reference:

- See Access Standard 19 for reach and control specifications.

KITCHEN PLANNING GUIDELINE 31
LIGHTING

Recommended:

In addition to general lighting required by code, every work surface should be well illuminated by appropriate task lighting.

Code Requirement:

- At least one wall-switch controlled light must be provided. Switch must be placed at the entrance.
  (IRC E 3803.2)

- Window/skylight area, equal to at least 8% of the total square footage of the kitchen, or a total living space which includes a kitchen, is required.
  (IRC R 303.1, IRC R 303.2)

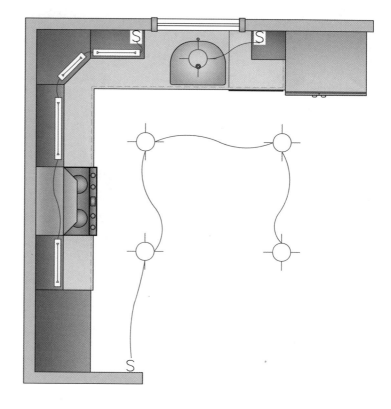

ACCESS STANDARD

Recommended:

Lighting should be from multiple sources and adjustable

Code Reference:

- See Access Standard 19 for reach and control specifications.

A

Absolute humidity: The actual amount of water vapor in the air.

Accessible design or accessibility: Characteristics of spaces or products that meet prescribed requirements for particular variations in ability, i.e. "wheelchair accessible."

Acromion: A human body measurement of the two large triangular bones on the upper back that function to support the shoulders.

Alternating Current (AC): The type of current used in household wiring. The current changes polarity, or alternates, continually from positive to negative and back again at the rate of 60 times a second.

Americans with Disabilities Act Accessibility Guidelines (ADAAG): Guidelines for compliance with the accessibility requirements of the Americans with Disabilities Act (ADA).

Adaptable design: Features that are either adjustable or capable of being easily added or removed to "adapt" the unit to individual needs or preferences.

ACH (air exchanges per hour): Used to measure the ventilation rate of a room or building; 1 ACH means that, in one hour, a volume of air equal to the volume of the room has been exhausted and replaced with outside air.

A.F.F.: Above the finished floor; sometimes written O.F.F. for over the finished floor.

Ambient Lighting: General lighting diffused within an entire room.

Ambient noise: The level of acoustic noise at a given location, such as in a room.

ANSI A117.1 Accessible and Useable Buildings and Facilities: Original American National Standards Institute (ANSI) guidelines for accessible design in commercial and residential spaces. Now the International Code Council (ICC)/ANSI A117.1 is the referenced technical standard for compliance with the accessibility requirements of International Building Code and many other state and local codes. 1998 edition used as reference for NKBA Access Standards.

Anthropometrics: The study of human measurements, such as size and proportion, and parameters, such as reach range and visual range.

Anti-microbial finish: A material that has an applied finish, or ingredient in the product that inhibits the growth of microorganisms, such as bacteria or fungi.

Auxiliary sink: Second sink in the kitchen providing additional work area for either cleanup or food preparation.

B

Back drafting: Used to describe a situation where combustion by-products, from furnaces, gas water heaters, fireplaces, stoves and other fuel-burning appliances, are pulled back into the house instead of exhausting through the flue or chimney; the situation can occur when the air pressure inside the home is less than outside, and is usually the result of running exhaust fans and appliances without providing adequate make-up air.

Ballast: A device that controls the current in a fluorescent lamp.

Banquette: A built-in table with chairs in an alcove.

Barn door: Hardware that allows the door to slide along a wall. Useful when a pocket door is too costly or not possible.

Barrier-free design: An older term for universal design, based on the concept of solutions that removed barriers in the environment.

Biological pollutants: Indoor air pollutants that originate from living sources, including molds, insects and animals; more likely to be found in moist places.

Building Code: Community and state ordinances governing the manner in which a home may be constructed or modified.

C

CADR (Clean Air Delivery Rate): A measure of the efficiency of a portable air cleaner, based on the percentage of particles removed from the air and the speed at which the particles are removed.

Canadian Electric Code (CEC): A code for electrical safety adopted by Canadian political jurisdictions. The CEC is almost identical to the National Electric Code (NEC).

Canopy Ventilation Systems: See updraft ventilation systems.

Center: Area where a task occurs, including the fixture, clear space, storage and other components that support the function of the task. In the kitchen the centers are: preparation, cooking and cleanup.

Certified Kitchen Designer (CKD): NKBA designation for a kitchen designer who has passed the certification examination.

CFM: Cubic feet per minute; used as a measure of the amount of air a fan can move in one minute.

Circuit breaker: A device that is designed to protect electrical equipment and people from damage caused by overload or short circuit. It can be reset to resume operation.

Clear floor space: Area which is free of obstruction within an overall space, typically used in reference to the recommendations for clearances at an appliance or work center.

Color Rendering Index: A method for describing the effect of a light source on the color appearance of objects compared to a reference source of the same color temperature.

Comfort zone: Refers to a body buffer zone that people maintain between others and themselves.

Condensation: The process whereby water, in the form of steam, changes from a gaseous stage to a liquid stage; heat is released by condensation.

Covenant: Sometimes called a restrictive covenant, this is a legally binding clause in a property deed that imposes a limitation or requirement on the use of the property.

D

Daylighting: Using light from the sun to illuminate the interior of a building.

Design programming: The stage of the design process in which information about the client; the wants, needs and desires of the design project; the jobsite; design guidelines; building codes; and other relevant knowledge is organized and analyzed in preparation for the development of the design.

Dew point: The temperature at which water vapor condenses; the dew point temperature is a function of humidity: when the relative humidity is 100%, the air is saturated and can hold no more water vapor, therefore, if there is more water vapor, or the temperature drops below the dew point, condensation occurs.

Downdraft ventilation systems: A kitchen ventilation system that pulls air with the by-products of cooking down through a vent and exhausts it to the outside; typically the ventilation system is integrated with the cooktop or installed immediately adjacent to it.

Energy recovery ventilation system: See whole house ventilation system.

Dual cueing: Also called redundant cueing, refers to the use of different modes (pictorial, verbal, tactile) to communicate necessary information effectively to the user, regardless of ambient conditions or the user's sensory abilities.

E

Egress: A path or opening from a room or building.

Ergonomic design: The application of human factor data to the design of products and spaces to improve function and efficiency.

F

Fair Housing Accessibility Guidelines (FHAG): Accessibility regulations affecting the design of multi-family housing built since 1991. FHAAG make up the technical guidance for compliance with the accessibility requirements of the Fair Housing Amendments Act of 1988 (the Act).

Fenestration: The arrangement of windows in a building.

Filler: Wood or veneer strips inserted merely to occupy space.

Fitting: A term used for a device that controls water entering or leaving a fixture. Faucets, spouts, drain, controls, water supply lines and diverter valves are all considered fittings.

Fixture: Any fixed plumbing feature that is part of the structural design, such as the primary and auxiliary sinks.

FlexHousing: Housing that incorporates, at the design and construction stage, the ability to make future changes easily with minimum expense to meet evolving needs of occupants.

Functional anthropometry: The measurements of the body in motion.

Fuse: A device that can interrupt the flow of electrical current when a circuit is overloaded.

G

Glazing: Industry term for a pane of glass in a window.

Ground Fault Circuit Interrupter (GFCI): A device that monitors the electric current on a circuit to make sure the amount of current going out is the same as that returning to the electric receptacle. Serving as a safety device, the slightest difference in current will shut off the circuit.

H

Halal: Halal is an Arabic word meaning lawful or permitted and can be applied to foods that are permitted to followers of Islam. Dietary practices can influence kitchen design. Foods meeting halal specifications may be difficult to find in some areas, necessitating special long-distance shopping trips and extra storage space.

Halogen lamp: A gas-filled tungsten filament incandescent lamp with a lamp envelope made of quartz to withstand the high temperature. This lamp contains some halogens (namely iodine, chlorine, bromine, and fluorine), which slow the evaporation of the tungsten. They are also commonly called a quartz lamp. Halogen lamps can be either low voltage or operate with a standard 120v electrical source.

"Hard" water: Water with a high content of minerals, usually calcium and magnesium; often leads to plumbing problems from mineral deposits.

Heat recovery ventilation system: See whole house ventilation system.

Homeowner's association: An organization of the property owners in a specific housing development or neighborhood; responsibilities of the association will vary, but often include management of common areas and oversight of requirements affecting the community as a whole; requirements for membership and dues may be a condition of property ownership.

Humidity: The amount of water vapor in the air.

Hydronic systems: A heating system that uses circulating hot water as the heat source; the water is distributed through tubes in the floor, baseboards, or freestanding radiators.

I

International Residential Code (IRC): Building code developed by the International Code Council for single-family housing and used as a reference for the NKBA Kitchen and Bathroom Planning Guidelines.

J

Joists: A level or nearly level member used in a series to frame a floor or ceiling structure.

K

Kosher: In Judaism, the term kosher can be applied to foods that meet a series of dietary laws. The ease of meeting some of these dietary laws, such as the separation of meats and dairy products, can be enhanced by the design of the kitchen.

L

L/s: Liters per second; metric measurement used to rate the capacity of a ventilation fan.

Lamp: Industry term for a light bulb.

Landing area: Measured as countertop frontage adjacent to a sink and/or appliance. Must be at least 16 inches deep and 28 to 45 inches above the finished floor.

Lifespan design: The aspect of universal design that provides for the changes that occur in the lifespan of the home and its owners.

Load-bearing wall: exterior and interior walls of the home that support the structure vertically. Openings in any load-bearing wall must be reinforced to carry the live and dead weight of the structural load.

Low-e coating: A low-emittance coating consisting of a thin, virtually invisible metal or metal oxide layer deposited on a window-glazing surface primarily to reduce the U-factor by suppressing radiant heat flow.

M

Mobility aid: A device, such as wheelchair, cane or walker, used by a person to assist their movement through a space.

N

National Electric Code (NEC): A code for electrical safety adopted by states and local jurisdictions in the United States.

Needs assessment: gathering information about the client and their needs, wants and desires for the design project as well as the physical characteristics of the jobsite.

O

Off-gas: A term used to describe the release or evaporation of chemicals into the air from building materials as they dry, cure or age. The process can be more rapid if temperature and/or humidity are increased.

On-demand/instantaneous water heater: A gas or electric unit that heats water, with no waiting as it is needed by the user.

Outpost kitchen: Small kitchen located away from the primary food preparation area, such as in the bedroom/bathroom area (morning kitchen) or a living or recreation area.

P

Peripheral vision: Scope of vision on both sides of the eyes. Range often diminishes with age.

pH: A scale used to measure acidity or alkalinity, with values from 1 to 14; neutral is 7; decreasing numbers below 7 mean greater acidity and increasing numbers above 7 mean greater alkalinity.

Pocket door: A door that slides horizontally on a track and is typically concealed inside a wall for storage.

Popliteal: A human body measurement relating to the back part of the leg behind the knee.

Preparation center: Long, uninterrupted span of countertop used to make food. Typically placed between the sink and the cooking surface, or the sink and the refrigerator.

Primary center: One of the three main work centers, these include, the main sink, cooking surface and refrigeration storage.

Primary cleanup/prep sink: The sink used most frequently. If only one sink is planned it will be used for both cleanup and food preparation. A kitchen with primary and auxiliary sinks may separate these tasks.

Primary drinking water standards: Federally mandated standards for acceptable levels of certain pollutants in water; used to assure that water is safe to drink or ingest.

Proximity ventilation systems: See downdraft ventilation systems.

R

Radon: A naturally occurring radioactive gas found in soil and ground water; tasteless, odorless, colorless and detectable only through testing equipment; can seep into homes and build to levels that can be a health threat; long-term exposure can lead to lung cancer.

Reach range: The measured distance off the floor within which a person can reach and grasp an item. The universal reach range refers to the distance where most people can reach an item, which is 15 to 48 inches off the floor.

Re-circulating (ductless) system: A kitchen ventilation system installed in a hood that pulls air through one or more filters, then exhausts the filtered air into the room; a metal mesh filter to remove grease is typical; an activated carbon filter to remove odors may be included.

Relative humidity: A ratio, usually expressed as a percent, of the actual amount of water vapor in the air to the maximum amount (saturation) of water vapor the air could hold at the current temperature.

Rough-in: Where plumbing materials, faucets and fixtures are layed out in the early stages of new construction.

S

Safe harbors: Standards that are legally recognized as compliance with the requirements of a code or guideline.

Sconce: A light fixture that is fixed to the wall.

Sealed combustion appliances: Appliances, such as a furnace or water heater, where the air needed for combustion is pulled from an outside vent and then the flue gases resulting from combustion are exhausted to the outside; the combustion process is thus "sealed' from room air.

Secondary center: A work area established for a specific task, such as baking or salad preparation. It may include an appliance or fixture, storage and counter space, but is not calculated as part of the work triangle.

Secondary drinking water standards: Voluntary standards for acceptable levels of certain pollutants in water; used to assure that water is functional and aesthetically pleasing for typical household uses, such as bathing and laundry.

Septic tank: A large holding tank where solid matter or sewage from a home is disintegrated by bacteria.

Service entry: A second, informal entrance to the home, used for bringing in groceries and supplies. It is often close to the kitchen and to garage or carport.

Shelf/drawer frontage: Calculation of cabinet size x number of shelves or drawers x cabinet depth in feet. Used to determine adequate storage in a kitchen.

Shut-off valve: A valve control that allows the user to shut off the water entering a fixture. These valves are usually located close to the fixture.

Sight lines: The range or visual field in direct line with a person's eyes, affected by the position a person will be in when the space or product is being used. This is useful in planning heights of fixtures, fittings, lighting, windows and more.

Sone: A unit of loudness, which is a subjective characteristic of a sound; the sone scale is based on data from people judging the loudness of pure tones; as an example, a noise at four sones is perceived to be four times as loud as a noise of one sone.

Static anthropometry: The study of the measurements of the body at rest.

Storage principles: A series of recommendations, developed through research, to increase both the efficiency of storage space and the ease of use. The most common principles are:

1. Store items at the first or last place of use.
2. Store items in duplicate locations, if needed.
3. Items used together should be stored together.
4. Items should be stored so they are easy to see.
5. Frequently used items should be stored so they are easy to reach.
6. Like items should be stored or grouped together.
7. Hazardous items should be stored out of reach of children.
8. Store items in the appropriate environment.

Surge protector: Or surge suppressor; an electrical device used to protect electronic equipment, especially computer systems, from surges or spikes in electrical current or voltage.

Sub-flooring: The flooring applied directly to the floor joist on top of which the finished floor rests.

T

Tactile cueing: Using textural elements to communicate necessary information through touch to the user.

Task lighting: Lighting focused on a work area.

Toe kick: An intentional space in cabinetry near the floor to accommodate the feet while standing next to a cabinetry.

Transformer: An electrical device by which alternating current of one voltage is changed to another voltage.

Trans-generational design: Another term for universal design, referring to design that acknowledges and supports the multiple generations more commonly living in a home.

Truss: A framework of beams forming a rigid structure such as a roof or floor truss.

U

Underlayment: A material placed over the subfloor plywood sheeting and under the finish covering to provide a smooth, even surface.

Uniform Federal Accessibility Standards (UFAS): The technical standard referenced by two federal mandates for accessibility for federal buildings; the Architectural Barriers Act (ABA) and Section 504 of the Rehabilitation Act of 1973 (Section 504).

Universal design: The design of products and environments to be useable by all people to the greatest extent possible.

Updraft ventilation systems: A kitchen ventilation system that includes a hood over a cooking surface to capture the airborne by-products of cooking and a fan to pull air up; captured air is either exhausted to the outside or filtered and re-circulated into the room, depending on the system.

V

Vegetarian: The term "vegetarian" is generally applied to people who restrict meat or animal products in their diets. Today, people who call themselves vegetarian may range from those who limit their meat consumption to maybe once a week to those who eat no animal products at all (usually called vegans). People may choose vegetarianism for many reasons, with health concerns being the most popular. Most vegetarians consume more fruits, vegetables, legumes and/or grains, which influences their need for food storage and preparation space.

Vernacular housing: Housing styles that are typical or common to a region and have developed over time in response to factors such as available building materials, climate and cultural heritage.

Volatile organic compounds (VOCs): A class of organic compounds that are easily evaporated into the air and used in the manufacturing, installation, and maintenance of many building products; many VOCs are toxic and may contribute to urban smog, the greenhouse effect and global warming.

W

Waste pipe: The pipe that carries water and waste away from a water-using fixture.

Water vapor: Water in its gaseous form.

Wet wall: A wall containing supply lines and soil and waste lines.

Whole-house ventilation system: A mechanical ventilation system that continuously ventilates the home by pulling outside air into the house and exhausting indoor air; heat recovery or energy recovery ventilation systems increase energy efficiency by using heat exchangers (sometimes called air to air heat exchangers) to pre-heat or pre-cool the incoming air with the exhaust air.

Work aisle: Space needed to function at the kitchen centers.

Work center: Comprised of an appliance or sink, surrounding landing/work area and storage.

Work Triangle: The distance between the three primary work centers (cooking surface, cleanup/prep primary sink and refrigeration).

X

Xenon: Xenon lamps are similar to halogen lamps in their characteristics and are made with electrodes in a small tube filled with an inert gas. These lamps do not burn as hot as halogen lamps and are not as fragile. They operate at a lower voltage than the standard 120v, and thus require a transformer.

Z

Zone: a) A section of a building that is served by one heating and cooling loop to meet distinct heating and cooling needs. b) A section of the home where similar activities occur such as social, private and work. c) A kitchen center.

Following is a completed sample of the NKBA's Kitchen Survey Form. Familiarity with this form is a requirement for certification.

MS DESIGN ASSOCIATES
18 MILL ROAD, MADISON KS 48920

Designer: Mary Smith

Kitchen Design Survey Form

Date: July 28, 2006
Name: Bonnie and Henry Peterson
Residence: 123 Main St.
Washington KS 48903
Jobsite Address: same

Client 1: Bonnie Peterson	Client 2: Henry Peterson
Home Phone: 555-2323	Home Phone: 555-2323
Work Phone: 555-0022	Work Phone: 555-8723
Cell Phone: 555-3876	Cell Phone: none
Email: bpeterson@anywhere.com	Email: hpeterson@anywhere.com

Appointment	Allied Professional
Schedule:	Name:
Call When Ready:	Firm:
Times Available: M-F 3-7 pm	Address:
Directions: corner of Lexington and Main	Office Phone:
	Cell Phone:
	Email:

Notes: Bonnie will be primary contact for this job.

©2006 NKBA BMF8   1

Copyright 2006 by NKBA. All rights reserved. No part of this document may be reproduced in any form by photostat, microfilm, xerography, or any other means, or incorporated into any informational retrieval system, electronic or mechanical, or transmitted, in any form or by any means, without the prior consent of the copyright owner.

General Client Information

1. *What type of project is this?* ☒Renovation ☐New Construction
2. *Have you ever purchased a kitchen before?* ☐Yes ☒No
3. *When would you like to start the project?* _August_   Complete the Project? _Before the holidays_
4. *How much time do you / will you spend at the jobsite residence?* _a lot_
5. *How did you learn about our firm?* _NKBA website_
6. *Has anyone else assisted you in preparing a design for the kitchen?* _no_
7. *Do you plan on retaining an interior designer or architect to assist in the kitchen planning?*
   If so, Name: _no_   Phone:
8. *Do you have a specific builder/contractor or other subcontractor/specialist with whom you would like to work?*
   If so, Name: _no_   Phone:
9. *What portion of the project, if any, will be your responsibility?* _none_
10. *What budget range have you established for your kitchen project?*
    ☐$5,000 – $10,000   ☐$10,000 -$ 20,000   ☐$20,000 – $40,000   ☐$40,000 – $60,000
    ☒$60,000 – $75,000   ☐$75,000 – $100,000   ☐$100,000 +
11. *How long do you intend to own the jobsite residence?* _5+ years_
a. Is return on investment a primary concern? _yes_
b. Do you plan on renting the jobsite residence? _no_
12. *What family members will share in the final decision-making process?* _Bonnie and Henry_
13. *Would you like our firm to assist you in securing project financing?* ☐Yes ☒No
14. *What do you dislike most about your present kitchen?* _Lack of storage space, outdated appliances_
15. *What do you like most about your present kitchen?* _Large space_
16. *Sustainable design ideas important to your family:*

☐Use of "Green" Products	General products made from recycled materials: ☐Cabinets ☐Counters ☐Floors ☐Building Materials
	☐ Wood products supplied by environmentally responsible manufacturers
☒Special water conservation products:	
☒Energy efficient appliances:	
☐Energy efficient lighting systems:	
☐Sustainable design details incorporated into the plan:	
☒Areas for recycling waste incorporated into the plan:	

17. *If you are remodeling:* Is there a room addition planned? ☐Yes ☒No
a. When was the house built? _1975_   How old is the present kitchen? _original_
b. Are you considering relocating ☒windows ☒doors ☐ walls in your new plan?
18. *If you are building a new home:*
   a. Are you able to relocate ☐windows ☐doors ☐walls at this stage of construction? ☐Yes ☐No
   b. Are you able to relocate walls at this stages of construction ☐Yes ☐No

©2006 NKBA BMF8   2

Copyright 2006 by NKBA. All rights reserved. No part of this document may be reproduced in any form by photostat, microfilm, xerography, or any other means, or incorporated into any informational retrieval system, electronic or mechanical, or transmitted, in any form or by any means, without the prior consent of the copyright owner.

Specific Kitchen Questions

1. *How many household members? Are you planning on enlarging your family while living here?* ☐Yes ☒No

Name	Age	Handed	Height	Physical Limitations/Mobility Aids
Bonnie	56	☒R ☐L	5'5"	none
Henry	62	☒R ☐L	6'1	arthritis
		☐R ☐L		
		☐R ☐L		
		☐R ☐L		
		☐R ☐L		
		☐R ☐L		

2. *How many pets in your household?_1_____*   What Types?_dog_____   Names:_Oscar_____

3. *Do any frequent guests have physical limitations?_mother-in-law uses a walker_____*

4. *Personal information about the kitchen:*

   What is the typical pattern of cooking in your household?

   ☐One person does most of the cooking. Who?_____

   ☐Two or more people share most of the cooking. Describe:_____

   ☒One person cooks and another person helps. Describe:_Bonnie is primary cook. Henry usually does cleanup_____

   ☐Different people take turns doing the cooking. Describe:_____

   ☐Another arrangement. Describe:_____

   What about clean-up?

   ☐The cook cleans up. Describe:_____

   ☐Cooking and clean-up are shared. Describe:_____

   ☒Clean-up is done by someone who does not cook. Describe:_mostly Henry_____

   ☐Another arrangement. Describe:_____

5. *Primary Cook:*

   Is the primary cook ☐left handed ☒right handed

   Does the primary cook have any physical limitation? ☐Yes ☒No _____

   How tall is the primary cook?_5'5"_____

   Does the primary cook have any cooking hobbies/specialty cooking preferences?

   ☐gourmet ☒baking ☐ethnic ☐grilling ☐bulk cooking to freeze

   ☐other:_____

6. *Other Family Cooks:*

   How many other household members cook?_none_____

   Who are they?_____

   Do they ☐ have a cooking hobby ☐assist primary cook with specific task ☐share a menu item with primary cook?

   Is a specialized cooking center required for the secondary cook?_____

©2006 NKBA BMF8   3

Copyright 2006 by NKBA. All rights reserved. No part of this document may be reproduced in any form by photostat, microfilm, xerography, or any other means, or incorporated into any informational retrieval system, electronic or mechanical, or transmitted, in any form or by any means, without the prior consent of the copyright owner.

7. *How does the family use the kitchen for meals at home?*_____

☐daily heat & serve meals ☒daily "from scratch" meals ☐daily "bring in" meals ☐weekend "quantity" cooking

☐weekend family meals ☐ ethnic or specialty cooking (please specify)

_____

_____

What type of foods is the family cooking? Simple foods. Henry is on a low-salt diet._____

_____

8. *What are your kitchen dining area requests?*_____

☒separate table- ☐new ☐existing_____ size_____ leaf extension_____ number of seated diners 4+_____

☐30" counter height ☐36" counter height ☐42" counter height

9. *Is the kitchen a socializing space?* yes_____

10. *What time of day is your kitchen most frequently used?* mornings and evenings_____

11. *Do you have any furniture that you want in your kitchen?*

☒Dining Table- Size?_____ ☒Chairs- How many?4+_____ ☐Hutch- Size?_____ ☐Buffet- Size?_____

☐Baker's Rack- Size?_____ ☐Easy Chair- How many?_____ ☐Sofa - Size?_____ Other Items-_____

12. *How would you like the new kitchen to relate to adjacent rooms?* staging area to dining room_____

_____

| ☐Family Room | ☒Dining Room | ☐Family Home Office |
| ☐Family Media Center | ☐Outdoor Kitchen | ☐Laundry/Hobby Space |

13. *Do you entertain frequently?* yes   per week 1-2 times   per month_____ per year - ☐formally ☒informally ☐buffet ☐plated

☐snacks/drinks mostly How many people typically might be in the kitchen when entertaining? 3-4   Do friends bring food to share? ☐Yes ☒ No

14. *Designing the kitchen so that it supports your entertainment style is part of the planning process. Tell me which statement fits you best:*

☐ I like to be the only one in the kitchen with my guests in a separate space that is away from the kitchen.

☐ I like to be the only cook in the kitchen, with my guests close by in a space that opens onto the kitchen.

☒ I like my guests to be sitting in the kitchen visiting with me while I cook.

☐ I like my guests to help me in the kitchen in meal preparation.

☐ I like my guests to help in the clean-up process after the meal.

☐ I retain caterers who prepare all meals for entertaining.

☐ The caterers come to the home to serve and clean up.

☐ I stop at the deli/take-out food source to bring part or all of the meal home before entertaining.

☐ Food items that I purchase from outside sources:

☐Appetizers ☐Entrees ☐Soups ☐_____

☐Desserts ☐Salads ☐_____ ☐_____

15. *What secondary activities will take place in your kitchen?*

☐Computer Usage	☐Hobbies:	☐Medicine Center / Use	☐Children Playing
☒Eating	☐Laundry	☒Message Center	☐Study/Homework
☐Growing Plants	☒Liquor/Wine Storage	☐Planning Desk	☐TV /Radio/Media/CD

©2006 NKBA BMF8   4

Copyright 2006 by NKBA. All rights reserved. No part of this document may be reproduced in any form by photostat, microfilm, xerography, or any other means, or incorporated into any informational retrieval system, electronic or mechanical, or transmitted. in any form or by any means, without the prior consent of the copyright owner.

16. *What is your cycle for shopping for food?*
☐Daily ☐Twice Weekly ☒Weekly ☐Bi-weekly ☐Monthly

17. *What types of products/materials do you purchase at the grocery/specialty store?*

☒ Predominantly fresh food purchased for a specific meal. fresh vegetables and meat from the butcher

☐ Predominantly fresh/frozen foods purchased for stock.

☒ Traditional pantry boxed/packaged/canned/bottled goods purchased for stock. soups, pasta, cereal

☐Cleaning products stocked in bulk:

☒Paper products stocked in bulk:

☐Other boxed/packaged food items stocked in bulk:

☐Other:

18. *Where do you presently store:*

T Baking Equipment	BA Flatware	W Leftover Containers	W Serving Trays
P Boxed Goods	BA Food Prep Utensils	L Linens/Towels	W Specialty Cooking Vessels (Wok, etc.)
P Canned Goods	BA Food Wrapping Materials	P Non-Refrigerated Fruits/Vegs	_Other:
BA Cleaning Supplies	W Glassware	L Paper Products	_Other:
BA Coffee Station	BA Grill Equipment	G Pet Food	_Other:
BA Cooking Utensils	BA Hand Appliances	BA Pots & Pans	_Other:
W Dishes	B Laundry/Iron Equip	BA Recycle Containers	_Other:

Legend:

AG=Appliance Garage	BC=Bookcase	G=Garage	T=Tall Cabinet
B=Basement	C=Countertop	L=Laundry Room	W=Wall Cabinet
BA=Base Cabinet	D=Desk	P=Pantry Closet	

19. *What type of specialized storage is desired?*

☐Bottles	☒Display Items	☐Linen	☒Wine
☐Bread Board	☐Dishes	☐Plasticware	☐_____
☒Bread Box	☐Food Wrappings	☒Soft Drink Cans	☐_____
☒Cookbooks	☐Glassware	☒Spice	☐_____
☒Cutlery	☐Lids	☐Vegetables	☐_____

20. *What small specialty electrical appliances do you use in your kitchen?*

☒Blender	☒Crock Pot / Slow Cooker	☒Mixer	☐_____
☐Can Opener	☐Electric Frying Pan	☐Toaster	☐_____
☐Coffee Grinder	☒Food Processor	☒Toaster Oven	☐_____
☒Coffee Pot	☒Griddle	☒Wok	
☒Countertop ☐Built-in	☐Juicer		

21. *Do you plan on sorting recyclable trash in your kitchen?* ☒Yes ☐No

Number of bins required: 2

Would you like a sorting station in the:

☒Kitchen ☐Utility Room ☐Garage ☐Basement ☐Outside

©2006 NKBA BMF8

Copyright 2006 by NKBA. All rights reserved. No part of this document may be reproduced in any form by photostat, microfilm, xerography, or any other means, or incorporated into any informational retrieval system, electronic or mechanical, or transmitted, in any form or by any means, without the prior consent of the copyright owner.

Design Information

1. *What type of feeling would you like your new kitchen space to have? Have you created a scrapbook of notes, photos and ideas of kitchens that you like?*

    ☐ American Country   ☐ Asian   ☐ Warm Contemporary   ☐ Sleek Contemporary

    ☐ American Formal   ☐ Old World European   ☐ Personal Design Statement (Eclectic)   ☒ Traditional

2. *What colors do you like?* neutrals

    And dislike? bright colors

    What colors are you considering for you new kitchen? yellow, beige

    What are the color preferences of other family members? same

3. *Design Notes:*

    Kitchen window can be moved, enlarged or changed but do not make any smaller.

    Would like glass doors on some cabinets for display

    Doors can be changed.

©2006 NKBA BMF8   6

Copyright 2006 by NKBA. All rights reserved. No part of this document may be reproduced in any form by photostat, microfilm, xerography, or any other means, or incorporated into any informational retrieval system, electronic or mechanical, or transmitted, in any form or by any means, without the prior consent of the copyright owner.

Special Details: We like the large size of our kitchen and the view of the backyard from the window.

Copyright 2005 by NKBA. All rights reserved under the Pan-American and International Copyright Conventions. No part of this publication may be reproduced, stored in a retrieval system, or transmitted in any form or by any means, electronic, mechanical, photocopying, recording, or otherwise, without the prior written permission of the copyright owner.

©2005 NKBA BMF6

©2006 NKBA BMF8

Copyright 2006 by NKBA. All rights reserved. No part of this document may be reproduced in any form by photostat, microfilm, xerography, or any other means, or incorporated into any informational retrieval system, electronic or mechanical, or transmitted, in any form or by any means, without the prior consent of the copyright owner.

7

Cabinetry

Source		

Key: KS= Kitchen Specialist

O= Owner OA= Owners Agent

Use Existing ☐Yes ☒No

Furnished by KS ☒   O/OA ☐

Installed by KS ☒   O/OA ☐

Construction	Base	Wall	Tall	Island
Framed	☒	☒	☒	☒
Frameless	☐	☐	☐	☐
Door Type				
Full Overlay	☐	☐	☐	☐
Partial Overlay	☒	☒	☒	☒
Lip	☐	☐	☐	☐
Inset	☐	☐	☐	☐
Hardware				
Knob	☐	☐	☐	☐
Pull	☒	☒	☒	☒
Finger Pull	☐	☐	☐	☐
Material	☐	☐	☐	☐

Face Material	Base	Wall	Tall	Island
Wood-Species cherry	☒	☒	☒	☒
Laminate	☐	☐	☐	☐
Paint	☐	☐	☐	☐
Acrylic	☐	☐	☐	☐
Metal	☐	☐	☐	☐
Other_____	☐	☐	☐	☐

Door Style: solid raised

Color and Finish: autumn glaze

Storage Accessories or Organizers:

	Base	Wall	Tall	Island		Base	Wall	Tall	Island
Appliance Garage	☐	☐	☐	☐	Pull-out Cutting Board	☐	☐	☐	☐
Breadbox	☐	☐	☐	☐	Roll-out Cart	☐	☐	☐	☐
Cutlery Tray	☐	☐	☐	☐	Roll-out Shelf	☒	☐	☐	☐
Door Shelf	☐	☐	☐	☐	Spice Rack / Drawer	☐	☒	☐	☐
Drawer Divider / Insert	☒	☐	☐	☐	Swing-out Shelf	☐	☐	☐	☐
Drawer Dish Storage	☐	☐	☐	☐	Tilt-down Drawer	☐	☐	☐	☐
Drawer Pot / Pan Storage	☒	☐	☐	☒	Towel Bar	☒	☐	☐	☐
Knife Block	☐	☐	☐	☐	Trash Can	☒	☐	☐	☐
Knife Drawer	☐	☐	☐	☐	Tray Dividers (Vertical)	☐	☒	☐	☐
Lazy Susan / Turntable	☒	☒	☐	☐	Toe Kick Step Stool	☐	☐	☐	☐
Mixer Lift-up	☐	☐	☐	☐	Vegetable Bin / Basket	☐	☐	☐	☐
Pantry	☐	☐	☒	☐	Wide / Deep Drawer	☐	☐	☐	☐
Plate Rack	☐	☒	☐	☐	Peg Board Drawer	☐	☐	☐	☐
Pot Rack	☒	☐	☐	☒	Other_____	☐	☐	☐	☐
Pull-out Recycle Bin	☒	☐	☐	☐	Other_____	☐	☐	☐	☐

©2006 NKBA BMF8

Copyright 2006 by NKBA. All rights reserved. No part of this document may be reproduced in any form by photostat, microfilm, xerography, or any other means, or incorporated into any informational retrieval system, electronic or mechanical, or transmitted, in any form or by any means, without the prior consent of the copyright owner.

8

Soffit / Fascia

Use Existing	Furnished by		Installed by	
☐Yes ☒No	KS ☒	O/OA ☐	KS ☒	O/OA ☐

Fascia / Soffit Construction	Fascia / Soffit Materials
☐Open ☐Extended ☐Flush ☐Recessed ☒Remove	☐Wallpaper ☐Wood ☐Display Rail ☐Paint ☐Lighted ☐Cornice
☐Other_____	☐Other_____

Countertops

Use Existing	Furnished by		Installed by	
☐Yes ☒No	KS ☒	O/OA ☐	KS ☒	O/OA ☐

Material	Kitchen	Island	Other	Edge Treatment	Kitchen	Island	Other
Ceramic Tile	☐	☐		**Thickness**	☐	☐	
Size				**Shape:**	☐	☐	
Grout				Bevel	☐	☐	
Concrete	☐	☐		Ogee	☒	☒	
Engineered Stone (quartz)	☐	☐		Bull Nose Full	☐	☐	
Granite	☒	☒		½ Full	☐	☐	
Limestone	☐	☐		Square	☐	☐	
Marble	☐	☐		Eased	☐	☐	
Plastic Laminate	☐	☐		**Contrast Color**			
Stainless Steel	☐	☐		**Other**			
Soapstone	☐	☐		**Backsplash**			
Solid Surface	☐	☐		Match to Counter	☒	☐	
Wood	☐	☐		Full Height	☐	☐	
Other_____	☐	☐		Endsplash 4" High	☐	☐	
Other_____	☐	☐		**Color or Pattern:**			
Other_____	☐	☐		Details:			

Color or Pattern:

Details: _gold_____

_____

Preparation:

Describe:_____

_____

Decking:_____

Insert:_____

©2006 NKBA BMF8

Copyright 2006 by NKBA. All rights reserved. No part of this document may be reproduced in any form by photostat, microfilm, xerography, or any other means, or incorporated into any informational retrieval system, electronic or mechanical, or transmitted, in any form or by any means, without the prior consent of the copyright owner.

Sink

Use Existing	Furnished by			Installed by		
☐ Yes ☒ No	KS ☒	O/OA ☐		KS ☒	O/OA ☐	

Material	Sink #1	Sink #2	Sink #3	Mounting	Sink #1	Sink #2	Sink #3
Composite	☐	☐	☐	Self-Rimming	☐	☐	☐
Enamel / Cast Iron	☐	☐	☐	Under-Mount	☒	☒	☐
Porcelain / Steel	☐	☐	☐	Integral	☐	☐	☐
Stainless Steel	☒	☒	☐	Counter Section	☐	☐	☐
Solid Surface	☐	☐	☐	Apron	☐	☐	☐
Other_____	☐	☐	☐	Other_____	☐	☐	☐
Other_____	☐	☐	☐	**Special Features**	Sink #1	Sink #2	Sink #3
Number of Bowls	Sink #1	Sink #2	Sink #3	Drainboard L	☐	☐	☐
One	☐	☒	☐	Drainboard R	☐	☐	☐
Two	☒	☐	☐	Strainer	☐	☐	☐
Same Size	☐	☐	☐	Accessories	☐	☐	☐
Large / Small	☐	☐	☐	1	☐	☐	☐
Three	☐	☐	☐	2	☐	☐	☐
Color	Sink #1	Sink #2	Sink #3	3	☐	☐	☐
	☐	☐	☐	4	☐	☐	☐
Details:_____				5	☐	☐	☐

Faucet

Use Existing	Furnished by			Installed by		
☐ Yes ☒ No	KS ☒	O/OA ☐		KS ☒	O/OA ☐	

Material	Sink #1	Sink #2	Sink #3	Style / Features	Sink #1	Sink #2	Sink #3
Brass	☐	☐	☐	One Handle ☐ L ☐ R	☐	☐	☐
Chrome	☐	☐	☐	Two-Handles	☐	☐	☐
Epoxy-Color	☐	☐	☐	Bridge Type	☐	☐	☐
Gold	☐	☐	☐	Pot Filler	☐	☐	☐
Brushed Nickel	☒	☒	☐	Goose Neck	☐	☒	☐
Pewter	☐	☐	☐	Pull-out Spray	☒	☐	☐
Stainless Steel	☐	☐	☐	Automatic Operation	☐	☐	☐
Other_____	☐	☐	☐	**Other Features**	Sink #1	Sink #2	Sink#3
Other_____	☐	☐	☐	Separate Spray	☐	☐	☐
Other_____	☐	☐	☐	Instant Hot	☒	☐	☐
Other_____	☐	☐	☐	Water Filter	☐	☐	☐
Other_____	☐	☐	☐	Dishwasher Air Gap	☐	☐	☐

Dispensers

Use Existing	Furnished by			Installed by		
☐ Yes ☒ No	KS ☒	O/OA ☐		KS ☒	O/OA ☐	

Type	Sink #1	Sink #2	Sink #3	Type	Sink #1	Sink #2	Sink #3
Dish Detergent	☒	☐	☐	Hand Soap	☐	☐	☐
Hand Lotion	☐	☐	☐				

Lighting Systems

Use Existing	Furnished by			Installed by		
☐ Yes ☒ No	KS ☒	O/OA ☐		KS ☒	O/OA ☐	

General				Ambient			
☒ Incandescent	☐ Halogen	☐ Fluorescent	☐ Xenon	☐ Cove	☒ Recessed	☒ Pendant	☐ Surface mtd.
Decorative				☐ Track	☐ Incandescent	☐ Halogen	☐ Fluorescent
☒ Incandescent	☐ Halogen	☐ Fluorescent	☐ Xenon	Other_____			
Under Cabinet				Other_____			
☐ Incandescent	☐ Halogen	☒ Fluorescent	☐ Xenon	Other_____			

©2006 NKBA BMF8

Copyright 2006 by NKBA. All rights reserved. No part of this document may be reproduced in any form by photostat, microfilm, xerography, or any other means, or incorporated into any informational retrieval system, electronic or mechanical, or transmitted, in any form or by any means, without the prior consent of the copyright owner.

10

Appliance & Fixture Specifications - Option 1
(Option 1 to be used by design professionals who select specific appliances for the client.)

Size	Color	Item / Description	Manufacturer	Model #	Notes
Surface Cooking			Configuration: P=Professional CT=Cooktop (controls on top)		
			RT=Range Top (controls on front)		
			Style: DI = Drop-in FS=Freestanding SI = Slide-in		
		Range___ Config.___ Fuel___			
		Cooktop___ Config.___ Fuel___			
		Rangetop___ Config.___ Fuel___			
Surface Ventilation	☐Remote Blower	☐Interior Blower	☐Recirculate	☐CFM	☐Height ☐Transition
		Hood: ☐Wall Mounted ☐Island			
		Duct Cover: _____			
		Hood Liner and/or Blower:_____			
		Down Draft:_____			
		Micro Combo:_____			
Oven Cooking					
		Oven: ☐Single___ ☐Double___			
		☐Oven / Microwave Combo			
		Warming Drawer___ Quantity:___			
Microwave and Specialty Ovens		Configuration: CT= Countertop BI= Built-In OTR= Over The Range			
		Microwave___ Config.___			
		Trim Kit:_____			
		Other:_____			
Refrigeration		Configuration: SxS= Side-by-Side UCDR= Undercounter Drawers UCD= Undercounter Door L/R TF= Top Freezer BF=Bottom Freezer			
		Style: Free Standing BI= Built-In (Standard) IN=Built-In (Integrated) AR=All Refrigerator AF=All Freezer			
		Refrig. Config _____ Style:_____			
		Refrig. Config _____ Style:_____			
		Refrig. Config _____ Style:_____			
		Front Panel_____			
Dishwasher / Compactor / Icemaker		Style: ST= Standard IN= Integrated SI= Semi-Integrated DR=Drawer			
		Dishwasher_____ Style_____			
		Compactor_____ Style_____			
		Front Panel_____			
Water Products		Configuration: S= Single D=Double BL= Big and Little	Style: UM= Undermount TM= Top Mount IN= Intergral AP= Apron C=Counter Section		
		Sink #1 Config_____ Style_____			
		Faucet:_____			
		Sink #2 Config_____ Style_____			
		Faucet:_____			
		Sink #3 Config_____ Style_____			
		Faucet:_____			
		Sink Accessories:_____			
		Instant Hot:_____			
		Water Filter:_____			
		Garbage Disposer_____ Quantity_____			
Miscellaneous		(Laundry, BBQ / Outdoor Equip, Intercom, Vacuum, Espresso, Ironing Center, Water Softener, Warranty, etc.)			

End Appliance & Fixture Specifications - Option 1

©2006 NKBA BMF8   11

Copyright 2006 by NKBA. All rights reserved. No part of this document may be reproduced in any form by photostat, microfilm, xerography, or any other means, or incorporated into any informational retrieval system, electronic or mechanical, or transmitted, in any form or by any means, without the prior consent of the copyright owner.

Appliance & Fixture Specifications - Option 2
(Option 2 is used by designers who gather all generic appliance info., rather than specifying specific appli

Range

Use Existing	Furnished by		Installed by	
☐Yes ☐No	KS ☐	O/OA ☐	KS ☐	O/OA ☐

☐New ☐Existing Finish:_____ Size:_____

Fuel

☐Electricity	☐Natural Gas
☐Propane	

Type

☐Free-Standing	☐Drop-In	☐Slide-In
☐Integrated	☐Professional Style	

Electric Surface Units

☐Conventional Coil	☐Solid Disk (Electric Hob)	☐Sealed Glass Ceramic
☐Magnetic Induction	☐Halogen Unit	☐Thermostatic Controlled Unit
☐Dual Size Unit		

Gas Surface Units

☐Open-Air (Conventional)	☐Sealed	☐High BTU

Surface Controls

☐Electronic	☐Conventional Knob

Other Cooking Surface Features

☐Griddle	☐Grill

Oven Features

☐Electric Oven	☐Gas Oven	☐Broiler
☐Convection Oven	☐Pyrolytic (Self-Cleaning)	☐Other_____

Controls: ☐Conventional Knob ☐Electronic

Other Range Features

Cooktop / Range Top

Use Existing	Furnished by		Installed by	
☐Yes ☒No	KS ☒	O/OA ☐	KS ☒	O/OA ☐

☒New ☐Existing Finish:_____ Size:_____

Fuel

☐Electricity	☒Natural Gas
☐Propane	

Type

☐Free-Standing	☒Drop-In	☐Slide-In
☐Integrated	☐Professional Style	

Electric Surface Units

☐Conventional Coil	☐Solid Disk (Electric Hob)	☐Sealed Glass Ceramic
☐Magnetic Induction	☐Halogen Unit	☐Thermostatic Controlled Unit
☐Dual Size Unit		

Gas Surface Units

☒Open-Air (Conventional)	☐Sealed	☐High BTU

Surface Controls

☐Electronic	☒Conventional Knob	☐Griddle	☐Grill

Other Cooking Surface Features

Ventilation System

Use Existing	Furnished by		Installed by	
☐Yes ☒No	KS ☒	O/OA ☐	KS ☒	O/OA ☐

Updraft / Canopy

☐Exhaust	☐Recirculating

Hood

☒Match to Cooktop	☐Match to Cabinetry
☐Custom Design	☐Slim Line / Telescoping

Downdraft / Proximity

☐Surface Mount	☐Pop-Up (Behind Cooktop)	☐Pop-Up (Next to Cooktop)

Ventilation System Installation

☒New Ductwork Needed	☐Duct Termination
☐Space to Run Ductwork	

Ovens

Use Existing	Furnished by		Installed by	
☐Yes ☒No	KS ☒	O/OA ☐	KS ☒	O/OA ☐

Conventional

☒New ☐Existing Finish:_____ Size:_____

Configuration

☐Single	☒Double	☐Combo Micro / Oven
☐Under-Counter Installation	☒Wall Installation	
☐Convection Cooking-elective	☒Convection Cooking-Gas	☐Steam Cooking
☐High-Speed Cooking	☐Pyrolytic (Self-Cleaning)	

Controls: ☐Conventional Knob ☒Electronic

Other Features

Microwave Oven

Use Existing	Furnished by		Installed by	
☐Yes ☒No	KS ☒	O/OA ☐	KS ☒	O/OA ☐

Microwave Oven

☒New ☐Existing Finish:_____ Size:_____

Installation

☐Free-Standing	☒Boxed/Built-In	☐Integrated

Configuration

☐Microwave-Ventilation Combo	☒Professional Style
☐Microwave-Convection Cooking	☐Microwave-Light Cooking

Features

☐Browning Element	☐Turntable

©2006 NKBA BMF8

Copyright 2006 by NKBA. All rights reserved. No part of this document may be reproduced in any form by photostat, microfilm, xerography, or any other means, or incorporated into any informational retrieval system, electronic or mechanical, or transmitted, in any form or by any means, without the prior consent of the copyright owner.

12

Refrigerator / Freezer

Use Existing	Furnished by			Installed by		
☐Yes ☒No	KS ☒		O/OA ☐	KS ☒		O/OA ☐

Type	#1	#2	#3	Features	#1	#2	#3
Single Door Refrigerator				Ice Maker	x		
Single Door Freezer				Ice Dispenser (Door)	x		
Refrigerator / Freezer:							
Side by Side				Mini-Door Access			
Top Mount				Water Disp. (Outside)	x		
Bottom Mount	x			LCD Screen			
Undercounter							
Modular Units:							
Refrigerator Drawers				Other Features	#1	#2	#3
Freezer Drawers							
Freezer:							
Upright							
Chest							
Installation	#1	#2	#3	Other Cooling Appliances			
Free-Standing				☐Ice Maker		☒Wine Storage	
Boxed-In	x						
Integrated							
Under-Counter							
Decorative Panels							

Dishwasher

Use Existing	Furnished by		Installed by	
☐Yes ☒No	KS ☒	O/OA ☐	KS ☒	O/OA ☐

Type	#1	#2	Interior Finish	#1	#2
Door	x		Plastic		
Drawers			Stainless	x	
Installation	#1	#2	Dishwasher Features	#1	#2
Built-In			Adjustable Shelves	x	
Integrated with Decorative Panel to Match Cabinets			Flatware Trays	x	
Stainless Steel	x		Multiple Racks		
Color Front			Special Cycles		
			Stem Storage		

Other Clean-Up Appliances

Use Existing	Furnished by		Installed by	
☐Yes ☒No	KS ☐	O/OA ☐	KS ☒	O/OA ☐

Type	#1	#2	#3	Type	#1	#2	#3
Disposer:				Trash Compactor			
Batch Feed	x						
Continuous Feed							

Other Appliances

Use Existing	Furnished by		Installed by	
☐Yes ☒No	KS ☒	O/OA ☐	KS ☒	O/OA ☐

Type:

☐Built –In Small Appliances	☐Computer	☐Intercom	☐VCR / DVD	☒Warming Drawer	☐Washer / Dryer
☒Radio	☒Telephone	☒Television	☐Other:_____	☐Other:_____	☐Other:_____

End of Appliance & Fixture Specifications - Option 2

©2006 NKBA BMF8

13

Copyright 2006 by NKBA. All rights reserved. No part of this document may be reproduced in any form by photostat, microfilm, xerography, or any other means, or incorporated into any informational retrieval system, electronic or mechanical, or transmitted, in any form or by any means, without the prior consent of the copyright owner.

Flooring

Use Existing	Furnished by		Installed by	
☐Yes ☒No	KS ☒	O/OA ☐	KS ☒	O/OA ☐

Floor Preparation

☒Removal:_____

☒Leveling:_____

☒Shim:_____

☐Subfloor Material:_____

☒Underlayment:_____

☒Baseboard Under Trim:_____

☒Transition Treatment_____

Floor Covering

Material

☐Bamboo	☐Carpet	☐Ceramic Tile	☐Cork
☐Laminate	☐Linoleum	☐Vinyl-Sheet	☐Vinyl-Tile
☒Wood	☐Wood-Engineered	☐Stone	☐Other:___

Color or Pattern:

Describe: oak

Windows

Check all that apply.

Slider = S   Casement = C   Double-Hung = DH   Skylight = SL   Bow = BO   Bay = BA
Vinyl = V   Aluminum = A   Aluminum Clad = AC   Wood = W   Glass Block = GB

Use Existing	Furnished by		Installed by	
☐Yes ☒No	KS ☒	O/OA ☐	KS ☒	O/OA ☐

Interior Wall Patch:_____   Exterior Wall Patch:_____   Sink Vent Relocation:_____

Window #	Configuration	Size	Screen
		Screen	
1 BO			Screen: ☐Yes ☒No
			Screen: ☐Yes ☐No
			Screen: ☐Yes ☐No
			Screen: ☐Yes ☐No
			Screen: ☐Yes ☐No
			Screen: ☐Yes ☐No

Doors

Check all that apply.

Bi-Fold = BF   Slider = S   Pocket = P   French = F   Swing = SW
Solid Core = SC   Steel = ST   Hollow Core = HC

Use Existing	Furnished by		Installed by	
☐Yes ☒No	KS ☒	O/OA ☐	KS ☒	O/OA ☐

Door #	Configuration	Hinge	Size	Screen
door #1 SW		☒L ☐R		Screen: ☐Yes ☒No
door #2 S		☐L ☐R		Screen: ☒Yes ☐No
		☐L ☐R		Screen: ☐Yes ☐No
		☐L ☐R		Screen: ☐Yes ☐No
		☐L ☐R		Screen: ☐Yes ☐No
		☐L ☐R		Screen: ☐Yes ☐No
		☐L ☐R		Screen: ☐Yes ☐No

Hardware Finish: brushed nickel _____   ☐Passage ☐Privacy ☐Knob ☒Lever

(Note: Door hinging determined as you face door and open toward you.)

Decorative Surfaces

Use Existing	Furnished by		Installed by	
☐Yes ☒No	KS ☒	O/OA ☐	KS ☒	O/OA ☐
Wall Preparation	☐New Plaster/Drywall	☐Clean ☒Patch Exist	☐Remove Exist. Covering:____	
Wall Finish	☒Paint	☐Wallpaper ☐Tile	☐Other	
Ceiling Finish	☒Paint ☐Wallpaper	☐Suspended ☐Vaulted	☐Other:____	
Ceiling Preparation	☐New Plaster/Drywall	☐Clean ☒Patch Exist	☐Remove Exist. Covering:____	
	☐Other:____	☐Repairs:____		
Window Treatment	☐Blinds ☒Fabric	☐Shutters	☐Other:____	

©2006 NKBA BMF8

Copyright 2006 by NKBA. All rights reserved. No part of this document may be reproduced in any form by photostat, microfilm, xerography, or any other means, or incorporated into any informational retrieval system, electronic or mechanical, or transmitted, in any form or by any means, without the prior consent of the copyright owner.

14

Construction	Source			Category
	Use Existing	**Responsibility**		
		KS	O/OA	
HVAC Details: update cooking ventillation ductwork as needed	☐Yes ☒No	☒	☐	Air Conditioning System Age: _original_ Planned Improvements: _none_ Heating System Age: _original_ Planned Improvements: _none_ Cooking Ventilation Ductwork Age: _original_ Planned Improvements: _yes, as needed_
Electrical Work Details:	☐Yes ☒No	☒	☐	New Service Panel: Code Updates: Modifications to Exist. Service:
Plumbing:	☐Yes ☒No	☒	☐	New Rough-In Requirements: New Drainage Requirements: New Vent Stack Requirements: Modifications to Exist. Lines: _add waterline for icemaker_
General Carpentry	☐Yes ☐No	☒	☐	Demolition Work: Exist. Fixture and Equip. Removal: Trash Removal: _to trash container in driveway_ **Reconstruction Work (Except as previously noted.)** Windows: Doors: Interior Walls: Exterior Walls: Cabinet Install. / Woodworking Trim Install:
Miscellaneous Work Details:	☐Yes ☐No	☒	☐	Jobsite / Room Clean-up: Building Permit(s): _as required_ Structural Engineering / Architectural Fees: Inspection Fees: _as required_ Jobsite Delivery: _to garage_ Other:

©2006 NKBA BMF8

Copyright 2006 by NKBA. All rights reserved. No part of this document may be reproduced in any form by photostat, microfilm, xerography, or any other means, or incorporated into any informational retrieval system, electronic or mechanical, or transmitted, in any form or by any means, without the prior consent of the copyright owner.

Existing Construction Details

1. *Age of Home:* built in 1975   *Access Roads to Home:* ample

   Delivery Truck Clearances: yes   *Elevator Size Limitations:*

2. *Type of Neighborhood:*
   ☐Rural ☒Suburban ☐Urban ☐Historic ☐Mixed Use ☐Multi-Family ☐Gated Community ☐Planned Development

3. *Type of Home:*
   ☒Single Family ☐Duplex ☐Townhouse ☐Condominium ☐Apartment/Flat ☐Other:

4. *Structure of Home:*
   ☐One-Story ☒Two-Story ☐Three-Story ☐Ranch ☐Split-Level ☐Split-Foyer/Raised Ranch ☐Other:

5. *Approximate Size of Home:* 2800 sf

6. *Style of Home (Exterior):* colonial

7. *Is the home historic?*   ☐Yes ☒No   What time period?
   Are there historic covenants or restrictions affecting the home?

8. *Is the home part of a Homeowner's Association?* ☐Yes ☒No
   Is there Homeowner's Association covenants or restrictions affecting the home? ☐Yes ☐No

9. *Style of Home (Interior)*   traditional
   Colors: neutral
   Materials: wood
   Furniture: traditional
   Accessories:
   Other:

10. *Room Below Kitchen* basement

©2006 NKBA BMF8

Copyright 2006 by NKBA. All rights reserved. No part of this document may be reproduced in any form by photostat, microfilm, xerography, or any other means, or incorporated into any informational retrieval system, electronic or mechanical, or transmitted, in any form or by any means, without the prior consent of the copyright owner.

16

Existing Construction Details- continued

11. *Condition of –*

Surface Walls   good

Floors: good

Ceilings: good

Soffit / Fascia: good

Squareness of Corners: good   (Parallel Wall to Within ¾)

Is there any hazardous material to be removed? no

12. *Construction of Floor:* ☐Slab ☒Frame

13. *Direction of Floor Joists*: ☐Parallel to Longest Kitchen Wall ☒Perpendicular to Longest Kitchen Wall   Joist Height: 10"

14. *Exterior:* ☐Brick ☐Aluminum ☐Stucco ☐Wood ☒Other: vinyl siding

15. *Interior:* ☒Drywall ☐Lath & Plaster ☐Wood ☐Other:

16. *Windows Can Be Changed:* ☒Yes ☐No *Doors Can Be Relocated:* ☒Yes ☐No *Walls Can Be Relocated:* ☐Yes ☒No

17. *Windows:* ☐Sliders ☒Double Hung ☐Skylights ☐Casement ☐Greenhouse ☐Bow/Bay ☐Other:

18. *Sewage System:* ☐City Service ☒Septic System ☐Other:

19. *Type of Roof Material:* asphalt   *Age of Roof:* 6 years

Access:

Can Equipment Fit Into The Room? yes

Basement: full access   Attic: limited   Crawl Space:

Material Storage: garage   Trash Collection Area: trash container in driveway

HVAC: Describe Existing System: Heating: central   Ventilation: Air Conditioning: central

Plumbing:

Location of Existing Vent Stack: right of window   Type of Trap: P

Add Additional Line:

Electrical

GFCI Existing: ☐Yes ☒No

New Wiring Access: ☐Hard ☒Average ☐Easy   Number of Circuits Open for Expansion: 8

Existing Electrical Service Capacity: 200   Number of 120V Circuits: 22   Number of 240V Circuits: 5

©2006 NKBA BMF8   17

Copyright 2006 by NKBA. All rights reserved. No part of this document may be reproduced in any form by photostat, microfilm, xerography, or any other means, or incorporated into any informational retrieval system, electronic or mechanical, or transmitted, in any form or by any means, without the prior consent of the copyright owner.

Appliance Diagram

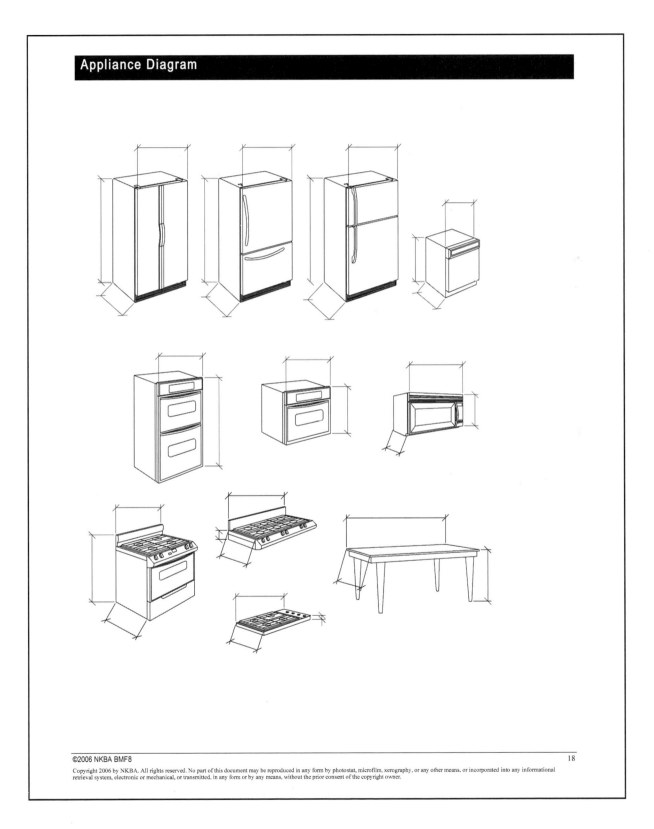

©2006 NKBA BMF8

Copyright 2006 by NKBA. All rights reserved. No part of this document may be reproduced in any form by photostat, microfilm, xerography, or any other means, or incorporated into any informational retrieval system, electronic or mechanical, or transmitted, in any form or by any means, without the prior consent of the copyright owner.

18

Windows and Doors Diagram

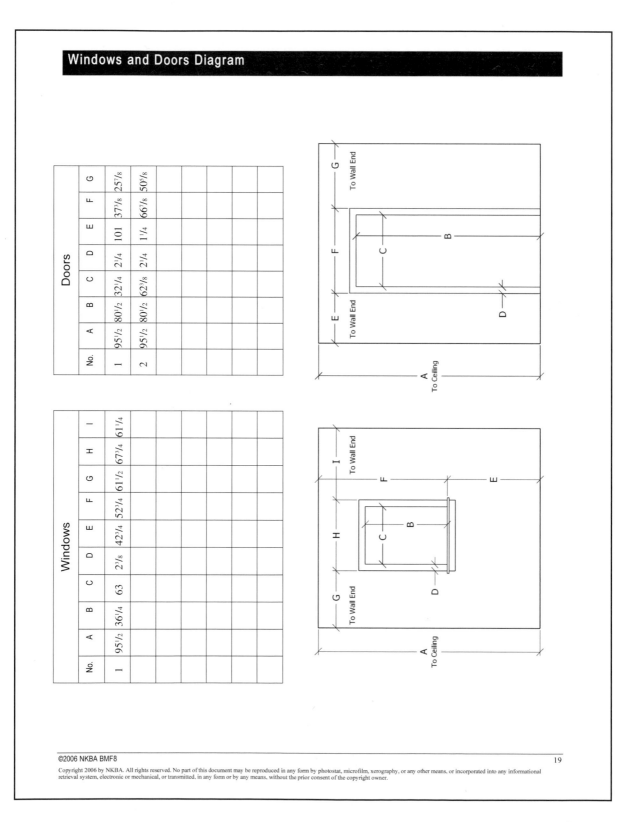

Doors

No.	A	B	C	D	E	F	G
1	95½	80½	32¼	2¼	101	37⅞	25⅞
2	95½	80½	62⅜	2¼	1¼	66⅞	50⅝

Windows

No.	A	B	C	D	E	F	G	H	I
1	95½	36¼	63	2⅜	42¾	52¾	61½	67¾	61¼

©2006 NKBA BMF8

Copyright 2006 by NKBA. All rights reserved. No part of this document may be reproduced in any form by photostat, microfilm, xerography, or any other means, or incorporated into any informational retrieval system, electronic or mechanical, or transmitted, in any form or by any means, without the prior consent of the copyright owner.

19

Heating Diagram

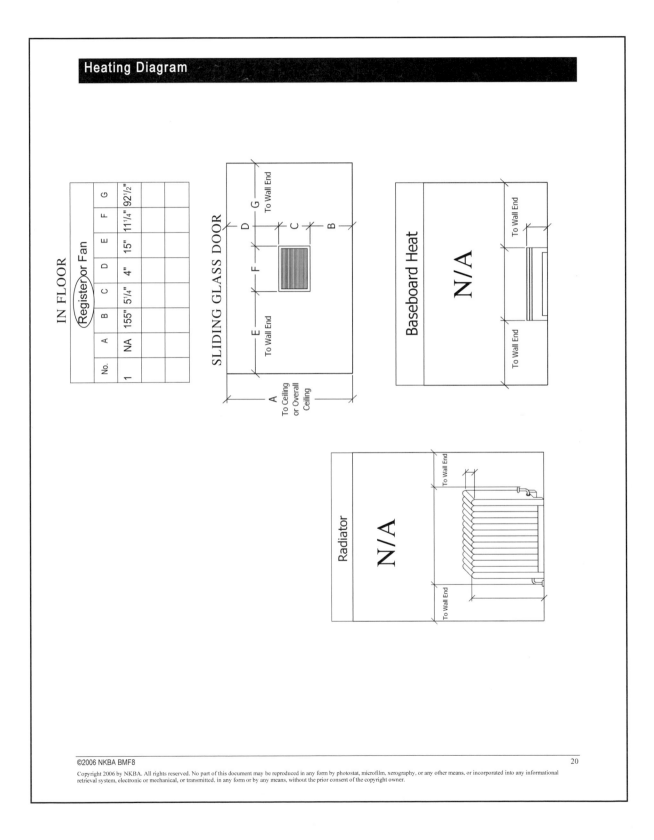

IN FLOOR

Register or Fan

No.	A	B	C	D	E	F	G
1	NA	155"	5¹/₄"	4"	15"	11¹/₄"	92¹/₂"

SLIDING GLASS DOOR

A — To Ceiling or Overall Ceiling

Baseboard Heat

N/A

Radiator

N/A

©2006 NKBA BMF8

Copyright 2006 by NKBA. All rights reserved. No part of this document may be reproduced in any form by photostat, microfilm, xerography, or any other means, or incorporated into any informational retrieval system, electronic or mechanical, or transmitted, in any form or by any means, without the prior consent of the copyright owner.

20

LIST OF PHOTOS

Chapter 1

1.1   1920s range 7

1.2   1930s kitchen 9

1.3   1980s Islands 13

1.4   Unfitted furniture look 15

1.5   Professional-style appliances 17

1.6   Kitchen open to a family room 21

1.7   Multiple height counters 22

1.8   Kitchen with minimal wall cabinets 23

1.9   Refrigerator with television and Internet . . . 25

1.10   Drawer dishwasher 26

1.11   Outdoor kitchen 27

Chapter 2

2.1   Sink most frequently used area 31

2.2   People still cook regularly 35

2.3   Hand washing dishes at the sink 38

2.4   Consumers want more storage 40

Chapter 4

4.5   Water filtration devices 69

4.6   A touchless faucet 72

4.9   Recycling systems 82

4.10   Recycling storage containers 84

4.11   Compost bin 86

Chapter 5

5.14   Side-by-side refrigeration 107

5.15   Pull-out step stool 108

5.16   Single-lever faucet 109

5.17   Digital and pictorial oven controls 110

5.18   Induction cooktop 111

5.19   Taller laundry appliances 112

5.20   Taller ovens 113

Chapter 7

7.1   U-shaped kitchen 205

7.2   Parallel or galley kitchen 206

7.3   G-shaped kitchen 207

7.4   L-shaped kitchen 208

7.5   One-wall kitchen 209

7.6   Corridor kitchen 210

7.7   Island kitchen 211

7.8   Angled kitchen 212

7.16   Pot racks and open shelving 219

7.31   A pop-up mixer stand 235

7.33   Cleanup sink and dishwasher 237

7.37   (A & B) Waste and recycling bins 239

7.38   A second or auxiliary sink 240

7.39   Undercounter refrigerators 242

7.42   Cooktop and sink at a right angle 246

7.43   Cooktop controls located in the center 246

7.49   (A, B & C) Microwave locations 251

7.64   Island base cabinets for storage 269

7.78   Storage organizers: a) Customizable drawer
       b) Rack storage c) Roll-out tray and lid
       dividers d) Tilt-out storage 290

7.79   Pantry shelf configurations 291

7.85   Outdoor kitchen 304

7.86   Portable patio heaters 305

7.87   Mini kitchen 307

Chapter 8

8.6   Hood styles 324

8.7   Proximity ventilation system 325

8.9   A "pop-up" or telescoping ventilation fan . . 329

8.10   Kitchen lit with window and ceiling
       fixtures 337

8.11   Accent lighting 339

8.12   Kitchen with general, task and accent
       lighting 341

Chapter 9

9.1	Family foyer	347
9.2	Mudroom	348
9.3	Storage for bulky coats and jackets	350
9.6	Small home planning center	355
9.7	Compact planning center desk	356
9.12	Raised front-loading washer and dryer	367
9.15	Concealed ironing board	375
9.16	Planning desk and craft area	377
9.16	Gardening area	380
9.17	Potting area	381
9.18	Sink with slatted insert	382
9.19	Kitchen integrated with living and bar/ serving area	385
9.20a	Kitchen open to a social space	386
9.20b	Kitchen adjoining separate social space	387

Chapter 10

10.1	Undercounter microwave	397
10.2	Pull-down storage	398
10.3	Undercounter refrigeration	399
10.4	Separate cooktop/oven	403
10.6	Raised dishwasher	409
10.7	Knee space	410
10.8	Digital and pictorial oven controls	411
10.9	Door and drawer pulls	413
10.10	Faucet with lever/loop handles	414
10.11	Smoothtop cooking surface	415
10.12	Rolling storage unit	416
10.13	Interior cabinet lighting	418
10.14	Controls raised from cooktop	419
10.15	Tambour sliding doors	420
10.16	Overhead ventilation with eased edge	423
10.17	Facing work centers	424
10.18	Cooktop with heat indicators and control locks	427

LIST OF DRAWINGS
AND ILLUSTRATIONS

Chapter 3

3.1   Piping or wiring within the floor structure . . 45

3.2   Extra floor supports 46

3.3   Leveling uneven floors 47

3.4   Load-bearing wall 48

3.5   Door styles and swings 52

3.6   Window options 54

3.7   Water shut-off valves 56

3.8   Drain, waste and vent pipes 58

3.9   On-demand water heater 60

Chapter 4

4.1   Energy-efficient windows 62

4.2   The Energy Star logo 63

4.3   Water classifications 66

4.4   Water treatment methods 68

4.7   Condensation 81

4.8   Vapor retarder 81

4.12   Noise control 88

4.13   Building techniques to reduce sound
        transmission 90

Chapter 5

5.1   Body measurements 93

5.2   Adult female vertical reach height sitting . . . 95

5.3   Vertical grip reach 96

5.4   Side arm grip reach 97

5.5   Thumb tip reach 98

5.6   Reach ranges 99

5.7   Range of motion in spine and shoulders . . . 100

5.8   Spatial clearances with mobility aids 101

5.9   Minimum clearances with a walker 102

5.10   Clearance dimensions for user and dog . . . 102

5.11   Measurements for a person using a chair . . 103

5.12   Shared space minimum dimensions 104

5.13   Height and breadth of children, standing
        and seated 105

Chapter 6

6.1   NKBA Kitchen Design Survey Forms 123

Form 1: Getting to Know Your Client 136-142

Form 2: Getting to Know Your Client's Home . 143-144

Form 3: Checklist for Kitchen Activities (Client
        Checklist) 145-149

Form 4: Kitchen Storage Inventory (Client
        Checklist) 150-165

Form 5: Cabinetry, Surfaces, and Kitchen Features
        Checklist (Client Checklist) 166-178

Form 6: Appliance Preference Checklist
        (Client Checklist) 179-188

Form 7: Job Site Inspection 189-195

Form 8: Dimensions of the Kitchen – Floor Plan . 196

Form 9: Dimensions of the Kitchen – Elevations . 197

Form 10: Dimensions of Mechanical Devices 198

Form 11: Window Measurements 199

Form 12: Door Measurements 200

Form 13: Fixture and Appliance Measurements
        201-202

Chapter 7

7.1   U-shaped kitchen 205

7.2   Parallel or galley kitchen 206

7.3   G-shaped kitchen 207

7.4   L-shaped kitchen 208

7.6   Corridor kitchen 210

7.7   Island kitchen 211

7.9   Determining kitchen size 213

7.10   Maximum reach over base cabinet 215

7.11   A work surface width 215

7.12   Base cabinet 217

7.13   Drawer base cabinet 217

7.14   Typical wall cabinet. 218
7.15   Tall cabinets 219
7.17   Work-surface height. 220
7.18   Kitchen Planning Guideline 1 223
7.19   Kitchen Planning Access Standard 2 224
7.20   Kitchen Planning Guideline 2 224
7.21   Kitchen Planning Guideline 6 225
7.22   Kitchen Access Standard 6 226
7.23   Kitchen Access Standard 6 226
7.24   Kitchen Access Standard 6 227
7.25   Kitchen Planning Guideline 7 227
7.26   Kitchen Planning Guideline 10 231
7.27   Kitchen Planning Guideline 11 232
7.28   Recommended landing area 233
7.29   Kitchen Planning Guideline 11 233
7.30   Preparation/work area 234
7.32   Knee space at a counter 236
7.34   Kitchen Planning Guideline 13 238
7.35   Kitchen Planning Guideline 13 238
7.36   Kitchen Planning Guideline 13 238
7.40   Kitchen Planning Guideline 16 243
7.41   Kitchen Planning Guideline 16 243
7.44   Kitchen Planning Guideline 20 247
7.45   Kitchen Planning Guideline 17 248
7.46   Kitchen Planning Guideline 17 248
7.47   Kitchen Planning Guideline 18 249
7.48   Kitchen Planning Guideline 18 250
7.50   Kitchen Planning Guideline 21 252
7.51   Kitchen Planning Guideline 21 253
7.52   Kitchen Planning Guideline 22 254
7.53   Landing area for a separate oven 256
7.54   Kitchen Planning Guideline 3 258
7.55   Kitchen Planning Guideline 3 259
7.56   Multiple work triangles 259
7.57   Kitchen Planning Guideline 4 260
7.58   Kitchen Planning Guideline 4 260
7.59   Kitchen Planning Guideline 5 261
7.60   Kitchen Planning Guideline 24 262

7.61   Kitchen Planning Guideline 25 264
7.62   Kitchen Planning Guideline 25 264
7.63   Kitchen Planning Guideline 26 265
7.65   Wall cabinet shelf frontage 271
7.66   Base cabinet shelf frontage 272
7.67   Drawer frontage 273
7.68   Pantry cabinet shelf frontage. 274
7.69   Blind cabinet shelf frontage 275
7.70   L-shaped cabinet shelf frontage 276
7.71   L corner with Lazy Susan shelf frontage. . 277
7.72   Diagonal cabinet shelf frontage 278
7.73   Storage in a small kitchen 279
7.74   Calculating storage 280
7.75   Cabinet Calculation Charts 282-287
7.76   Kitchen Planning Guideline 28 288
7.77   Kitchen Planning Guideline 29 289
7.80   Serving areas 293
7.81   Butler's pantry 295
7.82   Kitchen Planning Guideline 8 297
7.83   Sizes and shapes of various tables. . . . 298-299
7.84   Kitchen Planning Guideline 9 300

Chapter 8
8.1   GFCI. 313
8.2   Mechanical plan. 314
8.3   Heating/cooling vent locations 317
8.4   Radiant floor system tubing 319
8.5   Radiant floor heating system. 319
8.8   Hood size and placement 327

Chapter 9
9.4   Closet rod heights 350
9.5   Access to hangers 351
9.8   Desk top minimum size. 357
9.9   Adjustable height desk chair 358
9.10   File drawer clearance. 360
9.11   Computer workstation 363
9.13a   Clearance in front of laundry equipment . . 370

9.13b Cearances for a side-by-side washer
and dryer 370

9.13c Clearances for washer and dryer on
opposite sides 370

9.13d Clearances for washer and dryer at right
angles 370

9.14 Ironing area space 374

9.21 Common furniture sizes 389

Chapter 10

10.5 Clear floor space for person using
mobility aid 406-408

Chapter 11

11.1 User Analysis chart 435

11.2 Relationship matrix 436

11.3 Bubble diagram 437

11.4a Design template for sink center 439

11.4b Simplified template of the sink center 439

11.4c Simplified elevation view of sink center
template 440

11.5a Existing kitchen floor plan with project
parameters 442

11.5b Altered kitchen outline plan 443

11.6 Visual diagram of new kitchen 444

11.7 Rough elevation sketch of sink center wall . 446

11.8 a, b & c Sequence of placing items in the
sink center 448-449

11.9 Continued design of sink center 450

11.10 Continued design: kitchen shape evolves . . 451

11.11 Continued design: locking in the peninsula . 452

11.12 Continued design: completing sink
center wall 453

11.13 Continued design: adding wall cabinets . . . 454

11.14 Continued design: elevation of sink
center wall 459

11.15 Continued design: completing the elevation. 460

11.16 Kitchen Planning Guidelines Checklist
. . . . 462-463

11.17 Kitchen Planning Access Standards
Checklist 464-465

11.18 Leah and Matthew's existing kitchen 467

11.19 User Analysis for baking area 469

11.20 Bubble diagram for Leah and Matthew's
remodeled kitchen 470

11.21 Visual diagram of Leah and Matthew's
kitchen 470

11.22 Design drawing for Leah and Matthew's
new kitchen 471

11.23 Elevation of the baking area 471

11.24 Evaluation of kitchen design 472

11.25 Calculating shelf/drawer frontage 473

Chapter 12

Kitchen Planning Guidelines and Access
Standards 1-31 476-512

Chapter 2

Beecher, C. E., & Stowe, H. B. (1869).
The American woman's home.
New York: J. B. Ford & Co.

Carter, D. (1932).
Studies in the design of kitchens and kitchen equipment.
Arkansas Agricultural Experiment Station Bulletin
276. Fayetteville.

Cheever, E. M. (1992).
*Kitchen planning and safety standards:
Kitchen industry technical manuals, Vol. 4.*
Hackettstown, NJ: National Kitchen and Bath
Association.

Cheever, E. M. (1996).
*Kitchen planning and safety standards: Kitchen
industry technical manuals, Vol. 4 (3rd ed.).*
Hackettstown, NJ: National Kitchen and Bath
Association.

Cushman, E. (1936).
The development of a successful kitchen.
Cornell Bulletin for Homemakers 354. Ithaca, NY.

Emmel, J. M., Beamish, J & Parrott, K. (2001)
*Someone's in the kitchen: Summary of findings from
the kitchen space and storage research project.*
Virginia Tech, Blacksburg, VA.

Frederick, C. (1913).
*The new housekeeping: Efficiency studies in
home management.*
Garden City, NY: Doubleday, Page, & Co.

Heiner, M. K., & McCullough, H. E. (1948).
FinctionalFunctional Kitchen Storage.
Cornell University Agricultural Experiment Station
Bulletin 846, IthicaIthaca, NY.

Heiner, M.K., & Steidl, R. E. (1951).
Guides for arrangement of urban family kitchens.
Cornell University Agricultural Experiment Station
Bulletin 878. Ithaca, NY.

Howard, M.S. (1965).
*Development of the Beltsville Energy-Saving
Kitchens, Final report, Project CH 2-14.*
Agricultural Research Service, U.S. Department of
Agriculture. Beltsville, MD.

Jones, R. A., & Kapple, W. H. (1975).
Kitchen industry technical manual, Vol. 5.
National Kitchen and Bath Association and
Small Homes Council. Urbana-Champaign:
University of Illinois.

Jones, R. A., & Kapple, W. H. (1984)
Kitchen industry technical manual, Vol. 5. (2nd ed.).
National Kitchen and Bath Association and the
Small Homes Council. Urbana-Champaign:
University of Illinois.

Kapple, W. H. (1964).
Kitchen planning standards.
Small Homes Council – Building Research Council
Circular Series C5.32. Urbana: University of
Illinois Press.

Parrott, K., Beamish, J., & Emmel, J. (2003).
Kitchen Storage Research Project.
Virginia Tech, Blacksburg, VA.

McCullough, H. E. (1949).
Cabinet space for the kitchen.
Small Homes Council Circular Series C5.31.
Urbana: University of Illinois Press.

Wanslow, R. (1965).
Kitchen planning guide.
Small Homes Council – Building Research Council.
Urbana-Champaign: University of Illinois.

Wilson, M. (1938).
The Willamette Valley farm kitchen.
Corvallis: Oregon State University Agricultural
Experiment Station.

Wilson, M. (1947).
Considerations in planning kitchen cabinets.
Oregon State University Agricultural Experiment
Station Bulletin 445, Corvallis.

Wilson, M. (1947).
Patterns for kitchen cabinets.
Oregon State Agricultural Experiment Station
Bulletin 446. Corvallis.

Wilson, M. & McCullough, H. E. (1940).
A set of utensils for the farm kitchen.
Oregon State Agricultural Experiment Station
Circular 134. Corvallis.

Yust, B. L., & Olsen, W. W. (1992).
*Residential kitchens: Planning principles
for the 1990's.*

In Cheever, E. M.
*Kitchen planning and safety standards:
Kitchen industry technical manuals, vol. 4.*
Hackettstown, NJ: National Kitchen and
Bath Association.

Chapter 4

American Lung Association
61 Broadway, 6th Floor
NY, NY 10006
www.lungusa.org

Children's Environmental Health Network
110 Maryland Avenue NE, Suite 505
Washington, DC 20002
www.cehn.org

Energy Star
www.energystar.gov
www.oee.nrcan.gc.ca/energystar

**Environmental Health Center,
National Safety Council**
1121 Spring Lake Drive
Itasca, IL 60143-3201
www.nsc.org/ehc.htm

Health Canada
Brooke Claxton Building
Ottawa, Ontario
K1A 0K9
www.hc-sc.gc.ca

Healthy Indoor Air for America's Homes
Montana State University Extension Service,
Taylor Hall
Bozeman, MT 59717
www.healthyindoorair.org

**Help Yourself to a Healthy Home
(An Environmental Risk-Assessment Guide for
the Home)**
303 Hiram Smith Hall
1545 Observatory Drive
Madison, WI 53706
www.uwex.edu/homeasyst

**National Center for Environmental Health,
Center for Disease Control**
1600 Clifton Rd.
Atlanta, GA
www.cdc.gov/nceh

**National Institute of Environmental Health
Sciences**
111 T.W. Alexander Drive
Research Triangle Park, NC 27709
www.niehs.nih.gov

Office of Energy Efficiency
580 Booth St., 18th floor
Natural Resources Canada
Ottawa, ON K1A 0E4
www.oee.nrcan.gc.ca

U.S. Environmental Protection Agency
Ariel Rios Building
1200 Pennsylvania Avenue, N.W.
Washington, DC 20460
www.epa.gov

U.S. Green Building Council
1015 18th Street, NW, Suite 508
Washington, DC 20036
www.usgbc.org

Water Quality Association
International Headquarters & Laboratory
4151 Naperville Road
Lisle, IL 60532-3696
www.wqa.org

Chapter 5

United States Access Board
1331 F Street, NW, Suite 1000
Washington, DC 20004-1111
www.access-board.gov

Barrier Free Architecturals
2788 Bathurst St.
Suite 219
Toronto, ON M6B 3A3
www.barrierfree.org

Canada Mortgage and Housing Corp.
700 Montreal Rd.
Ottawa, ON KIA OP7
www.cmhc-schl.gc.ca

**U.S. Department of Housing
and Urban Development**
451 7th Street S.W.
Washington, DC 20410
www.hud.gov

Chapter 10

Abledata
8630 Fenton Street, Suite 930
Silver Spring, MD 20910
www.abledata.com

Access One
25679 Gramford Avenue
Wyoming, MN 55092
www.beyondbarriers.com

Adaptive Environments
374 Congress Street, Suite 301
Boston, MA 02210
www.adaptiveenvironments.org

AARP American Association of Retired Persons
601 E Street NW
Washington, DC 20049
www.aarp.org

Alzheimer's Association
225 North Michigan Avenue, Suite 1700
Chicago, IL 60601-7633
www.alz.org

Alzheimer's Disease Education & Referral Center
ADEAR Center
P.O. Box 8250
Silver Spring, MD 20907-8250
www.alzheimers.org

American Foundation for the Blind
11 Penn Plaza, Suite 300
New York, NY 10001
www.afb.org

American Heart Association National Center
7272 Greenville Avenue
Dallas, TX 75231
www.americanheart.org

American National Standards Institute
1819 L Street, NW, 6th floor
Washington, D.C., 20036
www.ansi.org

American Occupational Therapy Association
4720 Montgomery Lane
P.O. Box 31220
Bethesda, MD 20850
www.aota.org

American Stroke Association
National Center
7272 Greenville Avenue
Dallas, TX 75231
www.strokeassociation.org

Amputee Coalition of America
900 East Hill Avenue, Suite 285
Knoxville, TN 37915-2568
www.amputee-coalition.org

Area Agencies on Aging
www.aoa.dhhs.gov/agingsites/state.html

Arthritis Foundation
1330 West Peachtree Street
P.O. Box 7669
Atlanta, GA 30309
www.arthritis.org

**Center for Inclusive Design and Environmental
Access (IDEA Center)**
School of Architecture and Planning
University of Buffalo
378 Hayes Hall, School of Architecture & Planning
3435 Main Street
University at Buffalo
Buffalo, NY 14214-3087
www.ap.buffalo.edu/idea/

The Center for Universal Design
North Carolina State University
50 Pullen Road
Brooks Hall, Room 104
Campus Box 8613
Raleigh, NC 27695
www.design.ncsu.edu:8120/cud

Council for Exceptional Children
1110 North Glebe Road, Suite 300
Arlington, VA 22201
www.cec.sped.org

Cystic Fibrosis Foundation
6931 Arlington Road
Bethesda, MD 20814
www.cff.org

Disabled American Veterans
807 Maine Ave., S.W.
Washington, D.C. 20024
www.dav.org

Disability Rights Education Defense Fund
1730 M Street N.W. Suite 801
Washington, DC 20036
www.dredf.org

Easter Seal Society
230 West Monroe Street, Suite 1800
Chicago, IL 60606
www.easter-seals.org

Eldercare Locator
c/o Administration on Aging
220 Independence Avenue SW
Washington, DC 20201
www.eldercare.gov

Harris Communications, Inc.
15155 Technology Drive
Eden Prairie, MN 55344-2277
www.harriscomm.com

Home Modification List Serve
Homemodification-list@listserv.acsu.buffalo.edu

Independent Living Research Utilization Project
2323 South Shepard Street, Suite 1000
Houston, TX 77019
www.ilru.org

Lifease Inc.
2451 15th St N.W., Suite D
New Brighton, MN 55112
www.lifease.com

Lighthouse International
111 East 59th Street
New York, N.Y. 10022-1202
www.lighthouse.org

Muscular Dystrophy Association
3300 East Sunrise Drive
Tucson, AZ 85718
www.mdausa.org

National Association of the Deaf
814 Thayer Avenue
Silver Spring, MD 20910-4500
www.nad.org

National Council on Independent Living
1916 Wilson Boulevard, Suite 209
Arlington, VA 22201
www.ncil.org

National Institute on Aging
Building 31, Room 5C27
31 Center Drive, MSC 2292
Bethesda, MD 20892
www.nia.nih.gov/

National Institute on Deafness and Other Communication Disorders
National Institutes of Health
31 Center Drive, MSC 2320
Bethesda, MD USA 20892-2320
www.nidcd.nih.gov

National Institute on Disability and Rehabilitation Research
US Department of Education
400 Maryland Avenue, S.W.
Washington, DC 20202-2572
www.ed.gov/about/offices/list/osers/nidrr/index.html?
src=mr

National Kitchen & Bath Association
687 Willow Grove Street
Hackettstown, NJ 07840
www.nkba.org

National Rehabilitation Information Center
4200 Forbes Boulevard, Suite 202,
Lanham, MD 20706
www.naric.com

National Resource Center on Supportive Housing and Home Modifications,
Andrus Gerontology Center,
University of Southern California
3715 McClintock Avenue
Los Angeles, CA 90089-0191
www.homemods.org

Paralyzed Veterans of America
801 Eighteenth Street, NW
Washington, DC 20006-3517
www.pva.org

ProMatura Group, LLC
142 Hwy 30 E
Oxford, MS 38655
www.promatura.com

Regional ADA technical assistant centers
www.adata.org

Rehabilitation Engineering and Assistive Technology Society of North America (RESNA)
1700 North Moore Street
Suite 1540
Arlington, VA 22209-1903
www.resna.org

Trace Research and Development Center
University of Wisconsin
2107 Engineering Centers Bldg.
1500 Highland Avenue
Madison, WI 53706
www.trace.wisc.edu

U.S. Access Board
1331 F Street, NW
Suite 1000
Washington, DC 20004-1111
www.access-board.gov

U.S. Dept. of Housing and Urban Dev.
Tech. assist. on Section 504 & Fair
www.hud.gov/fhe/fheo.html

U.S. Dept. of Justice
Tech. Assist. on ADA
950 Pennsylvania Avenue, NW
Civil Rights Division
Disability Rights Section – NYAV
Washington, D.C. 20530
www.usdoj.gov/crt/ada/adahom1.htm

Visitability List Serve
visitability-list@ACSU.buffalo.edu

Volunteers for Medical Engineering
2301 Argonne Drive
Baltimore, MD 21218
www.toad.net/~vme

"A Set of Utensils for the Farm Kitchen" 30

Abraham & Straus 8

Accent lighting 338-342

Access Standards xix, 221, 222, 224, 226, 241, 256, 291, 300, 308, 349, 394, 405, 406, 432, 434, 435, 439, 461, 465, 466, 475-512

Accessibility 222-226

Accessible and Useable Buildings and Facilities 116, 117, 222, 475

Accessible design (*see also* Universal design) 101-103, 105-120

Accessible Design for the Built Environment 118

Accessories 12, 289

Acrylics 11

Activities in the Kitchen Form 3 127-128, 145-149

Activity trends 24

Adaptable design 114

Aerator 67

Aging 394, 417, 400-404, 425

Aging population 19

Agricultural Experiment Station 29

Agricultural Research Service of Beltsville, MID 31

Air quality 78-79

Aisles 223, 225, 227, 261

Aluminum (cast) 11

Amana 11, 12

Ambient lighting 335, 336, 418

American Home Lighting Institute 337

American Modern dinnerware 11

American National Standards for Accessible and Useable Buildings and Facilities (ANSI A117.1) 116, 117, 222, 475

American National Standards Institute 101

American Society of Heating, Refrigeration and Air-conditioning Engineers (ASHRAE) 75, 330

American Woman's Home Companion 4

Americans with Disabilities Act 114, 119, 120

Americans with Disabilities Act Accessibility Guidelines 118

Amperes 310

Anthropometric measurements 214

Anthropometry 91-99, 104-105, 120

Antimicrobial finishes 80

Antiques 13

Appliance garage 14, 235, 263, 264, 312, 417

Appliance Measurements Form 13 132, 201-202

Appliance Preference Checklist (client checklist) 179-188

Appliances 25, 27-28, 37, 39, 42, 45-47, 63, (waste management) 83-87, 99, 110-113, 129-130, 216, 218, 224, 225, 226, 235, 243, 245, 248, 249, 250, 259, (garage) 263, 264, 311, 329, 331

Architectural Barriers Act 117

Armstrong Cork Company 6

Art Deco 8, 10

Artificial lighting 335

Asbestos 10, 11, 75

Asphalt-asbestos tiles 11

Assessing client needs 121-202

Assessment forms 122-202

Auxiliary sink 216, 228, 235, 240, 258, 294

Axial fan 332

Back-draft flap 330

Back-drafting 332

Bakelite 8

Baking 235, 468, 469, 471, 472, 474

Baking table 6

Balance 399, 401

Bar (eating) 22, 294, (juice) 306

Barrier-free design 114

Barrier Free Design Standards 118

Base cabinet 215, 216, 217, 220, 232, 239, 270-281, 284, 285, 288, 448, 450, 453-454, 459

Base cabinet shelf frontage 272

Baseboard heater 317

Batch feed disposer 396

Bath Planning 372

Beamish 33

Bedroom suite 27

Beecher, Catherine 4, 29

Beecher kitchen 4

Beehive ovens 4

Beer kegs 242

Bendix 11

Beverage station 294

"Bizarre" ceramics 8

Blind corner cabinet 275, 288

Blind wall cabinet 275

Breadth 94, 95

Breakfast nook 9

Broom cabinet 6

Bubble diagram 431, 436, 437, 438, 444, 445, 469, 470

Buffer zone 104

Building codes 43

Built-in cabinetry 9

Built-in kitchen 11

Burners 14, 27

Butcher block 13

Butler's pantry 294-295

"Cabinet Space for the Kitchen" 30

Cabinetry, Surface and Kitchen Features Form 5 130, 166-178

Cabinets (*see also* Wall cabinets) 130, 166-178, 215, 216, 217, 218, 220, 232, 239, 260, 268, 270-281, 282, 284, 285, 288, 289, 398, 439, 448, 450, 453-454, 455, 459, 510

Calculations (cabinets) 279-281, 282, 453

Canada Mortgage and Housing Corporation 61, 76, 90

Canada Mortgage and Housing Corporation's Healthy Housing Program 61

Canadian Code Center 118

Canadian Standards Association 118, 119

Canopy vent system 355

Carbon filters 65

Carpeting (indoor/outdoor) 13, 79, 86, 89, 457

Carter, Deane 29

Cast aluminum 11

Cast iron sink 8

Caterer kitchens 331-332

Ceiling vents 350

Center concept 214-222

Center for Real Life Kitchen Design 34

Center for Universal Design 106, 107

Centerline 479

Central heating system 346, 352

Centrifugal fan 363

Ceramic tiles 11, 12, 13, 444

Certified Kitchen Designers 32, 41, 213

Certified Kitchen and Bath Designer certification 123

Certified Kitchen Designer exam 32, 221

Charcoal filters 69

Charter of Rights and Freedoms 129

Checklist 123, 124, 128-130, 145, 150, 166, 179, 433

Cheever, Ellen 32, 33

Child anthropometry 104-105

Children 104, 395-398

Chlorine 69, 71

Chlorofluorocarbon 10

Chromium 10

Circuit breaker panel 341

Circuits 310-312, 353, 364, 368

Circulation 227, 261, 349

Cleanup 229, 237, 240, 259, 293

Clearances 248, 296, 297, 359

Client (checklist) 128-130, (interviewing) 122-124, (home) 125-126, 127, (preferences) 130-131, 394, 430, 457

Cliff, Clarice 8

Closet 349-351

Clothes washer 11, 73, 112, 312, 366-370

Closed kitchen arrangements 205-207

Code Requirements for Housing Accessibility 2000 117

Codes 43-44, 57, 114, 116-120, 307, 313, 344, 369

Cognition 425-428

Cold Climate Housing Information Center 77

Colonial furniture 11

Colonial kitchen 2

Colonial Revival 8

Color 8, 9, 10, 11, 12, 14, 16, 419, 426

Combining centers 257-291

Command central 21

Comfort zone 104

Compact fluorescent light 16

Compactor 12, 14, 84, 239, 396, 426

Compost bin 83-86, 229, 239

Composter 229

Computer 25, (workstation) 362-364, (programs) 434, 445

Communications (system) 315, (household) 361

Continuous disposer 428, 457

Controls 25, 28, (appliance) 258, (lighting) 373-374, 386, 450

Conservation (water) 73

"Considerations in Planning Kitchen Cabinets" 30

Construction 131

Cooking center 244-256, 397, 402-403, 427

Cooking surface 245, 247-250, 326-328, 496-500

Cooktop 111, 113, 244-246, 248, 316, (ventilation) 323-329, 397, 402-403, 410, 419, 427, 457, 497

Cooling 321-323

Cooperative Extension bulletins 29, 31

Cooperative Extension Service 29, 90

Coppes Brothers 6

Cork 6, 10, 87, 89

Corner cabinets 260, 275, 288, 289, 450, 453, 510

Corridor kitchen 5, 210

Counter areas 248, 261-265, 379, 472

Counter design 265

Countertop materials 7, 16

Countertop microwave 12, 251, 254, 255, 411

Countertops 22, 220, 232, 234, 243, 263, 416, 505, 506

Country kitchen 384

Country look 14

Craft area 376-378

Cueing 419, 425

Curved kitchen 212

Cushman, Ella 29

Custom cabinets 10

Daylighting 334-335

De Chiaro 101

Design drawing 438-471

Design goal 121

Design plan 28

Design Principles 18, 461

Design process 430-432

Design program 121, 122, 432-437

Design solution 438, 469

Designing kitchen centers 221

Desk area 356-360

Dexterity 413-417

Diagonal corner cabinet with Lazy Susan 278

Diagrams 463, 476, 477, 478, 479, 480, 501

Dimensions 132-133

Dimensions Form 8 132-133, 196

Dining 292-295, 296-300

Dishwasher 26, 72, 112, 229, 237-238, 259, 295, 402, 409, 414, 447

Dispensers (water, ice) 12, 398, 416

Display space 359, 360, 378

Disposer 10-11, 59, 83-84, 396, 428

Distillers 71

Door interference 477

Door Measurements Form 12 132-133, 200

Door openings 223-225, 405

Doors 50-52, 224-225, 405, (tambour) 420, 421

Double ovens 28, 113, 255

Downdraft ventilation 325, 328, 422

Drain board 7, 10, 229, 232, 381

Drain pipes 57-58

Drawer cabinet 271, 273

Drawer frontage 270, 273

Drawers 216, 217

Dryer 11, 87, 112, 366-369, 370, 372

Ductless vent system 325

Ducts 360

Duomatic washer/dryer 11

DuPont 10

Dutch cabinets 6

Earthenware sink **8**

Eating bars **14, 320, 417**

18th century kitchen **2, 4**

Electric floor heating systems **318-319**

Electric range **9**

Electric refrigerator **10**

Electric toekick heater **317**

Electrical/wiring **309-315**

Electronics **25**

Elevation **440, 445-447, 458-459, 460, 469, 471**

Elevations Form 9 **132, 197**

Emmel **33**

Energy crisis **12**

Energy efficiency **12, 61, 63, 79**

Energy Guide labels **12**

Energy management **63**

Energy prices **13**

Energy saving kitchen designs **31**

Energy standards **16**

Energy Star **16, 63**

Entertaining **301-305**

Environmental awareness **24**

Equitable use **107**

Ergonomics **91, 105**

European design **14**

Eurostyle cabinetry **12, 14**

Evaporative coolers **352**

Exhaust vent system **316, 321, 325-327, 332**

Factory-built cabinets **11**

Fair Housing Act Accessibility Guidelines **117, 118, 119**

Fair Housing Act Design Manual **117**

Fair Housing Amendments Act **116, 222**

Fan **322, 323, 326-333, 378**

Farmhouse kitchen **7**

Faucet **72, 109, 381, 396, 411, 414, 415, 426**

Federal Housing Administration Minimum Property Standards **30**

Federal Register **118**

Fiber filters **69**

Fiberglass **11, 89**

Fiestaware **10**

Fillers **456**

Filter (fan) **75, 325, 333**

Filtering (water) **24, 68, 69, 71, 75**

Fire extinguisher **247, 404**

Fireplace **2, 6, 27**

Fixture and Appliance Measurements Form 13 **132, 201-202**

Fixtures (plumbing) **55-56,** (lighting) **338-340**

Flemish kitchen **1**

FlexHousing **115**

Flexibility in use **108**

Floor heater **318-319**

Floor plan **441-457, 458-459**

Floor Plan Dimensions Form 8 **132, 196**

Floor space **216, 241, 295, 296, 405, 406, 412**

Floor tile **6**

Floors **44-48**

Fluorescent light **13**

Food prep centers **222-233, 234-236, 242, 244, 245, 291, 301-302**

Food preservation **236**

Food processor **12**

Formica Co. **8**

Forms **123-202**

Foyer **345-354**

Frameless cabinet **14**

Franklin, Benjamin **2**

Franciscan dinnerware **11**

Frederick, Christine **5, 29**

Freezers **11**

Freon **10**

Frontage (countertops) **232, 233, 234, 243, 261, 263**

Functional anthropometry **95-104**

Functional Kitchen Storage **30**

Fuse box **341**

Future plan (client's home) **127**

Gardening area **379-383**

GE Monitor refrigerator 8, 9

GE wall refrigerator 11

G.P. McDougall & Sons 6

G-shaped kitchen 206

Galley kitchen 206

Garage (appliance) 14, 235, 263, 264, 312, 417

Garbage disposer 59, 83, 84, 234, 235

Gas (stove) 8, (burners) 14, (grill) 303-304, (cooktop, range) 316, (cooking) 316, 329

Gas-powered refrigerator 11

General lighting 333-344

Getting to Know Client Form 1 124-125, 136-142

Getting to Know Client's Home Form 2 126-127, 143-144

Gilbreth, Lillian 5

Glass 11

Glass block 14

Glass-chip terrazzo 11

Glossary 513-529

Goal 122, 433

Granite 14, 16

Great room 12, 14

Green building 24, 61-62

Grill 12, 27, 303-305

Ground fault circuit interrupters 313

Halogen heating 14

Hand washing 38, 228

Harlequin dinnerware 10

Healthy housing 115

Healthy Housing Program, Canada Mortgage and Housing Corporation 61

Hearing 400, 422-425

Hearth 4

Heaters 27, 59-60, 316-319

Heating 316-319

Heating units 304

Height 105, 220, 249, 252, 255, 296, 350, 358, 363, 373, 379, 409

Heiner & McCullough 30, 33

Hobby area 376-378

Hobby cooking 24

Home Adaptations for Seniors' Independence Program 119

Home planning center 354-364

Home Ventilating Institute 330, 331

Hood 249, 323, 326-327, 328, 329, 333

Hoosier 6, 7, 9

Hoosier Manufacturing Co. 6

Hot water 59-60, 69, 307, 318

Hot water heater 318

Household composition 19

Hub of home 24

Human dimensions 92-100, 215, (work surface) 220, 351, 358, 360, 363

Human factors 91-120

Hydronic heater 317-319

IC (insulation) housing 342

Ice dispenser 12

Icebox 8, 10

Icemaker (see also Servel) 11, 14, 27

In-cabinet accessories 12

Indoor grill 12

Induction cooking 14

Induction cooktop 111

Infrastructure considerations 43-60

Inglenook 384

Institute for Research in Construction 118

Internal functions 401

International Building Code 116, 117, 222

International Code Council 116, 117

International Energy Star program 16

Interviewing the client 122-124

Intuitive use 109

Inventory 40-41, 128-209

Inventory form 128-209, 150-165

Ironing area 374-375

Islands 13-15, 20, 22, 34, 209, 211, 212, 231, 243, 246, 247, 248, 249, 258, 269, 293, 329

Insulation 50, 316, 321

Jenn-Air 12

Job site 131, 132

Job Site Inspection Form 189-195

Joint Center for Housing Studies of Harvard University 18, 19

Juice bar 306

Kapple 32

Kelvinator 8

Kitchen & Bath Design News 20

Kitchen & Bath Drawing 447, 466

Kitchen & Bath Products 56, 61, 63, 216, 374

Kitchen & Bath Project Management 134

Kitchen & Bath Systems 43, 56, 59, 61, 72, 126, 131, 231, 309, 316, 322, 333, 344

Kitchen Cabinet Manufacturers Association (KCMA) 11

Kitchen history 1-28

Kitchen Industry Technical Manual, Vol. 5 (1975) 32, 221

Kitchen Planning Guidelines xxi, 33, 42, 74, 221, 222, 241, 256, 288, 291, 300, 302, 308, 399, 405, 432, 435, 457, 461, 466, 469, 475-512

Kitchen research 33-42, 82, 129, 230, 263, 267

"Kitchen Storage Research Study" 33-34

Kitchen Survey Form 123

Kompass & Stoll Co. 6

Knee space 108, 113, 236, 409-410

L corner cabinet 276, 277

L-shape 5, 208, 451, 452

L-shaped wall cabinet 276, 277

Ladies Home Journal 5

Laminate 10, 11, 12, 13, 14

Landing area 232-233, 240, 243, 247-248, 254-256, 261-262, 264, 490, 495-496, 502-504

Laundry area 364-375

Lazy Susan 277, 278, 289, 450

Levelness (floors) 47

Lifespan design 114

Lifestyle factors 18-28

Lighting 333-344, 360, 373-374, 386, 418, 512

Lighting controls 373-374, 386

Lighting fixtures 338-340

Linen cabinet 6

Linoleum 7, 8, 9, 10, 11

Living area 384, 387

Load-bearing walls 48-49

Locations trends 27

Low physical effort 112

Low voltage lighting 1, 338, 343-344

Mace, FAIA, Ron 96

Macy's 8

Make-up air 332

Master suite 27

Materials 9, 11, 16, 63, 83, 86-87, 89, 265, 303, 322, 353, 374, 376

McCobb, Paul 12

McCullough, Helen 30, 33

Measurements 103, 105, 199-200, 217-220, (guidelines) 223-227, 232-234, 238, 243, 258, 259, 262, 270-288, 362, 412, 441

Measuring 41, 133

Mechanical cooling 321, 322-323

Mechanical Devices Dimensions Form 10 132, 198

Mechanical systems 353-354

Medium kitchen 41-42, 213, 267, 288

Merillat Industries 11

Message board 361

Microwave 10, 11, 12, 14, 22, 244, 249, 250-255, 328, 397, 402, 414, 415, 419, 501, 502

Microwave cooking 244, 250

Microwave drawer 250, 251, 411

Mini-kitchens 27, 337

Minimum Property Standards 30

Miscellaneous shelf/drawer frontage 302

Mobility aids 101-103, 224, 225, 227, 330, 382, 398, 403

Modern kitchen 3, 5-28

Moisture 48, 73-81

Monel 8

Morning kitchen 336

Mudroom 346-348, 349-354

Multi-speed fan 333

Multiple cook kitchen 22, 34, 210, 228, 257, 424

Multiple height counters 22

Mutschler Brothers 12

Mylar 13

National Association of Home Builders 19, 20

National Center for Injury Prevention and Control 106

National Family Opinion Survey 20

National Institute of Wood Kitchen Cabinets 11

National Institute on Disability and Rehabilitation Research 106

NKBA Endorsed College Programs 222

NKBA Guidelines & Access Standards 475-512

NKBA's Professional Resource Library xix, 18, 43, 56, 61, 63, 131, 447

National Research Center 118

Natural cooling 322

Natural light 334-335

Natural resources 24, 61

Need assessment forms 123-202

1980s kitchen 13-14

1950s kitchen 11

1940s kitchen 10-11

1990s kitchen 14-17, 26

1970s kitchen 12-13

1960s kitchen 12

1930s kitchen 9-10

1920s kitchen 7-8

19th century kitchen 3, 4

Noise 50, 86-88, 332-333, 365, 391, 422, 425

Oil embargo 12

Old world styling 14

Olsen 32

One-wall kitchen 5, 209

Ontarians with Disabilities Act 119

Open kitchen 12, 14-15, 20, 21, 23, 208-212, 268, 301, 325, 383-384, 386

Organizer (storage) 289, 290

Outdoor kitchen 27, 57, 302-305

Outpost kitchens 27, 306-307

Oven (see also Microwave) 11, 12, 14, 113, 216, 225, 244, 250, 252, 253, 256, 257, 260, 261, 325, 397, 398, 402, 403, 410, 411, 445

Over-the-range microwave 12, 249, 251, 254

Panero 92, 101, 104

Pantry 23, 212, 213, 218, 260, 267-268, 270, 274, 279, 280, 281, 286, 288, 291, 294, 295

Pantry shelf frontage 279, 280, 281, 287

Parallel kitchen 206, 210

Parrott 33

Particleboard 12, 74

Pass-through 207

"Patterns for Kitchen Cabinets" 30

Perceptible information 110

Peninsula 207, 231, 247, 248, 258, 312, 331, 452, 472

Pipes 57-58

Placement (sink center) 230-231

Planning 203-344, 379

Planning center 354-364

Planning Guidelines xxi, 33, 42, 74, 221, 222, 241, 256, 288, 291, 300, 302, 308, 399, 405, 432, 435, 457, 461, 466, 469, 475-512

Plumbing 55-60

Plumbing fixtures 55-56

Pollution (air) 73-76, 325, 378

Pop Art color 12

Population diversity 18

Porta-Bilt cabinets 9

Prep area 222-233, 234-236, 242, 244, 245, 291, 301-302

Preserving natural resources 24, 60

President's Conference on Home Building and Home Ownership 29

Priscilla curtains 11

Processor 12

Product trends 28

Professional Resource Library xix, 18, 43, 56, 61, 63, 131, 447

Professional-style appliances 16, 17

Professional-style range 329, 332

Propeller fan 332

Proximity ventilation system 75, 249, 250, 323, 325, 328

Radarange 10

Radiant floor systems 319

Range 9, 10, 31, 207, 216, 228, 244, 247, 248, 249, 250, 255, 316, 325, 326, 402, 411, 452, 468

Range-of-joint motion 100

Raytheon 12

Reach 95-99, 214, 215, 218, 220, 226, 234, 247, 266, 291, 312, 343, 350, 373, 396, 401, 411, 412, 474

Receptacles 89, 307, 311, 312-313, 353, 364, 378

Recessed lighting 335-338, 340-344

Recirculating vent system 76, 325

Recycling 24, 61, 62, 82, 83, 84-86, 239

Recycling center 84-86

Refrigerated cooling 322

Refrigeration center 241-243, 398, 411-412, 416, 428

Refrigerator 9, 11, 14, 25, 45, 75, 107, 231, 235, 241-243, 258, 261, 263, 294, 295, 312, 320, 398, 411-412, 416, 428, 440, 451

Registers 133, 320

Relationship matrix 436

Remodeling 132

Remodeling Form 7 132, 189-195

Replacement air 332-333

Research 29-32, 33-42, 213, 234, 252, 257, 267

"Residential Kitchens: Planning Principles for the 90s" 32

Residential Construction 43, 47, 48, 49, 50, 51, 53, 61, 126, 131, 309, 322

Residential Rehabilitation Assistance Program for Persons with Disabilities 119

Resilient flooring 11, 412

Resins 11

Resources (natural) 24, 61

Retro-style appliances 16

Reverse osmosis 68, 71

Room outline 431, 441-445, 469, 470

Safe harbors 116-118, 222

Safety 253, 265, 313, 329, 344, 427

Scale 440, 459

Sealed gas burners 14

Seated work areas 236

Seating 296, 297, 298-300, 388-392

Second appliance 28

Self-cleaning oven 12

Self-defrost refrigerator 11

Sensory changes 400

Septic systems 59

Servel 11

Serving 292-300

Seven Principles of Universal Design 107

17th century kitchen 1, 2

Sheet metal cabinets 6

Shelf/drawer frontage 286

Side-by-side refrigerator 14, 107, 398

Single-lever faucet 109, 402

Sink center 228-241, 257, 396, 402, 409, 414, 422, 424, 426, 435, 439

Sink drain line 231

Sinks 10, 14, (integral) 13, 28, 31, 55-59, 206-207, 211, 214, 228-241, 245, 246, 257-262, 288, 295, 303, 304, 307, 347, 368, 372-373, 377, 381, 382, 396, 402, 409, 414, 422, 426, 436, 439, 440, 454

Site inspection 132

Sitting area 384, 388-391

Size and space for approach and use 113

Size of kitchen 213

Skylights 334, 383

Small appliances 11, 39, 42, 235, 245, 307, 311

Small Homes Council report 30, 32

Small kitchen 213, 247, 267, 279, 280, 288

"Smile" cookie jar 12

Social area 204, 383-387

Solid surface 13, 14, 16

"Someone's in the Kitchen" 33-39

Sound insulation **89-90**

Space usage trends **21**

Speed cooking **244, 250**

Squirrel-cage fan **332**

Stainless steel **10, 14**

Standards **30, 75, 116-120**

Standing desk **360**

State of the Nation's Housing 2002 **18**

Stature **92, 105**

Steel cabinets **11**

Steidel **31**

Step stool **108, 396**

Stiles **456**

Storage **23, 40-42, 216-219, 266-272, 288-291, 293-295, 352, 358-359, 372-374, 377-379, 382, 398, 412, 416, 421, 428, 473**

Storage accessories **12**

Storage in the Kitchen Form 4 **128-129, 150-165**

Stoves (wood and coal) **2, 4, 6,** (gas) **8**

Stowe, Harriet Beecher **4, 29**

Structural anthropometry **92-94**

Structural issues **44-54**

Styrofoam beams **13**

Surface cooking **244, 245, 248, 250**

Switches (lighting) **342-343, 353, 360**

T-turn **226, 227, 406, 410**

Table-top range **10**

Tall cabinet shelf frontage **274, 286**

Tall cabinets **218, 219, 244, 291**

Tambour doors **420, 421**

Tappan **11**

Tappan microwave wall oven **11**

Task lighting **338, 360**

Technology **25**

Television **25, 391**

Templates **431, 438-440, 445, 469**

"The Development of a Successful Kitchen" **29**

13th century kitchen **1**

Three-dimensional sketches **445**

Tiffany lamps **13**

Tiles **80**

Tolerance for error **111**

Touchless faucet **72**

Track lighting **13, 335, 338, 343**

Traffic **210, 211, 213, 217, 218, 255, 256, 261, 474**

Traffic aisles **213, 217, 218**

Traffic clearance **297, 485**

Traffic interference **261**

Trans-generational design **114**

Transformer **337, 343**

Trash **37, 83-85, 239**

Trash compactor **12, 14, 84, 239, 396, 426**

Trash disposal chute **8**

Trends (demographic and population) **1-28, 120**

Tudor style **8**

Tupperware **11**

20th century kitchen **3, 5-28**

2003 International Residential Code **221, 312, 313**

2006 International Residential Code **330, 331, 475**

Types of kitchens **204-212**

U.S. Access Board **120**

U.S. Census Bureau **106**

U.S. Department of Agriculture's Agricultural Experiment Station **29**

U.S. Department of Education **106**

U.S. Department of Housing and Urban Development **116, 117, 118, 120**

U.S. Environmental Protection Agency **64, 90**

U.S. Green Building Council **61**

U-shape **5, 205, 223, 226, 474**

Under-cabinet lighting **16**

Undercounter refrigerator **235, 242, 294, 306**

Uneven walls **48-49**

Unfitted kitchen **15, 212, 289**

Uniform Federal Accessibility Standards **101, 117, 222**

Universal design (*see also* Accessible design) **91, 99, 105-120, 312, 393**

Universal reach range **99, 113, 312, 343, 350, 373, 412, 474**

Updraft ventilation **325, 326-327**

Use Form & Appliance Checklist Form 6 **130, 179-188**

User Analysis **431, 434, 435, 436, 445, 461, 469, 471**

Utensil Survey Project **32**

Utility service **368**

Vapor retarder **80, 81**

Variety **28**

Vent hood **249, 323, 324, 326, 327, 328, 331, 468**

Vent pipes **57-58**

Ventilation **73-74, 75-76, 79, 87, 248-249, 250, 323-333, 368**

Vents **317, 320, 328, 350**

Victorian kitchens **3**

Vision **400, 417-422**

Visual cueing **422, 425**

Visual diagram **431, 438, 441, 444, 445, 446, 447, 470**

Visit-ability **114**

Vinyl **10, 11, 12, 80**

Vinylite **10**

Volatile organic compounds (VOC) **74**

Voltage **310**

Walkway **227, 349**

Wall cabinet **218, 252, 260, 270, 271, 275, 276, 278, 280, 281, 288, 454, 455, 459**

Wall cabinet shelf frontage **271, 278, 282-283**

Wall oven **11, 216, 250, 260, 261, 325, 445**

Walls **48-50**

Wanslow **32**

Warming drawer **16, 27**

Washer (clothes) **11, 73, 112, 312, 366-370**

Waste disposal **8, 75, 82**

Waste management **82-84**

Waste pipes **57-58**

Waste receptacles **239**

Water (dispenser) **12**, (safety, filtering) **24, 69**, (delivery) **55, 56-57, 59-60, 64-66**, (heater) **59-60, 63, 69, 72, 312** , (conservation) **72**, (treatment equipment) **69-71**, (softeners) **69-70**, (filtering) **69**

Westinghouse **9**

Whole house vent system **331**

Willamette Valley Farm Kitchen **30**

Wilson, Maud **30**

Window Measurements Form 11 **132, 199**

Windows **23, 50-54, 62, 246, 247, 316, 321, 322, 334, 383, 441**

Wiring/electrical **309-315**

Woks **27, 415**

Wood-Metal **11**

Work aisles **205, 206, 208, 211, 223, 225-226, 261, 301, 439, 481-483**

Work areas **31, 203-214, 222, 225, 226, 233, 234, 236, 260, 263, 289, 356, 357, 491**

Work centers **4, 5, 9, 214, 227, 257, 258, 260, 305, 395, 403, 413**

Work flow **257, 260, 305**

Work stations **28**

Work surface **220**

Work triangle **5, 84, 257, 258, 259, 260, 261, 291, 294, 378, 402**

Work zone **203-204**

World War II **10, 106**

Wright, Russel **11**

Wringer washer **8, 11**

Youngstown cabinets **6**

Your Client's Kitchen Form 5 **129-130, 166-178**

Yust **32**

Zelnick **92, 101**

Zone **23, 214**

Zook **6**